THE SECRETARY'S HANDBOOK

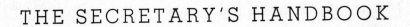

Sarah Augusta Taintor (sole author)
TRAINING FOR SECRETARIAL PRACTICE

Coauthor with Helen L. Paddock
ON WRITING ESSAYS; A MANUAL OF THE ESSAY

Kate M. Monro (sole author)
ENGLISH FOR SECRETARIES
A WORKBOOK COURSE IN BUSINESS ENGLISH

Coauthor with Isabel Stevenson Monro
THE CLUBWOMAN'S MANUAL
COSTUME INDEX SUPPLEMENT
INDEX TO REPRODUCTIONS OF AMERICAN PAINTINGS
INDEX TO REPRODUCTIONS OF EUROPEAN PAINTINGS

Sarah Augusta Taintor and Kate M. Monro
THE SECRETARY'S HANDBOOK
THE HANDBOOK OF SOCIAL CORRESPONDENCE
CORRECTIVE EXERCISES IN ENGLISH
ENGLISH FOR AMERICAN YOUTH
EDITORS OF "THE BOOK OF MODERN LETTERS"

THE
SECRETARY'S
HANDBOOK

A Manual of Correct Usage

SARAH AUGUSTA TAINTOR

FORMERLY OF DEPARTMENT OF ENGLISH, THEODORE ROOSEVELT HIGH
SCHOOL, NEW YORK CITY, AND INSTRUCTOR IN UNIVERSITY CLASSES IN
EXTENSION DEPARTMENT, COLUMBIA UNIVERSITY

and

KATE M. MONRO

FORMER ADMINISTRATIVE ASSISTANT, HAAREN HIGH SCHOOL,
NEW YORK CITY

EIGHTH EDITION
COMPLETELY REVISED BY KATE M. MONRO

The Macmillan Company · New York · 1961

*Set up and printed. Published July, 1929. Re-
printed, November, 1929.*
*Third Edition Revised, January, 1930. Reprinted,
May, June, July, September, October, November,
1930.*
*Reissue with Corrections, April, 1931. Reprinted,
July, September, 1931; January, February, July,
1932.*
*Fourth Edition Completely Revised, October, 1933.
Reprinted March, August, October, 1934; April,
June, October, 1935; March, September, 1936.*
*Fifth Edition Completely Revised and Reset, June,
1937. Reprinted February, 1938; May, 1938;
August, 1938; February, 1939.*
*Sixth Edition Completely Revised, Published 1941.
Reprinted August, 1941; December, 1941; July,
1942; November, 1942; July, 1943; June, 1944;
May, 1945; April, 1947.*
*Seventh Edition Completely Revised, Published
1949. Reprinted January, 1949; December, 1949;
June, 1950; March, 1951; June, 1951; November,
1951; March, 1952; February, 1953; February,
1954; May, 1955; May, 1956.*
*Eighth Edition Completely Revised and Reset,
Published 1958. Reprinted, June, 1960. Third print-
ing 1961.*
LIBRARY OF CONGRESS CATALOG CARD NUMBER:
58–6964

PRINTED IN THE UNITED STATES OF AMERICA

To the Secretaries of America
to Whose Untiring and Often Unheralded
Work the World of Business Owes Much
of Its Success, This Book Is Gratefully
Dedicated

This eighth edition is dedicated to Sarah Augusta Taintor, who conceived the idea of the book and brought to it wide experience, abounding enthusiasm, and unwearied industry. Her gracious personality, kindly humor, and generosity of spirit endeared her to her many friends and students and made working with her a rare privilege.

K. M. M.

Preface to Eighth Edition

The eighth edition of *The Secretary's Handbook* has been reset with revisions in almost every chapter. In Part I chapters on Capitalization, Punctuation, Hyphenation and Compounds, Figures, and Abbreviations have been enlarged with additional rules and examples. In Part II in the chapter on Correct Usage in Letter Parts, more examples have been added to illustrate forms of address for American officials, British nobility, and ecclesiastical dignitaries. The chapters on Invitations, Telegrams and Cablegrams, Minutes, Constitutions, Bylaws, Standing Rules, and Sources of Information have been revised to conform with modern practice. In the Appendix a list of foreign countries and their capitals has been substituted for Syllabication of Foreign Words.

The author is especially indebted to her sister Isabel Stevenson Monro for help and constant encouragement.

Acknowledgment is also gratefully made to the following persons for material and suggestions that will add to the usefulness of the book: James A. Eastman, First Assistant, Information Division, New York Public Library; John Boynton Kaiser, Director, and Miss Mary P. McLean, Supervising Librarian (Business), of the Public Library of Newark, New Jersey; Mrs. Flora Lindsay Magoun, Assistant Professor of Business Education, Rollins College, Winter Park, Florida; and George P. Oslin, Publicity Director, Western Union Telegraph Company, New York.

K. M. M.

Preface to First Edition

The number of good handbooks on English published during the last few years almost forbids the writing of another. Indeed, it would be futile if a new one should approach the subject of good usage from the same point of view or should offer no different material. This handbook is intended primarily for secretaries whose duties include the writing of letters and other business forms. Not a day passes in a business office that some question of usage does not arise. Secretaries have desired a book planned from their point of view, stressing their problems. With this in mind, the manual has been written as a reference book containing authoritative usage.

The material is divided into two parts: the first containing rules with illustrations of correct form in English; the second consisting of various types of letters relating to business, social, and official usage, as well as other forms of business writing often required of the secretary. These include, among other types, the making of resolutions, the writing of minutes, the framing of petitions, and the compiling of reports.

With particular problems of the secretary in mind, specific directions have been given for the preparation of manuscript for publication and the reading of it in proof, for the making of indexes and the compiling of bibliographies. Other chapters contain sources of information for the secretary, and a number of citations used in conferring honors upon individuals. These will prove interesting and suggestive both for their content and for their manner of expression.

While the problems of the secretary have been emphasized, it is hoped the manual will prove helpful to all who are seeking concise information on points of correctness.

The authors have consulted freely other style books to which they acknowledge their indebtedness. Among these are: *A Manual of Style of the University of Chicago Press; A Style-Book for*

Writers and Editors, compiled by C. O. Sylvester Mawson; *Text, Type, and Style,* published by The Atlantic Monthly Press; and the *United States Government Printing Office Style Manual.* Where usage is divided, the authors have endeavored to record such differences for the benefit of the secretary.

Special acknowledgment is made to the following persons who have offered helpful suggestions in making the book practical or who have made it possible to use valuable illustrative material: Nicholas Murray Butler, President of Columbia University; Professor John H. H. Lyon, Professor Ernest Hunter Wright, Miss Mildred Loxton de Barritt, of the English Department of Columbia University; Judge John J. Freschi; Mr. Augustus Loring Richards; Colonel Theodore Roosevelt; H. C. Major, Captain U.S.M.C.; L. G. Caton, Acting Secretary of the Library of Congress; Professor James C. Egbert, Columbia University; John A. Lynch, President of the Borough of Richmond; Mr. Eugene F. McLaughlin, Secretary of the Borough of Manhattan; Mr. E. F. Austin, Chief Engineer of the Borough of the Bronx; Mr. Peter McArdle, Secretary to the President of the Borough of Brooklyn; Julia M. Wilkinson, Executive Secretary, University of Wisconsin; Miss Ella Banks, Secretary to the President of Boston University; Mr. Hermann Hagedorn, Director of the Roosevelt Memorial Association; F. M. Wilmot, Manager of the Carnegie Hero Fund Commission; Mr. Cameron Beck, Director of the Personnel Department of the New York Stock Exchange; Congressman Sol Bloom; Mr. Andrew Keogh, Librarian of Yale University; Dr. Lawson Purdy, Secretary of the Charity Organization Society of New York; Mr. Hiller C. Wellman, Librarian of the City Library Association of Springfield, Mass.; Mother M. Corrigan, Instructor in the College of the Sacred Heart, New York; Dr. Otto Zobel, Research Department of the American Telephone and Telegraph Company; Miss Isabel Stevenson Monro, New York Public Library; Mr. William R. Hayward, Principal of the Theodore Roosevelt High School; Mr. John B. Opdycke, Chairman of the Department of English of Haaren High School; Miss Katherine Morse, of the English Department of the Manhattan Training School; Dr. Charles R. Gaston, Chairman of the English Department, Mrs. Alice Butler Richards, Mrs. Edna B. Kerr, Dr. Bruno Fedter, Mr. H. S. Leonard, Mr. Jack Silverman, Mr. Harold Fields, of Theodore Roosevelt High School; Miss Olive Carter of The Macmillan Company; Miss Madeline Lane, Secretary, The

Dorr Engineering Company; Miss Alice Ames, Secretary, The International Telephone and Telegraph Company; Miss Rose Wolcott, Architect; Miss Margaret Hanna, Washington, D.C.; Miss Marie Konzelman, student in Columbia University, and the classes of 1928 and 1929 in Secretarial Correspondence.

To Miss Katherine Spencer, who read the manuscript in proof, the authors wish to express their grateful appreciation.

They also wish to acknowledge their indebtedness to the following organizations which have allowed them to use illustrative material: The National Education Association, The Vocational Guidance Association, The Young Women's Christian Association, Rogers Peet and Company, and Lord and Taylor.

Sarah Augusta Taintor
Kate M. Monro

Contents

Preface, Eighth Edition   ix
Preface, First Edition   xi

PART I

1. Capitalization   3
2. Punctuation   29
3. Hyphenation and Compounds   64
4. Use of Italics   77
5. Figures   83
6. Spelling   92
7. Diction   110
8. Abbreviations   137
9. Points of Grammar   181

PART II

1. Letter Writing   211
2. Correct Usage in Letter Parts: Official, Ecclesiastical,
      Foreign   287
3. Invitations   332
4. Business Announcements   369
5. Telegrams and Cablegrams   376
6. The Framing of Petitions   387
7. The Writing of Minutes   390
8. The Framing of Resolutions   405
9. Constitutions, Bylaws, and Standing Rules   423
10. The Writing of Reports   434
11. Preparation of Manuscript   460
12. Compiling a Bibliography   465
13. Proofreading   468
14. Making an Index   474
15. Rules for Alphabetical Filing Used in Business Offices 477
16. Sources of Information Useful to Secretaries   486

xvi   *Contents*

17. Citations   494
18. Inscriptions   508
19. Programs   518
    Appendix   534
    Index   543

PART ONE

1. Capitalization

1. Capitalize the first word of every sentence.

Much may be made of a Scotchman if he be caught young.
SAMUEL JOHNSON

Modern writers often capitalize the first word of detached phrases and clauses used in place of sentences.

These essays are the records of moods and sometimes contradict each other. So much the better.
JOSEPH WARREN BEACH

Islands, islets, and mere rocks; some jutting high up, some nestling low. A dangerous coast, and a splendid fishing-ground.
HUGH S. SCOTT

2. Capitalize the first word of every line of poetry.

To the glory that was Greece,
And the grandeur that was Rome.
EDGAR ALLAN POE

In some modern English poetry forms, only the first word of the first line is capitalized, and sometimes even this is written lower case.

The sky
is that beautiful old parchment
in which the sun
and the moon
keep their diary.
ALFRED KREYMBORG

3. Capitalize all proper nouns that are names of individuals.

Jane Addams   Herbert Hoover

(1) Capitalize epithets added to proper names or applied to people or places.

3

Edward the Eighth	the Empire State
William the Conqueror	the Great White Way
the Commoner	the Golden Gate
the Lone Eagle	the Hub

(2) Capitalize *father* and *mother* when used in address; but do not capitalize such nouns when a possessive pronoun is used with them.

> Yes, Mother, I am going.
> My father is at home.

(3) Capitalize *uncle, aunt,* and other family appellations when used with a proper noun.

> I met Uncle John who told me of my aunt's good fortune.

4. Capitalize particles in names of persons as follows:

(1) In foreign names such particles as *d', da, della, van,* and *von* are capitalized unless preceded by a forename or title.

> D'Orbigny; Alcide d'Orbigny
> Da Ponte; Cardinal da Ponte
> Van Rensselaer; Stephen van Rensselaer

(2) In American and British names such particles are usually capitalized, even if preceded by a forename or title, but individual usage, if ascertainable, should be followed.

Justice Van Devanter	Henry van Dyke
Thomas De Quincey	Louis de Forest
William Von Glahn	Oscar von Engeln

References for authoritative capitalization: *Who's Who, Who's Who in America,* etc.

5. Capitalize all academic degrees following the name whether abbreviated or written out.

> John H. Finley, LL.D.; Dorothy Ann Burnett, Ph.D.; Kate Douglas Wiggin, Litt.D.; Katherine Morse, Master of Arts.

(1) When writing more than one degree after a name, arrange according to their importance, the most important last, or, when they are of the same rank, as various doctoral degrees, according to the time of their being granted. (*See* p. 163.)

Arthur Sutton Corbin, LL.B., M.A.
James Rowland Angell, Ph.D., Litt.D., LL.D.
Alexander William Evans, M.D., Ph.D.

6. Capitalize all academic and religious titles, as, *Doctor, Bishop, Professor, Dean,* when preceding a name.

Dr. Mary Morton, Bishop Lawrence, Professor Ernest H. Wright, Dean Gildersleeve.

(1) With *Reverend,* other academic titles and abbreviations for academic degrees may be used, as they do not repeat the title. The following are correct forms for the use of *Reverend:*

Rev. John Blake
The Reverend John Blake
The Reverend John Blake, D.D.
The Reverend Dr. John Blake
The Reverend President John Blake
The Reverend Professor John Blake
The Very Reverend Dean John Blake
The Right Reverend John Blake (Bishop)
The Most Reverend John Blake (Archbishop)
The Very Reverend John Blake (Monsignor)
The Reverend Mother Superior
The Reverend Father John Blake
The Reverend Martha Simpson

The article *the* when preceding *Reverend* in a sentence should not be capitalized. The abbreviation *Rev.* should not be used when preceded by *the.*

On Sunday *the* (not *The*) Reverend Roy Gates will preside.
We heard *the Reverend* (not *The Rev.*) Roy Gates.

(2) The title *Reverend* is an adjective, not a noun, and must, therefore, always be used with a given name or initials on the envelope or in writing the inside address; as,

Rev. John L. Blake   *or*   Rev. J. L. Blake
not
Rev. Blake

It is permissible, however, in referring to a clergyman in the body of a letter, to write

Rev. Mr. Blake   *or*   Rev. Dr. Blake

although it is considered better form to use the given name with the title in even such a reference.

(3) The titles *Reverend* and *Doctor* are usually abbreviated, but are often spelled out in formal use. *Reverend* is not used in the salutation of a letter. Where there is no other title, the salutation is *Dear Mr. ____.*

(4) Do not capitalize the following when they stand alone (see Rule 9):

judge	cantor	rabbi
justice	elder	rector
principal	minister (of religion)	attaché
professor	pastor	consul
superintendent	priest	consul general

The rector has engaged a new secretary.

Did the professor receive his class list from the registrar or from the clerk?

The judge asked the assistant director for all data on the case.

7. Capitalize all titles of rank, honor, or respect when preceding the name.

President ———	Speaker ———
Vice President ———	Governor ———
the Earl of ———	Mayor ———
General ———	Cardinal ———
Senator ———	Chief Justice ———
Congressman ———	Under Secretary ———

8. Capitalize all Government titles when referring to definite persons or offices, and all titles of honor or nobility when referring to specific persons.

the Secretary of Defense
the Secretary of the Treasury
the Assistant Secretary of the Treasury
Acting Secretary of State
the Architect of the Capitol
Associate Justice of the Supreme Court
Chairman of the Committee of the Whole

the Congressman from Maine
the Senator from Florida
House Chaplain
Solicitor of Internal Revenue
Director, U. S. Coast and Geodetic Survey
the Queen of England
the President of the French Republic
the Archbishop of Canterbury

Chief Justice of the United
  States
the Under Secretary of State
the Speaker of the House

the Mayor of Southampton
His Honor the Mayor
Your Grace
Your Royal Highness

Difference in Usage of Capitalization of Titles

9. Usage varies as to the capitalization of titles following a name.

BUSINESS USAGE OF CAPITALIZATION OF TITLES

In reports and in correspondence, business titles referring to positions of authority are usually capitalized as a form of courtesy when they refer to definite individuals.

Lewis Barr, President of the Southern Cotton Association, called the meeting to order.

The Director of Arnold & Cole was authorized by the stockholders to increase the dividend.

NEWSPAPER USAGE OF CAPITALIZATION OF TITLES

In printing, as in newspapers, books, and magazines, titles following a name are usually not capitalized.

Other features of the afternoon session included a radio message from England by Prime Minister Baldwin, chancellor of Cambridge University, of which John Harvard was an alumnus; addresses by Alexander Dunlop Lindsay, master of Balliol and vice chancellor of Oxford University; James Russell Agassiz, president of the Harvard Board of Overseers; and Judge Learned Hand, '93, president of the Alumni Association.

The New York Times

ACADEMIC USAGE

Henry Solon Graves, LL.D., Provost, Dean of the School of Forestry, and Sterling Professor of Forestry.

Bulletin of Yale University

10. Capitalize *president* when referring to the President of the United States, or any synonymous title referring to him.

Commander in Chief   Chief Magistrate

Note the manner in writing the following:

ex-President Hoover	the President-elect
former President Hoover	the Vice President

Usage varies in regard to adjectives derived from *President* and *Vice President* in referring to the officials of the Government.

NEWSPAPER USAGE	GOVERNMENT USAGE
the Vice-Presidential suite	the vice-presidential suite
the Presidential nomination	the presidential nomination

11. Capitalize *governor* when preceding the name of any state; as, the Governor of Wisconsin.

12. Capitalize *commissioner* when used definitely with a title, but do not capitalize it when standing alone.

> Commissioner of Education of the State of New York
> Commissioner of Immigration and Naturalization
> Commissioner of Patents
> Commissioner of the District of Columbia

13. Titles are sometimes used instead of the names of those who bear them. In such cases, when a definite person is referred to in the singular number, the title is to be capitalized.

(1) In the second person if used as synonyms of proper names.

> Mr. Secretary, please examine the report.
> You will report, Captain, to Headquarters.
> Do you think, Senator, this bill will pass?

Do not capitalize *sir, madam, monsieur,* and such expressions used alone in address.

> What's that to you, sir?
> Why, madam, look what it means.
> And so, my fellow citizens, the reason that I came away from Washington is that I sometimes get lonely down there.
>
> WOODROW WILSON

(2) In the third person.

When the Governor, escorted by local Democrats, appeared at the door of the station, there was a roar from the crowd.

14. *The GPO Style Manual* presents the following on Army and Navy:

United States Army, French Army; the Army, Regular Army, Army Band, Army Establishments, Reserve officer, the Volunteers, Eighty-first Regiment, etc. (U.S. understood in all cases); *but* volunteer officer, army shoe, Grant's army, Robinson's brigade, the brigade, the corps, the regiment, infantryman.

United States Navy, British Navy, the Navy, Navy (Naval) Establishment, Navy officer, the Marine Corps, the Air Force; *but* navy yard, naval officer, naval district.

15. Capitalize the words *department, bureau, service, station, office,* and *board* if referring to a bureau or executive department of the United States Government if the name is given.

the Department of State   Newport Naval Station
the Bureau of Customs   the Office of Education
the Foreign Service   the Federal Reserve Board

Business usage varies as to the capitalization of such words as *bureau, department, office,* and the like following a name.

Adjustment Bureau *or* adjustment bureau
Savings Department *or* savings department
Department of Applied Science *or* department of applied science
Employment Office *or* employment office

Do not capitalize *department, office, bureau,* and like words when used without a name or if used as an adjective.

I am going to the office.
He belonged to one of the Government bureaus.
The department clerk filed the report.

16. Capitalize *committee* with a name or in place of the name when referring to all standing and select committees of the Senate and the House of Representatives.

House Census Committee   Committee on Post Office and Civil
                                         Service

17. Capitalize *Federal* and *State Courts* when used with a definite name. Do not capitalize *city* and *county courts* (Government usage).

the United States Supreme Court
the United States Circuit Court
the State Court of Appeals

Federal Grand Jury
the police court
the magistrate's court

Capitalize *Court* meaning a judge or judicial tribunal in direct personal reference to such a judge or tribunal.

18. Capitalize the word *Cabinet* when referring to the Cabinet of the President of the United States.

Cabinet Officer
The President's Cabinet
the chief post of the Cabinet

19. Capitalize *Federal* when referring to the United States Government.

He was in the service of the Federal Government.

Notice, however, that the "down" style does not capitalize *federal.*

What it would cost the federal government to finance this scaling down of farm mortgages is conjectural.

20. Usage varies as to the capitalization of *administration*. When referring to the political party in power or when used with a name to designate a Government board, *administration* is usually capitalized.

the Democratic Administration
the Administration
the Taft administration
a former administration
Veterans' Administration

21. Capitalize *Government* when used synonymously with the United States Government or when referring to that of any foreign nation.

a Government official
Federal Government
National Government
Government ownership

the Italian Government
Imperial Government
Her Majesty's Government
a Government bureau

Do not capitalize *government* when referring to that of a state in the United States or to that of any possession of the United States.

22. Capitalize *commonwealth, confederation, powers, union,* etc., if used with proper names or as proper names or as proper adjectives.

> British Commonwealth of Nations
> Swiss Confederation
> United Nations
> Union of Soviet Socialist Republics
> Union of South Africa

23. Capitalize *Constitution* when referring to that of the United States.

> James Madison was called the Father of the Constitution.
> The Constitution of the United States of America was adopted in 1789.
> The Constitutional Convention of Philadelphia set up the Federal Government of the United States.
> Constitutional Committee, Constitutional Amendment.

Also *act, bill, code, law, report,* and *treaty* with a name or number to designate a particular document are capitalized.

Volstead Act	Public Law 9
Bill of Rights	Annual Report of the Secretary of
Internal Revenue Code	Defense
	Jay Treaty

Note the "down" style of capitalization in the following news item:

> The nullification of the fourteenth amendment in congress has given the United States a form of representative government for which the constitution does not provide.

24. Capitalize any United States Government commission when it is designated by its name.

> Commission of Fine Arts
> Federal Communications Commission
> Interstate Commerce Commission
> National Forest Reservation Commission
> Securities and Exchange Commission
> United States Tariff Commission

Also capitalize *commission* when standing alone, if it refers to a national or international commission already named.

25. Capitalize all names of state legislatures when used with the name of the state and all names of national legislatures and their branches.

> the Assembly of New York
> the Ohio House of Representatives
> the General Court of Massachusetts
> House of Commons
> Chamber of Deputies
> Rigsdag
> the Sixty-ninth Congress

But do not capitalize *assembly, general court, legislature,* if they stand alone without the name of the state to which they belong. Do not capitalize *national legislature,* meaning the United States Congress, or *city legislature,* meaning City Council or Board of Aldermen; or *executive session, special session.*

26. Capitalize *nation* when used as a synonym for the United States or when used with a name to designate a definite nation.

What are we going to do with the influence and power of this great Nation?

Woodrow Wilson

The Six Nations lived within the boundaries of New York.

But, What great nation in such circumstances would not have taken up arms?

Woodrow Wilson

Capitalize *national* when preceding a capitalized word.

National Capital
National Academy of Sciences
The National Government
But, national ideas, national pride
The national defence demands not merely force but intelligence.

27. Capitalize *state* when used with a name or when used in place of the name, but lower-case when used as a general term.

New York State	State ticket
the State of Ohio	State government
the State leaders	State Democratic headquarters

This State must cope with its own problems.

The United States is a Federal republic of sovereign states bound together by the Constitution.

Note the usage of capitalization in the following:

State prison
State rights
State's attorney
statehood

State's evidence *or*
state's evidence
State banking division
State-wide (United States)

28. Capitalize all names of political parties and their adherents; names of royal families and dynasties.

Democrats
Republicans
Fascisti

Bourbon
Ming Dynasty
House of Stuart

Usage varies as to capitalization of *party. The New York Times* capitalizes *party,* as, Republican Party; the *Manual of Style,* the *New York Herald Tribune,* and the *New York World-Telegram & Sun* do not capitalize it, as, Republican party.

29. Capitalize names of clubs, associations, institutions, orders, and companies.

Union League Club
Tammany Hall
University Club of New York
American Association of University Women
American Association for the Advancement of Science
Young Women's Hebrew Association
American Legion
American Academy of Arts and Letters
English-Speaking Union
Knights of Columbus
Masonic Order
Russell Sage Foundation
Order of the Sacred Heart
American Ice Company

Do not capitalize *club, association, union, college,* or *university* when used alone, unless it has the value of a proper name.

The Board will meet at the Club this afternoon.
The clubs and associations of this city are numerous.
He belonged to a carpenters' union.
The Association voted on the question of dues.

Note the following illustrations of the "down" style of capitalization in regard to names of clubs, associations, etc.

The Chicago chapter of the Connecticut College Alumnae *association* is to meet for dinner this evening at the Chicago College *club,* after which the annual election of officers will take place. Mrs. Clarence Silber is now the president.

30. Capitalize names of squares, parks, towers, monuments, statues, buildings, thoroughfares.

Union Square	Trinity Church
the Tower of London	the Washington Monument
Park Row	*or* the Monument
Gramercy Park	the House (National)
the Mall	Halls of Congress
Eiffel Tower	the Capitol Grounds
the Capitol (Washington)	the Lincoln Memorial
Metropolitan Museum of Art	Capitol Halls of Congress
the Library of Congress	the Senate (National)
El Bethel Synagogue	Governor's Mansion
Avery Library	Kingsway
the Hall of Fame	the Lincoln Highway
the Executive Mansion	Capitol Chamber
Mansion House (London)	Westminster Abbey
the Guild Theater	Champs Elysées
the White House	Rock Creek Park

But, the statue of Lincoln, the tomb of Washington.

In some telephone and city directories, and in many newspapers the words *avenue, street, boulevard, square, place* and *court* are not written with initial capitals, even when used to indicate particular places.

Construction of a new YMCA building at Grove *street* and Elmwood *avenue,* Evanston, will begin this week, it was announced yesterday by Edward Sherman, chairman of the building committee.

Mr. Augustus Dinkler, of Waterbury, Conn., formerly of Narberth, is the guest for a few days of Mr. and Mrs. Newlin Wismer, of 210 Essex *avenue,* Narberth.

The plural form of a common noun written as part of a proper noun is capitalized, according to Government usage; but many publications advocate writing the plural form of the common noun without initial capital.

Park and Madison Avenues
Sylvan and Orange Boulevards
Milk and Winter Streets
Union and Pershing Squares
Hudson and Harlem Rivers
Avery and Morgan Libraries
Trinity and Grace Churches

Park and Madison avenues
Sylvan and Orange boulevards
Milk and Winter streets
Union and Pershing squares
Hudson and Harlem rivers
Avery and Morgan libraries
Trinity and Grace churches

Capitalize a common noun when it is used as a well-known short form of a specific proper name.

the Canal (Panama Canal)   the Lakes (Great Lakes)

Place references when merely descriptive and preceded by *the* and a definite name are not capitalized.

the mountains of North Carolina   the valley of the Susquehanna

(1) In business writing the following geographical terms are usually capitalized in the singular or plural, immediately following the name:

archipelago	gap	ocean
basin	glacier	park
bend	gulch	passage
branch (stream)	harbor	peninsula
butte	hill	plateau
canal	hollow	pond
channel	inlet	range (mountains)
county	island	reef
crater	light	ridge
creek	mesa	run (stream)
draw (stream)	mountain	shoal
flats	narrows	sound

(2) In business writing the following words are usually capitalized, singular or plural, when they stand before a name or after it, or when they are used as a part of a name:

bay	fort
bayou	head
camp (military)	isle
cape	lake
desert	mount
falls	oasis

pass	sea
port (*but* port of New York)	strait
river	valley

(3) Capitalize the following words if part of a name; but do not capitalize them when they are used in a general sense, as the rivers of Maine, the valleys of California and North Carolina:

airport	gulf	rapids
beach	lagoon	reservation
borough	landing	reservoir
cavern	lighthouse	spring
ferry	plain	tunnel
forest	prairie	volcano
gorge	province	woods

(4) Do not capitalize the following terms, even when they are used with a name or a number (Government usage):

breakwater	drydock	spillway
buoy	levee	station 4
chute	lock	watershed
dike	pier	weir
dock	slip	wharf

31. Capitalize special names of countries or regions of countries, cities or sections of cities, countries, rivers, bays, oceans, mountains, islands, and other geographical words.

Old World	the South Pole
New World	the Tropics
Orient	the Promised Land
Occident	the Eternal City
Far East	the Right Bank (Paris)
the Levant	the Border (Scotland)
the Continent (*but,* the conti-	the Southland
nent of Europe)	Greater New York
the Reich	the Loop (Chicago)
the Empire State	the Hub (Boston)
Middle West	Beacon Hill (Boston)
the Northwest Pacific States	the North End (Boston)

If a common noun or adjective forming an essential part of a name becomes removed from the rest of the name by an intervening common noun or adjective, the entire expression is no longer a proper noun and is therefore not capitalized.

> Union Station: union passenger station
> Eastern States: eastern farming states
>
> *GOP Style Manual*

32. Capitalize points of the compass when they designate geographical parts of the country.

Southern States	the Northwest
out West	Midwestern States

The South has increased its manufactures.
Election returns from the East are eagerly awaited.
The North took a decided stand on the question.
Big concentrated buying orders credited to Eastern sources were in evidence.

Do not capitalize such words when used merely to indicate direction.

—in Virginia and the colonies to the north and south of her.

facing south	north of Boston
driving east	west of the Rockies

(1) Do not capitalize adjectives derived from regional names when they are merely descriptive in character.

continental customs	oriental life
western hospitality	southern cooking
eastern fashions	northern climate
tropical fruits	an east wind

(2) Capitalize *northern, southern, western, eastern,* etc., when used as a part of proper names to designate a world division; do not capitalize such words when used to indicate parts of states.

Central and Southwestern Europe	western New York
Eastern Asia	eastern Pennsylvania
West South Africa	southern California
Eastern Hemisphere	northern Idaho

(3) Nouns referring to the inhabitants of different sections of the United States may or may not be capitalized.

Northerner   *or*   northerner
Easterner   *or*   easterner

33. Capitalize all proper names denoting political divisions.

British Empire	the Papal States
French Republic	the Pine Tree State
the Dominion of Canada	Ward Ten
the Commonwealth of Massa-chusetts	Nineteenth District
	Fourth Precinct
the Republic (United States)	Thirteenth Congressional District
the South American Republics	Westchester County
Thornton Township	City of New York

34. Capitalize *college, university, seminary, school, high school,* when used with a proper name; but when such words are used alone do not capitalize unless the word stands for a definite college or university and has the value of a proper name.

Elmira College	Oak Park High School
the College of Fine Arts	Bacon Academy
the School of Philosophy	the Academy (Athens)
the Graduate School	Students Hall

35. Capitalize *church* when used with a name to designate a body of religious belief or a building and also when it designates the Church Universal; capitalize *cathedral, synagogue,* and *chapel* when used with a name.

the Roman Church	the Cathedral of St. John the Divine
the Church of England	
High Church	St. Patrick's Cathedral
Protestant Episcopal Church	the National Cathedral
the Presbyterian Church	Beth-El and Emanuel Synagogue
the dignitaries of the Church	Free Synagogue
Church and State	Riverside Church

When *church, cathedral, synagogue, chapel* are used without a name or in a general sense, do not capitalize them.

church history	synagogue services
church altars	chapel exercises
cathedrals of France	church societies

36. Capitalize all names for the Bible, for parts and versions of the Bible, and all names of other sacred books.

Bible
Scriptures
Holy Writ
Word of God
Holy Bible
Breeches Bible
Old Testament
New Testament
Pentateuch
the Ten Commandments
Gospels (*but,* gospel teachings)

Lord's Prayer
Twenty-third Psalm
Gospel of Mark
King James Version
Authorized Version
Septuagint
Vulgate Version
Revised Version
Apocrypha
Koran
Talmud

Authorities differ regarding the capitalization of some adjectives derived from such nouns. The following examples are given in Webster.

apocryphal
Biblical
rabbinical

scriptural
Talmudic
Vedic

37. Capitalize all names for the Deity.

Father
Almighty
Judge of Nations
Jehovah
Supreme Being
First Cause
Divine Providence
Lord of Hosts

Messiah the Comforter
Son of Man
King of the Jews
Holy Ghost
Holy Spirit
Holy Trinity
Redeemer
Saviour

Do not capitalize *fatherhood, sonship, messiahship, messianic.*

38. Capitalize the *Virgin Mary,* the *Virgin,* the *Blessed Virgin, Madonna,* the *Holy Mother, Our Lady.*

39. Do not capitalize the word *goddess* except when referring to statues, such as the Goddess of Liberty.

When the daughter of Jupiter presented herself among a crowd of goddesses, she was distinguished by her graceful stature and superior beauty.

JOSEPH ADDISON

40. In the Bible and in the Book of Common Prayer, pronouns relating to the Deity are not capitalized.

O Lord, thou hast been our dwelling-place in all generations.
And he looked up and saw the rich men that were casting their gifts into the treasury.

Opinions of publishers of other books differ in regard to the capitalization of pronouns relating to the Deity.

The nominative and the accusative of the personal pronouns—He and Him, Thou and Thee—are capitalized in this connection, but not the possessives, his and thine.

All pronouns referring to the same (the Supreme Being, or any member of the Christian Trinity) when not closely preceded or followed by a distinct reference to the Deity should be capitalized.

"Trust Him who rules all things" (*but,* "When God worked six days he rested the seventh").

41. Capitalize *Heaven* when referring to the Deity, and *Paradise* and *Heaven* only when referring to a future abode; also *Hades,* but not *hell.*

The Style Book of The New York Times

Her prayers, whom Heaven delights to hear.

WILLIAM SHAKESPEARE

New Thoughts of God, new hopes of Heaven.

JOHN KEBLE

O bed! bed! bed! delicious bed!
That heaven upon earth to the weary head.

THOMAS HOOD

He descended into hell.

BOOK OF COMMON PRAYER

And in Hades, he lifted up his eyes, being in torment.

GOSPEL OF LUKE, REVISED VERSION

42. Capitalize the *Pope,* or the *Popes,* always; also *Holy Father* and *Pontiff,* meaning the Pope; *Cardinal, Apostolic Delegate, Archbishop, Bishop, Moderator* and *Presiding Elder* before personal names; also when used separately after the person has been named or when used in direct reference to persons holding office.

The Style Book of The New York Times

Every heart that has not been blinded and hardened by this terrible war must be touched by this moving appeal of his Holiness, the Pope.

WOODROW WILSON

43. Capitalize all names of creeds and confessions of faith and general Biblical terms.

the Apostles' Creed	the Westminster Catechism
Nicene Creed	Thirty-nine Articles
Athanasian Creed	Lord's Supper
Westminster Confession of Faith	Creed of Pius IV

44. Capitalize *Devil,* the *Evil One,* the *Adversary,* the *Father of Lies,* and *Beelzebub* meaning Satan.

"The beggar is in the saddle at last," cries Proverbial Wisdom. "Why, in the name of all former experience, doesn't he ride to the Devil?"
JAMES RUSSELL LOWELL

And the great dragon was cast out, that old serpent, called the Devil, and Satan, which deceiveth the whole world.
REVELATION 12:9

Do not capitalize when used in a general sense or as an expletive.

The things, we know, are neither rich nor rare.
But wonder how the devil they got there.
ALEXANDER POPE

45. Capitalize all names of holy days and holidays.

Christmas	Feast of Tabernacles
Easter	Whitsuntide
Good Friday	Memorial Day
Labor Day	New Year's Day
Yom Kippur	Thanksgiving Day
Fourth of July	All Saints' Day
Columbus Day	Michaelmas
Passover	Lincoln's Birthday

46. Capitalize the first word following a colon when it introduces an independent passage or sentence. (*See* p. 47.)

47. Capitalize the first word of each of a group of headings following a colon in a sentence if the topics are to be developed.

48. Capitalize the first word of such topics even when written in a tabular form.

1. Attracting attention.
2. Creating desire.

3. Convincing the mind.
4. Stimulating action.

Advanced Business Correspondence, HOTCHKISS AND KILDUFF

Do not capitalize a short list of words or phrases following a colon directly.

The steps of a century of educational development in America: industrialism, urbanization, mass schooling.

49. Capitalize the first word of every complete quotation.

In one of his letters, Franklin K. Lane wrote, "To be gay, one must see how very little some things are."

(1) Do not capitalize the first word of a direct quotation if this quotation is introduced indirectly in the text.

Lincoln ended his famous speech at Gettysburg with a plea for government "of the people, for the people, and by the people."
It was said by Theodore Roosevelt that "no people on earth have more cause to be thankful than ours."

(2) Do not capitalize that part of a quotation resumed within the same sentence.

"Nature," said Lowell, "abhors the credit system."

(3) Capitalize the first word of a question made in direct form but not quoted.

1789 asked of a thing, Is it rational? 1642 asked of a thing, Is it legal? or, when it went further, Is it according to conscience?

(4) Do not capitalize the first word of an indirect question or statement.

He asked what was the meaning of the party's steady growth in power.
Stevenson says that it is charm which is the basis of enduring art.

(5) Do not capitalize a partial quotation when this quotation is used as a motto on a title page or as a heading of a chapter; as,

. . . a letter may be written upon anything or nothing just as that anything or nothing happens to occur.

WILLIAM COWPER

(6) Do not capitalize a parenthetical statement that occurs in the middle of a sentence.

The enclosed matter either falls between the parts of a sentence or follows a sentence. When within a sentence the enclosed matter does not begin with a capital letter even though a full sentence, unless the first word is a proper noun, nor does it take a period at the end. If, however, the language is either interrogative or exclamatory, it takes the proper mark to show this; and such mark is placed within the parentheses or brackets.

Why We Punctuate, W. L. KLEIN

The clanging of the ambulance bell (for I had been brought to the hospital in an ambulance) was still ringing in my ears as the attendants tied me to a bed.

"We're going to annoy you, Worth!" (He kept on reading.)
"We've invented a new game." (At this he appeared interested.)
"It's called 'Eenie, meenie, minee, moe'—you get out and I go to Central Islip, or vice versa." Worth actually smiled.

50. Capitalize the first word of exclamatory or of interrogative sentences used in a series.

Not believe in Santa Claus! You might as well not believe in fairies!

The pale nymphs dancing at dawn, in a landscape of Corot's,—are they not formed from the dawn itself, from the first shafts and glimmerings of light on the forest's edge? And may not myths have been evolved in the same manner?

SOPHIA KIRK

51. Capitalize *Whereas* and *Resolved* in resolutions and the first word following *Resolved*. (*See* pp. 405–422.)

> *Whereas,* The United States Tariff Commission . . .
> *Be it Resolved,* That the President of the Senate . . .

52. Capitalize the article *the,* or its equivalent in a foreign language, when it is the authorized part of a geographical name, of a title of a book or of a work of art, or when incorporated as part of the legal name of a company or of an institution.

Geographical names: The Dalles, The Hague, The Weirs, El Salvador, La Paz, Le Havre; *but* the Gulf States, the Midwest, the Orient, the Western Hemisphere.

Titles: The House of the Seven Gables, The Merchant of Venice, The Gleaners.

Names of companies or institutions: The Federal Sugar Refining Company, The English-Speaking Union.

This rule is usually disregarded in newspapers and in informal writing when mentioning periodicals, ships, firm names, etc., as, the Tribune, the Atlantic Monthly, the Carborundum Company.

When used with personal titles, if it is not the first word in a sentence, *the* should not be capitalized.

Two new ex-officio members of the Board were the Reverend Joseph O'Donnell and the Honorable James Ryan.

53. Capitalize all references to divisions or parts of a specific work.

The Preface of the textbook is interesting.
Look in the Table of Contents.
The Index is well arranged.
The Introduction to the text presents biographical information.
Look in the Appendix for further information.

Do not capitalize these when used in a general sense; as,

We learned how to make an index.

54. Capitalize the names of the seasons only when they are personified or when they are referred to specifically.

If Winter comes, can Spring be far behind?
PERCY BYSSHE SHELLEY

We are going in the spring.
The Spring of 1930.

55. Capitalize words personified.

Sport that wrinkled Care derides,
And Laughter holding both his sides.
JOHN MILTON

Members are requested to rise when addressing the Chair.

As the practice of capitalizing personified terms gives rather an old-fashioned appearance, some modern writers disregard it.

56. In typewritten work, such as business letters and reports, when a noun is followed by a code reference or by a number, the word is ordinarily capitalized. When used generally, such words are not capitalized. The word *number* and its abbreviation *No.* are always omitted after *Form,* and may or may not be used in other such case.

Bulletin CL-50, *but* a news bulletin
Catalogue B-4, *but* your catalogue
Certificate 654, *but* birth certificate, marriage certificate
Contract No. 65, *but* a long-term contract
Form 335, *but* a shortened form
Reorganization Plan No. 6, *but* the plan

57. Capitalize nouns followed by a capitalized Roman numeral.

Act I, Vol. V, Book II

Often *in references* such nouns and Roman numerals are not capitalized.

Subdivisions and their abbreviations in literary references are not capitalized.

article—art.	line—l.	page—p.	verse—vs.
chapter—chap.	note—n.	section—sec.	volume—vol.

58. Capitalize all principal words (that is, nouns, pronouns, adjectives, adverbs, verbs, and first words) in titles of books, pictures, plays, musical compositions, documents, reports, papers, proceedings, captions, display lines, headings.

Books	A Son of the Middle Border
	Mark Twain's Letters
Pictures	Raphael's Madonna of the Grand Duke
	The Last Supper
Plays	The Merchant of Venice
	They Knew What They Wanted
	She Stoops to Conquer
Musical Compositions	
	Beethoven's Fifth Symphony
	The Moonlight Sonata
	The Pirates of Penzance
	Chopin's Nocturne, Opus 37, No. 2
Documents, Reports, and Proceedings	
	Charter of the United Nations
	The Report of the Committee on Vocational Education
	The Proceedings of the Modern Language Association

Captions

> Aloft They Soar in Their Air Taxis
> At the Flying Fields Adventurers of All Types Get New
>   Thrills

Modern usage in letters and advertisements frequently omits quotation marks but instead capitalizes every letter in titles of books, as THE CLUBWOMAN'S MANUAL.

59. Capitalize scientific names of the world's eras, common names for historical epochs, periods in the history of literature or language, and important events.

the Neolithic age	the Wars of the Roses
the Paleozoic period	Colonial days
the Fourth Glacial age	Revolutionary period
the Dark Ages	the days of the Empire
the Christian Era	the Civil War
the Crusades	the World War
the Middle Ages	the Louisiana Purchase
the Renaissance	the Battle of Bull Run
the Exile	Veterans' Day

60. Capitalize all names of the bodies of the solar system except the words *earth, moon, stars,* and *sun* unless they are personified.

the Milky Way	Orion
the Great Bear	Cassiopeia's Chair
the Big Dipper	the North Star
Venus	the Southern Cross

61. Capitalize in botanical, geological, zoölogical, and paleontological matter the scientific (Latin) names of divisions, orders, families, and genera, but not their English derivatives.

> Cotylosauria, *but* cotylosaurs
> Cruciferae, *but* crucifers

62. In botanical, geological, zoölogical, paleontological, and medical matter the names of species are never capitalized.

Cedrus libani	*Styrax californica*
Felis leo	*Conodectes favosus*
Cocos nucifera	*Epigaea repens*

63. Do not capitalize abbreviations unless the words they represent are usually capitalized, as, *F.* or *Fahr.* (Fahrenheit), or unless the abbreviation has been capitalized by custom, as, *EB* (eastbound) or *No.*

64. Abbreviations for forenoon and afternoon may be written as follows:

A.M.	*or*	a.m.
P.M.	*or*	p.m.

65. Do not capitalize units of measurement such as 6 *ft.*, 4 *lbs.*, 3 *qts.*

66. Capitalize the trade names of manufactured products, but lower-case the words following a trade name that are not part of the name.

Bon Ami   Celotex   Dixie milk   Silvertown tires

67. Capitalize most adjectives formed from proper nouns. Do not capitalize such adjectives in French, Italian, Norwegian, Spanish, and Swedish text.

British	Olympian
Canadian	Pan-American
Chesterfieldian	Papal
Elizabethan	Parisian
Gregorian	Rooseveltian
Hellenic	Semitic
Latin	Swiss
Napoleonic	Victorian

68. In advertising and in journalistic writing, capitals are often used for emphasis. This should be done sparingly, as excessive capitalization tends to weaken rather than to emphasize.

69. Capitalize both parts of a hyphened word if each part is ordinarily capitalized: *Anglo-American* attitude, *Scotch-Irish* ancestry. When a prefix that is part of a hyphened word is ordinarily written without a capital, it is not capitalized when combined with a proper noun except when used as the name of an organization or in a title that would require capitalization.

anti-American	non-Swedish
intra-European	trans-Canadian

but

Inter-American Artists	Trans-Siberian Railway

70. A list of words and expressions showing their generally accepted capitalization follows. Note that words derived from proper nouns that have developed a specialized meaning and are no longer identified with such nouns are not capitalized.

Allies (World War)
American history
Americanism
Americanization
anglicize
Anglo-French entente
artesian well
boycott
Breton lace
Cheshire cheese
chinaware
delftware
English literature
Georgian architecture
Gothic architecture
gothic type
Grades I-XIII
Icelandic legends
india rubber
Indian corn
Iroquois nation
jersey cloth
Jersey cows
Jewish people
lyonnaise potatoes

macadamized roads
mercurial
mid-Atlantic
morocco leather
Negro (the race)
negro spirituals
plaster of paris
Pompeian red
poor whites
portland cement
pro-British
Province of Quebec
Red Man
Roman citizens
roman type
Room 224
Statement No. 2
Table No. 5
transatlantic
transoceanic
tropical fruits
Tropics, the
Wedgwood ware
X-ray

REFERENCE BOOKS

Canadian Government Editorial Style Manual (The). Ottawa, Queen's Printer and Controller of Stationery.

HART, HORACE. *Rules for Compositors and Readers at the University Press, Oxford*. Oxford University Press.

THE NEW YORK TIMES. *Style Book*.

UNITED STATES GOVERNMENT PRINTING OFFICE. *Foreign Languages for the Use of Printers and Translators*. Superintendent of Documents.

UNITED STATES GOVERNMENT PRINTING OFFICE. *Style Manual*. Superintendent of Documents. (In this Handbook referred to as *GPO Style Manual*.)

UNIVERSITY OF CHICAGO PRESS. *A Manual of Style with Specimens of Type*. University of Chicago Press. (In this Handbook referred to as *Manual of Style*.)

Webster's New Collegiate Dictionary, pp. 1155–56.

2. Punctuation

The Period

1. Place a period at the end of a declarative sentence and at the end of an indirect question.

> The pure scientists are the advance guard of civilization.
> The chairman asked where the conference would be held.

2. Place a period after a request.

> Will you please give me a copy of the Summer Session Catalogue of Columbia University.
> May I have your answer by next Friday.
> May I not help you with your problem of reorganization of the Advertising Department.

A technically interrogative sentence—disguised as a question out of courtesy but actually embodying a request—does not need the interrogation point.

Manual of Style

> Will you kindly sign and return the inclosed card.
> Will you please quote prices for (1) 200 copies in paper, (2) 300 copies in regular cloth binding, and (3) 25 copies in library binding.

3. Place a period after an abbreviation that stands for a single word. (See also Rules 5 and 6.)

ctge.	inst.	o.p.
cu. ft.	lb.	q.v.
Dr.	mdse.	vol.
Esq.	Mrs.	yd.

Keep the period of an abbreviation with any other punctuation mark needed, except another period.

Before a colon:

The following prices were quoted yesterday on standard forty-inch burlap by E. R. Hill and Co., Inc.:

Before a semicolon:

Tune in *Magazine of the Air*. Full half hour—Monday, Wednesday and Friday mornings, 11 E.S.T.; 10 C.S.T.; 9 M.T.; 12 Noon P.T.

At the end of a sentence:

Formal notice was issued today of a sale of the property of Payson Brothers & Co., Ltd.

4. Do not place a period after Mme and Mlle in French (American usage, Mme. and Mlle.); after letters of technical matter of well-known publications, as PMLA (Publications of the Modern Language Association); or after abbreviations for linguistic epochs, as OE (Old English), MHG (Middle High German).

5. Ordinarily do not place a period between letters indicating the names of government boards; as, AAA, FBI, TVA; or after the call letters of broadcasting stations: WOR, WQXR.

6. According to individual preference, periods may or may not be placed after initials representing full personal names. Formerly periods were usual, as, *R. L. S., T. R., F. D. R.*
    In monograms periods are always omitted.

OWR   BI

In indicating the initials of a person dictating a letter and those of the typist, periods are always omitted.

AJ:STM   LPD MK

7. Do not place a period after Roman numerals unless in a table of contents or in other enumerative parts of lists.

Vol. X   Elizabeth II

I. The Development of the Letter
II. Letter Arrangement
III. What Enters into the Making of a Letter

8. Do not place a period after letters when they designate a person, as, *Mr. A* has paid his monthly interest.

9. Place periods after letters or figures in an outline when they mark the chief division of a subject. Omit the periods when the letters or figures are enclosed in parentheses.

I.
  A.
  B.
      1.
      2.
          a.
          b.
          c.
              (1)
              (2)
                  (a)
                  (b)
  II. etc.

10. Place a period before a decimal; and after abbreviations for *shillings* and *pence.*

    24.55   £6 5s. 10d.

British money may also be written:

    £6 5 10   *or*   £6.5.10   *or*   £6:5:10   *or*   6/5/10

11. A period may be used between figures denoting hours and minutes; as, 10.15. It is more usual, however, to use a colon; as, 10:15. (*See* pp. 48, 87.)

12. Place the period inside the parentheses when they inclose an independent sentence. (*See* p. 61.)

"Orchestra?" repeated Ben, in a puzzled voice.
"The crickets." (She tried not to make it sound like an explanation.) "I'd forgotten that nights on the Island were like this."
                                              CHRISTOPHER MORLEY

13. Place the period outside the parentheses when the enclosed matter forms a part of the preceding statement.

H. Poincaré, *Science and Method* (trans., pp. 54–55) (Footnote in *The Art of Thought*).

Orator, statesman, philosopher, rhetorician, and letter writer was the great Marcus Tullius Cicero (106–43 B.C.).

Since the tendency today is to avoid double punctuation, that is, more than one punctuation mark at the same place, parentheses are often used without the addition of any other punctuation mark even at the end of a sentence where formerly a period would be placed after the parentheses as in the preceding example.

14. Place a period inside quotation marks. (*See* pp. 56–57.)

I am going to read Tomlinson's "Gifts of Fortune."

"I am not afraid of work," said Gissing. "But I'm looking for horizons. In my work, I could never find any."

15. Omit the period after all display lines; after running heads; after centered headlines; after side-heads set in separate lines; after cut-in heads; after box-heads in tables; after superscriptions and legends that do not make more than a single line of type; after items in enumerated lists; after date lines heading communications; and after signatures.

Manual of Style

16. Do not place a period after chemical symbols, the words indicating size of books, or the words "per cent."

H_2O 16mo   10 per cent

17. Omit the period after a signature and after a title following a signature in a letter.

Yours very truly,
Martha Alexander
Personnel Director

18. Use three dots to denote an omission in quoted matter. When the omission occurs at the end of a sentence, the sentence period is retained as well. Use seven dots across the page to denote the omission of one or more paragraphs of quoted matter.

Henry Clay declared that the veto is totally irreconcilable with the genius of representative government if it is . . . employed with respect to the expediency of measures, as well as their constitutionality.

The Comma

1. Use a comma to separate words and phrases in a series.

Chess players, mathematicians, and organists are clannish, as all are workers in mysteries.

Sharing in the indicated larger yields were corn, potatoes, apples, tobacco, and peanuts.

Present usage advocates the use of the comma before *and* connecting the last two words of a series.

Some writers, however, prefer to omit the comma before *and,* as, The room is large, dignified and hospitable.

Their equipment includes fire extinguishers, safety flares, hydraulic jacks, portable danger signs, crow-bars and an emergency first-aid kit.

(1) Do not use a comma when the conjunction connects all the words in a series.

The soul of the largest and wealthiest and proudest nation may well go halfway to meet that of its poets.

WALT WHITMAN

There was in it (the song of a thrush) youth and hope and spring and glories of dawns and sunsets and moonlight and the sound of the wind far away.

SAMUEL SCOVILLE, JR.

(2) When *etc.* is the concluding member of a series, it should be preceded and followed by a comma. Note that *etc.* is the abbreviation for *et cetera.* As *et* means *and,* the word *and* should not precede *etc.*

(3) In company names consisting of a series of surnames, most organizations omit the comma between the last two members: *Hudson, Blair & Grant; Lawrence, Stevenson and Kane.* When the word *company* completes the series, the comma is omitted: *Green, Lake and Company.*

2. Use a comma between two adjectives preceding a noun when they are coordinate qualifying words.

Neutral, solid colors predominate, but a definite trend toward lighter shades is seen.

Do not use a comma between two adjectives preceding a noun if such punctuation destroys the relationship intended, as the adjectives are too closely related to be separated.

A State road runs northward by my door, dropping at length, through rolling fields, to a *pretty little* valley threaded by a *clear mountain* brook, and swinging across a neat bridge into an elm-shaded village.

so-called long-term obligations
daily average output
outstanding common stock

3. Use a comma to separate pairs of words in a series.

Arbutus and violets, crocuses and snowdrops, daffodils and jonquils bloom early.

4. Use a comma or commas to separate the name of the person addressed or his title from the rest of the sentence.

I believe, Mr. Cameron, that insurance is advisable for protection.
We welcome you, Mr. President, to our Conference.
Is there not a motion, Mr. Chairman, already before the House?

5. Use a comma to set off words in apposition.

Brigadier General Hugh A. Drum, Commander of the First Division, U.S. Army, formerly War Plans Officer of the General Staff, addressed reserve officers of the Metropolitan district last night at the De Witt Clinton High School.

Kessler and Adler, great tragedians both, once trod the boards with no more than a sentimental notice from the world uptown.

(1) The personal pronouns *myself, himself, herself,* etc., are not set off from words which they emphasize.

Stevenson himself confesses, but with no trace of egotism. that it is charm which is the basis of enduring art.

(2) Also do not use the comma when the word or phrase is in italics or is set apart by some other device.

The word *caprice* is derived from the Latin word *caper.*
Some few years ago painters coined the word "expressionism."

(3) Omit the comma in the following:

a. When the appositive has become part of the proper name.

Cedric the Saxon   William the Conqueror

b. When the connection is unusually close between the appositive and the word it modifies.

Our salesman Brown covers the New England territory.
But, Our salesman, Herbert Brown, covers the New England territory.

6. Use a comma to set off inverted names in bibliographies, in directories, or in other reference lists. (*See* p. 467.)

Cleveland, Grover	Lane, Franklin K.
Eliot, Charles W., LL.D.	Taylor, Howard, M.D.

7. Use a comma to separate a name from a title or degree that follows it.

Robert M. Carruth, President of the University of Erville
Simon Flexner, M.D.

8. Use a comma to set off a contrasted word, phrase, or clause.

Idling, in the true sense, is a gracious, not an inane thing.
In regard to inspiration man is passive, not active.
The rule works both ways: The higher the yield, the less the safety; the greater the safety, the less the yield.

9. Use a comma to set off a transitional word or expression; as, *then, indeed, nevertheless, moreover, of course* when a pause is needed for clearness or for emphasis. Dr. Summey says that there is no safe rule for such expressions. "If felt as integral parts of the structure they are usually open. If felt as parenthetical, and if they and the context are worth the emphasis effected by pointing, they are ordinarily punctuated. But each case is an individual problem."

Moreover, a series of short unrelated problems does not sustain the interest.
On the contrary, it is very clear that native good judgment and good feeling are not proportional to education.

Finally, Western's manufacturing engineers are learning new ways to produce new devices.

In conclusion, then, let it be stated again that the secretary in going into a new position has a vast amount of information to acquire.

EDWARD J. KILDUFF

We need not wonder, then, if perfect sentences are rare, and perfect pages rarer.

R. L. STEVENSON

All that we can say, therefore, as to the choice of words, is that we should use the words which fit the thought, whether they are Saxon or Latin.

GEORGE PHILIP KRAPP

In the following examples no commas are needed:

It is indeed strange that so few children read well today.
The decision in this case is probably not significant.

10. Use commas to set off parenthetical words, phrases, and clauses when such expressions clearly indicate pauses and when clearness is achieved by such punctuation. But when these expressions do not interrupt the thought or require punctuation for clearness, the commas should be omitted.

He, however, hurried forward, led by instinct towards an unknown goal.
The foreign-born, in fact, compose only fifty per cent of the East Side population.
All students, except aliens, are required to attend exercises in military drill.
A recent writer, it is true, has done much to show that the general reader daily indulges in poetry of a kind without knowing it.
Travel, we are often told, gives light to the mind.
The jury therefore gave a unanimous decision.
We are accordingly signing the contract.

11. Use a comma to indicate the omission of a word.

The former lead to the degree of Bachelor of Science or Bachelor in Architecture; the latter, to the degree of Master in Architecture, Master in Science, Doctor of Philosophy, Doctor of Science, Doctor of Public Health.

Often, however, commas are omitted, if the meaning is clear without them.

The Englishman's virtue is wisdom; the Frenchman's is reason; the Spaniard's serenity.

12. Use a comma to set off light exclamations.

Ah, if it were only the ocean to cross, it would be a matter of small thought to me—and great pleasure.

13. Use a comma to set off a phrase denoting residence or position and after, but not before, postal-delivery zone numbers.

Mr. Alexander Vanderpoll, of Larchmont, New York, addressed the meeting.

Also written:

Mr. Alexander Vanderpoll of Larchmont, New York.
Miss Ella Lane, 121 Fifth Street, N.E., Washington 2, D.C.

14. Use a comma in dates.

On February 25, 1920, the business was organized.

A comma may be used to separate the month from the year when the day of the month is omitted, as June, 1927; but modern usage permits June 1927.

15. Use a comma to set off figures in groups of more than four; as, 1,000,000; 31,842. (*See* p. 88.)

16. Use a comma to separate two figures or words indicating figures in order to make their meaning clear.

In 1935, 37,000 people in the United States were killed in automobile accidents.
On November 11, 379 issues closed higher.
Instead of thousands, millions were spent.

17. If such introductory words as *as, for example, for instance, namely, viz., that is,* and the terms following form parenthetical expressions and do not introduce enumerations, a comma precedes and follows the introductory word. (*See* p. 45 for use of semicolon and p. 46 for use of colon.)

Many of our American universities, for example, Harvard and Columbia, offer excellent courses in business.
You know that our November holiday, that is, Thanksgiving, was a New England institution.
Perhaps the most important factor of all is the psychological one, namely, the charm of aviation, for this means that the whole weight of American sentiment is behind this industry.

The use of the comma after *e.g.* (exempli gratia, for example) and *i.e.* (id est, that is) is optional. The present tendency is to omit the comma.

18. The use of the comma after phrases and clauses at the beginning of a sentence.

In such cases there is "great diversity of practice," as expressed by George Summey, Jr., in *American Punctuation* (pp. 170–71).

"Some writers and copy editors," he says, "appear to act on the theory that all adverbial clauses and most adverbial phrases at the beginning must be set off. . . . Writers who use good judgment punctuate according to thought and desired degrees of distinction, not on the principle 'Here's the pattern; apply the rule.' "

The comma with phrases:

(1) Use a comma after a long introductory prepositional phrase out of its natural order or when punctuation is needed for clearness.

For the roofing of your home and for the exterior walls, many inexpensive materials are available.
For railroads, new teletypewriter equipment will automatically relay such information.
Besides the usual business training a secretary receives in most schools in preparation for her work, a course in psychology would be advantageous for her.

But usually a short introductory prepositional phrase need not be followed by a comma.

In recent months many physical changes have taken place in this city.
During the last twenty years the business letterhead has undergone fundamental changes in content and appearance.

(2) Use a comma after introductory participial and absolute phrases.

The matter being decided, the President continued his report.
Realizing the need for more storage room, we built a new wing.
Generally speaking, his successes go unnoticed.
All things considered, the decision was just.

(3) Use commas to set off descriptive phrases following the noun they modify.

The stock, having reached 175, remained there for three weeks.
The child, pale with fatigue, waited for her mother.

19. When a dependent adverbial clause precedes a main clause, a comma is generally used.

While the general trend has been upward, decreases in the tax rates are not unknown.
Before the sale is advertised, we must take an inventory of our present stock.

But a short introductory adverbial clause may need no comma after it, provided that there can be no slightest uncertainty, without a comma, where the main clause begins, as is likely to be the case where the subject of both clauses is the same.

Webster's New Collegiate Dictionary

If we go back in American history we find this country has never kept silence as to what it stands for.

Before I began to write novels I had forgotten all I learned at school and college.

Note that when the dependent clause follows the main clause, the comma is usually omitted, except when the clause is plainly nonrestrictive, that is, adds a reason or concession introduced by *because, since, as, though.*

He was always at hand when there was difficult work to do.

He saw that some causes of international jealousy and of war would be removed if the grosser forms of exploitation of labor and the more distressing kinds of competition in this field . . . were eliminated.

Loyalty is one of the cardinal virtues of a secretary, because of the confidential nature of her position.

A chairman is likely to make an occasional error in his decisions, since he is only human.

20. Use commas to separate the members of a compound sentence when the clauses are short and closely connected.

Annoyances were laughed at, our noisy behavior was overlooked, conversation took an agreeable turn, and a delightful air of cheerfulness and good humor pervaded the entire household.

According to George Summey, Jr. (*American Punctuation,* p. 94), "Though there is apparently an increasing tendency to omit punctuation in compound sentences with *and* (to a less extent with the disjunctive *but*), it is still true that the great majority of compound sentences with connectives mark the junctions with punctuation."

Distinguish between a compound sentence (two or more independent clauses) and a simple sentence with a compound predicate (two or more verbs with the same subject). Do not use a comma between the verbs of a compound predicate.

He entered the firm to be an accountant and remained to be manager.

They changed their plans and erected an office building.

21. Use a comma to separate similar or identical words standing next to each other, even when the sense or continuation does not require it.

Whatever is, is right.

22. Use a comma to set off a nonrestrictive adjective clause. Such a clause is one that is not needed to make the meaning clear.

Engraved letterheads, which convey the impression of dignity and reliability, add to the attractiveness of letter pictures.

Dr. Peter Bell, who is regarded as one of the leading educators of the country, will address the meeting.

23. Do not use a comma to set off a restrictive adjective clause. Such a clause is one that is needed to make the meaning clear.

Most of the sales are made to people that are footloose or retired and that see in the trailer a means of casting off the cares of a home.

Anyone that does not appreciate music is unfortunate.

Present usage generally favors *who* or *which* when the relative clause conveys a qualification or statement simply additional or parenthetic, and *that* when it is definitely restrictive.

Our advertisements, *which* we strive to make truthful and convincing, have increased our business enormously this year.

Mrs. Martin, *who* visited the exhibition, came away delighted.

Women *that* visited the exhibition came away delighted.

24. Use a comma to set off informal direct quotations.

"Isn't it remarkable," marvelled Tonseten, "that such things can spring up out of the very ground? This is truly a Promised Land."

"Let our object be our country, our whole country, and nothing but our country," said Webster in his *First Bunker Hill Oration.*

Washington declared, in his *Farewell Address,* "Harmony, liberal intercourse with all nations, are recommended by policy, humanity, and interest."

Note that in an indirect quotation no comma is needed.

Washington said that we should not enter into political alliances with foreign nations.

25. Do not use a comma after a verb followed by an object noun clause introduced by *that, how, whether,* or *what.*

They believe that such a system, in order to be efficient, must be carefully planned and controlled.

Experience has shown how speed classes keep a stenographic force alert.

The firm did not know whether or not it would be successful in its new venture.

I learned what radio means to thousands of active-minded men and women, temporarily in drydock.

26. Use a comma to set off words, phrases, and clauses that would otherwise not be clear.

> Wrong: For a dollar you can secure dinner or bed and breakfast.
> Right: For a dollar you can secure dinner, or bed and breakfast.
> Wrong: When I was about to begin the speech ended.
> Right: When I was about to begin, the speech ended.

27. For use of the comma with parentheses, see pp. 61–62.

28. Notice the correct uses of the comma in the various parts of a letter. The comma at the ends of lines in written headings and in inside addresses, formerly so common, is seldom used today. The Department of State, however, advocates the use of the comma in the inside address of letters to officials. (*See also* pp. 287–304.)

IN FRIENDLY LETTER

Avon, New York
April 10, 19—

Dear Helen,

Sincerely yours,

IN BUSINESS LETTERS WITH WRITTEN ADDRESS

(1)

121 Fifth Street, N.E.
Washington 2, D.C.
July 24, 19—

Donald Charles, M.D.
   7746 South Shore Drive
   Chicago 49, Illinois

Dear Dr. Charles:

Yours sincerely,
Katherine Coleman
Secretary to Mr. Ayre

(2)

                                        Box 14, Rollins College
                                        Winter Park, Florida
                                        June 12, 19___

The Reverend Albert Reed, D.D.
New Boston, Mass.

Dear Sir:

                                        Very truly yours,
                                            Emily Rush Thompson
                                                (Mrs. Peter Thompson)

(3)

                                        Room 906, Grace Building
                                        1896 South Main Street
                                        Blanksville, Ohio
                                        February 26, 19___

Eastern Steamship Lines
Pier 25, North River
New York 13, N. Y.

Gentlemen:

                                        Yours very truly,
                                        Howard A. Wentworth, Jr.
                                        Credit Manager

(4)

                                        RD 1, Kings Road
                                        West Chester, Pa.
                                        December 4, 19___

Mason, Brooks and Co., Inc.
170 State Street
Boston 2, Mass.

Gentlemen: Attention of Mr. J. H. Green, Manager

                                        Yours very truly,
                                        Madeline Longwood
                                        (Mrs. Andrew Longwood)

(5)

General Delivery
Bangor, Maine
August 30, 19—

Mrs. J. E. Atkins, Secretary
Beaufort Garden Club
Beaufort, South Carolina

Dear Mrs. Atkins:

Sincerely yours,
Harriet Price, President
Longmeadow Civic Society

The Semicolon

Much modern writing, such as that found in newspapers, magazines, and business letters, makes use of the comma instead of the semicolon as formerly used.

The following are the generally accepted rules for the use of the semicolon.

1. Use a semicolon between the clauses of a compound sentence when the conjunction is omitted or when the connection is not close.

Some of us are wise in this way naturally and by genius; some of us never become so.

A man of action may be thinking; a man of passion may be acting.

Most businesses have a liability for accrued wages; large corporations also often give accrued bonuses to officers and employers and accrued commissions to salesmen.

2. Use a semicolon to separate coordinate clauses when they are long or when they contain commas.

In writing about himself, he may assume a serious or semiserious attitude; but more frequently he deals with his subject in a humorous, mock-serious, or even playful, personal gossip.

With one person or with one commodity, exposition may have to be featured, assisted by description and argument; with another person and commodity, narration may have to be featured, assisted by exposition and argument.

The best twentieth century letterwriter does not employ hackneyed expressions, for they make letters sound machinelike, as if all were cut to one pattern; they therefore deprive letters of individuality and personal flavor; they clog the message, blur the meaning, confuse the construction.

3. Use the semicolon in lists of names with titles or addresses and in other lists which would not be clear if separated by commas.

Other speakers on this program were L. R. Alderman, Specialist in Adult Education in the U.S. Bureau of Education; Miss Willie Lawson, Deputy State Superintendent of Public Schools, Little Rock, Ark.; and Reed Lewis, Director of Foreign Language Information Service, New York City.

Officers elected for the coming year are as follows: president, James Thomas; secretary, Raymond Colt; treasurer, Kenneth Graham.

The survey was made in Hartford, Torrington, and Winsted in Connecticut; and in Springfield, Worcester, and Boston in Massachusetts.

Invitations to the dedication should be sent to Mrs. Burton Allen, 11 Lake Road, Newton Centre, Massachusetts; Miss Helen Wollaston, 16 Adelaide Avenue, Barrington, Rhode Island; and Dr. Luke Randall, Pleasant Valley, Connecticut.

Horton's experience, according to his letter, has been two years as salesman for Bradford & Crane, Orlando, Florida; four years as sales manager for The Norton Company, Kansas City, Missouri; and five years as buyer for Hall Brothers, Richmond, Virginia.

Note that the *United States Government Printing Office Style Manual* states that the semicolon is to be avoided where a comma will suffice, as in the following sentence:

Regional offices are located in New York, N.Y., Chicago, Ill., and Dallas, Tex.

Bibliographical References.

Political Conditions in the South in 1868.—Dunning, *Reconstruction, Political and Economic* (American Nation Series), pp. 109–123; Hart, *American History Told by Contemporaries,* Vol. IV, pp. 445–458, 497–500; Elson, *History of the United States,* pp. 790–805.
Psalms 23:1–4; 37:2–5; 91:1–10.

4. Use a semicolon to separate groups of words, whether phrases or clauses, dependent on a general term or statement.

We hold these truths to be self-evident,—that all men are created equal; that they are endowed by their Creator with certain inalienable rights; that among these are life, liberty, and the pursuit of happiness.

THOMAS JEFFERSON

It is important that the young man entering the field of aeronautics should be interested in science, particularly in physics and mechanics; that he should be capable of close concentration; that he should like the atmosphere of a factory; and that he should be willing to do manual labor whenever required.

5. Use a semicolon to precede *for example, namely, for instance, viz., to wit, as, i.e.,* when they introduce an enumeration of examples not felt to be parenthetical or when they precede a principal statement or a sentence. (*See* p. 37 for use of comma, p. 46 for use of colon.)

The examinations will include practical demonstrations of professional skills in actual life situations; for example, a secretary in an actual office situation, a teacher in an actual classroom, and a nurse in an actual hospital ward.

Periodic reports may be either public or private; that is, they may deal with the affairs either of a community or of a business organization.

The qualities of the examination report are those which have been stressed in connection with the report as a type of literature; that is, completeness, clearness, and conciseness.

The course in Mechanical Engineering prepares the student to enter any one of the various branches of the profession; i.e., engine design, automatic design, locomotive construction.

The Catholic Church lays down rules and regulations; to wit, the Canon Law and the regulations made by the bishops of the several dioceses throughout the world for the conduct of its members.

6. Use a semicolon to separate clauses joined by such transitional words as *hence, moreover, however, also, therefore, consequently.* Follow these words by commas when they themselves should be emphasized.

The principles are almost universally accepted; hence you should learn them.

The speaker saw no objection to the suggestion; therefore she accepted it.

7. Place the semicolon outside quotation marks. (*See also* pp. 56–57.)

A chairman recognizes a member by calling his name, as "Mr. Ray"; or by addressing him, as "Mr. Member"; or by nodding to him.

At the conference he said definitely, "I will never run again for office"; however, we hope he will change his mind.

8. Place a semicolon after the parentheses when the parenthetical matter is explanatory of something that precedes.

Example: All marks [proofreader's] should be made in the margin on the same line as the error, and if there is more than one correction in a line, they should appear in their order separated by a slant line (i.e., *cap/wf/tr/*); if there are many, both margins may be used for marks.

The Colon

1. Use a colon to introduce a list, or to introduce formally a statement, an enumeration, or an illustration.

In the preparation of every report, there are three distinct steps:

1. Formulating the plan
2. Making the examination
3. Writing the report

When such introductory expressions as *namely, for example, for instance* are omitted before a list, a colon is used.

There were three reasons for his failure: laziness, ill health, and lack of training.

When the enumeration is informal or closely connected with the verb, the colon should be omitted.

Qualities every employee should exhibit are honesty, promptness, and courtesy.

2. Use a colon to introduce a formal or long direct quotation.

After visiting the island yesterday the Mayor said:

"It has long been my ambition to have the city provide a camp where youngsters not otherwise provided for could get the healthful benefits of sunshine, swimming and other recreational activities under ideal conditions. There are many private organizations which are doing excellent work in caring for children at Summer camps every year."

In answer to your request in regard to what must be done after an automobile accident in Florida, I quote from the "New Financial Responsibility Law":

"Immediately after an accident in which a person is killed or injured, the driver of every vehicle involved must notify the local police if it occurred in a municipality; otherwise, the county sheriff or nearest state highway patrol station."

3. Use a colon after a formal salutation in a letter. (*See* p. 41.)

Dear Sir: Gentlemen:

4. A colon is sometimes used instead of a comma after the place of publication in bibliographical matter, such as the following:

Van Doren, Dorothy. *The Lost Art.* New York: Coward-McCann, Inc., 1929.

5. Use a colon preceding a restatement of an idea.

Special intensity of silence seemed to emanate from Ben and Ruth, who sat close together on the top step. In the general pause theirs was like a hard core: it was not true silence, but only repressed speech.

CHRISTOPHER MORLEY

6. A colon is often used to precede an extended explanation.

True democracy presupposes two conditions: first, that the vast majority of the people have a genuine opinion upon public affairs; secondly, that electors will use their power as a public benefit.

ANDRÉ SIEGFRIED

7. Capitalize the first word following a colon when it introduces an independent passage or sentence. Do not capitalize the first word following a colon when it introduces an explanatory element or one logically dependent on what precedes.

Of what use is a college training? A certain amount of meditation has brought me to this as the pithiest reply which I myself can give: The best claim that a college education can possibly make on your respect, the best thing it can aspire to accomplish for you, is this: that it should help you to know a good man when you see him.

WILLIAM JAMES

News will be announced as follows: at the opening of the market, during trading, and after the close.

8. A colon may be placed between figures denoting hours and minutes. 11:30. (*See* pp. 31, 87.)

The Interrogation Point

1. Use an interrogation point at the end of a direct question.

"What are you going to do about it?" she asked.
She asked, "What are you going to do about it?" in a sarcastic manner.

Note that an indirect question is followed by a period.

They asked what we were going to do about it.

Note also that a request is usually followed by a period, rather than by an interrogation point. (*See* p. 29.)

Will you send me these articles by parcel post.
May I ask you to come early.
Would you mind letting me know whether or not he is still with the company.
Will you please look into this matter and let us have your comments.
May we suggest that you immediately notify the bank to cancel this check.

2. Use an interrogation point after a question not a direct quotation, which occurs within a sentence, when the question is emphatic.

Will advertising to such an extent pay? is a question.
The question put to the company will not be: What would you like to do? The question will be: What are you able to do? And the answer to that question will have to be: We can do little or nothing without the active collaboration of the employees.

When the question is not emphatic, a comma is generally used instead of an interrogation point.

How can such heavy expenditures be met, is a question that the administration must consider.
His main test for a salesman is, Will he create good will for the company.

3. Use an interrogation point after a quoted question at the end of a sentence.

The subject he will discuss is "How can credit be controlled?"

4. Use an interrogation point to indicate the end of a parenthetical question.

They wanted to know (would you believe it?) whether we should go by airplane. (*See* p. 62.)

Mr. Newton (or was it Mr. Lewton?) contended that jobs are "an end result, not a means to an end."

The manager was pleased (who would not have been?) by the 90 per cent increase in sales.

5. An interrogation point in parentheses is sometimes used to indicate doubt or irony.

Booker T. Washington was born in 1858 (?).

The necklace consisted of real (?) emeralds.

6. Place the interrogation point inside the quotation marks when it belongs to the quoted matter.

"Page," said Mr. McClure, "there are only three great editors in the United States."

"Who's the third one, Sam?" asked Page.

Life and Letters of Walter Hines Page

But place the interrogation point outside the quotation marks when it is not a part of the quoted matter.

Have you heard "Carmen"?

Were you ever "Way Down South in Dixie"?

The Exclamation Point

1. Use an exclamation point to mark an exclamatory word, phrase, or sentence.

Eastward Ho!

New Hampshire! historic state of scenic beauty, enshrined in the hearts of Americans! [Advertisement]

Simplicity, simplicity, simplicity! I say, let your affairs be as two or three, and not a hundred or a thousand; instead of a million count half a dozen, and keep your accounts on your thumbnail.

HENRY DAVID THOREAU

This is a pretty state of things, seven o'clock and no word of breakfast!

R. L. STEVENSON

2. If the whole sentence is exclamatory in form, place an exclamation point at the end.

And I awoke in struggles, and cried aloud, "I will sleep no more!"
                                                    THOMAS DE QUINCEY

3. Use an exclamation point at the end of sentences, interrogatory in form, but exclamatory in meaning.

What could have been better than our supper, cooked in the open air and eaten by firelight!

                                                    HENRY VAN DYKE

4. When the exclamation is not emphatic, place a comma instead of an exclamation point after it.

Well, well, Henry James is pretty good, though he is of the nineteenth century, and that glaringly.

                                                    R. L. STEVENSON

5. Use an exclamation point to express irony, surprise, and dissension.

What if words are doomed—merely to be used to fill in the interstices of architecture, the intervals between jazz music, or just written on a board! What if the dramatist is to become second fiddler, a hack hired and commissioned!

                                                    JOHN GALSWORTHY

The Apostrophe

1. To form the possessive singular of nouns add *'s:* the *woman's* child, the *secretary's* report, the *professor's* book, the *witness's* testimony.

2. To form the possessive singular of compound nouns add an apostrophe and *s* (*'s*) at the end of the word: his *daughter-in-law's* manners, the *vice-consul's* arrival, a *letter-carrier's* appointment.

3. To form the possessive singular of expressions used as compound nouns add an apostrophe and *s* (*'s*) to the last word of an expression: *Charles the First's* failure, *Peter Miller Jr.'s* education, the *Duke of York's* palace.

4. To denote the possessive when a phrase is regarded as a compound noun and means a person or persons, the apostrophe and *s* (*'s*) are added to the last word of the phrase: the *University of Chicago's* second revolution in education, the *Bank of the Republic's* gold reserve.

5. To form the possessive plural of nouns add an apostrophe if the plural ends in *s: girls'* coats, the *Ladies' Home Journal.*

6. If the plural does not end in *s,* add an apostrophe and *s* (*'s*): *children's* games, *women's* clubs.

7. To form the possessive plural of compound nouns add an apostrophe and *s* (*'s*) at the end of the word: his *sons-in-law's* taxes.

8. To form the possessive of two or more words in a series connected by conjunctions and denoting joint possession use the apostrophe and *s* (*'s*) after the last noun only: *Lord & Taylor's, Park and Tilford's.*

9. When joint possession is not denoted, use the apostrophe and *s* (*'s*) after each noun: *Macy's and Gimbel's, Altman's and Bonwit Teller's, Wordsworth's and Shelley's* poetry, *Hoover's and Roosevelt's* policies, *ladies' and children's* apparel.

10. In proper nouns ending in *s,* add an apostrophe and *s* (*'s*) to indicate the possessive: *Adams's* chronicle, *Dawes's* bank, *Cross's* theory, *Wells's* heroes, *Ayres's* references, *Ellis's* psychology, *Sinclair Lewis's* new novel, *Watkins's* lectures, *Lily Pons's* song recital, *Keats's* poems, *Dickens's* stories, *Brooks's* composition, *Mrs. Gates's* estate. I read *Holmes's* (not *Oliver Wendell's*) School History and *Wells's* History of the World.

This usage is advocated by *Text, Type, and Style;* by *A Handbook of Style of Princeton University Press;* by *Rules for Compositors and Readers at the University Press, Oxford,* and by Woolley and Scott's *College Handbook of Composition.*

(1) Some authorities allow the omission of *s* after the apostrophe in singular nouns ending in *s, x,* or *z;* as, Grant *Richards'* insinuatingly simple tale (*New York Herald Tribune*), *Clemens'* autobiography, *Keats'* poems, *Dickens'* stories, *Thomas'* broadcasting, *Knox'* coats, *Diaz'* biography.

Modern usage, as noted above, prefers *Keats's, Dickens's, Brooks's.*

(2) Notice the omission of apostrophes in some titles: *Teachers*

College, *Governors* Island, *Citizens* Bank, American *Bankers* Association. But many organizations follow the general rule: The *Actors'* Dinner Club, Southern *Women's* Educational Alliance.

(3) To avoid unpleasant sound, the apostrophe without the *s* is used by most authorities in the following: for *conscience'* sake, in *Jesus'* name.

11. The object of an action should be expressed by an *of-phrase* rather than by the possessive case: the assassination *of President McKinley,* the expulsion *of the Romanoffs.*

12. Note that either the possessive case or the *of-phrase* may sometimes be used interchangeably, the choice often depending upon the sound of the expression in the sentence: the *secretary's* work or the work *of the secretary, Roosevelt's* Administration or the Administration *of Roosevelt.* The possessive, however, does not always mean the same as the objective with the *of-phrase.* Compare *Mary's* picture, a picture *of Mary.*

13. In certain idiomatic expressions both the apostrophe and *s* (*'s*) and the *of-phrase* (sometimes called the double possessive) are used: This is a favorite pen *of John's;* I have examined that report *of the bookkeeper's.*

14. To denote the possessive of inanimate objects an *of-phrase* is used instead of the possessive form: the success *of that store,* the routine *of the office,* the chapters *of the book,* the thunder *of the surf.*

(1) When an inanimate object is personified, the apostrophe and *s* (*'s*) may be used: *Death's* approaching stride, the *wind's* tongue.

(2) Certain idiomatic expressions referring particularly to time are written with the apostrophe and *s* (*'s*):

a day's vacation, a day's work, a day's journey, a two weeks' trip, a week's work, a month's notice, four months' wages, a year's interest, three years' salary, a two years' lease. Notice also *a stone's throw, my heart's desire, the world's work, a dollar's worth, ten dollars' worth, thirty days' grace, the week's development.*

15. The *'s* is usually added to figures, signs, symbols, and letters of the alphabet to form the plural. There is, however, a growing tendency to omit the apostrophe in plurals of capital letters, signs, symbols, and figures: *ABCs, 6s, ¶s.*

Your *a's* look very much like your *o's.*
In our grandmothers' days the three *Rs* (or *R's*) formed the basis of education.
The *8's* (or *8s*) are to be placed in this column.
In the *1800s* (or *1800's*) business made great strides.

16. An apostrophe is used in expressions like the following:

OK'd, 4-H'ers, SOS'd, X'd out.

17. Use an apostrophe to denote the omission of a letter in contractions.

can't, couldn't, didn't, it's, isn't, o'clock, they're, 'tis, won't.

Such words as *bus,* from *omnibus,* and *phone* from *telephone* are written without an apostrophe.

18. Do not use an apostrophe to denote the omission of a letter or letters in an abbreviation.

Asst.	chg.	pkg.	Supt.
Dept.	Comdt.	shpt.	Wm.
Chas.	pfd.	sgd.	yd.

19. Sometimes the apostrophe is used in place of the first two figures for the year: *the Class of '38, late in '57.*

20. A noun modifying a gerund must be in the possessive case.

I had not heard of *John's* going.
Kreisler's playing of the *Kreutzer Sonata* delighted his audience.

21. For the use of the apostrophe in words referred to as words see p. 186.

Quotation Marks

1. Use double quotation marks to enclose a direct quotation.

"The truth is," says Roland Hall in *Business Writing,* "that business and industry are full of romance, adventure, and interesting pictures if the observer will only train his mind to see and appreciate."

Weseen states in *Everyday Uses of English,* "Speaking and writing are done, not for the sake of the speaker or writer, but for the sake of other persons."

"Page could reject a story with a letter that was a compliment," O. Henry said, "and make everybody feel so happy that you could take it to a bank and borrow money on it."

Life and Letters of Walter Hines Page

Do not use quotation marks to set off indirect quotations.

Wrong: He remarked "that he was tired."
Right: He remarked that he was tired.
Right: He remarked, "I am tired."

Do not capitalize the first word of a quotation introduced indirectly in the text. (*See* p. 22.)

Field Marshal Lord Allenby praised the Kellogg anti-war pact as the "finest achievement of modern times."

Mr. Humphrey expressed confidence that the commission would have the cooperation of "practically every publisher in the country" in its attempt to suppress fraudulent advertising.

2. When two or more paragraphs are quoted, quotation marks should be placed at the beginning of each paragraph, but only at the end of the last.

In *The Writing of English,* Manly and Rickert state the following:
"The chances are that on almost any subject, if you have done your bibliographical work well, you will have many references. Where shall you begin to read?

"It is usually best to begin with the most recent books and articles, for the reason that they often include summaries of earlier work on the same subject and may save you the trouble of looking that up.

"As between two recent writers on the same subject, choose the one of better reputation."

Modern usage advocates the omission of quotation marks around single extracts quoted in smaller type or placed in paragraphs indented on both sides.

John Burroughs, who had plenty of time and leisure to read and think about books and nature, said of writing:

One thing is certain: where there is no distinct personal flavor, we soon tire of it. The savor of every true literary production comes from the man himself. The secret is not in any prescribed order or words—it is the quality of mind and spirit that warms the words and shines through them.

If Burroughs had written these words in regard to letters, he could not have spoken more truly, for one of the requisites of great letters is the revelation of personality.

Training for Secretarial Practice, S. A. TAINTOR

3. Styles vary regarding the use of quotation marks to enclose complete letters or telegrams with date and signature.   The *GPO Style Manual* states the following:

Quotation marks are not used to enclose complete letters having date and signature, . . . extracts that are indented or set in smaller type, or solid extracts in leaded matter . . .

Many business firms, however, prefer the use of quotation marks before the date, the inside address, and the salutation, and after the final word in the signature.

"January 1, 19—

"Baldwin Paint Company
298 Fourth Avenue
New York, N. Y.

"Gentlemen:

. . . .
. . . .

Yours very truly,
Henry Grant
Manager"

If the letter requires an additional page, quotation marks should precede each paragraph to make clear the continuation of quoted matter.

4. Use single quotation marks to enclose a quotation within a quotation. When it is necessary to use quotation marks within these, use double marks again.

"Fourth 'world's greatest movie' this season is at the Manzanita tonight," Nat said.

" 'Did you ever know,' said the indignant Mr. Balfour, turning to me, 'of such a thing as a minister not even being informed of his Government's decisions?' 'Yes,' I said, 'if I ransack my memory diligently, I think I could find such cases.' The meeting went into laughter."

Life and Letters of Walter Hines Page

5. Use quotation marks or italics to set off from the context any quoted or emphasized word or short phrase.

"Inquiry" and "address" are words often mispronounced.

People never cease to marvel at the so-called "suddenness" of fate. In the next street a house "suddenly" falls down, an old neighbor "suddenly" dies, a famous European dynasty is "suddenly" wiped out. As a matter of fact, as all scientists, most newspaper men, and a few historians know, nothing ever happens "suddenly."

HENDRIK VAN LOON

The phrase, "A hundred per cent American," is often carelessly used. The government is "playing with fire" in sending troops.

6. Quotation marks are often used to enclose titles of books, but in present usage titles are ordinarily italicized.

My favorite? It is "Joan of Arc." My next is "Huckleberry Finn," but the family's next is "The Prince and the Pauper."

Mark Twain's Letters

David Copperfield is one of Dickens's most popular novels.

Underline in manuscript what is intended to be in italics in print.

In the best present usage titles of whole printed works and periodicals are italicized and titles of parts are inclosed in quotation marks. (*See* pp. 79–80, 466–467.)

A Dictionary of English Grammar, MAURICE WESEEN

To denote titles of lectures and of similar items on programs, quotation marks, italic, small caps, or roman may be used. Since too many quotation marks on a page are unattractive, italic or roman is often preferred.

QUOTATION MARKS WITH REFERENCE
TO OTHER PUNCTUATION MARKS

7. The following usage of quotation marks represents modern practice in writing.

Quotation marks are always set *outside* the comma and the period; always *inside* the colon and the semicolon; *outside* or *inside* the marks of exclamation and the interrogation according as those marks do or do not belong to the quoted matter; *outside* the dash when it stands for something left unsaid, and *inside* when it is used as an ordinary punctuation mark; *inside* parentheses when the parenthetical clause alone is quoted, otherwise *outside*.

Text, Type, and Style, ATLANTIC MONTHLY PRESS

With the comma (*see also* p. 40):

Never were "we, the people of the United States," so thoroughly united as in that vast cooperation.

HENRY VAN DYKE

With the period (*see also* p. 32):

Elbert Hubbard's essay bore the title of "A Message to Garcia."

With the semicolon:

"Punctuality," says the proverb, "is the courtesy due to kings"; and the saying has an extra super-diplomatic force when the sovereign happens to be a very beautiful young lady.

HENRY VAN DYKE

There are Americans who appear to love their country for much the same reason that Stevenson's "child" loves the "friendly cow";
"She gives me cream with all her might
To eat with apple tart."

AGNES REPPLIER

Newspapers unsparingly denounced "trade union politicians" as "demagogues," "levellers," and "rag, tag and bobtail"; and some of them, deeming labor unrest the sour fruit of manhood suffrage, suggested disfranchisement as a remedy.

History of the United States, BEARD AND BEARD

With the dash:

"The trouble with this country is," observed Herndon, "that there are too many people going about saying, 'The trouble with this country is—' "

"Yes," declared the supervisor, "Jones would be a possible candidate, but—" Here he paused significantly.

With the exclamation and interrogation points:

O, if I could only write my own biography from beginning to end— without reservation or false colouring—it would be an invaluable document for my countrywomen in more than one particular; but "decency forbids"!

JANE CARLYLE

"Mother!" he appealed. "Tell the truth. Do you have a good time?"

CHRISTOPHER MORLEY

Why should we be told that "the world gapes in wonder" as it contemplates "an Aladdin romance of steel and gold"?

AGNES REPPLIER

But who shall say that a hundred dollars a minute is beyond the "order of reason"?

AGNES REPPLIER

The Dash

Formerly other punctuation marks were used with the dash, but now such combinations as comma with dash, semicolon with dash, and colon with dash are rare.

1. Use a dash to indicate an abrupt change in a sentence.

July 25—your birthday!
"We haven't found out yet, but—here comes the doctor," Mother replied.

2. Sometimes a dash is used in place of the parentheses to set off interpolated explanatory matter.

Care should be exercised in the construction of any sort of insert—be it notice or announcement or frank sales appeal—to make it comply with the general principles involved in writing good advertising copy.

JOHN B. OPDYCKE

Then there is a never-failing crop of birds—robins, gold-finches, king-birds, cedar-birds, hair-birds, orioles, starlings—all nesting and breeding in its branches.

JOHN BURROUGHS

3. Use a dash to indicate an unfinished sentence.

"Oh, but I can't," I said. "They're the most interesting letters I've read this year. In fact, she is the most alive and compelling personality I've met since—since—" I hesitated for a worthy comparison.
"You surely wouldn't give a present of books you didn't like," Gretta interrupted. "If you can't give away the poor ones, and won't give away the good—" She raised her eyes in despair.

4. A dash is sometimes used in appositive expressions.

They sit there forever on the dim horizon of my mind, that Stonehenge circle of elderly disapproving Faces—Faces of the Uncles and Schoolmasters and Tutors who frowned on me in my youth.

Local governments—the cities, the school districts, the counties, and the states—should face up to their responsibilities.

5. Use a dash to indicate hesitancy in speech.

"You're—you're fine!" she said admiringly. "Just—just fine!"

"Think, for instance, of—well—of Helen's foolish extravagance or Paul's selfishness."

"Never to marry!" exclaimed Anne. "To be—to be an old maid—why—why that would be tragic."

6. Use a dash instead of the word *to* in reference to dates, pages, paragraphs, verses, and cantos.

1455–1585	Genesis 2:10–14
pages 10–49	verses 5–10
paragraphs 1–14	Cantos I–IV

7. Use a dash under names in a catalogue to indicate repetition.

Galsworthy, John. *The Forsyte Saga*
——————. *The Silver Fox*
——————. *Justice*

Note that the dash for this purpose must never be used at the top of a page.

Parentheses

1. Use parentheses to denote parenthetical matter not necessary to the grammatical structure of the sentence. For slight or informal parenthetical elements, the comma or the dash is preferred.

The French (and I never could write a book without some reference to that peculiar wisdom of the French people which seems to harmonize whatever it touches), the French long ago gave us a recipe for the writing of history.

HENDRIK VAN LOON

But, my dear fellow, a gout (the most obscure of diseases) of thirty-two years standing (and when the patient is sixty-five years old) is not to be driven off by the Medicine-men incantations.

Letters from Joseph Conrad

The old New England covered bridge (covered, of course, to protect the traffic from the winter blasts during the long crossing) had the boxlike simplicity of the New England farmhouse and barn.

WALTER PRICHARD EATON

Sentiment (so far as literature is concerned) may be defined, I suppose, as the just verbal expression of genuine feeling.

JOHN GALSWORTHY

2. Parentheses may be used to enclose figures or letters marking the divisions of a subject.

Alexander Hamilton believed that Washington's *Farewell Address* should include among other topics the following:
 (a) The Union
 (b) Relation of the parts of the Union to each other
 (c) Morals, religion, industry, commerce, economy
 (d) Good faith with all other nations

Webster spoke on the following subjects at Bunker Hill: (1) the significance of the occasion, (2) honor to the dead, (3) the principle of popular government.

Modern usage omits parentheses with Roman numerals.

3. Use parentheses to enclose matter interpolated by way of explanation.

The figure of a knight in armor (see plate 4) shows the style worn by King Richard.

Yale University beneficiary funds (available in part for financial aid to undergraduates in addition to that provided by the above funds of the separate schools) include the University Loan Fund and those founded in memory of Francis Bacon, Joseph Lyman, and David Willcox.

The Perfect Tribute (a story of Lincoln's Address at Gettysburg) by Mary Raymond Shipman Andrews, Charles Scribner's Sons.

4. In legal documents or whenever double form is required, use parentheses to enclose a figure inserted to confirm a statement given in words: thirty (30) days; sixty (60) dollars, *not* sixty dollars (60); twenty dollars ($20), *not* twenty ($20) dollars.

PARENTHESES WITH REFERENCE TO OTHER
PUNCTUATION MARKS

Since the tendency today is to avoid double punctuation, that is, more than one punctuation mark at the same place, no additional

punctuation is used with parentheses unless it is needed to punctuate the whole sentence. Carrying out the avoidance of double
punctuation, many authorities even advocate the omission of the
period at the end of a sentence following the parenthesis.

(a) The mark of punctuation follows the second parenthesis of the
pair when this mark applies to the sentence containing the parenthesis
and not to the passage in parentheses.

(b) The mark of punctuation precedes the second parenthesis of the
pair when this mark applies to the passage in parentheses.

WOOLLEY AND SCOTT

With Period Outside:

The whole of this passage is worth studying. Part of it is quoted by
T. Hazlitt (*loc. cit.,* pp. 84–88).

GRAHAM WALLAS

The paper was marked "Defendant's Exhibit No. 4" (exact title).

With Period Inside:

The remark set me wondering to what extent dealers in other articles
are perplexed by their customers' preferences. (Some milliners, I hope.)

E. V. LUCAS

All nominations take current date. (Sample of each form is shown
on following pages.)

If copy reads 3½ million dollars, change to read $3½ million. (To
be used only in amounts of a million or more.)

Note that the word *confirmed* is set in italic in the recommendation
line. (See sample 6, p. 246.)

With the exclamation point:

I find that on my list of loves, scents would take a very important
place— . . . the leaves of the lemon verbena, the scent of pine trees,
the scent of unlit cigars, the scent of cigarette smoke blown my way
from a distance, the scent of coffee as it arrives from the grocer's (see
what a poet I am!), the scent of the underside of those little cushions of
moss which come away so easily in the woods, the scent of lilies of the
valley . . .

With the comma, semicolon, and colon:

A comma, semicolon, or colon is not placed in front of an opening parenthesis.

Right: He takes the *Winter Park* (Florida) *Herald.*
Wrong: He takes the *Winter Park,* (Florida) *Herald.*

Right: This case (124 U.S. 329) is not relevant.
Wrong: This case, (124 U. S. 329) is not relevant.

A comma, semicolon, or colon should not be inserted after the closing parenthesis unless such punctuation would be needed if there were no parentheses.

Right: Essays, magazines (recent ones), poems, and plays were listed.
Wrong: Essays and magazines (recent ones), were listed.
Right: Ships sail on June 2 for Buenos Aires, Argentine Republic (mails close at 4 P.M.); for Caracas, Venezuela (mails close at 2 P.M.); and for Montevideo, Uruguay (mails close at 6 P.M.).

With the interrogation point (see p. 49):

He was vain (who would not be under the circumstances?) and loved to hear the applause of the multitude.

Brackets

1. Use brackets to enclose words and phrases independent of the sentence, such as explanatory notes, omissions, and such comments as are not written by the author of the text.

I once asked him [John] what he thought.
The following year [1620] the Pilgrims landed at Plymouth.
Such a recommendation should win our support. [Applause.]

2. Use brackets to enclose *sic* following an error in spelling or usage in copied matter.

The Rosevelt [*sic*] family contributed two presidents.

Asterisks and Dots

Indication of ellipses varies in different offices and publications. The *Style Book of The New York Times* states: "Use three stars, thus: * * * to denote an ellipsis either in the body of a paragraph or at the end. Between paragraphs make a line of three stars, when called for, thus:

*   *   *"

George Summey, Jr., in *American Punctuation,* on the other hand, explains that a group of three spaced periods is more often used than asterisks to show the omission of words from quoted matter and that a full line of spaced periods is more usual than spaced asterisks to denote ellipsis of a paragraph or more.

REFERENCE BOOKS (see also those for Chap. 1)

SUMMEY, GEORGE, JR. *American Punctuation*. The Ronald Press Company.
Webster's New Collegiate Dictionary. pp. 1148–53.

3. Hyphenation and Compounds

The Hyphen

GENERAL USES

A hyphen is used to indicate the following:

(1) Words compounded of two or more words to represent a new idea.

(2) The division of a word into syllables.

(3) The division of a word at the end of a line.

Since usage varies, it is impossible to give inflexible rules for the hyphening of phrases.

"Word forms constantly undergo modification. Two-word forms acquire the hyphen, later are printed as one word, and not infrequently the transition is from the two- to the one-word form, by-passing the hyphen stage. . . .

"Current language trends point definitely to closing up words which, through frequent use, have become associated in the reader's mind as units of thought. The tendency to amalgamate words, particularly two short words, assures easier continuity, and is a natural progression from the older and less flexible treatment of words."

GPO Style Manual

When there is doubt whether a phrase should be written solid, as two words, or hyphened, it is advisable to consult an authoritative source, such as a dictionary.

The following rules may be regarded as a guide to current practice.

Compounds with and without Hyphens

1. Use a hyphen as follows between units forming a compound adjective before the noun modified:

first-class bond

deep-blue color

four-year-old girl

house-to-house search

long-distance telephone

one-man job

up-to-date fashion

worth-while program

Note that the hyphen should be inserted after a series of hyphenated adjectives modifying the same noun when the noun occurs after the last adjective only: *5- and 10-cent store; four-, five-, and six-story buildings.*

2. When a compound adjective follows the noun or the predicate ordinarily it is not hyphened.

Many fashions, popular and up to date, will be on display.

His fame, well deserved and world wide, rests on his scientific achievements.

The program proved to be worth while.

3. An adverb ending in *ly* is not joined with a hyphen to the adjective which it qualifies; as, a *highly* developed intelligence, a *fully* balanced ration, a *beautifully* told story.

4. Surnames written with a hyphen are in most cases considered as one name; as, Harley *Granville-Barker,* Sheila *Kaye-Smith,* and Madame *Schumann-Heink.*

5. Proper names used adjectively are not joined by a hyphen; as, *New England* winters, *Fifth Avenue* shoppers, *South American* Indians.

But notice such forms as *German-American, Anglo-Indian, Indo-European,* which are purely adjective in nature and always hyphened.

6. Use a hyphen in compound numerals; as, *forty-six, twenty-one* hundredths, *twenty-first.*

7. Use a hyphen when compounding numerals with other words; as, *five-o'clock* tea, *twenty-foot* pole, *150-yard* dash.

8. Fractions are hyphened when the word is used as an adjective; as, They were entitled to *ten and one-half* shares of stock. When the fraction is used as a noun no hyphen is necessary; as, He invested *one third* of his money in real estate. But there is a growing tendency in business writing to use the hyphen in both the adjective and the noun.

9. Use a hyphen in compounds made up of nouns and prepositional phrases.

sons-in-law
daughter-in-law
man-of-war
hand-to-hand

cap-à-pie
vis-à-vis
tête-à-tête
will-o'-the-wisp

10. Use a hyphen in titles compounded with *ex* and *elect*.

ex-Governor
ex-Mayor
ex-President

Governor-elect
President-elect
Vice President-elect

11. Civil and military (single) titles are not hyphened.

GPO Style Manual

CIVIL TITLES

Ambassador at Large
Ambassador Extraordinary and Plenipotentiary
Assistant Secretary
Associate Justice
Attorney at Law
Attorney General
Chargé d'Affaires
Chief Clerk
Chief Executive
Chief Justice
Chief Magistrate
Chief of Police
Chief of Protocol
Congressman at Large
Consul General
Counselor of Embassy
Deputy Commissioner
Director General

Editor in Chief
Envoy Extraordinary and Minister Plenipotentiary
First Secretary
Second Secretary
Third Secretary
Governor General
Lieutenant Governor
Military Attaché
Naval Attaché
Postmaster General
Public Printer
Secretary of Labor
Secretary General of the United Nations
Sergeant at Arms
Under Secretary
Vice Consul
Vice President

Words denoting the office itself are hyphened; as, *under-secretaryship, vice-presidency.*

MILITARY AND NAVAL TITLES

Adjutant General
Brigadier General
Brigadier General
   Commandant
Commander in Chief
Lieutenant Colonel
Lieutenant Commander

Lieutenant General
Major General
Quartermaster General
Rear Admiral
Surgeon General
Vice Admiral

According to British usage the following titles are hyphened:

Field-Marshal
Lieutenant-Colonel
Lieutenant-Commander
Lieutenant-General

Major-General
Rear-Admiral
Vice-Admiral

12. Use the hyphen in compounds made up of prefixes joined to proper names and in compounds of unusual formation.

anti-American
mid-Atlantic
mid-August
neo-Platonism
pan-Hellenic

pseudo-Gothic
un-American
anti-suffragist
anti-trust
ultra-fashionable

13. Do not ordinarily use the hyphen between a prefix and the stem when the added word is not a proper noun.

antisocial
biannual
bicentennial
biennial
extracurricular
forecast
foreclose
intercollegiate

intramural
nonconformist
nonessential
nonofficial
preview
retroactive
semiyearly
supermarket

Compounds are hyphened when otherwise a vowel would be confusingly doubled in combination: *anti-imperialist, co-owner, intra-atomic, pre-empt, re-enter, semi-independent.*

Exceptions: *Cooperate* and *coordinate* and their derivatives are often written thus as solid forms, because of their great frequency and familiarity.

Webster's New Collegiate Dictionary

Except after the short prefixes *co, de, pre, pro,* and *re,* which are generally printed solid, a hyphen is used to avoid doubling a vowel or tripling a consonant: *cooperation, deemphasis, preexisting, anti-inflation, micro-organism, semi-independent, brass-smith, Inverness-shire, thimble-eye, ultra-atomic, shell-like.*

GPO Style Manual

14. Use the hyphen in the following examples to distinguish words spelled alike but differing in meaning:

re-cover, to cover again	recount, to relate in detail
recover, to regain	re-count, to count again

15. Use the hyphen to form adjectives compounded with *well* preceding the noun; as, *well-bred, well-born, well-to-do, well-earned, well-expressed, well-known.*

His *well-known* courtesy made him a favorite.

Do not use the hyphen with such expressions when they follow the word modified.

She showed herself a woman *well versed* in the ways of the world.

16. Use the hyphen generally in words compounded with *self* as a prefix; as, *self-conceit, self-confidence, self-control, self-reliance, self-respect, self-starter, self-assured, self-explaining, self-governing, self-made, self-taught, self-willed.*

Do not use the hyphen in *selfsame* and *selfless* or in pronouns compounded with *self;* as, *myself, himself, herself, itself, oneself, ourselves, themselves.*

17. Foreign phrases used adjectively should not be hyphened; as, an *a priori* argument, a *noblesse oblige* attitude, an *ex cathedra* pronouncement.

Guide to Compounding

In the following list, forms marked (G) are written in accordance with the *United States Government Printing Office Style Manual,* those marked (W) are in accordance with *Webster's New Interna-*

tional Dictionary, those not marked are in accordance with both books.

aforementioned
afterthought
airbase (G)
air base (W)
airbrake (G)
air brake (W)
airfield
airline
airmail
airplane
airport
all right
anybody
anyhow
any one (of them)
anyone (anybody)
anything
audiofrequency (G)
audio-frequency (W)
audiovisual (G)
audio-visual (W)
bankbook
banknote (G)
bank note (W)
basketball (G)
basketball, basket
  ball (W)
bas-relief
beforehand
billboard
birthrate (G)
birth rate (W)
blood bank
blood count
blood poisoning
blood pressure
blood test
blood type
blood vessel
blueprint
boathouse

bodyguard
bombproof
bombshell
bondholder
bond paper
bookbinding
bookcase
book review
bookshop
boxcar
box office
box spring
briefcase (G)
brief case (W)
broadcaster
businesslike
businessman
bylaws
byline (G)
by-line (W)
byproduct (G)
by-product (W)
cardboard
carport
cash account
cashbook
cash register
chain letter
chainstore (G)
chain store (W)
checkbook
chinaware
choir boy
choir master
clapboard
class day
classmate
classroom
clearinghouse
closeup (G)
close-up (W)

clubroom
coauthor
coeducation
coffeeshop (G)
coffee shop (W)
committeeman
commonsense (G)
common sense (W)
court-martial
crosscurrent
cross-examination
cross-fertilize
cross index (noun)
cross-index (verb)
cross-pollinate
cross-purpose
cross-reference (G)
cross reference (W)
cross-section (G)
cross section (W)
crossword
dateline (G)
date line (W)
daybook
day letter
death rate
dining room
double entry
dry goods
east-northeast
en route
everybody
everywhere
ex officio
extracurricular
extra dividend
fairway
filmstrip
fireproof
first aid
flagstaff

foolproof
footnote
forthcoming
free trade
free will (noun)
galley proof
good will (kindness)
goodwill (asset)
handwriting
headline
high frequency (G)
high-frequency (W)
horsepower
house organ
inasmuch
insofar
job lot
landowner
lawbreaker
letterhead
living room
loudspeaker (G)
loud-speaker (W)
makeup (G)
make-up (W)
mid-April
mid-Atlantic
midsummer
money order
moreover
network
nevertheless
newscaster
newsreel
night letter

noonday
northwest
notebook
note paper
notwithstanding
office boy
officeholder
offset
packinghouse (G)
packing house (W)
papercutter (G)
paper cutter (W)
parcel post
passbook
paymaster
payroll
per annum
percent (G)
per cent, percent (W)
policyholder
post card (G)
post card, postcard
  (W)
postmark
postmaster
post office
racecourse
salesclerk
sales tax
school board
schoolhouse
shopwindow
signpost
stockbroker
stock exchange

stock market
stockpile
stopgap
subcommittee
subdivision
taxpayer
textbook
thereafter
time clock
timekeeper
timetable
timesaving
titleholder
title page
toastmaster
toll road
trade-mark (G)
trade-mark, trademark
  (W)
transatlantic
trans-Canadian
transcontinental
turnover
viewpoint
violet ray
wage earner
wavelength (G)
wave length (W)
wax paper
waybill
weekend (G) (noun)
week end (W) (noun)
workday
X-ray
yearbook

Division of Words

Avoid all unnecessary divisions. Pronunciation is usually the best guide in determining how to divide words into syllables. An important principle to follow is that the part of the word left at the end of the line should suggest the part beginning the next line.

1. Do not divide monosyllables: *friend, through, stopped.*

2. Divide words of two syllables at the end of the first: *pave-ment, Eng-lish.*

3. Do not divide words of four letters or, if avoidable, those of five or six: *item, index, supper, needed.*

4. Do not divide a word on a single letter or on two letters: *able,* not *a-ble; omit,* not *o-mit; ratio,* not *rati-o* or *ra-tio; only,* not *on-ly.*

5. In words beginning with prefixes, divide, if possible, on the prefix: *mis-pronounce, sub-sidize.*

6. Never let more than two consecutive lines end with a hyphen if it can be avoided.

7. Do not divide such suffixes as the following:

cial	in	spe-cial
tial	"	pala-tial
cion	"	coer-cion
sion	"	occa-sion
tion	"	administra-tion
cious	"	falla-cious
geous	"	gor-geous
gious	"	conta-gious
tious	"	frac-tious

8. Separate suffixes, as a rule, from the stem of the word: *hop-ing, dear-est.*

9. In general, the following endings make reasonable divisions: *able, ance, ant, ence, ent, ible, ical, ive.*

accept-ance	prefer-ence
account-ant	correspond-ent
consider-able	crea-tive

10. In general, divide a word between double consonants unless the stem *ends* in a double consonant.

embar-rass	but	assess-ment
forgot-ten		bill-ing
mil-lion		full-est
neces-sary		odd-ity
occur-rence		pass-able
refer-ring		profess-ing
win-ning		tell-ing

11. Words containing a single consonant are divided as follows:

(a) If the preceding vowel is short and the syllable accented, let the consonant end the syllable: *bal-ance, pun-ish.*

(b) If the preceding vowel is long, write the consonant with the following syllable: *le-gal, oppo-nent.*

12. Solid compounds should usually be divided between the members: *book-keeper, care-taker, date-line, forth-coming, type-write.*

13. When a hyphened compound must be divided at the end of a line, divide on the hyphen: *forty-five, law-abiding, long-distance.*

14. Unless absolutely necessary, do not divide names of persons or other proper nouns.

15. Do not separate such titles as *Capt., Dr., Esq., Mr., Mrs., Rev., St.,* or abbreviations for degrees, from names to which they belong.

16. Do not separate abbreviations for societies, radio stations, and the like: YWCA, WDBO.

17. Do not divide initials preceding a name.

18. Do not divide a word at the end of a page or a paragraph if it is possible to avoid doing so.

19. Do not add another hyphen to words already hyphenated: not *self-con-trol,* but *self-control.*

20. When two vowels come together but are sounded separately, divide them into separate syllables: *gene-alogy, cre-ation.*

DIVISION AND ACCENT OF WORDS
ACCORDING TO
WEBSTER'S NEW INTERNATIONAL DICTIONARY
AND
THE STANDARD DICTIONARY

ab-bre'vi-ate	ac-cept'ance (W)	ac-com'plish
a-bil'i-ty	ac-cep'tance (S)	ac-cord'ance
ab'so-lute-ly	ac-ces'so-ry	ac-knowl'edge
a-bun'dance	ac-ci-den'tal	ac-qui-esce'
ac-cel'er-ate	ac-com'mo-date	ac-qui-si'tion
ac-cept'a-ble	ac-com'pa-ny	ac-quit'tal

a-dapt'a-ble
ad-di'tion-al
ad-dress-ee'
ad-journ'ment
ad-ju'di-cate
ad-just'a-ble
ad-min'is-ter
ad-mis'sion
ad-mit'tance
ad-van'tage
ad-vis-a-bil'ity
af-fir-ma'tion
af-firm'a-tive
au'thor-ize
au-to-mat'ic
au-to-mo-bile'
au'tumn
aux-il'ia-ry
a-vail'a-ble
av'e-nue

bac-te'ri-a
bal'ance
bank'rupt-cy
be-gin'ning
be-hav'ior (W)
be-ha'vior (S)
be-liev'a-ble
ben'e-fit
bil'lion
bi-tu'men
bi-tu'mi-nous
blot'ted
book'keep-er
brev'i-ty
brib'er-y
budg'et
busi'ness (W)
bus'i-ness (S)

ca'ble-gram
ca-lam'i-ty
can'di-date
ca-pa-bil'i-ty

ca-pac'i-ty
cap'i-tal-ist
car'di-nal
ca-reer'
cash-ier'
cas'u-al
cat-e-gor'i-cal
cat'a-log or
cat'a-logue
ca-tas'tro-phe
cel'e-brate
ce-leb'ri-ty
cen'te-na-ry
cen-ten'ni-al
cer-tif'i-cate
cer'ti-fy
cham'pi-on
change'a-ble
char'ac-ter-ize
chil'dren
chi-rop'o-dist
chron'ic
cig-a-rette'
cir-cu'i-tous
ci-ta'tion
ci-vil'ian
civ-i-li-za'tion
clas'si-fy
cli-en-tele'
co-ad'ju-tant
co-a-lesce'
co-a-li'tion
cod'i-cil
cod'i-fy
co-erce'
co-her'ence
col-lab'o-rate
col'league
colo'nel
com-bi-na'tion
co-me'di-an
com'e-dy
com'men-ta-ry
com-mer'cial

com-mit'ment
com-mod'i-ty
com-mu'ni-cate
com'pa-ra-ble
com-par'a-tive
com-pen'di-um
com-pet'i-tive
com-pi-la'tion
com-plai'sant
com'pli-cate
com'pli-ment
com-po-si'tion
com-pre-hend'
com-pu-ta'tion
con-ceiv'a-ble
con'cen-trate
con-ces'sion
con-cil'i-ate
con-cord'ance (W)
con-cor'dance (S)
con-de-scend'
con-di'tion-al
con-do'lence
con-du'cive
con-fec'tion-er-y
con'fi-dence
con-fir-ma'tion
con-fla-gra'tion
con-fu'sion
con-gre-ga'tion
con-gres'sion-al
con-gru'i-ty
con'science
con-sci-en'tious
con'se-quence
con-ser-va'tion
con-serv'a-tive (W)
con-ser'va-tive (S)
con-serv'a-to-ry (W)
con-ser'va-to-ry (S)
con-sid'er
con-sid'er-a-ble
con-sign-ee'
con-sist'en-cy (W)

con-sis'ten-cy (S)
con-stit'u-en-cy
con-sti-tu'tion
con-ta'gious
con-tem-po-ra'ne-ous
con-tem'po-ra-ry
con'ti-nent
con-ti-nen'tal
con-tin'gen-cy
con-ti-nu'i-ty
con-tin'u-ous
con-tra-dic'to-ry
con-trib'ute
con-trib'u-tor
con-triv'ance (W)
con-tri'vance (S)
con-trol'
con'tro-ver-sy
con-va-lesce'
con-ven'ient (W)
con-ve'nient (S)
con-vert'i-ble
co-or'di-nate
cor'o-ner
cor-po-ra'tion
cor-re-spond'ence(W)
cor-re-spon'dence(S)
cor-rob'o-rate
cos-mo-pol'i-tan
coun-ter-bal'ance
coun'ter-sign
cour'te-sy
cre-den'tial
cred'i-ble
cred'it-a-bly
cred'i-tor
cri-te'ri-on
crit'i-cal
crys'tal-lize
cul-mi-na'tion
cu'mu-la-tive
cu-ra'tor
cur'ren-cy
cus'tom-er

dec'ade
dec-la-ra'tion
de-fi'cient
def'i-cit
def'i-nite
de-nom-i-na'tion
de-par'ture
de-pend'a-ble
de-pend'ence (W)
de-pen'dence (S)
dep-o-si'tion
de-pre-ci-a'tion
de-scend'ant (W)
de-scen'dant (S)
de-scrip'tion
de-sir'a-ble
de-vel'op
dif'fi-cul-ty
di-min'ish
di-rec'tion
dis'ci-pline
dis-crep'an-cy
dis-crim'i-nate
dis-miss'al (W)
dis-mis'sal (S)
dis-patch'
dis-pos'al (W)
dis-po'sal (S)
dis-pos-sess'
dis-turb'ance (W)
dis-tur'bance (S)
dis-tinc'tion
di-verge'
div'i-dend
di-vi'sion
do-na'tion
du'pli-cate
dy-nam'ic

ear'nest
e-co-nom'i-cal (W)
ec'o-nom-i-cal (S)
e-co-nom'ics (W)
ec'o-nom-ics (S)

e-con'o-my
ed-i-to'ri-al
ef-fi'cient
e-lec'tric
e-nor'mous
en-thu'si-asm
es'ti-mate
ex-ec'u-tive
ex-pe'ri-ence
ex-ter'mi-nate
ex-traor'di-na-ry

fal'la-cy
fi-nan'cial
fin-an-cier'
for'ger-y
for'mal

gra-tu'i-ty
guar-an-tee'

his-to'ri-an
hos-pi-tal'i-ty
hun'dred
hy'dro-plane

i-den'ti-cal
im-me'di-ate-ly
in-ac'cu-ra-cy
in-cal'cu-la-ble
in-ca'pa-ble
in-ca-pac'i-ty
in-de-scrib'a-ble
in-di-vid'u-al
in-di-vis'i-ble
in-dus'tri-al
in-es'ti-ma-ble
in-ex-pe'di-ent
in-ex-pe'ri-ence
in-fe'ri-or
in-fir'ma-ry
in-ge-nu'i-ty
in-ju-di'cious
in-se-cu'ri-ty

in-spi-ra'tion
in-sta-bil'i-ty
in-sub-or'di-nate
in-suf-fi'cient
in-teg'ri-ty
in-te'ri-or
in-ter'mi-na-ble
in-ter-pre-ta'tion
in'ti-ma-cy
in-tro-duc'tion
in'tu-i'tion
in-val'i-date
in'ven-to-ry
in-vi-ta'tion
ir-ref'u-ta-ble
ir-rep'a-ra-ble
ir-re-press'i-ble (W)
ir-re-pres'si-ble (S)
ir-re-spon'si-ble
i'so-late (W)
is'o-late (S)
i-tal'i-cize
i-tin'er-a-ry

ju-di'cial
ju-di'ci-a-ry
jun'ior
ju'rist
jus-ti-fi'a-ble

knowl'edge

lan'guage
leg'is-la-ture
le-git'i-mate
lei'sure
le'ni-ent
li'cense
liq'ui-date

ma-te'ri-al
me-chan'i-cal
me'di-um
me-mo'ri-al

mile'age
mis-cal'cu-late
mo-nop'o-ly
mu-nic'i-pal

nat'u-ral-ize
nec'es-sa-ry
ne-ces'si-ty
neg-lect'
ne-go'ti-a-ble
nul'li-fy

ob'li-ga-to-ry
ob-lit'er-ate
op-por-tu'ni-ty

par-lia-men'ta-ry
par'ti-san
pe-cul'iar (W)
pe-cu'liar (S)
pe-cu'ni-a-ry
pe-des'tri-an
pe'nal-ize
per-emp'to-ry (W)
per'emp-to-ry (S)
per-mis'si-ble
per'pe-trate
pic-to'ri-al
plain'tiff
plau'si-ble
pneu-mat'ic
pol'i-tic
po-lit'i-cal
pol-i-ti'cian
po-lice'
po-si'tion
pos-si-bil'i-ty
prac'ti-cal
pre-ced'ence (W)
pre-ce'dence (S)
prec'e-dent
pre-ci'sion
pref'er-a-ble
pre-lim'i-na-ry

priv'i-lege
prod'uct
pro-duc'tion
prof'it-a-bly
pro-gres'sive
pro-hib'it
prom'i-nent
prom'is-so-ry
pro-pos'al (W)
pro-po'sal (S)
pros'pect
punc'tu-al

qual'i-fy
quo'ta
quot'a-ble
quo-ta'tion

rat'i-fy
re'al-ize
re-cip'ro-cal
rec-om-men-da'tion
re-mu'ner-ate
re-pris'al (W)
re-pri'sal (S)
rep'u-ta-ble
req-ui-si'tion
res'tau-rant
res-to-ra'tion
ro'de-o (W)
ro-de'o (S)
rou-tine'

sat-is-fac'to-ry
sce-na'ri-o
se-cu'ri-ty (W)
se-cur'i-ty (S)
serv'ice (W)
ser'vice (S)
sev'en-ti-eth
sev'er-al
si-mul-ta'ne-ous
spon-ta'ne-ous
stand'ard-ize

sta-tis′tics
sub-sid′i-a-ry
sub′si-dize
sub-or′di-nate
suf-fi′cient
su-per-fi′cial
su-per-in-tend′
su-pe′ri-or
sym-pa-thet′ic

ten′ta-tive
ter′mi-nal
ter′ri-to-ry
tes′ti-fy
treas′ur-y (W)
trea′sur-y (S)

un-com′pro-mis-ing
un-de-ni′a-ble

va-lid′i-ty
va-ri′e-ty
vo-li′tion
vol′un-ta-ry

ward′en
wa′ter
wa′ver
weath′er

REFERENCE BOOKS

BALL, ALICE MORTON. *Compounding in the English Language.*
TEALL, EDWARD N. *Meet Mr. Hyphen and Put Him in His Place.*
United States Government Printing Office Style Manual.
Webster's New International Dictionary.

4. Use of Italics

1. Italics are often used to give prominence or emphasis to words or expressions. To indicate italics, underline in manuscript the words to be so printed.

When I was an undergraduate in Brown, it seemed quite out of order either to write or to read a *popular* book on science.

DALLAS LORE SHARP

If anything can make hard things easy to follow, it is a *style* like Bergson's.

WILLIAM JAMES

2. Italicize the words *Continued, To be continued, Continued on page,* and *To be concluded.*

3. Italicize the words, *See also, See,* before a cross reference in an index; also the words *For* and *Read* in a list of errata placed at the beginning or at the end of a volume.

> *See also* Advertising.
> *For* Rosevelt *read* Roosevelt.

4. Abbreviations of Latin words in common use are not ordinarily italicized; as, e.g., i.e., viz., and vs. Italicize *v.* or *vs.* as in Yale *vs.* Princeton, 5 to 0, when it stands between terms not italicized. (*See* p. 81.)

5. Italicize the following abbreviations, words, and phrases used for reference unless they occur in italic matter.

ad loc. (to the place)	loc. cit. (place cited)
circa, c., ca. (about)	op. cit. (work cited)
et al. (and others)	passim (here and there)
ibid. (the same reference)	sc. (namely)
idem (the same person)	supra (above)
infra (below)	vide (see)

6. Italicize such foreign words and phrases as have not become a part of the English language. The following are found italicized in *Webster's New International Dictionary.*

amor patriae
Anschluss
ancien régime
ante meridiem
a posteriori
bambino
beau geste
beaux-arts
bonne
bon soir
bon vivant
bon voyage
cabaña
café noir
casus belli
chez
comédien
comme il faut
congé
coup de grâce
coup de main
coup d'état
crème
danseur
de facto
dégagé
de jure
de trop
double entente
eau de vie

élan
embarras de richesse
émigré
empressement
en effet
en famille
en passant
en rapport
entre nous
fait accompli
fauteuil
faux pas
femme de chambre
feu de joie
fiesta
garçon
in loco
in loco parentis
in medias res
jeu d'esprit
jeune fille
joie de vivre
lapsus linguae
mal de mer
mise en scène
nisi
noblesse oblige
nom de guerre
nouveau riche
on dit

pâté
passim
petits fours
pièce de résistance
pourboire
première
prie-dieu
raconteuse
raison d'être
rapprochement
rara avis
salon
sang-froid
savoir-faire
savoir-vivre
soi-disant
soigné
status quo
sub rosa
tant mieux
tabula rasa
Te Deum
thé dansant
valet de chambre
vide
videlicet
wagon-lit
Zeitgeist

7. Use italics when a word is spoken of as a word. (*See also* p. 56.)

The word *very* is incorrectly used in the expression *very pleased.*

When a word, however, is quoted, it is better to enclose it in quotation marks rather than to write it in italics.

I said "minuteness" and "selfishness" of suggestion: but it would have been enough to have said "injustice" or "unrighteousness" of sensation.

JOHN RUSKIN

8. *Webster's New International Dictionary* lists the following words and phrases as not italicized:

addendum	divorcée	nom de plume
ad infinitum	dramatis personae	opus
ad interim	éclat	papier-mâché
agenda	elite	par excellence
à la carte	en route	penchant
à la mode	ensemble	per annum
ante bellum	entente	per capita
a priori	entourage	per contra
apropos	entree, entrée	per diem
artiste	entrepreneur	porte-cochere
attaché	ex cathedra	poseur
au revoir	ex officio	post-mortem
beau ideal	exposé	précis
belles-lettres	habeas corpus	prima donna
bête noire	habitué	prima facie
billet doux	hors d'oeuvre	procès verbal
blasé	in memoriam	pro rata
bloc	levee	pro tempore
bona fide	mâitre d'hôtel	protocol
canapé	mandamus	quasi
carte blanche	manège	regime
chargé d'affaires	mélange	résumé
chef d'oeuvre	melee	subpoena
cliché	ménage	table d'hôte
coup	morale	tour de force
cul-de-sac	mores	vice versa
décolleté	naïve, naive	vis-à-vis
distrait	nee, née	viva voce

9. Use italics or quotation marks for titles of books, of music, of periodicals, pamphlets, and newspapers. (*See* p. 56.)

Then from over the edge of the world appeared *The Popular Science Monthly, The Warfare of Science* by Andrew D. White, and the *Lay Sermons* by Huxley.

I am going to hear Beethoven's *Symphonie Pastorale* tonight.

My authority is "Text, Type, and Style."

It appeared in the "Springfield Republican."

Use of Italics as Shown in Bibliographical Matter

"Some Neglected Characteristics of the New England Puritans"; *Annual Report of the American Historical Association for 1891.*

(1) Do not use italics for titles of divisions of books and titles of magazine articles and other contributions. Use quotation marks, however.

"How He Went to the Devil"; Two Tales, April 30,—From Bibliography attached to *Barrett Wendell and His Letters.*
"Were the Salem Witches Guiltless?" *Historical Collections of the Essex Institute,* February.
"The Dean at Bourges" (poem): *Scribner's Magazine,* January.

(2) Do not use italics, but use quotation marks around the titles of lectures, toasts, articles, sermons, and papers.

Russell H. Conwell's famous lecture, "Acres of Diamonds," was given hundreds of times.
Miss Jane Brown read her paper, "Women in Business," before the Business and Professional Women's Club.
"Francis Parkman"; *Proceedings,* American Academy of Arts and Sciences, May 9.

Notice, however, the following:

Review of *The Transit of Civilization from England to America in the Seventeenth Century,* by Edward Eggleston: *American Historical Review,* July.

(3) Do not use italics or quotation marks in long bibliographies where they would detract from the appearance of the page.

(4) Do not use italics or quotation marks for the Bible, its books, or for titles of ancient manuscripts.

The clergyman took the text for his sermon from Matthew 5:5.

To this list, *The Style Book of The New York Times* adds the following:

Book of Common Prayer, Prayer Book, Blue Book, Scriptures, New Testament, Corporation Manual, Revised Statutes, Encyclopaedia Britannica, Lippincott's Gazeteer, Almanacs, Annuals or similar publications.

10. Legal usage customarily places in italics the names of plaintiff and defendant in the citation of cases at law, and titles of procedure.

Brown v. *Jones*
The Atlantic Pencil Company vs. *Henry Taylor*
In re Sumner

Ex parte John Chase
In the matter of Elmer White for a writ of—

The *GPO Style Manual* uses italics for *v.*, in titles of cases referring to bills introduced into Congress and for contested election cases. It states, however, that Supreme Court records use roman both for titles of cases and for *v.*: Jones v. Brown.

Under Court Briefs and under Court of Claims Opinions, the *GPO Style Manual* presents the following to illustrate capitalization, italic, small caps, and abbreviations generally used in court work.

The *Legal Tender* cases.
In Clarke's case the court said.
In the case of Clarke.
In *Ex parte 74* the court said.
In the *Fifteen Percent Rate Increase case* the court decided.
In the case of Jones against Robinson. (A general or casual reference to a case.)
In *Jones* v. *Robinson* (122 U. S. 329). (A specific citation of a case.)
In *In re Robinson* (19 Wall. 304), the court * * *.
(*Ex parte 74*, 58 I. C. C. 220.)
Bowman Act (22 Stat. L., ch. 4, § [or sec.] 4, p. 50).
Act Aug. 5, 1882 (Supp. Rev. Stat. 284; Stat. L. 28; R. S. 15).
Clarke's case (14 Howe 14).
WALLACE, *J.*, delivered the opinion.
(31 Stat. 154).
Rev. Stat., Stats., Stat. L., Stats. L., or R. S., as written.
In *Roe* v. *Doe* the court ruled.
United States v. *12 Diamond Rings.*
The United States v. *Forty Hogsheads of Tobacco.*

In titles of cases, follow copy as to figures and abbreviations.

11. Modern usage differs widely as to the correct manner of indicating the names of ships in print or in typewritten manuscript.

The *Manual of Style* advocates the use of quotation marks; the *GPO Style Manual*, italics; while most newspapers seem to prefer roman.

(1) The "Mauretania" had a record for speed.
(2) The *Leviathan* was one of the largest ships.
(3) The Independence arrived in port early.

12. Italicize the binomial (scientific) names of species and genera.

Salix babylonica, Acer rubrum, Liriodendron tulipifera.

Do not italicize the names of genera without the species, or of groups of higher rank (classes, orders, families, tribes, etc.); as, the family Leguminosae.

13. Italics may be used for abbreviations for s. and d. (shillings and pence) after a numeral: 5*s.* 6*d.*

14. Use italics for address lines in speeches and in reports.

To the Honorable Senate and House of Representatives of the United States of America Now Assembled at Washington, D. C.
Mr. President, Ladies and Gentlemen:

15. In preparing matter for publication, use italics for a title following a signature: William Hawthorne, *Secretary.*

16. Do not use italics for foreign titles or designations of foreign leaders, as, Emir; or for names of foreign legislatures or institutions, as, Rigsdag, Bibliothèque Nationale.

5. Figures

1. NUMBERS IN ORDINARY TEXT

In bookwork and other plain reading matter, as editorials and book reviews, usually spell out all numbers under one hundred.

Book

For thirty-six years after the Treaty of San Stefano and the Berlin Conference, Europe maintained an uneasy peace within its borders.

H. G. WELLS

Editorial

Whether the Antarctic is one continent or two great bodies of land separated by a frozen sea, he may be able to determine.

The New York Times

Business Letters

When an isolated mention of a sum in round numbers is written, spell out the number if it can be done in one or two words; as, *six, three hundred, ten thousand, five million*. For other numbers, use the sign *$* and figures; as $321; $4,425; $2,640,000. (*See* p. 37.)

Please invest twenty thousand dollars for me in ———————— stock.
His shares depreciated over twelve hundred dollars.
His estate amounted to $67,554.

For ordinal numbers to designate days of a month, figures are used.

I forwarded your order on March 4.

Financial News Item

They frequently have risen as much as 10 points a day.
After selling as low as 75 this year, the debentures touched a new price yesterday at 92⅞.

Sport News

Henri Cochet, ace of the French Davis Cup team, advanced into the semifinal round by defeating Gerald Stratford of San Francisco, 6—4, 6—1.

2. ROUND NUMBERS

Usage differs as to the writing of such figures. The *GPO Style Manual* states that numbers greater than one thousand, if spelled out, should be in the form *one thousand eight hundred and fifty* not *eighteen hundred and fifty; one thousand two hundred tons,* not *twelve hundred tons.*

The *Manual of Style* and the *Style Book of The New York Times* state that numbers of four digits, if spelled out, as in straight reading matter, should read *eighteen hundred and fifty,* not *one thousand eight hundred and fifty.*

(1) The word *and* may or may not be used between tens and units. Modern usage seems to prefer its omission; as, *three hundred five.*

(2) Spell out all round numbers or approximate figures; as, *four or five feet, six or seven hundred miles, a thousand reasons, almost a million slaves.*

(3) Spell out round sums of money in general matter if this can be done in one or two words; as, *two hundred dollars, seven thousand dollars, three million dollars. (See also* p. 37.)

In business writing and in statistics in letters and reports, figures are generally used for definite amounts or for complicated numbers:

The movement of gold from London to New York, which started in mid-September, was increased to $10,000,000 yesterday when it was announced that $5,000,000 of bars was being sent here on the *Mauretania,* steaming today.

At the start of the movement, estimates were made by bankers that it would total $25,000,000 or so, and it is still believed this is a fairly accurate gaging of the situation.

In their feverish activity, however, may be seen pretty clear proof that the party managers are as doubtful about the outcome of the campaign, in which perhaps 40,000,000 votes will be cast, as are the rest of us.

3. FIGURES AT THE BEGINNING OF A SENTENCE

Spell out all figures at the beginning of a sentence if they are short, even when other numbers in the sentence are expressed by figures; if long, they are better written in figures.

Forty cows comprised his livestock.
Three years ago he left for South Africa.
Two cars of new sample grade corn were received here during the day and sold at 68 to 71 cents.
1,977,639 shares were traded in this month compared with 2,320,003 last month.

4. FIGURES WITHIN A SENTENCE

Numbers or amounts within a sentence should be expressed either entirely in figures or entirely in words unless this would result in lack of clearness.

They employed 10 girls for 3 weeks at $15 a week. *Or,* they employed ten girls for three weeks at fifteen dollars a week.

Note that it is better not to place next to each other two numbers referring to different things:

Incorrect:	In 1929 15 states ratified the law.
Correct:	In 1929 fifteen states ratified the law.
Allowable:	In 1929, 15 states ratified the law.
Incorrect:	2 3-room apartments.
Correct:	Two 3-room apartments.

When one number immediately precedes another, spell out one, preferably the one with the fewer letters; as, ten 3-inch nails, 20 six-foot poles.

5. DATES

In decades and centuries. Spell out numbers referring to decades and centuries; as, the gay *nineties;* the *nineteenth century.*

In years. For general purposes, in expressing years in words, write *nineteen hundred and fifty;* but in formal and legal documents, write *one thousand nine hundred and fifty.*

In letters. Use figures, as a general rule, in the heading of a business letter to express the date; as, *January 27, 1949,* not 1/27/1949 or January 27th, 1949.

(1) Many business houses write out the day and the year in the headings of letters; as, *June sixth, Nineteen Hundred and Forty-nine* or *June sixth, 1949.*

(2) According to European practice, the day precedes the month in letter headings; as, *2 May, 1949.*

(3) In the body of a business letter, when the name of the month precedes the date, the date should be written in figures without the ordinal abbreviation.

Make the appointment for January 22. (*Not* January twenty-second *or* January 22d.)

When the name of the month follows the date or when the name of the month is omitted, the date should be written in full or in figures with the ordinal abbreviation.

Make the appointment for the twenty-second of January *or* the twenty-second *or* the 22d of January *or* the 22d. (*Not* the 22 of January *or* the 22.)

Our representative will be in Boston on November 19, 20, and 21. Would it be convenient for you to see him on the 20th or the 21st?

Note the acceptable methods of writing dates: May 1959 *or* May, 1959; May 25, 1959 (*not* May 25th, 1959); June 6 to July 15, 1959 (*not* June 6, 1959, to July 15, 1959); April, May, and June, 1959 (*but* May and June 1959 *or* May and June, 1959).

In referring to a fiscal year, consecutive years, or a continuous period of two years or more, when contracted, the forms 1906–38, 1931–32, 1801–2, 1875–79 are used (*but* 1895–1914, 1900–1901); for two or more separate years not representing a continuous period, a comma is used instead of a dash (1875, 1879); if the word *from* precedes the year or the word *inclusive* follows it, the second year is not shortened and the word *to* is used in lieu of the dash (from 1933 to 1936; 1935 to 1936, inclusive).

In dates, *A. D.* precedes the year (A. D. 937); *B. C.* follows the year (254 B. C.).

GPO Style Manual

(4) In formal invitations, announcements, and acceptances, dates are invariably spelled out; as, *February Twenty-first, Nineteen Hundred and Forty-nine,* or, *February Twenty First, Nineteen Hundred and Forty Nine.*

In legal documents. In legal documents, such as wills and deeds, dates are invariably written out; as, *the twelfth day of January, one thousand nine hundred and fifty-eight.*

6. TIME OF DAY

Spell out the time of day in text matter.

(1) Use *A.M.* or *a.m., P.M.* or *p.m.* in connection with figures; as,

> 1:30 A.M., *or* 1.30 a.m.
> 1:30 P.M., *or* 1.30 p.m. (*See* p. 27.)

Note that when the time is spelled out, the abbreviations a.m. or A.M., p.m. or P.M., must not be used:

The train left at three in the afternoon.
Not: The train left at three P.M.

7. STREETS

In the text spell out numbers of streets, avenues, wards, and districts; as, *Forty-second Street, Sixth Avenue, Thirteenth District, Ninth Ward.*

In writing streets and avenues, spell out the names of those up to twelve; as, *Fifth Avenue, Ninth Street.*

In correspondence express numbers above twelve in figures; as, *121 Street* or *121st Street.*

8. PAGE NUMBERS

Use figures for page numbers; as, page 533.

9. REFERENCES IN FOOTNOTES

In footnotes and in all bibliographical material abbreviate a word designating a part when followed by a number.

Chap. III
Vol. II (pl. Vols.)
Fig. 80 (Figs.)
sec. 3 (secs.)
No. 1 (Nos.)
col. 2 (cols.)
art. 14 (arts.)

p. 1 (pp.)
pp. 6f. (page 6 and the following page)
pp. 6ff. (page 6 and the following pages)
pp. 5–8 (pages 5 to 8 inclusive)

Section is usually abbreviated in enumeration, except the first:

Section 1
Sec.   2
Sec.   3

10. SUMS OF MONEY

Write sums of money in general matter as follows:

$55,000, *not* $55,000.00.
They also announced September earnings were $650,000, equal to about $8 a share on the present stock, and sales of more than $4,000,-000. Earnings for four months were said to be about $20 a share.
59 cents, *not* $.59 or 59¢.
The company declared a special dividend of 75 cents a share.
The heavy offerings of highway bonds by various States since the war have been made possible to a large extent by State gasoline taxes ranging from 3 to 7 cents a gallon.

(1) In bills and in other distinctly financial statements the symbol for cents is used when given in cents only; as, *steers low, 25¢ to 40¢ lower.*

(2) Do not use both figures and words for sums of money except in commercial and legal documents. When both are used, parentheses follow the completed expression; as, thirty dollars ($30) or thirty (30) dollars, *not* thirty ($30) dollars. The custom of using both figures and words for sums of money is seldom used today in letters. (*See* pp. 238–239.)

11. DECIMALS

Use figures for expressing decimals and percentages, but spell out percentages when they begin a sentence.

0.832; 10.5
The Saskatchewan official reports said 80 per cent of the wheat in that province had been threshed.
Ten per cent will be the profit.

In writing a decimal fraction not preceded by a whole number, a cipher is placed before it except when the decimal begins with a cipher; as, 0.235, .0235.
In letters and formal writing, *per cent* or *percent* should be used instead of the symbol %. In commercial work, such as tabular matter, the symbol % is used.

12. FRACTIONS

Fractions standing alone or expressed in a single compound word are usually written out; as, *half* a mile, a *quarter* of an ounce, a *one-third* interest.

The fractional part of a mixed number should be written in figures; as, 20½ miles, *not* 20 and a half miles.

Written-out fractions used as adjectives must be hyphened; as, a *two-thirds* vote, *one-half* inch; but when they are used as nouns they are usually not hyphened; as, *one sixth* of the estate, *two fifths* of the field. There is a growing tendency in business writing to use the hyphen for both the adjective and the noun; as, a *one-third* interest in the estate, *one-third* of the estate.

When fractions are expressed in figures, the diagonal line rather than the hyphen should be used; as, 5/6, rather than 5–6.

Mixed numbers, when expressed in figures, should be typed with a space rather than a hyphen between the integer and the fraction; as, 23 3/4, rather than 23-3/4.

When a fraction is the subject of a sentence, the verb agrees with the noun in the prepositional phrase.

Two thirds of his income *is* from real estate.
Two thirds of their incomes *are* from real estate.

With *one* as subject followed by a fraction, the predicate is singular.

One and five-sixth yards is enough.
One and a half teaspoonsfuls was given in the recipe.

13. AGES

In stating definite ages, usage differs. In general, figures should be used for ready reference; as, "My age is 52 years, 6 months, 10 days; a boy 6 years old; 3-year-old colt; 2-months-old child."

In formal writing or when the age is indefinite, references to ages should be spelled out; as, eighty years and four months old; children between six and fourteen.

14. RESULTS OF BALLOTS

These should be expressed by figures; as, 38 for, 25 against. Yeas 56; nays 24.

15. DIMENSIONS

In text to represent dimensions write 10 by 15 inches, *not* 10 x 15 inches *or* 10″ x 15″.

In technical work, use ′ for feet, ″ for inches, and x for by: 9′ x 11″. In ordinary writing, abbreviate but do not capitalize dimensions, 6 ft. 11 in.

16. DISTANCES

Write in figures all measures of distances except a fraction of a mile; as, 16 miles, 12 yards, 3 feet; *but,* one-half mile.

17. MEASURES

Enumerations of measure must be expressed by figures; as, 10 gallons, 4 quarts, and 3 pints; 60 bushels, 5 pecks. In ordinary writing, they are abbreviated; as, 6 lbs. 3 oz.

18. TEMPERATURE

Use *F.* for Fahrenheit preceded by the degrees in figures; use *C.* for Centigrade preceded by degrees in figures; as, 32° F., 45° C.

19. WEIGHTS

Enumerations of weight should be expressed in figures; as, 2 tons, 40 pounds, 10 ounces.

20. METRIC SYSTEM

Abbreviate after a numeral all designations of weights and measures in the metric system. The period may be omitted according to the National Bureau of Standards.

The *United States Government Printing Office Style Manual* advocates the period. (*See* pp. 537–538.)

21. ROMAN NUMERALS

The following table represents Roman numerals commonly used:

1—I	6—VI	11—XI
2—II	7—VII	14—XIV
3—III	8—VIII	18—XVIII
4—IV or IIII	9—IX	19—XIX
5—V	10—X	20—XX

30—XXX	200—CC	1000—M
40—XL	300—CCC	2000—MM
50—L	400—CCCC or CD	3000—MMM
60—LX	500—D	4000—M̄V̄
70—LXX	600—DC	5000—V̄
80—LXXX	700—DCC	1928—MCMXXVIII
90—XC	800—DCCC	1930—MCMXXX
100—C	900—CM	1,000,000—M̄

6. Spelling

Rules for Spelling

DOUBLING FINAL CONSONANTS

1. Monosyllables and words accented on the last syllable when ending with a single consonant preceded by a single vowel, double the consonant before a suffix beginning with a vowel.

bag	baggage	occur	occurred
begin	beginning	refer	referring
bid	bidden	remit	remittance
control	controlling	repel	repellent
equip	equipped	sad	sadden
impel	impelled	sit	sitting
man	mannish	wed	wedded
plan	planned	wit	witty

Exceptions

gas	gaseous, *but* gassed
transfer	transferable, *but* transferring, transferred

2. Final consonants when preceded by two vowels are not doubled in adding a suffix beginning with a vowel.

beat	beaten
congeal	congealing
retail	retailing
soak	soaking

3. Final consonants are not doubled when the word ends in more than one consonant.

conform	conformed	conforming
help	helped	helping

4. Final consonants are not doubled when the accent is not on the last syllable or when the accent is thrown forward in the case of a derivative. (But note No. 8, following.)

benefit	benefiting	benefited
cancel	canceling	canceled
worship	worshiping	worshiped
travel	traveler	traveled

Note that the American and the British usage often differ. (*See* pp. 93–95, 99.)

5. Adjectives ending with *l,* like other adjectives, add *ly* to form the corresponding adverbs.

accidentally	exceptionally	occasionally
casually	finally	really
coolly	legally	unusually

Prefixes and suffixes ending in *ll* generally drop one *l* in combination.

although	always
altogether	helpful
already	wonderful

6. Words ending in *n* keep that letter before the suffix *ness*.

barrenness	meanness
greenness	plainness
keenness	suddenness

7. Words ending in a double consonant usually retain both consonants on adding suffixes.

assess	assessment	shrill	shrilly
embarrass	embarrassment	success	successful

Note the spelling of the following words according to American and British usage:

American	*British*
enroll	enrol
enrollment	enrolment

8. British usage authorizes the doubling of the final *l* when adding a suffix beginning with a vowel; American usage does not authorize the doubling of the final *l* in such cases.

The following show both American and British usage in the doubling of the *l:*

American	British
appareled	apparelled
appareling	apparelling
barreled	barrelled
beveled	bevelled
chiseled	chiselled
chiseling	chiselling
councilor	councillor
counseled	counselled
counselor	counsellor
dueling	duelling
enameled	enamelled
enameling	enamelling
equaled	equalled
equaling	equalling
impaneled	empanelled
impaneling	empanelling
imperiled	imperilled
imperiling	imperilling
jeweled	jewelled
jeweler	jeweller
jewelry	jewellery
kidnaped	kidnapped
labeled	labelled
labeling	labelling
leveled	levelled
leveling	levelling
libeled	libelled
marshaled	marshalled
marshaling	marshalling
marveling	marvelling
marvelous	marvellous
medalist	medallist
metaled	metalled
modeled	modelled
modeler	modeller
paneled	panelled
paneling	panelling
parceled	parcelled
parceling	parcelling
penciled	pencilled

American	British
penciling	pencilling
periled	perilled
periling	perilling
quarreled	quarrelled
quarreling	quarrelling
raveled	ravelled
raveling	ravelling
reveling	revelling
rivaling	rivalling
shoveled	shovelled
shriveled	shrivelled
shriveling	shrivelling
signaled	signalled
signaling	signalling
stenciled	stencilled
stenciling	stencilling
toweling	towelling
trammeled	trammelled
trammeling	trammelling
tranquilize	tranquillize
traveled	travelled
traveler	traveller
traveling	travelling
tunneled	tunnelled
tunneling	tunnelling
woolen	woollen
worshiped	worshipped
worshiping	worshipping

FINAL E

9. Words ending in silent *e* usually omit the *e* before suffixes beginning with a vowel.

arguing	giving	pleasing
arrival	guidance	salable
blamable	hoping	subduing
coming	judging	tracing
deplorable	lovable	truism
desirable	loving	typing
dining	managing	writing

British usage does not conform entirely to this rule.

10. When words end in soft *ce* or *ge*, keep the *e* before *able* and *ous*.

advantageous	noticeable
allegeable	outrageous
changeable	peaceable
chargeable	pronounceable
courageous	serviceable
enforceable	traceable

11. Keep final *e* in the present participle of *singe, tinge, dye.*

singeing
tingeing
dyeing

12. When words end in *oe*, keep the *e* before a suffix beginning with any vowel except *e.*

hoeing
toeing

13. When words end in silent *e*, keep the *e* before a suffix beginning with a consonant.

baleful	lonely
encouragement	lovely

movement

Exceptions

acknowledgment	duly
argument	judgment

truly

14. Verbs ending in *ie* change the termination to *y* before adding *ing.*

die dying (*but,* died)   lie lying (*but,* lied)
tie tying (*but,* tied)

FINAL Y

15. Words ending in *y* preceded by a consonant change *y* to *i* before a suffix, unless the suffix begins with *i.*

busy	busier	business
defy	defiant	defies
mercy	merciful	merciless

But

carry	carrying
hurry	hurrying
study	studying
thirty	thirtyish

16. Words ending in *y* preceded by a vowel generally keep the *y* before a suffix.

buyer	buying
delayed	delaying
obey	obeying

Exceptions

daily	paid
laid	said

17. Monosyllabic adjectives usually keep *y* when adding a suffix.

dry	dryly
sly	slyly

Ei and Ie

18. Follow the well-known rhyme in spelling words in *ie* and *ei*.

> I before E
> Except after C
> Or when sounded as A
> As in n*ei*ghbor and w*ei*gh

ei used after *c*

> receive, perceive, conceive
> ceiling, receipt, deceit

ie used after all letters but *c*

achieve	fiend	niece	shriek
apiece	frontier	pierce	shrieve
believe	grief	relieve	sieve
chief	mischief	reprieve	yield

ei sounded as *a*

feign	reign
heinous	their
neighbor	weight

Exceptions

counterfeit	forfeit	leisure
foreign	height	seize

Words Ending in C

19. When words end in *c*, add *k* to *c* when adding *ing* or *ed*.

frolicked	picnicking	trafficking

Variations in American and British Spelling

20. Note the variations in American and British usage in the following:

(1) Words ending in *or*.

American	British	American	British
arbor	arbour	labor	labour
ardor	ardour	misdemeanor	misdemeanour
behavior	behaviour	neighbor	neighbour
candor	candour	odor	odour
clamor	clamour	parlor	parlour
endeavor	endeavour	rancor	rancour
favor	favour	rumor	rumour
flavor	flavour	splendor	splendour
harbor	harbour	vapor	vapour
honor	honour	vigor	vigour
humor	humour		

Note that *discoloration, horror, invigorate, mirror, pallor, tenor, terror,* and *tremor* do not take *u.*

Note that adjectives formed from *clamor, humor, labor, odor, rigor, vigor* do not take *u.*

clamorous	laborious	rigorous
humorous	odorous	vigorous

(2) Words ending in *er*.

American	British	American	British
caliber	calibre	meter	metre
center	centre	miter	mitre
fiber	fibre	niter	nitre
liter	litre	reconnoiter	reconnoitre
maneuver	manoeuvre	theater	theatre

(3) Words ending in *ise* and *ize*.

Most words ending in this sound take *ize*. Some may be spelled either *ize* or *ise;* as, *advertise, advertize; comprise, comprize; criticize, criticise*. American usage generally prefers *ize*.

The following spellings are those given in Webster:

advise	compromise	exercise	patronize
amortize	demoralize	extemporize	penalize
anglicize	despise	familiarize	recognize
apologize	devise	fertilize	satirize
authorize	disfranchise	franchise	scrutinize
baptize	disorganize	harmonize	specialize
capitalize	dramatize	merchandise	supervise
centralize	economize	mobilize	surmise
characterize	emphasize	modernize	surprise
chastise	enterprise	monetize	sympathize
civilize	equalize	naturalize	utilize
colonize	excise	organize	visualize

Geographical Names Often Misspelled

Adirondacks	Cheyenne
Albuquerque	Chile
Allegany County, N. Y.; Md.	Cincinnati
Alleghany County, Va.	Czechoslovakia
Alleghany Mountains	Des Moines
Allegheny County and River, Pa.	Dobbs Ferry, N. Y.
Appomattox	Eastchester, N. Y.
Asheville	Edinburgh
Baireuth, Bavaria	Governors Island, N. Y.
Barbados	Guatemala
Bedloe's Island, N. Y.	Hoosac Tunnel
Beirut, Syria	Hoosick Falls
Bering Sea	Kearny, N. J.
Budapest	Khartum
Buenos Aires	Kingsbridge, N. Y.
Cape Verde Islands	Korea
Caribbean Sea	Kyoto (Japan) not Kioto
Cayuga	Leipsic
Chattanooga	Louisiana
Chautauqua	Luxemburg (a country)
Chesapeake	Luxembourg Gardens and Museum (Paris)

Massachusetts
Matawan, N. J.
Matewan, W. Va.
Mattawan, Mich.
Matteawan, N. Y.
Mississippi
Muscle Shoals, Ala.
Newcastle, England
New Castle, Pa.
Newfoundland
Niu-chwang
Nuremberg
Panhandle (of Texas)
Paterson, N. J.
Patterson, N. Y.
Philippines
Pittsburgh, Pa.
Plattsburg, N. Y.
Pocatello
Puerto Rico
Prince George's County, Md.
Prince George County, Va.
Princes Bay, S. I.
Pulaski
Roanoke

Rumania
Sacket Harbor
Sands Point, L. I.
Santo Domingo
Saskatchewan
Schenectady
Schuyler
Shenandoah
Spuyten Duyvil
St. Andrews, Scotland
St. Andrew's, Westchester
    County, N. Y.
St. John, N. B.
St. John's, Newf.
Strasbourg
Tallahassee
The Hague
Tokio
Trieste
Waynesboro
Wilmington
Wood's Hole
Westchester, N. Y.
West Chester, Pa.
Yosemite

Argentina (when used as the name of the country without the word "Republic")

Argentine (the adjective form—an Argentine product, Argentine wheat, &c.)

Words Often Misspelled

(Divided according to *Webster's New International Dictionary*)

a bridg ment
a cad e my
ac ci den tal ly
ac com mo date
a chieve ment
ac knowl edg ment
ac quaint ed
ac quit ted
a cross
ad dressed
a e ri al

air plane
all right
al read y
a lu mi num
am a teur
an es thet ic
ap pa ra tus
ap par ent
ar gu ment
as cend an cy
as cend ant

ath let ic
aux il ia ry

bal ance
ba zaar
be lieve
be liev ing
bi ased
bound a ry
bou quet
Brit ain

broad cast
buc ca neer
bus i ness

caf e te ri a
cem e ter y
chang ing
cli en tele
col umn
com mit tal
com pel
con trol ler
cor rob o rate
cor ru gate
coun ter feit

de bat er
de ceive
de ferred
de mean or
de scend ant
de scribe
de scrip tion
de spair
dex ter ous
diph the ri a
di rect
dis ap pear
dis ap point
dis patch
dis trib u tor

ear nest
ec sta sy
eighth
em bar rass
em i grant
ex ag ger ate
ex ceed
ex cel
ex cel lent
ex er cise
ex hil a rate
ex ist ence

fas ci nate
Feb ru a ry
fi nal ly
for eign er
fore tell
for ward
friend

gov ern ment
gov er nor
gram mar
gra tu i tous
griev ous
guard i an

hair breadth
har ass
height
he roes
hop ing
hun dredths
hy giene

ic ing
im ag i na ry
im me di ate ly
im mi gra tion
im mi nent
im ping ing
in ci den tal ly
in de pend ent
in dis creet
in fi nite
in noc u ous
in oc u late
in sist ence
in stal la tion
in ter cede
ir i des cent

judg ment

keen ness
knowl edge

lab o ra to ry
le gion naire
li bra ry
li cense
light ning
lik a ble
liq ue fy

man i kin
man u al
mar riage
mat i nee
mat tress
mes sen ger
mil len ni um
mil lion aire
mis cel la ne ous
mis chie vous
mis spell
mis state ment
mon as ter y
mon eyed

ne groes
nick el
nine teenth
no tice a ble

oc ca sion al ly
oc cur rence
oc cur ring
om e let
o mis sion
o mit ted
op ti mis tic
out ra geous

pac i fist
paid
par al lel
par lia ment
pas sen ger
pas time
peace a ble

per ceive

per emp to ry

per se ver ance

per son nel

per spi ra tion

pic nic

pneu mo ni a

pol i ti cian

pol i tics

pos ses sor

pre ced ence

prep a ra tion

priv i lege

pro ced ure

pro fes sion

prof fered

prom is so ry

psy chol o gy

ques tion naire

real ly

re ceive

rec og nize

rec om mend

ref er ence

rep e ti tion

sec re ta ry

seize

ser geant

serv ice a bly

siege

sim i lar

sin cere ly

su per in tend ent

tend en cy

trace a ble

u nan i mous

un nec es sa ry

use ful

venge ance

vil lage

war rant

weath er

WORDS ENDING IN *IBLE*

accessible

admissible

audible

collapsible

collectible

combustible

comprehensible

compressible

convertible

corruptible

deducible

destructible

dirigible

discernible

divisible

edible

eligible

exhaustible

feasible

forcible

horrible

illegible

imperceptible

inaudible

incompatible

incorrigible

incredible

indefensible

indelible

indigestible

infallible

inflexible

intangible

intelligible

invincible

invisible

irascible

legible

negligible

permissible

plausible

possible

reprehensible

resistible

responsible

reversible

susceptible

tangible

terrible

transmissible

WORDS ENDING IN *ANT*

abundant

accountant

adjutant

appellant

applicant

arrogant

assailant

attendant

benignant

blatant

claimant

coadjutant

commandant

complainant

complaisant

concomitant
conversant
covenant
currant
    (*see* current)
defendant
determinant
discordant
disinfectant
disputant
dissonant
distant
exorbitant
extravagant
exultant
flagrant
flippant
fragrant
gallant
hesitant
hydrant
ignorant
immigrant
important
incessant
inconstant

indignant
intolerant
intoxicant
irrelevant
irritant
itinerant
lieutenant
malignant
mendicant
militant
mordant
observant
occupant
pedant
penchant
pennant
petulant
pheasant
pleasant
poignant
precipitant
predominant
pregnant
preponderant
protestant
protuberant

pursuant
quadrant
recalcitrant
redundant
relevant
reliant
reluctant
repentant
repugnant
resistant
resonant
restaurant
servant
significant
stagnant
sycophant
tenant
termagant
tolerant
trenchant
triumphant
truant
vagrant
vigilant
visitant

Words Ending in *ENT*

abstinent
accident
affluent
antecedent
astringent
coherent
comment
competent
complacent
component
concurrent
confident
consistent
constituent
contingent

convergent
corespondent
correspondent
current
    (*see* currant)
despondent
deterrent
different
diffident
diligent
discontent
eminent
equivalent
evident
expedient

immanent
imminent
impatient
impertinent
improvident
imprudent
impudent
incident
inclement
incompetent
incontinent
incumbent
indecent
independent
indigent

indifferent
indolent
indulgent
inexpedient
inherent
innocent
insistent
insolent
insolvent
insurgent
intelligent
intermittent
irreverent
magnificent

malevolent
negligent
obedient
omnipotent
opponent
penitent
permanent
persistent
pertinent
pre-eminent
recurrent
redolent
remittent
repellent

reverent
somnolent
strident
stringent
succulent
transcendent
translucent
transparent
truculent
turbulent
urgent
vehement
violent

WORDS ENDING IN *ANCE*

abeyance
acceptance
accordance
acquaintance
acquittance
admittance
affiance
alliance
allowance
ambulance
appearance
arrogance
assistance
assurance
attendance
balance
circumstance
clearance
complaisance
compliance
concordance
connivance
contrivance
conveyance
countenance
counterbalance
deliverance

discontinuance
discordance
discountenance
disturbance
encumbrance
endurance
enhance
entrance
expectance
extravagance
exuberance
finance
forbearance
fragrance
furtherance
grievance
ignorance
importance
inheritance
instance
insurance
intemperance
intolerance
irrelevance
issuance
maintenance
nuisance

obeisance
observance
ordinance
ordnance
parlance
perchance
performance
precipitance
preponderance
protuberance
pursuance
quittance
radiance
reconnaissance
redundance
reliance
reluctance
remembrance
remittance
remonstrance
renaissance
repentance
repugnance
resemblance
resistance
resonance
riddance

romance
significance
substance

sustenance
temperance
tolerance

transmittance
variance
vigilance

Words Ending in *ENCE*

abhorrence
absence
abstinence
adherence
adolescence
affluence
audience
benevolence
coherence
commence
competence
complacence
concurrence
condolence
conference
confidence
confluence
conscience
consistence
continence
contingence
convergence
correspondence
credence
deference
dependence
despondence
difference
diffidence
diligence
disobedience
divergence
excellence

experience
imminence
impatience
impertinence
impotence
improvidence
imprudence
impudence
incandescence
incidence
incompetence
inconsequence
incontinence
independence
indifference
indolence
indulgence
inexperience
inference
influence
inherence
innocence
insistence
insolence
insurgence
intelligence
interdependence
interference
intermittence
irreverence
magnificence
malevolence
negligence

obedience
occurrence
omnipotence
penitence
permanence
persistence
pertinence
pestilence
precedence
presence
prevalence
prominence
providence
prudence
recurrence
redolence
repellence
residence
resilience
reticence
reverence
science
silence
somnambulence
subsequence
subsistence
transcendence
transference
translucence
transparence
truculence
turbulence
violence

Words Ending in *ER*

accuser
acquitter

admirer
adventurer

adviser *or*
advisor

appeaser
artificer
assayer
assigner
astronomer
astrologer
banker
barkeeper
barrister
beginner
believer
bibliographer
bidder
biographer
bombarder
bookbinder
bookkeeper
bookmaker
bookseller
bowler
broker
buyer
bystander
carpenter
cataloguer *or*
cataloger
commander
commissioner
commuter
comptroller
conjurer *or*
conjuror
coroner
costumer
counterfeiter
crusader
customer
daughter
dealer
deceiver
deserter
destroyer
discoverer
dreamer

driver
dyer
embroiderer
employer
engraver
examiner
explorer
exporter
extortioner
falsifier
fighter
flyer
follower
foreigner
fruiterer
furrier
gambler
harvester
householder
idolater
importer
inciter
insurer
interloper
interpreter
intruder
islander
jailer
jeweler *or*
jeweller
joiner
juggler
keeper
kidnaper *or*
kidnapper
laborer
landowner
lawgiver
lawmaker
lawyer
leader
leper
lexicographer
lithographer

manager
manufacturer
masquerader
meddler
messenger
miner
mourner
observer
offender
officer
organizer
painter
passenger
pauper
pensioner
performer
perfumer
photographer
pitcher
planner
planter
plasterer
pleader
plodder
plumber
pointer
porter
poser
potter
preacher
premier
preserver
printer
prisoner
producer
promoter
prompter
provider
prowler
publisher
purchaser
purser
racer
rancher

ranger
reaper
receiver
recorder
redeemer
reformer
reporter
retainer
reveler *or*
reveller
reviewer
reviler
revolver
rioter
robber
romancer
ruler
sharper
shipper
shopkeeper
skipper

soldier
sorcerer
southerner
spinster
stammerer
stationer
stenographer
stockbroker
stockholder
stranger
striker
subscriber
swimmer
swindler
teamster
telegrapher
teller
tiller
topographer
trader
trainer

traveler *or*
traveller
treasurer
trickster
trooper
trumpeter
tumbler
typesetter
typographer
unbeliever
underwriter
user
versifier
warder
watcher
whisperer
widower
worshiper *or*
worshipper
wrecker
youngster

WORDS ENDING IN *OR*

actor
adjudicator
administrator
adviser *or*
advisor
agitator
aggressor
ambassador
ancestor
annotator
arbitrator
assessor
auditor
author
aviator
bachelor
benefactor
calculator
chancelor *or*
chancellor

collaborator
collector
commentator
competitor
compositor
conductor
confessor
conjurer *or*
conjuror
conqueror
conservator
consignor
constructor
contractor
contributor
councilor *or*
councillor
creditor
curator
debtor

decorator
demonstrator
depositor
director
distributor
editor
elector
emancipator
emperor
executor
governor
grantor
guarantor
illustrator
imitator
impostor
inspector
instructor
interlocutor
inventor

investigator	oppressor	sailor
investor	orator	savior *or*
janitor	originator	saviour
junior	participator	sculptor
juror	pastor	senator
legislator	perpetrator	spectator
liberator	possessor	speculator
liquidator	preceptor	stipulator
malefactor	precursor	successor
mediator	predecessor	suitor
minor	procrastinator	supervisor
monsignor	proctor	survivor
mortgagor	professor	tailor
narrator	progenitor	testator
navigator	projector	traitor
neighbor *or*	proprietor	tutor
neighbour	protector	valuator
objector	purveyor	visitor
officiator	realtor	warrantor
operator	rector	warrior

WORDS ENDING IN *CEDE*

accede	precede
concede	recede
intercede	secede

WORDS ENDING IN *CEED*

exceed   proceed   succeed

WORD ENDING IN *SEDE*

supersede

Variant Spelling According to Webster's New International Dictionary

Preferred	*Allowed*
adviser	advisor
buses	busses
canyon	cañon
catalogue	catalog

Preferred	*Allowed*
check	cheque (British)
coconut	cocoanut
dispatch	despatch
employee	employe
fulfill	fulfil
maneuver	manoeuvre
medieval	mediaeval
mold	mould
peddler	pedlar
practice (v. & n.)	practise (verb only)
skillful	skilful
subpoena	subpena
taboo	tabu
willful	wilful

7. Diction

Words Often Confused in Meaning and in Spelling

accede	to attain, to agree
exceed	to surpass
accept	to receive
except	to exclude
adverse	opposed
averse	disinclined
adapt	to suit oneself to
adept	proficient
addition	something added
edition	number of books printed at a time
advice	counsel
advise	to give counsel. Not used correctly for *inform*.
affect	to influence, to change, to assume, always a verb.
effect	to bring about, as a verb; a result, as a noun
all together	in a body
altogether	entirely
aloud	audibly
allowed	permitted
altar	a sacred place for worship
alter	to change
apprise	to inform
apprize	to value
appraise	to value
ascent	act of rising
assent	consent
berth	a place in which to sleep in a Pullman or a ship
birth	act of being born
biannual	half-yearly
biennial	two-yearly

110

canon	a law; a rule
cannon	a large gun
canvas	a coarse cloth
canvass	to solicit
capital	a chief city, a sum of money
capitol	a state-house
cast	a group of actors; to throw
caste	hereditary class
censer	an incense pan
censor	a critic, to criticize
censure	to blame
cite	to summon
sight	a view
site	a place
cession	a ceding, a yielding up
session	a meeting assembled
coarse	common, rough
course	a direction of going
collision	an act of colliding; a clash
collusion	a secret agreement for fraudulent purposes
complement	that which completes
compliment	flattery, praise
correspondent	one who writes letters
corespondent	a third party in a divorce suit
council	an assembly or group for conference
counsel	advice; legal adviser
decent	respectable
descent	act of descending
dissent	act of disagreement
desert	a barren place
dessert	a course at the end of dinner
device (noun)	a plan
devise (verb)	to plan
divers	various
diverse	of different nature
dual	twofold
duel	a combat between two persons
dying	ceasing to live
dyeing	coloring

elicit	to draw forth
illicit	illegal
elusive	baffling
illusive	unreal
eminent	prominent
imminent	threatening
exercise	to practice in order to develop
exorcise	to purify a person or a place from an evil spirit
faint	fatigued; a swoon
feint	a pretense
fair	just; blond
fare	sum paid for journey
farther	in space
further	in degree
fore	in front
four	a number
formally	perfunctorily, ceremoniously
formerly	in times past
forth	away; forward
fourth	a number
guarantee	preferred in the verb sense
guaranty	preferred in the noun sense
hypercritical	too critical
hypocritical	insincere
indict	to charge with an offense
indite	to write, to compose
ingenious	clever
ingenuous	frank
instance	an example
instants	periods of time
its	pronoun
it's	contraction of *it is*
know	to be aware of
no	a negative
later	comparative of late
latter	the second of two mentioned
least	little
leased	held on lease

| loath | adjective |
| loathe | verb |

loose	free
loosen	to free
lose	to cease to have

| mantel | a shelf above a fireplace |
| mantle | a cloak |

| mean | average; shabby; to intend |
| mien | manner |

meat	food
meet	to assemble
mete	to measure

| miner | a workman in a mine |
| minor | one under age; lesser |

| ordinance | act of ordaining, ordering or arranging |
| ordnance | military supplies |

ought	should
aught	anything
naught	a cipher

pair	two; a couple
pare	to slice thinly
pear	a fruit

| past | adjective, adverb, or preposition |
| passed | past tense of *to pass* |

| peal | sound of bells |
| peel | to skin |

| pedal | a foot lever |
| peddle | to sell from house to house |

| personal | individual, private |
| personnel | staff of an institution |

| persecute | to subject to persistent ill-treatment |
| prosecute | to pursue, to bring lawsuit against |

| precede | to go before |
| proceed | to begin |

| precedence | priority |
| precedents | previous examples taken for basis of present action |

| prescribe | to lay down authoritatively a course of action |
| proscribe | to outlaw |

presence	state of being present
presents	gifts
principal	chief; head of a school; sum of money
principle	a general truth
prophecy	a noun
prophesy	a verb
quite	completely
quiet	not noisy
rapped	struck
rapt	transported in feeling
wrapped	folded
respectfully	manner of feeling
respectively	proper to each
role	a part in a play
roll	a round thing
sewage	matter carried in sewers
sewerage	system of sewers
shone	reflected light
shown	exhibited
stationary	not moving
stationery	writing paper
statue	a piece of sculpture
stature	height
statute	a law
straight	direct
strait	a narrow water passage; circumscribed
talesman	a person added to a jury
talisman	a charm
terminal	the end, particularly of a line of railroad
terminus	either end of a railroad line; particularly the station, town, or city at the end of a line of railroad
their	a pronoun
there	an adverb
they're	contraction of *they are*
therefor	to that end
therefore	for the reason
till until	(interchangeable)

topography	local geography, features
typography	the art of printing or the use of type in printing
troop	a body of soldiers or of cavalry
troupe	a company of stage performers
who's	contraction of *who is*
whose	pronoun, possessive of *who*
your	pronoun
you're	contraction of *you are*

Words Commonly Misused

ability	power to do
capacity	power to receive
all right	Note this is the correct and only spelling. There is no such spelling as *alright*.
almost	an adverb meaning *very nearly* (almost all)
most	an adjective, a pronoun, and an adverb of comparison: *most* people; *most* of them came; *most* beautiful
allusion	an indirect reference
illusion	an error of vision
delusion	an error of judgment
amoral	nonmoral
unmoral	having no moral perception
immoral	dissolute
amount	the sum total referring to number
number	refers to something counted
quantity	refers to something measured
anecdote	a narrative of a particular incident
antidote	a remedy to counteract poison
antagonist	an enemy
protagonist	principal character in a drama
anywhere	There is no such word as *anywheres*.
apt	suitable, appropriate, skilled
likely	possible
liable	implies undesirable consequences, legally bound
as—as	used in affirmative comparison
so—as	used in negative comparison
avocation	a minor occupation
vocation	a regular calling or profession

balance	the difference between the debit and credit side of an account
remainder	the comparatively small part left over
beside	at the side of
besides	in addition to
bring	to convey toward the speaker
take	to carry from the speaker
can	denotes ability
may	denotes permission
casual	happening by chance
causal	relating to a cause or causes
comprehensive	having a wide scope
comprehensible	intelligible
credible	worthy of belief
creditable	praiseworthy
credulous	too ready to believe
customer	person entering shop to buy, especially one dealing with a firm
client	person using the services of a lawyer or other professional man
deposition	sworn testimony obtained out of court; removal from office; sediment
disposition	arrangement; temper
directly	never a conjunction; as, *Directly* he came, I left. *Correct: As soon as* he came, I left.
due to	adjective modifier *Correct:* His failure, *due to* ill health, caused financial embarrassment. *Incorrect: Due to* the bad weather, we could not go.
because of	*Because of* financial embarrassment he could not go to Europe.
each	refers to the members of a group
each other	Use *each other* of *two.* Use *one another* of *more than two.*
both	two considered together
economic	pertaining to economics
economical	thrifty
emigration	the moving from a country
immigration	the moving into a country

exceedingly	very greatly
excessively	too greatly
exceptional	unusual
exceptionable	open to objection
excite	to stir up emotionally
incite	to stir to action
expect	to regard as likely to happen
suspect	to doubt the truth of
farther	referring to distance
further	in addition, to greater extent
few	used in reference to number
less	used in reference to quantity
first	both adjective and adverb. *Firstly* is not in good use.
hanged	of a person
hung	of an object
healthy	in good health or condition
healthful	health-giving, as of climate
wholesome	producing a good effect, as of food
hire	to employ, to obtain the use of
let	to give the use of
lease	to give the use of by lease
human	pertaining to mankind (an adjective, not a noun)
humane	benevolent
irrelevant	not pertaining to
irreverent	wanting in reverence
last	after all others
latest	the most recent
learn	to acquire knowledge
teach	to give instruction
legible	easy to read, readable
eligible	qualified to be chosen
luxuriant	profuse of growth
luxurious	self-indulgent, conducive to luxury
mad	insane. Do not use in the sense of *angry*.
angry	enraged
Madam	polite form of address to women
Madame	prefix to foreign name

majority	receiving more than half of the number of votes
plurality	receiving a greater number than any other, but less than half of the votes cast
much	referring to quantity
many	referring to persons or things
near	in proximity to time or space
nearly	almost
new	recent, not old
novel	unusual, strange
none (*See* p. 189)	may be singular or plural according to sense
noted	favorably known
notorious	unfavorably known
famous	celebrated
observance	rite, a ceremonial
observation	act of observing
partake	to take a share, as of food
participate	to have a share in
party	a body of persons; in law term, a person
person	an individual
practical	that which can be done advantageously
practicable	that which can be done
proposition	statement, assertion, something offered for discussion
proposal	something offered for acceptance or rejection
raise	transitive verb, to lift
rear	to bring up, to train
rise	intransitive verb, to ascend
real	not counterfeit
quite	adverb of degree, meaning entirely
very	adverb of degree, meaning extremely. Do not use to modify a participle.
recipe	a statement of ingredients and procedure for a medicine or dish
receipt	a written acknowledgment of receiving money, a fact of receiving
salary	a fixed periodical payment made to a person employed in other than manual or mechanical work
wages	workman's or servant's periodical pay

some	an adjective or a pronoun
somewhat	an adverb of degree
valuable	of great value
valued	estimated

Pronunciation *

acclimate—ăk-klī′-māt, *not* ăk′-klĭm-āt
acumen—ă-kū′-měn, *not* ăk′-yū-měn
address (n.)—ăd-drěs′
address (vb.)—ăd-drěs′
adept (n.)—ăd′-ěpt *or* ăd-ěpt′
adept (adj.)—ăd-ěpt′
admirable—ăd′mĭr-à-bl, *not* ăd-mī′rà-bl
admirably—ăd′mĭr-à-blĭ, *not* ăd-mī′-rà-blĭ
adult—ȧdŭlt′, *or* ăd′-ŭlt
advertisement—ăd-věr′tĭz-ment *or* ȧd-ver-tīz′-ment
alias—ā′-lĭ-ăs, *not* ăl-ī′-ăs
Alma Mater—ăl′-mȧ mā′-tēr *or* äl-mȧ mä′-tēr
alumnae—ȧ-lŭm′-nē
alumni—a-lŭm′nī
annex (n.)—ăn′-něks *or* ăn-něks′
annex (vb.)—ăn-něks′
annihilate—ăn-nī′-hĭl-āt
applicable—ăp′-plĭk-à-bl *or* ăp-plĭk′-ā-bl
appreciate—ăp-prē′-shĭ-āt, *not* ăp-prē′-sĭ-āt
apropos—ăp-rō-pō′
aristocrat—ȧ-rĭs′-tō-krăt *or* ăr′-ĭs-tō-krăt
ask—ȧsk, *not* ăsk
associate—ăs-sō′-shĭ-āt, *not* ăs-sō′-sĭ-āt
association—ăs-sō-sĭ-ā′shŭn *or* ăs-sō-shĭ-ā′-shŭn
athlete—ăth′-lēt, *not* ăth′l-ēt *or* ăth′-a-lēte
avenue—ăv′-ė-nū, *not* ăv′-ē-noo
aviator—āv′iātor *or* ăv′ī-ā-tēr
bade—băd, *not* bād
banquet—băng′-kwět, *not* băn′-kwět
bicycle—bī′-sĭk-l, *not* bī′-sī-kl
biography—bī-ŏg′rȧ-fĭ *or* bĭ-ŏg′-rȧ-fĭ
blatant—blā′-tănt, *not* blăt′-ănt
bouquet—boo-kā′ *or* bō-kā′
cello—chěl′-ō
chaos—kā′-ŏs
chastisement—chăs′-tĭz-měnt, *not* chăs-tīz′-měnt

* See key to symbols, on p. 123.

chiropodist—kī-rŏp′-ō-dĭst
clique—klēk, *not* klĭk
cognomen—kŏg-nō′-měn, *not* kŏg′-nō-měn
combatant—kŏm′-băt-ănt; kŭm′-băt-ănt
comparable—kŏm′-pȧ-rȧ-bl, *not* kŏm-pâr′-a-bl
complaisance—kŏm-plā′-zăns *or* kŏm′-plā-zăns
compromise—kŏm′-prō-mīz
comptroller—kŏn-trō′-lēr
condolence—kŏn-dō′-lĕns *or* kŏn′-dō-lĕns
connoisseur—kŏn′ĭ-sûr′ *or* kŏn′ĭ-sūr′
conscientious—kŏn-shĭ-ĕn′-shŭs, *not* kŏn-sĭ-ĕn′-shŭs
considerable—kŏn-sĭd′-ēr-ȧ-bl, *not* kŏn-sĭd′-rȧ-bl
conspiracy—kŏn-spĭr′-ȧ-sĭ, *not* kŏn-spī′-rȧ-sĭ
corps (military)—kōr; pl., kōrz
coupon—kōō′-pŏn
cowardice—kow′-ärd-ĭs, *not* kow′-ärd-īs
credence—krē′-dĕns, *not* krĕd′-ĕns
creek—krēk, *not* krĭk
crematory—krē′-mȧ-tō-rĭ *or* krĕm′-ȧ-tō-rĭ
culinary—kū′-lĭn-ā-rĭ *or* kŭl′-ĭn-ā-rĭ
data—dā′-tȧ *or* dä′-tȧ
deaf—dĕf
decade—dĕk′-ād
deficit—dĕf′-ĭs-ĭt, *not* dē-fĭs′-ĭt
detail (n.)—dē-tāl′ *or* dē′-tāl
depot—dē′-pō
detour—dĕ′-tōōr *or* dĕ-tōōr′
digest (n.)—dī′-jĕst
digest (vb.)—dĭ-jĕst′ *or* dī-jĕst′
digestion—dĭ-jĕs′-chŭn, *not* dī-jĕs′-chŭn
direct—dĭ-rĕkt′ *or* dī-rĕkt′
discourse—dis-kōrs′ *or* dĭs′-kōrs
economic—ē-kō-nŏm′-ĭk *or* ĕk-ō-nŏm′-ĭk
egotism—ē′-g̱ō-tĭzm *or* ĕg̱′-ō-tĭzm
envelope—ĕn′-vĕl-ōp *or* ŏn′-vĕl-ōp *or* ĕn-vĕl′-ŭp
epitome—ē-pĭt′-ō-mē, *not* ĕp′-ĭ-tōm
epoch—ĕp′-ŏk *or* ē′-pŏk
err—ûr
errata—ĕr-rā′-tȧ
exigency—ĕk′-sĭ-jĕn-sĭ
exit—ĕk′-sĭt *or* ĕg′-zĭt
exquisite—ĕks′-kwĭz-ĭt, ĕks-kwĭz′-ĭt (*occasionally for emphasis*)
extol—ĕks-tŏl′ *or* ĕks-tōl′
extraordinary—ĕks-trôr′-dĭn-ā-rĭ

faucet—fô′sĕt, *not* făs′-ĕt

fiat—fī′-ăt

finale—fē-nä′-lā, *not* fī-năl′-ē

finance—fĭn-ăns′ *or* fī-năns′ *or* fī′-năns

financial—fĭn-ăn′-shăl *or* fī-năn′-shăl

financier—fĭn-ăn-sēr′ *or* fī-năn-sēr′

forbade—fôr-băd′, *not* fôr-bād′

forehead—fŏr′-ĕd *or* fŏr′-ĭd

formidable—fôr′-mĭd-à-bl

forward—fôr′-wĕrd

fragile—frăj-ĭl, *not* frăj′ĭl

frequent (adj.)—frē′kwĕnt

frequent (vb.)—frē-kwĕnt′

gala—gā′-là, *not* găl′-à

gamut—găm′-ŭt, *not* gā′-mŭt

genuine—jĕn-ū-ĭn, *not* jĕn-ū-īn

gigantic—jī-găn′-tĭk, *not* jĭg-ăn′-tĭk

gist—jĭst, *not* ḡĭst

gondola—gŏn′-dō-là, *not* gŏn-dō′-la

gratis—grā′-tĭs *or* grăt′-ĭs

Hades—hā′-dēz

harass—hăr′-ăs *or* hà-răs′

hearth—härth, *not* hĕrth

height—hīt, *not* hītth

helm—hĕlm, *not* hĕl′-ŭm

herb—ērb *or* hĕrb

Herculean—Hēr-kū′-lē-ăn *or* Hēr-kū-lē′-ăn

humor—hū′-mēr *or* yū′-mēr

hypocrisy—hĭp-ŏk′-rĭs-ĭ

hysteria—hĭs-tē′-rĭ-à

illustrate—ĭl′-lŭs-trāt *or* ĭl-lŭs′-trāt

incomparable—ĭn-kŏm′-pà-rà-bl, *not* ĭn-kŏm-pâr′ā-bl

indict—ĭn-dīt′

indictment—ĭn-dīt′-mĕnt

indisputable—ĭn-dĭs′-pū-tà-bl *or* ĭn-dĭs-pū′-tà-bl

indissoluble—ĭn-dĭs′-ō-lū-bl *or* ĭn-dĭ-sŏl′u-bl

industry—ĭn′-dŭs-trĭ, *not* ĭn-dŭs′-trĭ

inertia—ĭn-ēr′-shĭà *or* in-ēr-shĭ-à

inexorable—ĭn-ĕks′-ō-rà-bl

inexplicable—ĭn-ĕks′-plĭk-à-bl

inextricable—ĭn-ĕks′-trĭk-à-bl

infamous—ĭn′-fà-mŭs

infantile—ĭn′-făn-tīl *or* ĭn′făn-tĭl

inhospitable—ĭn-hŏs′-pĭt-à-bl, *not* ĭn-hŏs-pĭt′-à-bl

inquiry—ĭn-kwīr′ĭ *or* ĭn′-kwĭ-rī

insatiable—ĭn-sā′-shĭ-á-bl *or* ĭn-sā′-shá-bl

interested—ĭn′-tēr-ĕst-ĕd, *not* ĭn-tēr-ĕst′-ĕd

interesting—ĭn′-tēr-ĕst-ĭng, *not* ĭn-tēr-ĕst′-ĭng

irreparable—ĭr-rĕp′-á-rá-bl, *not* ĭr-rē-păr′-á-bl

isolate—ī′-sō-lāt *or* ĭs′ō-lāt

italic—ĭ-tăl′-ĭk, *not* ī-tăl′-ĭk

juvenile—jū′-vē-nĭl *or* jū′-vē-nīl

kept—kĕpt, *not* kĕp

length—lĕngth, *not* lĕnth

mischievous—mĭs′-chēv-ŭs, *not* mĭs-chē′-vŭs

municipal—mū-nĭs′-ĭp-ăl, *not* mū-nĭs-ĭp′-ăl

nauseate—nô′-shē-āt *or* nô′-sē-āt

nephew—nĕf′-yū *or* nĕv′-yū

often—ŏf′-n, *not* ŏf′-tĕn

oral—ō′rál

pageant—păj′-ent, *occasionally* pā′-jent

parquet—pär-kā′ *or* pär-kĕt′

pertinacious—pēr-tĭn-ā′-shŭs, *not* pēr-tĭn-ăsh′-ŭs

poem—pō′ĕm, *not* pō′-ŭm

precedence—prē-sē′-dĕns *or* prĕs′-ē-dĕns *or* prē′-sė-dĕns

precedency—prē-sē′-dĕn-sĭ, *not* prĕs′-ē-dĕn-sĭ

precedent (n.)—prĕs′-ē-dĕnt *or* prē′-sė-dĕnt

precedent (adj.)—prē-sēd′ĕnt

premature—prē-má-tūr′ *or* prē′-má-tūr

promissory—prŏm′-ĭs-sō-rĭ

promulgate—prō-mŭl′-g̅āt

qualm—kwäm *or* kwôm

radiator—rā′-dĭ-ā-tor

radio—rā′-dĭ-o

raillery—rāl′-ēr-ĭ *or* răl′-ēr-ĭ

ratio—rā′-shō *or* rā′-shĭ-ō

recognize—rĕk′-ŏg̅-nīz

referable—rĕf′ēr-á-bl *or* rė-fûr′-á-bl

retailer—rē′tāl-er *or* re-tāl′-er

revocable—rĕv′-ō-ká-bl, *not* rē-vō′ká-bl

revolt—rē-vōlt′ *or* rē-vŏlt′

rinse—rĭns, *not* rĕns

romance—rō-măns′ *or* rō′-măns

roof—rōof, *not* rŏof

room—rōom, *not* rŏom

root—rōot, *not* rŏot

route—rōot *or* rowt *(Century)*

salmon—săm′-ŭn, *not* sä′-mŭn

says—sĕz, *not* sāz
several—sĕv′-ēr-ăl, *not* sĕv′-răl
shone—shōn *or* shŏn
suggest—sŭg̃-jĕst′ *or* sŭj-jĕst′
suite—swēt, *not* sūt
superfluous—sū-pẽr′-flū-ŭs
tedious—tē′-dĭ-ŭs *or* tēd′-yŭs *or* tē′-jŭs
tepid—tĕp′-ĭd, *not* tē′-pĭd
tomato—tō-mā′-tō *or* tō-mä′-to
toward—tōrd, *not* tō-wôrd′
tribune—trĭb′-yūn *or* trĭ-būn′
ultimatum—ŭl-tĭm-ā′-tŭm, *not* ŭl-tĭm-ä′-tŭm
usage—ūs′-ĭj *or* ūz′-ĭj
vagary—vȧ-gâr′-ĭ *or* vȧ-gā′-rĭ, *not* vā′-gȧ-rĭ
vagrant—vā′grănt, *not* văg′-rănt
vice versa—vī′-sē vẽr′-sȧ, *not* vīs′-vẽr-sȧ
wan—wŏn
yacht—yŏt
yolk—yōk *or* yōlk
yule—yūl
zealous—zĕl′-ŭs

KEY TO PRONUNCIATION SYMBOLS FOR VOWELS

Symbol	Example	Name
ā	āle	long a
ȧ	chȧotic	half-long a
â	câre	circumflex a
ă	ădd	short a
ä	ärm	two-dot a
ȧ	ȧsk	one-dot a
ē	ēve	long e
ė	ėvent	half-long e
ĕ	ĕnd	short e
ẽ	makẽr	tilde e
ī	īce	long i
ĭ	ĭll	short i
ō	ōld	long o
ȯ	ȯbey	half-long o
ô	ôrb	circumflex o
ŏ	ŏdd	short o
ô̧	sô̧ft	short circumflex o
oi	oil	
o͞o	fo͞od	long double o

Symbol	Example	Name
o͝o	fo͝ot	short double o
ou	out	
ū	cūbe	long u
u̇	u̇nite	half-long u
û	ûrn	circumflex u
ŭ	ŭp	short u
ŭ	circ*ŭ*s	italic short u

With some omissions, from Merriam-Webster Pronunciation Key. *Webster's New Collegiate Dictionary*. Front lining paper.

Foreign Words and Phrases Commonly Used

(Selected from the *Standard Dictionary*)

LATIN WORDS AND PHRASES

a priori	From what is before; from cause to effect
annus mirabilis	Wonderful year
ante bellum	Before the war, especially before the Civil War
ante meridiem	Before the sun reaches the meridian, that is, before noon
arbiter elegantiae	A judge in matters of taste
bona fides	Good faith
carpe diem	Enjoy the present
casus belli	A cause justifying war
causa sine qua non	An indispensable condition
cave canem	Beware of the dog
circa	About
conditio sine qua non	An indispensable condition
confer (cf.)	Compare
consensus facit legem	Consent makes the law
copia verborum	Fluency of speech
cor unum, via una	One heart, one way
cui bono?	For whose advantage, to what end?
cum privilegio	With privilege
de gustibus non est disputandum	There is no disputing about tastes
de mortuis nil nisi bonum	Concerning the dead say nothing but good
Dei gratia	By the grace of God
Deo volente (D.V.)	God willing

Deus vobiscum	God be with you
dis aliter visum	It seemed otherwise to the gods
Dominus vobiscum	The Lord be with you
dulce et decorum est pro patria mori	Sweet and seemly is it to die for one's country
ecce homo	Behold the man
ex cathedra	Officially, with authority
ex curia	Out of court
ex more	According to custom
exempli gratia (e.g.)	By way of example
exeunt omnes	All go out (used as a stage direction)
facile princeps	Easily the first
fide et amore	By faith and love
fidus Achates	Faithful Achates; trusty friend
fortuna favet fortibus	Fortune favors the brave
gaudeamus igitur	Let us be joyful
genius loci	The spirit of the place; guardian deity
gloria in excelsis	Glory to God in the highest
hic et ubique	Here and everywhere
hic sepultus	Here lies buried
hinc illae lacrimae	Hence these tears
hoc anno	In this year
hoc loco	In this place
hoc tempore	At this time
hodie mihi, cras tibi	Mine today, yours tomorrow
homo sum; humani nihil a me alienum puto	I am a man; I count nothing human indifferent to me
honores mutant mores	Honors change manners
horribile dictu	Horrible to be told
humanum est errare	To err is human
id est (i.e.)	That is
in curia	In court
in extremis	At the point of death
in hoc signo spes mea	In this sign is my hope
in hoc signo vinces	By this sign you will conquer
in hoc statu	In this state of things
in loco parentis	In the place of a parent
in medias res	Into the midst of things; into the heart of the matter
in memoriam	In memory of
in nomine Domini	In the name of the Lord
in pace	In peace

in omnia paratus	Prepared for all things
in perpetuum	Forever
in personam	*Law*. Against the person instead of against specific things
in posse	In possibility; in potential existence
in propria persona	In one's own person
in re	In the matter of
in rem suam	*Civ. Law*. In his own affair; said of a certain power of attorney
in rerum natura	In the nature of things
in secula seculorum	To ages of ages; for ever and ever
in situ	In its place; in proper position
in statu quo	In the state in which it was before
in statu quo ante bellum	In the state in which it was before the war
in totidem verbis	In so many words
in toto	Altogether; entirely
in transitu	In transit
ipso jure	By the law itself
jure divino	By divine law
jus canonicum	Canon law
jus civile	Civil law
jus gentium	Law of nations
jus gladii	The law of the sword
justitia omnibus	Justice for all
labor est etiam ipsa voluptas	Labor is pleasure itself
labor ipse voluptas	Labor itself is pleasure
labor omnia vincit	Labor conquers all things
laborare est orare	To work is to pray
laesa majestas	Lese-majesty; treason
lapis philosophorum	The philosophers' stone
lares et penates	Household gods
laus Deo	Praise be to God
legalis homo	A person in good standing before the law
lex loci	The law of the place
lex scripta	The written law
lex terrae	The law of the land
licentia vatum	Poetic license
lite pendente	During the trial
loco citato	In the place cited
locum tenens	One taking the place of another
locus in quo	Place in which
locus sigilli	The place of the seal

longe absit	Far be it
longo intervallo	At a long interval
loquitur	He (or she) speaks
lux mundi	The light of the world
magna civitas, magna solitudo	A great city is a great solitude
magni nominis umbra	The shadow of a great name
magnum bonum	A great good
malis avibus	Under bad auspices
malum in se	Evil in itself
maximus in minimis	Very great in little things
me judice	In my judgment
memento mori	Remember that you must die
memoria in aeterna	In everlasting remembrance
mens agitat molem	A mind keeps the mass in motion: mind animates matter
mens legis	The spirit of the law
mens sana in corpore sano	A sound mind in a healthy body
meo periculo	At my own risk
meo voto	By my wish
merum sal	Pure salt; true good sense or wit
meum et tuum	Mine and thine
miles gloriosus	A braggart soldier
mirabile dictu	Wonderful to say
mirabile visu	Wonderful to be seen
mirabilia	Miracles
modus operandi	A mode of operating
modus vivendi	A mode of living
more majorum	According to the custom of our fathers
more meo	In my own way
more suo	In his own way
morituri te salutamus	We who are about to die salute thee
motu proprio	Of one's own accord
multum in parvo	Much in little
mutatis mutandis	The necessary changes having been made
mutato nomine	The name being changed
mutuus consensus	Mutual consent
natale solum	Native soil
natura abhorret a vacuo	Nature abhors a vacuum
ne cede malis	Do not give way to misfortunes
nemine contradicente	No one speaking in opposition
nemine dissentiente	No one dissenting
nemo me impune lacessit	No one attacks me with impunity

nemo mortalium omnibus horis sapit — No one is wise at all times

nihil ad rem — Nothing to the point

nihil quod tetigit non ornavit — He touched nothing without embellishing it

nil admirari — To wonder at nothing

nil desperandum — Nothing to be despaired of

nil dicit — He says nothing

nisi Dominus, frustra — Unless the Lord build the house, it is in vain (to build it)

nitor in adversum — I struggle against adversity

nolens volens — Unwilling or willing

noli me tangere — Do not touch me

non constat — It does not follow

non libet — It does not please me

non omnia possumus omnes — We cannot, all of us, do everything

non possumus — We are not able

non quis, sed quid — Not who but what

non quo, sed quomodo — Not whom but in what manner

nulla dies sine linea — Not a day without a line

nulli secundus — Second to none

nunc aut nunquam — Now or never

O tempora! O mores! — What times! What morals!

obiit — He or she has died

omnia ad Dei gloriam — All things to the glory of God

omnia bona bonis — All things are good to the good

omnia vincit amor — Love conquers all things

operae pretium est — It is worth while

opere citato — In the volume cited

opus artificem probat — The craftsman is proved by his work

ora et labora — Worship and work

orator fit, poeta nascitur — The orator is made, the poet is born

otium cum dignitate — Leisure with dignity

panem et circenses — Bread and circus; food and amusements

pari passu — With equal pace; at the same speed

particeps criminis — A sharer in the crime

pater patriae — Father of his country

paucis verbis — In few words

pax vobiscum! — Peace be with you!

peccavi — I have sinned

pendente lite — During the suit

per diem — Daily

per se	By itself
periculum in mora	There's danger in delay
persona grata	An acceptable person
pleno jure	With full right
posse videor	I seem to myself to be able
possunt quia posse videntur	They can because they think they can
post meridiem	After the sun has reached the meridian, that is, after noon
primus inter pares	First among equals
principia, non homines	Principles, not men
pro bono publico	For the public good
pro Deo et ecclesia	For God and the church
pro et con	For and against
pro forma	As a matter of form
pro memoria	As a memorial
pro tempore	For the time, temporary
probatum est	It has been proved
quantum libet	As much as you please
quantum meruit	As much as he deserved
quantum sufficit	As much as suffices
quantum vis	As much as you wish
qui docet discit	Who teaches, learns
quid faciendum?	What is to be done?
quid pro quo	Something for something
quo animo?	With what intent?
quo Fata vocant	Whither the Fates call
quo jure?	With what right?
quo modo?	In what manner?
quo vadis?	Whither goest thou?
quod erat demonstrandum	Which was to be proved
quorum pars magna fui	Of which things I was a great part
re infecta	The business being unfinished
religio laici	The religion of a layman
requiescat in pace	Rest in peace
sal Atticum	Attic salt; wit wisdom
scripsit	He or she wrote it
sculpsit	He or she sculptured it
secundum artem	According to art or custom
secundum naturam	According to nature
secundum usum	According to usage
semel pro semper	Once for all
semper eadem	Always the same
semper fidelis	Always faithful

semper paratus	Always prepared
si Deus nobiscum, quis contra nos?	If God be with us, who can be against us?
si diis placet	If it pleases the gods
sic passim	Thus everywhere
sic semper tyrannis	Thus ever to tyrants
sic transit gloria mundi	Thus passes the glory of the world
sine cura	Without care
sine die	Without a day being appointed definitely
sine dubio	Without doubt
sine mora	Without delay
sine qua non	Something indispensable
status quo	The state in which
sub judice	Under consideration
sub praetexto juris	Under the pretext of justice
sub rosa	Under the rose; in strict confidence
sui juris	In one's own right
summa summarum	Sum total
summum bonum	The supreme good
summum jus, summa injuria	The extreme of justice, the extreme of injustice
suo jure	In one's own right
suo loco	In its proper place
sursum corda!	Lift up your hearts!
suum cuique	To each one his own
tempora mutantur	Times change
tempus fugit	Time flies
tertium quid	A third something; a nondescript
timeo Danaos et dona ferentes	I fear the Greeks even when bearing gifts
totum	The whole
ubi libertas, ibi patria	Where liberty is, there is my country
ubique	Everywhere
ultimum vale	A last farewell
ultimus Romanorum	The last of the Romans
una voce	With one voice
usus loquendi	Usage in speaking
ut dictum	As said or directed
ut infra	As below
ut supra	As above
vade in pace	Go in peace

vade mecum	Go with me; companion
vae victis	Woe to the conquered
vale!	Farewell!
vera causa	A true cause or complaint
verbatim et literatim	Word for word and letter for letter
vide ut supra	See as above
vincet amor patriae	Love of country will conquer
vita brevis, longa ars	Life is short and art long
vox populi, vox Dei	The voice of the people is the voice of God

French Words and Phrases

à bon droit	With justice
à bon marché	At a good bargain
à gauche	To the left
à propos de rien	Apropos of nothing
à tout prix	At any price
affaire de cœur	A love affair
amende honorable	Public reparation; an apology
au contraire	On the contrary
au fait	Skilled, expert
au revoir	Till we meet again
au rez-de-chaussée	On the ground floor
autre temps, autres moeurs	Other times, other manners
avec plaisir	With pleasure
beau monde	The fashionable world
bête noire	Black beast; object of abhorrence
bon ami	A good friend
bon jour	Good morning
bon soir	Good evening
bon voyage	A prosperous voyage to you
catalogue raisonné	An illustrated or classified catalogue
cause célèbre	Celebrated case in law
cela va sans dire	That is a matter of course
c'est-à-dire	That is to say
c'est une autre chose	That is a different thing
chacun à son goût	Everyone to his own taste
chef de cuisine	Head cook
chemin de fer	Railway
cher ami, or (fem.) chère amie	Dear friend
cherchez la femme	Seek the woman

chevalier d'industrie	Knight of industry; a swindler
communiqué	Official communication
compagnon de voyage	Traveling companion
compte rendu	An official report
conseil d'état	Council of state
coûte que coûte	Cost what it may
dégagé	Free; unrestrained
de haut en bas	From top to bottom
de trop	Too much; too many
dernier ressort	A last resource
Dieu avec nous	God with us
Dieu défend le droit!	God defend the right!
Dieu et mon droit	God and my right
distingué	Distinguished
distrait	Absent-minded
double entendre	Double meaning
édition de luxe	An elaborate and costly edition, as of a book
embarras de richesses	Embarrassment of riches
en masse	In a body
en passant	In passing
en plein jour	Before the whole world
en rapport	In sympathetic relation
en règle	According to rule
entre nous	Between us
fait accompli	An accomplished fact
femme de chambre	A chambermaid; a lady's maid
fête champêtre	An open-air festival
garde du corps	A bodyguard
gardez bien	Take good care
gardez la foi	Keep the faith
grâce à Dieu	Thanks to God
grand merci	Many thanks
grand monde	The world at large; refined society
homme d'affaires	Man of business
homme de lettres	Man of letters; literary man
homme d'esprit	Man of intellect; wit
honi soit qui mal y pense	Evil be to him who evil thinks
honneur et patrie	Honor and fatherland
ici on parle français	French is spoken here
il faut de l'argent	Money is necessary
il n'y a pas de quoi	There is no occasion; don't mention it
il n'y a rien à dire	There is nothing to be said

je maintiendrai le droit	I will maintain the right
je me fie en Dieu	I trust in God
je ne sais quoi	I know not what
je suis prêt	I am ready
jeu de mots	Play on words
jeu d'esprit	A play of wit or fancy
j'y suis	I am here
le bon temps viendra	There's a good time coming
le jeu n'en vaut pas la chandelle	The game is not worth the candle
le jour viendra	The day will come
le roi est mort! vive le roi!	The king is dead! Long live the king!
le style est l'homme même	The style is the man himself
le tout ensemble	The whole taken together
lettre de cachet	A sealed or secret letter, usually containing orders for the arrest or imprisonment of the person concerned
lettre de change	Bill of exchange
lettre de créance	Letter of credit
lettre de marque	Letter of marque
l'homme propose, et Dieu dispose	Man proposes and God disposes
loyal en tout	Loyal in everything
ma foi!	Really! faith! to be sure!
maître d'hôtel	A house-steward
mal de mer	Seasickness
maladie du pays	Homesickness
mise en scène	Stage-setting; hence, visible surroundings, generally
mon ami	My friend
monde	World; society
moyen âge	The Middle Ages
n'est-ce pas?	Isn't that so?
ni l'un ni l'autre	Neither the one nor the other
n'importe	It does not matter
nom de guerre	Literally, a war-name; any assumed name
nom de piume	A pen name
n'oubliez pas	Do not forget
objet d'art	A work of art
par accord	By agreement
pardonnez-moi	Pardon me
pâté de foie gras	A paste of fat goose-livers
peu de chose	A small matter

pièce de résistance	A piece of resistance; the most substantial dish of a dinner
pied-à-terre	A temporary lodging
pis aller	To go worse; last shift; end of resources
place aux dames	Make way for the ladies
poste restante	To remain at the post office until called for; General Delivery
pour faire visite	To pay a visit
pour passer le temps	To pass the time
pour prendre congé (P.P.C.)	To take leave
procès verbal	A statement in writing
projet de loi	Bill (for legislation)
quand même	Notwithstanding
que voulez-vous?	What do you wish?
quelque chose	Something; a trifle
qui s'excuse, s'accuse	Who excuses himself accuses himself
qui va là?	Who goes there?
raison d'état	Reason of state
raison d'être	Reason for being; an excuse for existing
répondez s'il vous plait	Reply if you please (R.S.V.P.)
salle à manger	Dining-hall
sans cérémonie	Without ceremony
sans Dieu rien	Nothing without God
sans doute	Without doubt
sans façon	Informally
sans gêne	Without embarrassment
sans pareil	Without equal
sans peine	Without difficulty
sans peur et sans reproche	Without fear and without reproach
sans souci	Without care
savoir faire	The knowing how to do; tact
savoir vivre	The knowing how to live
tant mieux	So much the better
tant pis	So much the worse
tour de force	A feat of strength or skill
tout à fait	Entirely
tout à l'heure	Instantly
voilà	There
vous l'avez voulu	You have wished it

Pronunciation of Geographical Names

(For Key to Pronunciation Symbols for Vowels, *see* p. 123.)

Alabama   ăl′ à-bä′ mà;
ăl′ à băm′ a
Albuquerque   ăl′ bŭ-kûr′ kē
Allegheny   ăl′ ê-gā′ nĭ
America   à-mĕr′ ĭ-kà
Arkansas   är′ kăn-sô

Basque   bàsk
Baton Rouge   băt′ ŭn rōozh
Buenos Aires   bwā′ nōs ī′ rās;
â′ rēz
Butte   būt

Carácas   kä-rä′ käs
Caribbean   kăr′ ĭ bē′ ăn;
kà-rĭb′ ê-ăn
Caucausus   kô′ kà-sŭs
Cayuga   kà-yōō′gà; kī
Cherbourg   shĕr′ bōor
Cheyenne   shī-ĕn′
Chicago   shĭ-kä′gō;   shĭ kô′ gō
Colorado   kŏl′ ô rä′ dō
Connecticut   kŏ nĕt′ ĭ kŭt

Des Moines   dĕ moin′
Detroit   dĕ troit′

Edinburgh   ĕd′ ĭn bŭ-rŭ

Genoa   jĕn′ ô à
Gloucester   glŏs′ tĕr
Guiana   gê-ä′ nà
Guinea   gĭn′ ĭ

Hagerstown   hā′ gĕrz-toun
Hawaii   hä-wī′ ē
Himalaya   hĭ-mä′ là-yà;
hĭm′ à-lā′ yà
Hoboken   hō′ bō-kĕn

Iowa   ī′ ô-wà

Kansas   kăn′zàs

Leicester   lĕs′ tĕr
Loire   lwàr
Los Angeles   lōs ăn′ gĕl-ĕs;
lŏs ăn′ jĕl ĕs

Manitoba   măn′ ĭ-tō′ bà
Miami   mī-ăm′ ĭ;   mī ăm′ à
Montreal   mont′ rê-ôl′

Nevada   nê-vä′ dà
New Orleans   ôr′ lê-ănz
Niagara   nī ăg′ à-rà
Nice   nēs

Palestine   păl′ ĕs-tīn
Potomac   pô-tō′ măk
Poughkeepsie   pô-kĭp′ sĭ

Reading   rĕd′ ing
Regina   rê-jī′ nà
Rheims   rēmz;   F. răns

Saar   zär
Saguenay   săg′ ê-nā′
Sahara   sà hâr′ à; sà-hä′ rà
San José   sän hô-sa′
Sault Sainte Marie   sō′ sànt′
mà rē′;   sōō;   sō′ sănt′ mà rē′
Schenectady   skê-nĕk′ tà-dĭ
Seine   sān

Thames   tĕmz
Tucson   tōō-sŏn′
Tyrol   tĭr′ ŏl

Uruguay   ōō′ rōō-gwī;   ū′ rōō-gwā

Venezuela   věn′ ě zwē′ là   Winchester   wĭn′ ches-tēr
Versailles   věr′ sä′ y′;   věr-sālz′   Worcester   wŏŏs′ tēr

Warwick   wŏr′ ĭk (Eng.)   Yosemite   yŏ-sĕm′ ĭ tě
Westminster   wěst′mĭn stēr

8. Abbreviations

Modern usage advocates the spelling out of most words in letters and in literary text. Abbreviations are commonly used in tabulations, technical matter, and routine writing.

Capitalization of Abbreviations. (*See* p. 26.)

Punctuation after Abbreviations. (*See* p. 30.)

Plurals of Abbreviations. Most abbreviations form the plural by adding *s* to the singular form; as, *bds., mfrs., mos.*

Some abbreviations are the same in both singular and plural; as, *ft., kg., s.* (shillings), *deg., enc.*

Some abbreviations form their plurals by doubling the letter which represents the singular of the abbreviation; as, *MM.* (Messieurs), *pp.* (pages), *SS.* (Saints).

Some uncapitalized abbreviations form their plurals by adding an apostrophe and *s* (*'s*) to the singular form; as, *b.o.'s* (buyer's options), *b.v.'s* (book values), *g.a.'s* (general averages).

Capitalized abbreviations usually form their plurals by adding *s;* as, *C.P.A.s, K.C.s, Ph.D.s, YWHAs.*

The Possessive of Abbreviations. The singular possessive of abbreviations is formed like other possessives by the addition of an apostrophe and *s* (*'s*); as, *Sr.'s, M.P.'s, C.E.'s.*

The plural possessive of abbreviations is formed like other plural possessives by the addition of an apostrophe to abbreviations whose plurals end in *s;* as, *M.P.s', C.E.s'.*

Common Abbreviations

A

A.	answer in court trials
A-1	first class
A.A.R., aar	against all risks
abb., abbr.	abbreviated; abbreviation
abr.	abridged; abridgment

abst.	abstract
a/c, acct.	account
accum.	accumulative
ack., ackgt.	acknowledgment
acpt.	acceptance
ad, advt.	advertisement
a.d.	after date
A.D.	*Anno Domini* (in the year of the Lord)
ad int.	*ad interim* (in the meantime)
ad lib.	*ad libitum* (at pleasure)
Admr.	Administrator
Admx.	Administratrix
ads.	address
ad val., a/v	*ad valorem* (according to the value)
adv. chgs.	advance charges
ae., aet., aetat.	*aetatis* (aged; of age)
a.f.	audio-frequency
afft.	affidavit
agcy.	agency
agr.	agricultural; agriculture
agt.	against; agent
aj., adj.	adjustment
Al	aluminum
A.L.	American Legion
alt.	alternate; altitude
a.m. *or* A.M.	*ante meridiem* (before noon)
amp.	ampere
amp-hr.	ampere-hour
amt.	amount
anon.	anonymous
ans.	answer (*See* A.)
a/o	account of
a.p.	additional premium
AP	Associated Press
A.P.	accounts payable
app.	apparatus; appendix; appointed
aprox., ap.	approximately
appt.	appointed
Apt.	Apartment
aq.	*aqua* (water)
A.R.	accounts receivable; all risks; annual return
ar.	arrival; arrive

arr.	arranged; arrival; arrive
art.	article; artist
a/s	account sales
asgd.	assigned
asgmt.	assignment
asmt.	assessment; assortment
Assn. *or* Assoc.	Association
asso.	associate
Asst.	Assistant
asst., ast.	assented; assessment
asstd.	assorted
att.	attached
Attn., Atten.	Attention
atty.	attorney
at. wt.	atomic weight
aux.	auxiliary
Av., Ave.	Avenue
av., avg.	average
avdp., avoir.	avoirdupois
avn.	aviation

B

b.	book; born
bal.	balance
bar.	barometer
b.b.	ball bearing; bank book
bbl., *pl.* bbl. *or* bbls.	barrel
B.C.	before Christ
bd.	board; bond; bound
bd. rts.	bond rights
bdl., bdle.	bundle
bds.	beds; boards; bonds; bound in boards
b.e. *or* b/e	bill of exchange
bg.	bag
bk.	bank; book
bkg.	banking; bookkeeping
bkt., bsk.	basket
bl.	bale; block
b/l	bill of lading
B/L Att.	bill of lading attached
Bldg.	Building
bldr.	builder

Blvd.	Boulevard
b.m.	board measure
b.o.	back order; buyer's option
B.O.	branch office
Bor.	Borough
B.P., b.p., b.pay.	bills payable
b.p.d., bpd., b/d, bbls/day	barrels per day
bpl.	birthplace
B.R., b.r., b.rec.	bills receivable
Bro., *pl.* Bros.	Brother
brt. fwd., b.f.	brought forward
b.s.	balance sheet; bill of sale
bt.	bought
btl., *pl.* btls.	bottle
bu., *pl.* bu.	bushel
bull., *pl.* bulls.	bulletin
Bur.	Bureau
bus.	business
bx., *pl.* bxs.	box

C

c	candle; cycle
c.	cash; cent; chapter (in law citations only); coupon; centimes
c., ca., cir.	*circa* (about)
C.	Catholic; Centigrade; Congress
c.a.	chartered accountant; chief accountant; commercial agent; controller of accounts
c.a.f.	cost and freight
Can.	Canada; Canadian
cap., *pl.* caps	capital
Cash.	Cashier
cat.	catalog
c.b.	currency bond
cc., c.c.	cubic centimeter
C.C.	Construction Corps
cd.	cord
CDE	code
c.e.	*caveat emptor* (at buyer's risk; let buyer beware)
cen.	center; central; century
cent.	*centum* (one hundred)

Cent.	Centigrade
cert., ct., ctf.	certificate; certification; certified
cf.	compare
c. and f.	cost and freight
c.f. and i.	cost, freight, and insurance
cg.	centigram
c.g.	center of gravity
ch., *pl.* chs.	chain; check
c.h.	candle hours
C.H.	Clearing House; Courthouse; Custom House
chap., ch., *pl.* chaps.	chapter
chem.	chemical
chf.	chief
chg., *pl.* chgs.	charge
chge.	change
Chm.	Chairman
chron.	chronological
Cía.	(Sp.) Compañía (Company)
Cie	(Fr.) Compagnie (Company)
c.i.f.	cost, insurance, freight
cit.	citation; citizen
civ.	civil; civilian
ck., *pl.* cks.	cask; check
cl.	class; carload; clause
cld.	called (bonds); cleared
clk.	clerk
clt.	collateral trust (bonds)
cm.	centimeter
cml.	commercial
cm. pf.	cumulative preferred (stock)
c.m.	circular mil (wire measure)
c/o %	care of
C.O.	cash order; Commanding Officer
co	cobalt
Co.	Company; County
c.o.d.	certificates of deposit (securities)
C.O.D., c.o.d.	cash on delivery
C. of C.	Chamber of Commerce
col	colony; column
Col.	Colonel
coll.	collateral; collection; collector
com.	commerce; commission; committee; common

Com., Comdr.	Commander
coml., cml.	commercial
con., cons., consol.	consolidated
con.	*contra* (against)
Con.	Consul
Cong.	Congress; Congregational
cons.	consolidated; consigned; consignment
const.	construction
cont.	contents; continent; contract
contd.	continued
conv.	convention; convertible
co-op.	co-operative
Corp.	Corporal; Corporation
corr.	corrected; corresponding
cp.	candlepower; compare; coupon
cp., cpn.	coupon
C.P.A.	Certified Public Accountant
cr.	credit; creditor
C.R., c.r.	company's risk
cr. 8vo	crown octavo book size
cres., cresc.	*crescendo* (a gradual increase in volume of sound)
crt., *pl.* crts.	crate
cs.	case
C.S.T., CST	Central standard time
ct.	cent; certificate; count
c.t.	commercial traveler
C.T., CT	Central time
ctg., ctge	cartage
ctn.	carton
ct. stp.	certificate stamped
cts.	cents
cu., c., cub.	cubic
cum	with
cum.	cumulative
cum d., cum div.	with dividend
cum. pref., cu. pf	cumulative preferred
cur.	currency; current
cv., cvt.	convertible
c.v.d.	cash against documents
cv. db.	convertible debentures
cv. pf.	convertible preferred

c.w.o.	cash with order
cwt.	centum weight (hundred-weight)

D

d.	date; daughter; died; pence; penny
D	five hundred
D.	Democrat; diameter
D/A	documents upon acceptance
d.b.	day book
db. rts.	debenture rights
d.c.	direct current
d.d.	day's date; days after date
d.&w.tf.	daily and weekly till forbidden
deb.	debenture
dec.	deceased; declaration; decoration; decrease
Dft.	Defendant
del.	delegate
Dem.	Democrat
dia., diam., D.	diameter
dep.	deposit
Dept., Dpt.	Department
diag.	diagram
Dir.	Director
dis., disc., disct.	discount; district
dis., disch.	discharge
dist.	distance; district; distributed
distr.	distribution
div.	dividend; division
dk.	deck; dock
DL	day letter
dld.	delivered
D.L.O.	Dead Letter Office
do.	ditto
d/o	delivery order
doc.	document
dol., *pl.* dols.	dollar
dom.	domestic; dominion
doz.	dozen
D/P	documents upon payment (of draft)
dr.	debit; debtor; dram; drawn; drum

Dr., *pl.* Drs.	Doctor
d.s.	days after sight
d.s.p.	*decessit sine prole* (died without issue)
D.S.T., DST	daylight saving time
dstn.	destination
D.V.	*Deo volente* (God willing)
D.W.	dock warrant
dwt.	pennyweight

E

E.	Earl; East; engineer; English
ea.	each
EB	eastbound
ed.	editor
edit.	edition
E.D.T., EDT	Eastern daylight time
e.g.	*exempli gratia* (for example)
8vo	octavo
e.m.f.	electromotive force
enc.	enclosure; enclosures
end.	endorsed; endorsement
ENE.	east-northeast
Eng.	England; English
engr.	engineer; engraved; engraver
ens.	ensign
entd.	entered
e.o.d.	every other day
E. & O.E., e. & o.e.	errors and omissions excepted
ESE.	east-southeast
esp.	especially
Esq., Esqr.	Esquire
est.	estate; estimate
E.S.T., EST	Eastern standard time
E.T., ET	Eastern time
et al.	*et alii* (and others)
etc., &c.	*et cetera* (and so forth)
et seq., seq., sq.	*et sequentia* (and the following)
et ux.	*et uxor* (and wife)
et vir	and husband
ex.	example; exchange; executive
exam.	examination
exc.	except

exch., ex.	exchange; exchangeable; exchanged
excl.	exclusive
ex div., xd.	without dividend
exec.	executive; executor
exp.	expense; export; express
exr., exor.	executor
exrx.	executrix
ext.	exterior; extract

F

f., fo., fol., *pl.* ff.	and the following (page); folio
F. *or* Fahr.	Fahrenheit
f.a.a.	free of all average
f.a.q.	fair average quality
f.a.s.	free alongside ship
f.b.m., fbm	feet board measure
fcp.	foolscap
fd.	fund
f.d.	free dock
fdg.	funding
Fed.	Federal
fem., f.	feminine
ff.	following (pages); folios
ff.	*fortissimo* (very loud)
f.g.a.	free of general average
fgt. *or* frt.	freight
f.i.c.	freight, insurance, carriage
fict.	fiction
fig., *pl.* figs.	figure
Fin. Sec.	Financial Secretary
fir.	firkin
fm.	fathom
f.o.b.	free on board
f.o.c.	free of charge
f.o.r.	free on rail; free on road
for.	foreign
for'd, fwd.	forward
f.o.s.	free on steamer
f.o.t.	free on truck
f.p., fp	freezing point
f. pd.	full paid
Fr.	French
fr.	fragment; franc; frequent; from

ft.	foot; feet
fth.	fathom
fur.	furlong
FX	foreign exchange

G

g.a., G/A	general average
gal., *pl.* gals., *or* gall.	gallon
gaz.	gazette; gazetteer
G.B.	Great Britain
g.c.d.	greatest common divisor
gd. bds., g.b.	gold bonds
Ger.	German; Germany
GI	general issue; Government issue
Gk.	Greek
GM	Grand Master
G.M.T. *or* g.m.t.	Greenwich mean time
G.O.P.	Grand Old Party (Republican)
gov., govt.	government
g.p.d., gpd	gallons per day
g.p.m., gpm	gallons per minute
G.P.O.	General Post Office
GPU	secret service (Russia)
gr.	grain
Gr.	Greece
gro.	gross
gr. wt.	gross weight
G.S.	General Secretary; Grand Scribe; General Staff
g.s.	ground speed
GTC	good till canceled
gtd.	guaranteed
gu., guar.	guarantee; guaranty

H

h.	harbor; height; high; hour; house; hundred
h.a.	*hoc anno* (this year)
hab. corp.	habeas corpus
h.c., H.C., H.C.L.	High Cost of Living
hdbk.	handbook
hdkf.	handkerchief
Hdqrs., Hq.	Headquarters

hdwe.	hardware
h.e. (*hoc est*)	this *or* that is
H.E.	His Excellency
hf.	half
H.F.C.	High-Frequency Current
hhd.	hogshead
H.M.S.	His *or* Her Majesty's Service *or* Ship
Hon.	Honorable
hp., HP	horsepower
h.p.	half pay; high pressure
hr.	hour
H.R.	Home Rule; House of Representatives
ht.	height; heat
hun., hund.	hundred
h.w.m.	high water mark

I

I., is., isl.	island
i.b.	invoice book
ib., ibid.	*ibidem* (in the same place)
i. bu.	imperial bushel
I.D., i.d.	Intelligence Department
i.e.	*id est* (that is)
imp.	imperative; imperial; imported; improved
in.	inch *or* inches
inc., incl.	inclosure
Inc.	Incorporated
incog.	*incognito* (in secret; unofficially)
inf.	inferior
in f.	*in fine,* final, at the end
init.	initial
in lim.	*in limine* (at the outset)
in loc.	*in loco* (in the place of)
in re	in regard to; pertaining to
INP	International News Photos
INS	International News Service
ins.	inscribed; inspector; insurance
inst.	installment; instant
Inst.	Institute; Institution
int.	interest; interim

Intl.	International
in trans.	*in transitu* (on the way)
intro., introd.	introduction; introductory
inv.	invested; investment; invoice
i.o.	in order
IOU	I owe you
I.Q.	intelligence quotient
I.R.	Internal Revenue
I.R.O.	Internal Revenue Officer
iss.	issue
ital.	italics
I.W.W.	Industrial Workers of the World

J

J.	Judge; Justice
j/a	joint account
jnt. stk.	joint stock
Jour.	Journal
J.P.	Justice of the Peace
Jr., jr., jun.	Junior
jt.	joint
junc.	junction

K

K	karat (carat); king
k.	knot
kg.	kilogram
kg.	keg; kegs
kl.	kiloliter
km.	kilometer
Kr.	krone
kw.	kilowatt
kw-hr., kwhr.	kilowatt-hour

L

l.	left; length; line; liter
L	fifty; lire; listed
L.	Latin; law; libra (pound sterling)
l.a.	law agent
lab.	labor; laboratory
lang.	language
lat.	latitude
lb., *pl.* lbs.	*libra* (pound)

l.c.	lower case
LC	deferred cable (letter cable)
L/C, *pl.* Lo/C *or* l/c	letter of credit
L.C.L.	less than carload lots
leg.	legal; legislation; legislature
l.f.	ledger folio
l-f.c.	low-frequency current
l.h.	left hand
lin.	linear
liq.	liquid; liquor
lit.	liter; literally; literary; literature
L.M.	long meter
ln.	lien; loan
loc.	local; location
loc. cit.	*loco citato* (in the place cited)
lon., long.	longitude
l.p.	low pressure
l.s.	left side
L.S.	*locus sigilli* (place of the seal)
L.S.S.	Life Saving Station
l.t.	long ton
ltd.	limited

M

m.	mark (German money); married; masculine; meter; mile; minute; month; moon; *meridies* (noon)
M	*mille* (1000)
M., *pl.* MM.	Monsieur
mach.	machine; machinery
mag.	magazine; magnitude
maj.	major; majority
man.	manager; manual
Man.	Manhattan
mar.	maritime; market
mas., masc.	masculine
mat.	maturity (bonds)
max.	maximum
m.d.	months after date
mdnt., mid.	midnight
mdse.	merchandise
meas.	measure
med.	medium; medicine; medieval

mem.	member
mem., memo	memorandum
mer.	mercantile
Messrs.	Messieurs
mf., *pl.* mfs.	manufacture
mf., m.f.	*mezzo forte* (moderately loud)
mfd.	manufactured
mfg.	manufacturing
mfr., *pl.* mfrs.	manufacturer
mfst.	manifest
mg.	milligram
mgr.	manager
Mgr.,* Monsig., Msgr.	Monseigneur; Monsignor
M.H.	Medal of Honor
Mid'n	Midshipman
mil.	mileage; military; militia; million
min.	minimum; mining; minor; minority; minute
misc.	miscellaneous
Mlle., *pl.* Mlles.*	Mademoiselle
mm.	millimeter
MM.	Messieurs
Mme., Mmes.*	Madame, Mesdames
mo., *pl.* mos.	month
m.o.	mail order; money order
mol. wt.	molecular weight
m.o.m.	middle of month
M.P.	Member of Parliament; military, mounted, *or* municipal police
M.P.C.	Member of Parliament, Canada
m.p.g., mpg	miles per gallon
m.p.h., mph	miles per hour
Mr., *pl.* Messrs.	Mister
Mrs., *pl.* Mmes. *or* Mmes (French)	Mistress *or* Madam
ms., MS., *pl.* mss., MSS.	manuscript
m/s	meters per second; months after sight
m.s.l.	mean sea level
M.S.T., MST	Mountain standard time
Mt., *pl.* Mts.	mountain
mtg.	mortgage

* In a French context, written without a period.

mun.	municipal
mus.	museum; music; musical
m.v.	market value

N

n.	net; news; north; noon; note; noun; number
N	Navy
N.	North
N.A. *or* n/a	no account
nat., natl.	national
naut.	nautical
nav.	naval; navigation
n.b.	*nota bene* (note well); take notice
NB	northbound
N.C.O.	Noncommissioned Officer
n.d.	no date; next day's delivery
NE.	Northeast
neg.	negative
nem. con.	*nemine contradicente* (no one contradicting)
n.e.s.	not elsewhere specified
neut., n.	neuter
n.g.	no good
N.H.P.	nominal horse power
NL	night letter
n.l.; n. lat.	north latitude
NLT	night letter cable
NM	night message
NNE.	north-northeast
NNW.	north-northwest
no., *pl.* nos.	number
non seq.	*non sequitur* (it does not follow)
n.o.p.	not otherwise provided for
N.O.S., n.o.s.	not otherwise specified
n.p. or d.	no place or date
N.P.	Notary Public; no protest
n.s., n/s	not specified; not sufficient; new series; new style
N.S.F.	not sufficient funds
n.t.p.	no title page
n.u.	name unknown
nv	non-voting (stocks)

| N.W., NW | northwest |
| n. wt. | net weight |

O

o.	old; order; oxygen
o/a	on account
ob.	*obiit* (died)
O.B/L, ob/l	order bill of lading
obs.	obsolete
oc.	overcharge
oct.	octavo size
o/d	on demand
o.e.	omission excepted
off.	office; officer
OK, o.k.	correct
op.	*opus* (work)
op., opp.	opposite
o.p.	out of print
op. cit.	*opus citatum* (the work cited)
opt.	optician
o.r.	owner's risk
org.	organ; organic; organization
o/s	out of stock
o.t.	overtime
oz.	ounce; ounces

P

p., *pl.* pp.	page; parallel; part; participle; party; pay; penny; period; person; piano; pint; pipe; pole; population; post; profession
p.a.	private account; particular average
p.a., per an.	*per annum* (by the year)
P.A.	Press Agent; Purchasing Agent
P.a.C.	put and call
pat.	patent
Pat. Off.	Patent Office
payt.	payment
pc., *pl.* pcs.	piece
P.C.	petty cash
p.c.	per cent; post card
pcl.	parcel
pd.	paid

per cent, per ct.	*per centum* (by the hundred)
per pro., p.p., p. pro.	*per procurationem* (on behalf of)
pert.	pertaining
pet.	petroleum
petn.	petition
pf., pfd., pref.	preferred
pharm.	pharmacist; pharmacy
pinx.	*pinxit* (he, or she, painted it)
pk.	pack
pkg., *pl.* pkgs.	package
pl.	plate; place; plural
p.l.	partial loss
P.&L., p/l	profit and loss
plf.	plaintiff
P.L.&R.	Postal Laws and Regulations
p.m., prem.	premium
p.m., *or* P.M.	*post meridiem* (afternoon)
P.M.	postmaster
p.n.	promissory note
P. O.	post office
P.O.D.	Post Office Department; pay on delivery
pol.	political; politics
p.o.o.	post office order
pop.	population
P.O.R.	pay on return
pp.	pages; prepaid
P.P.	parcel post
p.p.c., P.P.C.	*pour prendre congé* (to take leave)
pph.	pamphlet
p.p.i.	parcel post insured *or* policy proof of interest
p.p.m.	parts per million
pr.	pair; printed; printer
PR	payroll
pref.	preface; preferred
prem.	premium
Pres.	President
prin.	principal
prob.	problem
proc.	proceedings
prod.	produce; product
Prof.	Professor
prop.	property; proposition

Prot.	Protestant
pro tem.	*pro tempore* (for the time)
Prov.	Province
prox.	*proximo* (in next month)
pr. pf.	prior preferred
prs.	pairs
p.s., *pl.* p.ss.	*post scriptum* (post script)
pseud.	pseudonym
P.S.T., PST	Pacific standard time
pt.	part; payment; pint; point
P.T., PT	Pacific time
ptg.	printing
pt. pf.	participating preferred
pub.	publisher
pwr., pow.	power
pwt.	pennyweight
p.x.	please exchange

Q

q.	quart; quasi; queen; query; question; quire
Q.E.D., q.e.d.	*quod erat demonstrandum* (which was to be proved)
Q.E.F., q.e.f.	*quod erat faciendum* (which was to be done)
Q.E.I., q.e.i.	*quod erat inveniendum* (which was to be found out)
Q.M.	Quartermaster
qr.	quarter; quarterly; quire
qt.	quart
quar., quart., qu.	quarterly
ques.	question
q.v.	*quod vide* (which see)
qy.	query

R

r	rare; received; recipe
R.	Regina; Republic; Republican; Rex
R.A.	regular army; Royal Academy; royal artist
R.C.	Red Cross; Roman Catholic
rc., rcpt., rect.	receipt
R.D.	rural delivery

re	regarding
R.E.	real estate
rec.	receipt
recd.	received
Rec. Sec., **R.S.**	Recording Secretary
ref.	reference; referee; referred; reformed
reg.	registered; regular
R.E.O.	real estate owner
rep.	reporter
Rep.	Republic; Republican; Representative
req.	requisition
ret.	retired; return
rev.	revenue; revised; revolution
Rev.	Reverend
rf., rfg.	refunding
r.f.	radio frequency
R.F.D. *or* **RFD**	rural free delivery (*see also* R.R.)
r.h.	right hand
R.I.P.	*requiescat in pace* (may he or she rest in peace)
rm.	ream; room
R.N.	Registered Nurse; Royal Navy
R.N.R.	Royal Naval Reserve
rom.	roman type
RP	reply paid
r.p.m., rpm	revolutions per minute
R.P.O., **RPO**	railroad post office
rpt.	report
R.R., RR., RR	railroad
R.R.	rural route
r.s.	right side
R.S.V.P., r.s.v.p.	*répondez s'il vous plaît* (reply if you please)
r.s.w.c.	right side up with care
rt., *pl.* rts.	right
Ry., ry., *pl.* Rys.	railway

S

s.	shilling; silver; stock
S.	Sabbath; Saint; Saxon; Signor; South

s.a.	subject to approval
SB	southbound
s.b.	sales book
sc., sci.	science
sc., scil., ss.	*scilicet* (namely)
sc., sculp.	carved; sculptor
s.c.	small capitals
s.d.	*sine die* (without naming a date)
SE.	southeast
sec.	seconds; section
Sec., Secy.	Secretary
2d, 2nd	second
sel.	selected; selection
Sen.	Senate; Senator
seq., *pl.* seqq.	*sequens* (the following)
ser.	serial; series; service
sergt., serg., sgt.	sergeant
s.f.	sinking fund
sg., sig.	signature
sgd.	signed
sh., *pl.* shs.	share
ship., shipt.	shipment
s.i.	short interest
sic	so; thus
sine die	without a day for meeting
sing.	singular
s.j.	*sub judice* (under consideration)
S.J.	Society of Jesus
s.l.	salvage loss; south latitude
sld.	sailed; sold
so.	south
s.o.	seller's option
soc.	society
s.o.d.	seller's option to double
sol.	solution; soluble
SOS	distress signal (suspend other service; "save our ship")
sp., spec.	special
Sp.	Spain; Spanish
sp. gr.	specific gravity
s.p.q.r.	small profits and quick returns
sq.	square
Sr. *or* sr.	Senior; Señor
Sra.	Señora

Sres.	Señores
SRO	standing room only
Srta.	Señorita
SS., S.S., SS	steamship
SSE.	south-southeast
SSW.	south-southwest
St.	Saint
St.	State; Street
s.t.	short ton
sta.	station; stamped
stat.	statistics; statutes
stat.	*statim* (immediately)
stbt.	steamboat
std.	standard
Ste.	Sainte (feminine of Saint)
sten.	stencil; stenographer
stet	let it stand
stg., ster.	sterling
stge., stor.	storage
stk.	stock
str.	steamer
subj.	subject
sund.	sundries
sup., supp.	supplement
Supt.	Superintendent
surg.	surgeon
Sw., Swed.	Swedish; Sweden
SW.	southwest
synd.	syndicate
syst.	system

T

t.	temperature; time; ton
T.B., t.b.	trial balance
t/c	till counterbalanced
tech.	technical
tel	telegram; telegraph; telephone
temp.	temperature
Ter.	Territory; territorial
t.f.	till forbidden
3d; 3rd	third
t.l.	total loss
t.l.o.	total loss only

t.m.o.	telegraph money order
TN	true north
t.o.	telegraph office; turn over; turnover
tonn.	tonnage
tr.	trust; trustee; transpose
T.R.	tons registered
Treas., Tr.	Treasurer; Treasury
t.t.	telegraph transfer
t.u.	trade union

U

u.	uncle
u.c.	upper case (printing term)
UGT	urgent
UN *or* U.N.	United Nations
UNESCO	United Nations Educational, Social, and Cultural Organization
UP	United Press
US	Universal Service
U.S.	United States
U.S.A.	United States of America; United States Army
U.S.C.	United States Code
U.S.M.	United States Mail
U.S.M.C.	United States Marine Corps
U.S.N.	United States Navy
U.S.SS.	United States Steamship
U.S.S.R.	Union of Soviet Socialist Republics

V

V	five
v	volt
v.	verse, *pl.* vss. *or* vv.; verb; versus; volume
vac.	vacuum
val.	value; valuation
v.g.	*verbi gratia* (for example)
v.i.	*vide infra* (see below)
vid., vide	*vide* (see)
vis.	visibility
viz.	*videlicet* (namely)
vol., *pl.* vols.	volume
vou.	voucher

V.P. *or* V. Pres.	vice president
vs., v.	versus (against)

W

w	watt
W.	West
w.	week; west; wide; wife; with; work
war., wt., w.	warrant
WB *or* w/b	waybill; westbound
w/c, wpc	watts per candle
w.f., wf	wrong font
w.g.	wire gauge
whf.	wharf
whge.	wharfage
whs.	warehouse
whsle.	wholesale
whs. rec., W.R.	warehouse receipt
wk.	week
w.l.	wave length
WNW.	west-northwest
w.r., wr	with rights
WSW.	west-southwest
wt.	weight
W.W., ww	with warrants

X

x	box; boxes
X	express (*as,* Ry.X); ten
XC, XCP.	ex *or* without coupon
x.d., x.div.	ex *or* without dividend
x in.	without interest
Xmas	Christmas
xr, xrts.	without rights
Xw	without warrants
XX	good quality; twenty
XXX	very good quality; thirty
XXXX	best quality

Y

y., yd., *pl.* yds.	yard
y., yr., *pl.* yrs.	year

Z

| Z | zero; zone |
| z. | zinc |

Geographical Names

1. Use the following official abbreviations for states, and regions administered by the United States:

Ala.	Nev.
Ariz.	N. C.
Ark.	N. Dak.
Calif.	N. H.
Colo.	N. J.
Conn.	N. Mex.
C. Z. (Canal Zone)	N. Y.
D. C. (District of Columbia)	Okla.
Del.	Oreg.
Fla.	Pa.
Ga.	P. R. (Puerto Rico)
Ill.	R. I.
Ind.	S. C.
Kans.	S. Dak.
Ky.	Tenn.
La.	Tex.
Mass.	Va.
Md.	V. I. (Virgin Islands)
Mich.	Vt.
Minn.	Wash.
Miss.	Wis.
Mo.	W. Va.
Mont.	Wyo.
Nebr.	

2. Do not abbreviate Alaska, Guam, Hawaii, Idaho, Iowa, Maine, Ohio, Utah.

3. In general, do not abbreviate geographical names except to gain space in tabular matter: Fort William Henry, Port Jervis, Mount Vernon.

4. In place names abbreviate *Saint*.

St. Helena	St. Paul
St. John	Sault Ste. Marie
St. Louis	

5. Use the abbreviated form *U. S.* for United States, when preceding the name of a Government vessel; also when used in footnotes, tables, or in names of departments, bureaus, commissions, and other services. (*Government usage.*)

U. S. Navy, U. S. Army

But, when used in ordinary text, United States should be spelled out.

6. Use the following abbreviations for Canadian provinces and territories:

Alta.	Alberta	N.W.T.	Northwest Territories
B.C.	British Columbia	Ont.	Ontario
Man.	Manitoba	P.E.I.	Prince Edward Island
N.B.	New Brunswick	Que. *or* P.Q.	Province of Quebec
Nfld.	Newfoundland	Sask.	Saskatchewan
N.S.	Nova Scotia	Y.T.	Yukon Territory

Names of Firms and Corporations

7. In writing the words *Company, Brother, Brothers, Limited, Incorporated,* and *Corporation,* in firm or corporate names, follow the usage of the company:

> The Macmillan Company
> James Scoville & Co.
> Gimbel Brothers
> Brooklyn Edison Company
> Judd & Detweiler, Inc.
> C. F. Church Mfg. Co.
> The Shelbourne Motor Company, Ltd.
> Trust Company of Larchmont
> County Trust Company

(1) It is better not to use & unless the firm's name consists of the names of persons. Many firms, however, do not follow this usage:

> American Bond & Mortgage Company
> The Mechanics & Metals Bank

(2) In footnotes and bibliographies use *Co., Bro.,* and & when they form part of the name of a firm.

(3) The character &, known as ampersand, should never be used to connect two names in text matter unless in connection with a firm name:

Beaumont and Fletcher (Elizabethan dramatists whose names are closely associated)
Neilson and Thorndike (joint authors of a history of English literature)
Lord & Taylor (firm name)

8. In writing given names of firms, follow the usage of the writer or firm addressed:

Thos. Cook & Son (abbreviation of given name as used by firm)
Henry Clews & Co. (unabbreviated name as used by firm)
The H. W. Wilson Co. (initials as used by firm)

Titles

TITLES PRECEDING PERSONAL NAMES

9. Use the following abbreviations for titles preceding personal names:

Mr., Messrs., M. (Monsieur), MM. (Messieurs), Mme., Mlle. (Madame, Mademoiselle with plurals Mmes., Mlles.—written in a French context without periods, whether singular or plural), St. (Saint).

10. In formal usage such as invitations and announcements it is better to spell out titles, such as *Honorable, Governor, Lieutenant Governor, Reverend, Professor.*

The Honorable James L. Tong, Governor Alfred P. King, Professor John Dewey.

11. In writing salutations, titles should not be abbreviated except Mr., Mrs., and Dr.

Dear Professor Harris   Dear Mr. Bailey
Dear Colonel Brown   Dear Mrs. Luetscher
Dear Dr. Thomas   Dear Governor Lehman

12. In writing *doctor, general, professor,* and the like without the surname, no abbreviation should be used.

The doctor will be here tomorrow.
I hope, General, that you will accept the invitation.

13. The title of *doctor* is given to holders of high university degrees in any faculty. (*Doctor of Divinity, Music, Medicine, Literature, Law, Philosophy,* etc.)

Abbreviations for scholastic degrees are not used in the United States in combination with such personal titles of address as *Mr., Dr.,* or *Honorable.*

John McKay, A.B. *not* Mr. John McKay, A.B.
James Holmes, A.M. *not* Hon. James Holmes, A.M.

14. In the case of *Reverend* usage varies. The following are considered correct: (*See* pp. 5, 319–325.)

Rev. Dr. Ramsay, *or* Rev. Mr. Ramsay
Rev. Hugh Miller
Reverend President Henry Pitney Van Dusen
The Right Reverend Bishop Sherrill
The Reverend Harry Emerson Fosdick, D.D.
The Reverend Professor Nels F. S. Ferré

Reverend should never be used as follows:

The Reverend Brown   Reverend Brown

In writing abbreviations for academic degrees and religious orders after a name, observe the following sequence:
First,   Religious orders
Second, Theological degrees
Third,   Other doctorate degrees
Fourth, Honorary degrees in chronological order of their bestowal

The Right Reverend John Smith, D.D., Ph.D., LL.D., L.H.D.
The Very Reverend Thomas O'Brien, S.J., S.T.D., Litt.D.

TITLES FOLLOWING PERSONAL NAMES

15. Use the following abbreviations following personal names:
Esq. This title is written, according to the British usage, after a gentleman's name. In America, it follows most commonly names of lawyers, architects, and members of other professions. If used, it should not be written with any other title.

Wallace Wolcott, Esq., *not* Mr. Wallace Wolcott, Esq.

Junior. In formal use, such as wedding invitations, this word is written out. In newspapers, business correspondence, and in signatures, it is abbreviated to denote a son whose name is the same as his father's. It is then usually capitalized and preceded and followed by commas:

Philip Grant, Jr., *or* Philip Grant Jr. *or* Philip Grant jr.

The plural is formed by pluralizing the surname or by adding *s* to the abbreviation:

The Philip Grants, Jr. (formal)   The Philip Grant, Jrs. (informal)

The possessive is formed as follows: (No comma follows the abbreviation.)

Philip Grant, Jr.'s check   The Philip Grant, Jrs.' tickets
   (singular)   (plural)

The abbreviation Jr. should not be used unless the surname is preceded by initials or by a first name, as *P. E. Grant, Jr.* or *Philip Grant, Jr.,* not *Grant, Jr.* or *Mr. Grant, Jr.*

The abbreviation may also be used when a first name or initials are preceded by a title, as *Dr. Philip Grant, Jr.*

Although *Jr.* is usually dropped after the death of the father of the same name, this is a matter of preference.

Second. A young man, not a son, whose name is the same as that of an older living relative, such as a cousin or an uncle, may use II or 2nd (2d) after his name to identify him and thus avoid confusing him with a relative. Also if he is named for his grandfather whose name differs from that of the young man's father, he may use II or 2nd (2d).

Third. If the name of a grandson is the same as that of his grandfather and his father, the numerals III or 3rd (3d) without periods may be written after his name. Commas are not used with the Roman numeral, but they may or may not be inserted before and after the ordinal numeral.

Philip Grant III *or* Philip Grant 3rd (*or* 3d) *or* Philip Grant, 3rd (*or* 3d)

Senior. This, or its abbreviation *Sr.,* is not needed and is almost never used after a man's name. Sometimes, to avoid confusion with a daughter-in-law, a widow may prefer to use *Sr.* after her name.

16. ACADEMIC DEGREES AND HONORS

A

A.B.	Bachelor of Arts
Ae.E.	Aeronautical Engineer
A.F.D.	Doctor of Fine Arts
A.M.	Master of Arts
A.M.L.S.	Master of Arts in Library Science
A.R.A.	Associate of the Royal Academy
A.R.A.M.	Associate of the Royal Academy of Music
Ar.M.	Master of Architecture
A.R.S.A.	Associate of the Royal Scottish Academy

B

B.A.	Bachelor of Arts
B.Acc.	Bachelor of Accounting
B.Ag. *or* B.Agr.	Bachelor of Agriculture
B.Ar. *or* B.Arch.	Bachelor of Architecture
B.A.S. *or* B.A.Sc.	Bachelor of Applied Science
B.B.A.	Bachelor of Business Administration
B.C.	Bachelor of Chemistry
B.C.E.	Bachelor of Chemical Engineering; Bachelor of Civil Engineering
B.C.L.	Bachelor of Civil Law
B.D.	Bachelor of Divinity
B.D.S.	Bachelor of Dental Surgery
B.E.	Bachelor of Engineering
B.E.E.	Bachelor of Electrical Engineering
B.F.A.	Bachelor of Fine Arts
B.J.	Bachelor of Journalism
B.L.	Bachelor of Laws
B.Lit(t)	Bachelor of Literature, or Letters
B.L.S.	Bachelor of Library Science
B.M.	Bachelor of Medicine
B.M.E.	Bachelor of Mining Engineering
B.Mus.	Bachelor of Music
B.Pd. *or* B.Pe.	Bachelor of Pedagogy
B.P.E.	Bachelor of Physical Education
B.S. *or* B.Sc.	Bachelor of Science
B.S.Ed.	Bachelor of Science in Education

B.T. *or* B.Th.	Bachelor of Theology
B.V.Sc.	Bachelor of Veterinary Science

C

C.B.	Bachelor of Surgery
C.E.	Civil Engineer
Ch.E. *or* Chem.E.	Chemical Engineer

D

D.C.L.	Doctor of Civil Law
D.D.	Doctor of Divinity
D.D.S.	Doctor of Dental Surgery
D.F.A.	Doctor of Fine Arts
D.Lit(t)	Doctor of Literature, or Letters
D.L.S.	Doctor of Library Science
D.M.D.	Doctor of Dental Medicine
D.Mus.	Doctor of Music
D.O.	Doctor of Osteopathy
D.P.H.	Doctor of Public Health
D.S. *or* D.Sc.	Doctor of Science
D.Th. *or* D.Theol.	Doctor of Theology
D.V.M.	Doctor of Veterinary Medicine

E

Ed.B.	Bachelor of Education
Ed.D.	Doctor of Education
Ed.M.	Master of Education
E.E.	Electrical Engineer
E.M.	Engineer of Mines
Eng.D.	Doctor of Engineering

F

F.A.C.P.	Fellow of the American College of Physicians
F.A.C.S.	Fellow of the American College of Surgeons
F.A.G.S.	Fellow of the American Geographical Society
F.A.I.A.	Fellow of the American Institute of Architects
F.B.A.	Fellow of the British Academy
F.C.A.	Fellow of the (Institute of) Chartered Accountants

F.C.I.S.	Fellow of the Chartered Institute of Secretaries
F.R.C.P.	Fellow of the Royal College of Physicians
F.R.C.S.	Fellow of the Royal College of Surgeons
F.R.G.S.	Fellow of the Royal Geographical Society
F.R.I.B.A.	Fellow of the Royal Institute of British Architects
F.R.S.	Fellow of the Royal Society
F.S.A.	Fellow of the Society of Antiquaries

J

J.C.B.	Bachelor of Canon Law; Bachelor of Civil Law
J.C.D.	Doctor of Civil Law
J.D.	Doctor of Laws; Juris Doctor; Doctor of Jurisprudence
Jur.D.	Doctor of Law

L

L.B.	Bachelor of Letters
L.H.D.	Doctor of Humanities
Lit(t).B.	Bachelor of Literature; or of Letters
Lit.D.	Doctor of Literature, or Letters
Litt.D.	Doctor of Letters
LL.B.	Bachelor of Laws
LL.D.	Doctor of Laws
LL.M.	Master of Laws

M

M.A.	Master of Arts
M.Agr.	Master of Agriculture
M.B.	Bachelor of Medicine
M.B.A.	Master in, *or* of, Business Administration
M.C.L.	Master of Civil Law
M.D.	Doctor of Medicine
M.D.S.	Master of Dental Surgery
M.E.	Mechanical Engineer
M.Ed.	Master of Education
M.L.S.	Master of Library Science

M.Pd.	Master of Pedagogy
M.P.E.	Master of Physical Education
M.R.C.P.	Member of the Royal College of Physicians
M.R.C.S.	Member of the Royal College of Surgeons
M.S. *or* M.Sc.	Master of Science
M.S.E.	Master of Science in Engineering
Mus.B. *or* Mus.Bac.	Bachelor of Music

N

| N.E. | Naval Engineer |

P

Pd.B.	Bachelor of Pedagogy
Pd.D.	Doctor of Pedagogy
Pd.M.	Master of Pedagogy
Pe.B.	Bachelor of Pediatrics
Phar.B.	Bachelor of Pharmacy
Phar.D. *or* Pharm.D.	Doctor of Pharmacy
Phar.M.	Master of Pharmacy
Ph.B.	Bachelor of Philosophy
Ph.C.	Pharmaceutical Chemist
Ph.D.	Doctor of Philosophy
Ph.G.	Graduate in Pharmacy
Pod.D.	Doctor of Podiatry

R

| R.A. | Royal Academician |
| R.N. | Registered Nurse |

S

S.B. *or* Sc.B.	Bachelor of Science
Sc.D. *or* S.D.	Doctor of Science
Sc.M.	Master of Science
S.J.D.	Doctor of Juridical Science
S.M. *or* Sc.M.	Master of Science
S.T.B.	Bachelor of Sacred Theology
S.T.D.	Doctor of Sacred Theology
S.T.M.	Master of Sacred Theology

T

Th.D.   Doctor of Theology

V

V.M.D.   Doctor of Veterinary Medicine

MILITARY ABBREVIATIONS

17. In abbreviations such as the following, authorities differ regarding the use or the omission of periods. Modern tendency leans toward the omission of periods.

AC	Air Corps
ANC	American Nurse Corps
CAC	Coast Artillery Corps
CEC	Civil Engineering Corps
CG	Coast Guard
ChC	Chaplain Corps
DC	Dental Corps
GHQ	General Headquarters
GSC	General Staff Corps
HC	Hospital Corps
MC	Medical Corps
NG	National Guard
ORC	Officers' Reserve Corps
OTC	Officers' Training Corps; Officer in Tactical Command
QMC	Quartermaster Corps
RA	Regular Army
ROTC	Reserve Officers' Training Corps
SC	Supply Corps
SPAR	Women's Reserve of the Coast Guard
U S Army or USA	United States Army
USCG	United States Coast Guard
USMC	United States Marine Corps
USMCR	United States Marine Corps Reserve
USN	United States Navy
USNR	United States Naval Reserve
VC	Veterinary Corps
WAC	Women's Army Corps
WAF	Women in the Air Force
WAVES	Women's Reserve of the Naval Reserve

18. Orders of Knighthood, Decorations, and Honors

C.B.	Companion of the Bath
C.M.G.	Companion of the Order of St. Michael and St. George
C.V.O.	Companion of the Royal Victorian Order
D.B.E.	Dame Commander Order of the British Empire
D.S.O.	Distinguished Service Order
G.B.E.	Knight or Dame Grand Cross Order of the British Empire
G.C.B.	Knight Grand Cross of the Bath
G.C.L.H.	Grand Cross of the Legion of Honor
G.C.M.G.	Knight Grand Cross of St. Michael and St. George
G.C.V.O.	Knight Grand Cross of Royal Victorian Order
K.B.	Knight of the Bath
K.C.	King's Counsel
K.C.V.O.	Knight Commander of the Royal Victorian Order
K.G.	Knight of the Order of the Garter
K.G.M.G.	Knight Commander of the Order of St. Michael and St. George
K.P.	Knight of the Order of St. Patrick
K.T.	Knight of the Order of the Thistle
M.V.O.	Member of the Royal Victorian Order
O.M.	Order of Merit

Titles of British Officials

19. The following abbreviations are frequently used for titles of British officials and members of the nobility:

C.J.	Chief Justice
E.R.	Elizabetha Regina (Queen Elizabeth)
H.B.M.	His or Her Britannic Majesty
H.E.	His Excellency
H.I.H.	His or Her Imperial Highness
H.I.M.	His or Her Imperial Majesty
H.M.	His or Her Majesty
Hon.	Honorable
Hon. Sec.	Honorable Secretary
H.R.H.	His or Her Royal Highness
H.S.H.	His or Her Serene Highness
K.C.	King's Counsel
Kt.	Knight

M.P.	Member of Parliament
Q.C.	Queen's Counsel
R.	Regina (queen); Rex (king)
R. et I.	Rex et Imperator (King and Emperor); Regina et Imperatrix (Queen and Empress)
T.I.H.	Their Imperial Highnesses
T.R.H.	Their Royal Highnesses

20. LEARNED AND PROFESSIONAL SOCIETIES

A.A.A.L.	American Academy of Arts and Letters
A.A.A.S.	American Association for the Advancement of Science
A.B.A.	American Bar Association
A.C.S.	American Chemical Society
A.C.S.	American College of Surgeons
A.G.S.	American Geographical Society
A.H.A.	American Historical Association
A.I.A.	American Institute of Architects
A.I.E.E.	American Institute of Electrical Engineers
A.L.A.	American Library Association
A.M.A.	American Medical Association
A.M.S.	American Mathematical Society
A.N.A.	American National Academy
A.P.A.	American Philological Association
A.S.C.E.	American Society of Civil Engineers
A.S.M.E.	American Society of Mechanical Engineers
A.R.I.B.A.	Associate of the Royal Institute of British Architects
M.L.A.	Modern Language Association
N.A.D.	National Academy of Design
N.A.S.	National Academy of Sciences
N.E.A.	National Education Association
N.I.A.L.	National Institute of Arts and Letters
R.A.	Royal Academy
R.A.M.	Royal Academy of Music
R.B.A.	Royal Society of British Artists
R.B.S.	Royal Society of British Sculptors
R.C.P.	Royal College of Physicians
R.C.S.	Royal College of Surgeons
R.G.S.	Royal Geographical Society
R.I.B.A.	Royal Institute of British Architects
R.S.A.	Royal Scottish Academy
R.S.E.	Royal Society of Edinburgh

ORGANIZATIONS OF SOCIAL AND RELIGIOUS NATURE

21. The following abbreviations are often used in place of the names of social, welfare, and religious organizations:

In abbreviations such as the following, authorities differ regarding the use or the omission of periods. Modern tendency leans toward the omission of periods.

A.S.S.U.	American Sunday School Union
B.P.O.Elks	Benevolent and Protective Order of Elks
C.E.	Church of England; Christian Endeavor Society
C.S.	Christian Science
C.S.S.	Community Service Society
D.A.R.	Daughters of the American Revolution
D.R.	Daughters of the Revolution
F. & A.M.	Free and Accepted Masons
I.O.F.	Independent Order of Foresters
I.O.O.F.	Independent Order of Odd Fellows
K. of C.	Knight(s) of Columbus
K.P.	Knight(s) of Pythias
M.E.	Methodist Episcopal
O.S.A.	Order of St. Augustine
O.S.B.	Order of St. Benedict
O.S.D.	Order of St. Dominic
O.S.F.	Order of St. Francis
R.C.	Roman Catholic
S.A.	Salvation Army
S.A.R.	Sons of the American Revolution
S.J.	Society of Jesus
S.P.C.A.	Society for the Prevention of Cruelty to Animals
S.P.C.C.	Society for the Prevention of Cruelty to Children
S.R.	Sons of the Revolution
U.D.C.	United Daughters of the Confederacy
WCTU	Woman's Christian Temperance Union
YMCA	Young Men's Christian Association
YMHA	Young Men's Hebrew Association
YPSCE	Young People's Society of Christian Endeavor
YWCA	Young Women's Christian Association
YWHA	Young Women's Hebrew Association

22. United States Administrative Boards, Commissions, Services, Etc.

AEC	Atomic Energy Commission
AMS	Agricultural Marketing Service
ARC	American Red Cross
ARS	Agricultural Research Service
BDSA	Business and Defense Services Administration
BEC	Bureau of Employees' Compensation
BLS	Bureau of Labor Statistics
CAA	Civil Aeronautics Administration
CAB	Civil Aeronautics Board
CAP	Civil Air Patrol
CCC	Commodity Credit Corporation
CEA	Council of Economic Advisers
CIA	Central Intelligence Agency
CSC	Civil Service Commission
CSS	Commodity Stabilization Service
DATA	Defense Air Transportation Administration
DMB	Defense Mobilization Board
DMEA	Defense Minerals Exploration Administration
FAS	Foreign Agricultural Service
FBI	Federal Bureau of Investigation
FCA	Farm Credit Administration
FCC	Federal Communications Commission
FCDA	Federal Civil Defense Administration
FDA	Food and Drug Administration
FDIC	Federal Deposit Insurance Corporation
FHA	Federal Housing Administration
FHLBB	Federal Home Loan Bank Board
FMB	Federal Maritime Board
FMCS	Federal Mediation and Conciliation Service
FNMA	Federal National Mortgage Association
FPC	Federal Power Commission
FRS	Federal Reserve System
FTC	Federal Trade Commission
GAO	General Accounting Office
GPO	Government Printing Office
GSA	General Services Administration
HHFA	Housing and Home Finance Agency
IADB	Inter-American Defense Board
ICA	International Cooperation Administration
ICC	Interstate Commerce Commission *or* Indian Claims Commission

IRS	Internal Revenue Service
MA	Maritime Administration
NACA	National Advisory Committee for Aeronautics
NATO	North Atlantic Treaty Organization
NBS	National Bureau of Standards
NLRB	National Labor Relations Board
NSA	National Shipping Authority
NSC	National Security Council
NSF	National Science Foundation
ODM	Office of Defense Mobilization
PBS	Public Buildings Service
PHA	Public Housing Administration
PHS	Public Health Service
RB	Renegotiation Board
REA	Rural Electrification Administration
RRB	Railroad Retirement Board
SBA	Small Business Administration
SEC	Securities and Exchange Commission
SSA	Social Security Administration
SSS	Selective Service System
TVA	Tennessee Valley Authority
USCG	United States Coast Guard
USES	United States Employment Service
USIA	United States Information Agency
USMC	United States Marine Corps
VA	Veterans Administration

23. AMERICAN RAILROADS

ACL	Atlantic Coast Line Railroad
AT & SF	Atchison, Topeka & Sante Fe Railway (called the Santa Fe route)
B & O	Baltimore & Ohio Railroad
CB & Q	Chicago, Burlington & Quincy Railroad (called the Burlington route)
CMStP & P	Chicago, Milwaukee, St. Paul & Pacific Railroad
C & N W	Chicago & North Western Railway
C & O	Chesapeake & Ohio Railway
DL & W	Delaware, Lackawanna & Western Railroad (called the Lackawanna route)
ERR	Erie Railroad (called the Erie)
FEC	Florida East Coast Railway
GN	Great Northern Railway
LV	Lehigh Valley Railroad (called the Lehigh)

MoPac	Missouri Pacific Railroad
NYCRR	New York Central Railroad
NYNH & H	New York, New Haven & Hartford Railroad
PRR	Pennsylvania Railroad
SAL	Seaboard Air Line Railway
SP	Southern Pacific Company
SR	Southern Railway
UP	Union Pacific Railroad

24. WORLD'S PRINCIPAL AIRLINES (SELECTED LIST)

AA	American Airlines
Aeroflot	Soviet Air Lines
AF	Air France
AII	Air-India International
AL	Allegheny Airlines
ANA	Australian National Airways
ASA	Alaska Airlines
Avianca	Aerovias Nacionales de Colombia, S.A.
BEA	British European Airways
BNIA	Braniff International Airways
BOAC	British Overseas Airways Corporation
CAL	Capital Airlines
CAT	Civil Air Transport
CNA	Central Airlines
COAL	Continental Air Lines
CPA	Canadian Pacific Airlines
DAL	Delta Air Lines
EAL	Eastern Air Lines
Iberia	Lineas Aereas Españolas
KLM	Royal Dutch Airlines
LH	Lufthansa A.G. (West Germany)
MEA	Middle East Airlines Co.
MOAL	Mohawk Airlines
NA	National Airlines
NEAL	Northeast Airlines
NOCA	North Central Airlines
NW-OAL	Northwest-Orient Airlines
NYA	New York Airways (helicopter)
OZAL	Ozark Air Lines
PAA	Pan American World Airways System
PAB	Panair do Brasil
PANAGRA	Pan American-Grace Airways
PIAL	Piedmont Airlines

PNAL	Pacific Northern Airlines
SAA	South African Airways
SAB	Sabena Belgian World Airlines
SAS	Scandinavian Airlines System
SOA	Southern Airways, Inc.
SWA	Southwest Airways
SWISSAIR	Swiss Air Transport Co.
TCA	Trans-Canada Air Lines
TWA	Trans World Airlines
UAL	United Air Lines
WA	Western Airlines, Inc.

Months

25. Do not abbreviate the names of the months except when necessary. It is better, in accordance with modern usage, to spell out the names of the months in the heading of a letter.

Note that *rd* and *nd* are used after the date in Great Britain; *d,* in the United States. The forms *st, d, th* are no longer considered correct in the heading, but are still used in the body of a letter. In letters it is not considered good form to abbreviate the date as follows: 1/5/24. When necessary on account of space to use abbreviations, write the names of months as follows: Jan., Feb., Mar., Apr., Aug., Sept., Oct., Nov., Dec. Do not abbreviate May, June, and July.

The following system of abbreviations is recommended for tabular matter, particularly for library use:

Ja.	My.	S.
F.	Je.	O.
Mr.	Jy.	N.
Ap.	Ag.	D.

Days of the Week

26. The names of the days of the week should usually be written in full, but when space makes abbreviations necessary, use the following:

Sun.	Thurs.
Mon.	Fri.
Tues.	Sat.
Wed.	

Compass Directions

27. For compass directions use the following letters with a period:

N.	E.	NE.	SE.	NNW.
S.	W.	NW.	SW.	NNE.

Sizes of Books

28. Use the following without a period to denote the sizes of books where abbreviations are desirable:

4to	quarto	24mo	twenty-four-mo
8vo	octavo	32mo	thirty-two-mo
12mo	duodecimo	36mo	thirty-six-mo
16mo	sextodecimo	48mo	forty-eight-mo
18mo	octodecimo	64mo	sixty-four-mo

The Books of the Bible and Principal Versions

29. Abbreviations for the books of the Bible and for names of translations and versions may be found in the following lists:

THE BOOKS OF THE OLD TESTAMENT

Gen.	I and II Kings	Song of Sol.	Obad.
Exod.	I and II Chron.	Isa.	Jonah
Lev.	Ezra	Jer.	Mic.
Num.	Neh.	Lam.	Nah.
Deut.	Esther	Ezek.	Hab.
Josh.	Job	Dan.	Zeph.
Judg.	Ps. (Pss.)	Hos.	Hag.
Ruth	Prov.	Joel	Zech.
I and II Sam.	Eccles.	Amos	Mal.

THE BOOKS OF THE NEW TESTAMENT

Matt.	Gal.	Philem.
Mark	Eph.	Heb.
Luke	Phil.	Jas.
John	Col.	I and II Pet.
Acts	I and II Thess.	I, II and III John
Rom.	I and II Tim.	Jude
I and II Cor.	Titus	Rev.

PRINCIPAL VERSIONS OF THE BIBLE

A.V.	Authorized Version
R.V.	Revised Version
A.R.V.	American Revised Standard Version
E.R.V.	English Revised Version
E.V.	English Version(s) of the Bible
Vulg.	Vulgate
LXX (*See* pp. 18–19.)	Septuagint

References to books or chapters of the Bible are not usually abbreviated in text matter:

The story of the Creation is found in Genesis, Chapter I.

References to Parts of Books

30. Write out references to chapters, pages, verses, and notes occurring in the text; but in parentheses, footnotes, cut-in notes, side notes, and tables, abbreviate as follows:

art. (arts.)	article	pl. (pls.)	plate
ch. (chs.)	chapter	pt. (pts.)	part
fig. (figs.)	figure	sec. (secs.)	section
p. (pp.)	page	vol. (vols.)	volume

Note that the Roman numeral with capital letter is used with these abbreviations except in the case of *p.* or *pp.*

Signs and Symbols

a/c	account
´	acute accent
&	and
*	asterisk, a mark used to denote a reference
***	asterisks used to denote omissions
@	at, about; as, velvet @ $10 per yd.
[ ]	brackets used to enclose matter incidental to the thought of the sentence
˘	breve, a mark used to indicate a short vowel; as, ĭll
%	care of
∧	caret, a sign inserted below a line between words or letters to denote an incorrect omission
ς	cedilla, under a *c* (ç) to show it is pronounced like *s*

¢	cent or cents
√	check
..	diaeresis in English or French, above a vowel to denote that it is pronounced separately from the preceding letter—as, coöperate; umlaut in German, over a vowel to indicate a pronunciation different from the one normally to be expected
"	ditto
÷	division
$	dollar or dollars
=	equals
° C.	degrees Centigrade
° F.	degrees Fahrenheit
′	feet; as, 16′; also minutes; as, 6′
`	grave accent
>	greater than
∴	hence, therefore
=	hyphen
″	inches; as, 10′ 16″ (ten feet, sixteen inches); a dictionary mark indicating secondary accent
–	macron, a mark used to indicate a long vowel; as, īce
—	minus
×	a sign denoting multiplication; a sign denoting *by* in dimensions; as, 3 ft. × 3 ft.; a character used instead of a signature by one unable to write his name
#	number; as, #7; also a printing mark used to indicate a needed space
¶	paragraph
‖	parallel to
%	per cent
+	plus
£	pound; as, £6 (English money)
~	tilde, a mark placed over *n* in Spanish words to denote the addition of the sound of *y;* as, *cañon* pronounced *canyon*

Some Abbreviations and Symbols Used for Indicating Money

The following are some of the abbreviations and symbols used for indicating money.

$, dol. (dollars)
c., ct., ¢ (cent, cents)
£T175 (Turkish)
$US15,000
$Mex2,650

₱ (pesos)
£ (pounds)
s. (shillings)
d. (pence)
£ 12 16s. 8d. (*not* 12/16/8)

REFERENCE BOOKS

ABBREVIATIONS IN COMMON USE

SCHWARTZ, ROBERT J. *The Complete Dictionary of Abbreviations.* New York, Thomas Y. Crowell Company, 1955.

SHANKLE, GEORGE EARLIE. *Current Abbreviations.* New York, The H. W. Wilson Company, 1945.

STEPHENSON, HERBERT JOHN. *Abbrevs. (A Dictionary of Abbreviations.)* New York, The Macmillan Company, 1943.

ABBREVIATIONS FOR BRITISH TITLES

BURKE, SIR JOHN BERNARD. *Genealogical and Heraldic History of the Peerage and Baronetage, the Privy Council and Knightage.*

Debrett's Peerage, Baronetage, Knightage and Companionage.

Kelly's Handbook to the Titled, Landed, and Official Classes.

Whitaker's Peerage, Baronetage, Knightage and Companionage.

9. Points of Grammar
Suggestions for Correct Usage

Nouns

1. Most nouns form the plural by adding *s* to the singular; *banks, letters, desks.*

2. Nouns ending in *s, sh, ch, x,* and *z* form their plurals by adding *es* to the singular: *kisses, bushes, branches, boxes, waltzes.*

3. Nouns ending in *f* or *fe* change *f* to *v* before adding *es: thieves, halves, shelves, wives.*

But the following nouns in *f* add *s* to form the plural:

beliefs	proofs
chiefs	scarfs (sometimes *scarves*)
dwarfs	serfs
handkerchiefs	wharfs (*wharves* more usual
hoofs	in the United States)

4. Nouns ending in *y.*

(1) Nouns ending in *y* preceded by a consonant, and those ending in *quy,* form their plurals by changing *y* to *i* and adding *es: cities,* their *Excellencies, colloquies.*

(2) Nouns ending in *y* preceded by a vowel form the plural in the usual way by adding *s* to the singular: *valleys, alleys.*

5. Nouns ending in *o.*

(1) Nouns ending in *o* preceded by a vowel add *s* to form the plural: *cameos, portfolios, studios.*

(2) Nouns ending in *o* preceded by a consonant form the plural by adding *es: mulattoes, tomatoes.*

Some of the most common exceptions to this rule are the following: *pianos, solos, sopranos, cantos.*

181

(3) Several words ending in *o* form their plurals in both ways: *cargoes, cargos; mottoes, mottos.*

The following list gives plural spellings of other words ending in *o* according to *Webster's New International Dictionary:*

altos
archipelagoes or archipelagos
calicoes or calicos
casinos
curios
dynamos
echoes
embargoes
embryos
Eskimos or Eskimo
frescoes or frescos
grottoes or grottos
halos or haloes
heroes
innuendoes
kimonos
manifestoes
mementos or mementoes
mosquitoes
Negroes
octavos
oratorios
porticoes or porticos
potatoes
provisos or provisoes
quartos
radios
stilettos or stilettoes
tornadoes
torpedoes
torsos
twos
volcanoes or volcanos
zeros or zeroes

6. Nouns that retain in English their foreign endings form their plurals in the following ways: those ending in *a* to *ae; us* to *i; um* to *a; on* to *a; is* to *es.*

Note the plurals of the following nouns which retain their foreign forms and in some cases have also an English plural:

a to *ae*
alumna-alumnae (f)
antenna-antennae-antennas (radio)
formula-formulae-formulas
larva-larvae
minutia-minutiae
vertebra-vertebrae

us to *i*
alumnus-alumni (m)
cactus-cacti-cactuses
focus-foci-focuses
fungus-fungi-funguses
genius-genii-geniuses
nucleus-nuclei-nucleuses
stimulus-stimuli
syllabus, syllabi
terminus-termini

um to *a*	addendum-addenda
	agendum-agenda
	aquarium-aquaria-aquariums
	bacterium-bacteria
	curriculum-curricula-curriculums
	datum-data
	erratum-errata
	gymnasium-gymnasia-gymnasiums
	maximum-maxima-maximums
	medium-media-mediums
	memorandum-memoranda-memorandums
	planetarium-planetaria-planetariums
	referendum-referenda-referendums
	residuum-residua-residuums
	stratum-strata-stratums
	ultimatum-ultimata-ultimatums
on to *a*	criterion-criteria
	phenomenon-phenomena
is to *es*	analysis-analyses
	axis-axes
	crisis-crises
	diagnosis-diagnoses
	ellipsis-ellipses
	emphasis-emphases
	hypothesis-hypotheses
	oasis-oases
	parenthesis-parentheses
	synopsis-synopses
	thesis-theses

The following nouns also retain their foreign forms and in some cases have also an English plural:

appendix	appendices, appendixes
beau	beaux, beaus
château	châteaux
dilettante	dilettanti, dilettantes
genus	genera
index	indexes, indices
madame	mesdames
monsieur	messieurs
tableau	tableaux, tableaus

7. Plurals of Titles.

When the title *Mr.* or *Dr.* is used with a name, in formal speech or writing the whole term is usually pluralized by making plural the title only; as, *Mr. Harper*, the *Messrs. Harper; Messrs. Jones and Gray; Dr. Lee*, the *Drs. Lee.* In commercial use "the" is commonly omitted, giving *Messrs. Harper, Drs. Lee, Drs. Simpkins and Thompson*, or the like. In informal speech or writing the name itself is often the part pluralized; as, *Mr. Harpers, Dr. Lees.*

In using the title *Mrs.* to designate two or more married ladies, the proper name should be pluralized; as, the *Mrs. Barlows.* But in using the title *Misses* to designate two or more unmarried ladies of the same name the preferred plural, especially in formal writing, is the *Misses Barlow,* though the *Miss Barlows* is permissible in less formal address.

When the names of two or more married women of different names occur in a list, the title *Mesdames* precedes them: Mesdames James Norton, Alfred Blakeslee, and Henry Johnson.

8. Proper nouns form their plurals in the usual way by adding *s: Helens, Henrys, Barrys, Marys, Murphys, Dalys, Rowleys, Carolinas, Ciceros.*

Those ending in a sibilant form their plurals by adding *es: Joneses, Adamses.*

9. Certain words are used with the plural only:

annals	proceeds
dregs	scissors
goods	shears
nuptials	thanks

10. Certain words may be used either as singular or as plural according to their meaning.

Athletics (that is, *athletic training*) *has become* popular.
Athletics (that is, *sports*) *are indulged* in by many students.
Acoustics (that is, the *science*) is studied by architects.
The acoustics (*acoustic qualities*) of the hall are poor.

Politics may be used as singular or as plural. The tendency today is to consider it as singular.

11. Some nouns plural in form may be singular in meaning. They then take a singular verb.

aëronautics	measles
alms	molasses
economics	news
ethics	physics
means (in the sense of *way*	statistics
to an end)	tactics

12. Some nouns form their plurals by the change of an internal vowel: *men, women, geese, mice.*

Notice that *Germans, Normans, Ottomans, talismans,* which are not compounds of *man,* form their plurals in the usual way.

13. Some nouns have the same form in the plural as in the singular: *chassis, corps, deer, heathen, salmon, series, sheep, species, trout, Chinese, Iroquois, Japanese, Portuguese.*

14. Most compound nouns form the plural by adding the sign of the plural to the fundamental part of the word: *aides-de-camp, courts-martial, editors in chief, maids-of-honor, sons-in-law.*

When a compound is made up of a noun and a preposition or a noun and an adverb, the noun is the part usually pluralized: *fillers-in, passers-by, runners-up.*

When neither word in a compound is a noun, the last part of the word is pluralized: *higher-ups, shut-ins, strike-overs.*

15. In forming the plurals of complex titles, the principal word (always a noun) takes the plural form.

Principal word first:	Principal word second:
attorneys general	deputy judges
chargés d'affaires	judge advocates
consuls general	lieutenant colonels
postmasters general	major generals
sergeants at arms	military attachés
sergeants major	under secretaries
surgeons general	vice chairmen

16. When the compounds are written solid, the sign of the plural is always at the end: *cupfuls, handfuls, spoonfuls.*

17. Some nouns form their plurals by adding an additional syllable: *children, oxen.*

18. Some nouns have two plurals differing in meaning: *brothers, brethren; cloths, clothes; dies, dice; fish, fishes; indexes, indices; pennies, pence.*

19. Letters, signs, symbols, and figures usually form their plurals by adding *'s* to the singular: *a's, &'s, $'s, 6's.* There is a growing tendency to omit the apostrophe in plurals of capital letters, signs, symbols, and figures: *Ns, SOSs, $s, 6s.*

20. Words referred to as words and those already containing an apostrophe form their plurals by adding *s* or *es* to the singular: *ands, yeas* and *nays, antis* and *pros, don'ts.* If the apostrophe through its absence would cause confusion in reading, it should be inserted: *do's, which's.*

Pronouns

1. The nominative case of pronouns is used:
   (1) As subject

They paid the premium promptly.
I met the chairman *who, I* think, is a friend of yours.
Who will be appointed secretary?
They sent cards to those *who* they thought would come.
I do not know *who* is treasurer.
We trustees must carry out the policy of the college.

   (2) As a predicate complement

It is *I* (*he, she, we, they*).
I am *he* (*she*).
Are you *he* (*she*)?
It seemed to be *he* (*she, they*).

(This construction has been a matter of disputed usage. A few modern writers believe this form too stilted and advocate It is *me,* etc.)

Current English Usage, STERLING A. LEONARD

Note that the verb *to be* takes the same case after, as before it.

It is *I.*
I am often taken to be *she.*
They took it to be *him. Him* is in the objective case because *it,* the subject of the infinitive, is in the objective case.)

   (3) In apposition with the subject of a verb or with a predicate nominative.

The Ambassador at the time was Walter Hines Page, *he* who assisted so many Americans in Europe during the early days of the World War.
We trustees must carry out the policy of the college.

2. The objective case of pronouns is used:
(1) As the object of a verb

The president trusted *him*.
I do not know *whom* you want.
Whom do you wish to see?
Who did you wish to see? (An accepted colloquialism.) *The Oxford English Dictionary* states that such usage is common in *colloquial use*.

(2) As the indirect object of a verb

The treasurer gave *him* fifty dollars.

(3) As the object of a preposition

The medal was awarded to *her* whom the faculty considered worthy of the honor.
The task was to be divided between *you* and *me* (not *you* and *I*).
The result depended upon *us* (not *we*) younger men.
The book was left for *you* and *him* (not *you* and *he*).
Whom are you looking for?
Who are you looking for? (An accepted colloquialism.)

(4) In apposition with the object of a verb or of a preposition

They fined Lawrence—both *him* and his brother.

(5) As subject of an infinitive

They asked *him* and *me* (not *he* and *I*) to report to the office.
Let *her* and *me* (not *she* and *I*) finish the proofreading.

3. The possessive case of pronouns is used:
(1) To denote possession

Their estate was divided equally.
They were interested in the campaign and *its* results.

Note that there is no apostrophe in possessive pronouns. The correct forms are *its, hers, ours, yours, theirs*.
Note that *whose*, the pronoun, must not be confused with *who's* meaning *who is*.

Whose book is that?
Who's going to the theatre with me next Thursday?

(2) To complete the predicate when the noun is omitted

The book is *mine* (*hers, his, yours, theirs*).

(3) To form a double possessive

This chair of *yours*.
A book of *his* has just been published.

(4) To modify a gerund

His going to Florida postponed the meeting.
The success of the meeting depends on *his* (not *him*) being present.
Father would not hear of *my* (not *me*) taking the case.

4. Compound personal pronouns are used:
  (1) For emphasis

I *myself* answered the telephone.
He gave the money to the boys *themselves*.

(2) Reflexively when as objects of a verb or of a preposition they refer back to the subject and denote the same thing or person as the subject.

He convinced *himself* that the scheme would work.
Anybody can see for *himself* that the plan is a good one.

Most authorities believe that compound personal pronouns should not be used as substitutes for personal pronouns.

Right: Amy, Anne, and *I* went.
Wrong: Amy, Anne, and *myself* went.
Right: He gave it to Mother and *me*.
Wrong: He gave it to Mother and *myself*.

5. Interrogative pronouns (*who, which* and *what*) are used in asking questions. In questions, particularly in spoken English, the use of *who*, instead of *whom*, is now current. According to the *Oxford English Dictionary* and to Fowler's *Dictionary of Modern English Usage, who* in such cases is correct.

Who is going with you?
Who are you going with?
Who has been appointed chairman?
Who do you wish to speak to?

Agreement

6. A pronoun must agree with its antecedent in person, number, and gender, but not in case.

Each girl should do *her* (not *their*) work accurately.
Everybody should pay *his* (not *their*) share.

7. Such words as *each, every, everyone, everybody, anybody, either, neither, no one, nobody,* are singular in number and, therefore, must take a singular verb and be referred to by a singular pronoun.

Each of the girls *was* (not *were*) present today.
Everyone *takes his* part well.
Nobody *was* willing to read *his* own poem.

H. W. Fowler's *Dictionary of Modern English Usage* discusses *each* as follows:

Each as subject is invariably singular, even when followed by *of them* . . . When *each* is not the subject, but in apposition with a plural noun or pronoun as subject, the verb (and complement) is invariably plural: the wheels *have* 12 spokes each; the wheels each *have* 12 spokes (this latter order is better avoided); the wheels *are* each 12-spokers.

8. *None* may be singular or plural according to the meaning.
None is usually used with a plural verb, unless a singular idea is clearly intended; in that case *no one* is frequently substituted for *none.* (Woolley and Scott's *College Handbook of Composition.*)

None of the directors *wishes* to cast *his* vote for the appropriation.
None *were* willing to sign the petition.

9. A relative pronoun must agree with its antecedent in person and number.

It is *I who am* surprised.
It is *she who is* afraid.
It is *they who are* in need.
This is the only *one* of my brothers *who likes* to travel.
He is one of the best *governors that have* ever served the State.

(In such expressions, the antecedent of *that* is *governors,* not *one.* But when *one* is preceded by *only,* the antecedent of *who* or *that* is *one.*)

10. With pronouns the verb must agree in person, as well as in number, with the subject nearest it.

Either you or *I am* to blame.
Either you or *she is* to blame

But it is better to reconstruct such sentences.

Either *you are* to blame, or *I am.*
Either *you are* to blame, or *she is.*

Verbs

AGREEMENT OF SUBJECT AND PREDICATE

1. A verb should agree with its subject in person and number.
(1) Two or more nouns connected by *and* take a plural verb.

Weather and unemployment *are* (not *is*) cited as causes of the decline in trade.
The secretary and the treasurer *were* (not *was*) absent from the meeting when their names were called.

(2) Do not mistake the form of the plurals of foreign nouns for the singular. (*See* pp. 182–183.)

The data *are* (not *is*) ready for the expert.
The errata *are* (not *is*) placed in the front of the book.
The phenomena of the Northern Lights *are* (not *is*) striking.

(3) Collective nouns may be regarded as singular or plural: singular, if the word denotes a group acting as an individual; plural, if the word denotes the individuals that make up the group.

The jury *has* (not *have*) agreed upon the verdict.
The jury *have* (not *has*) disagreed as to their verdict.
The Community Service Committee *were* (not *was*) divided on *their* (not *its*) understanding of the question.
When your committee *has* (not *have*) completed *its* (not *their*) work *it* (not *they*) should prepare a report.

Since the names of associations, boards, companies, corporations, and the like are collective nouns, they should be regarded as singular if the name denotes a group acting as an individual or as an entity; plural if the name denotes the individuals composing the group. Care must be taken to have the pronouns and the verbs agree with the collective nouns.

The American Association of University Women *has* urged *its* members to contribute to the Scholarship Fund.
The Southeastern Coast Line *is* agreeable to your suggestion . . . *It* has adopted a progressive public relations program and *is* receiving encouraging support.

The Hall Company *has* scheduled the largest promotional program *it* has ever placed behind any of *its* more than 1,000 products.

Some authorities regard a company name with a plural ending or makeup as plural; as, *Haines Brothers, Upjohn Publishers, L. M. Gordon and Sons.* Most firms with such endings, however, regard their titles as singular. This is true, for instance, of *Charles Scribner's Sons* and of *Harper & Brothers.*

Because the use of *it* or *its* to refer to an association, a company, a corporation, or any other entity may seem unsuitable or stilted, the plural pronouns, *they, their, them* may sometimes be preferred. Then, of course, the verb must also be plural.

As the copyright of the book is held by The Macmillan Company, you must have *their* permission to reproduce this extract. If you ask *them, they are* not likely to refuse you this privilege.

With such words as *number, remainder,* and *rest,* use a singular or a plural verb according as they refer to a whole or to the several members of a group.

(*The number* is usually singular.)
(*A number* is usually plural.)

The number of students in economics *has* increased rapidly.
A number of students in economics *have* signified their intention to take advanced work.
The remainder of the hour *was* spent in discussion.
The rest of the votes *were* lost.

(4) A verb should agree with its subject, not with a noun placed between the verb and its subject.

The joint meeting between the American and British engineers *is* one of the most amazing examples of the development of the radio.
A group of seven communities south of Springfield *is* served by the company.

But with fractions, the verb agrees with the noun in the prepositional phrase.

Half of the chairs *were* painted red.
Half of the chair *was* painted red.

(5) Expressions introduced by such phrases as, *as well as, together with, in addition to,* are not part of the subject and, therefore, do not affect the number of the verb.

The book, together with the newspapers and magazines, *was* destroyed.

(6) A compound subject consisting of two or more singular parts connected by *or* or *nor* always takes a singular verb.

The letter or the report *was* lost.
Either the secretary or the treasurer *is* always present at the monthly meeting.
Neither America nor England *fears* the outcome.

(7) When two parts of a compound subject differing in number are connected by *or* or *nor,* the verb agrees with the part next to it.

Neither his sisters nor his mother *was* present.
Neither the garage nor the houses *were* burned.

(8) When the verb precedes the subject, care should be taken to have it agree with its subject in person and number.

In this catalogue *are* (not *is*) the requirements of admission, the courses, and the fees.

(9) When nouns of quantity, distance, time, and amount are thought of as a unit, use the singular verb.

Forty pounds *is* all we need.
Two hundred miles *makes* a good day's journey.
Fours years *is* required in preparation for such work.
Twenty dollars *pays* for this set of books.

TENSE

2. The present tense should be used to express action or being of the present time.

(1) The present tense should not be used in telling of a past event.

Mary *said* (not *says*) to me, "The tire was punctured on the way from Newton."

(2) The present tense should not be used to express time begun in the past and still continuing.

I *have been* (not *am*) in New York for ten years.

(3) The present tense should be used to express a present fact or an unchangeable truth.

The guide explained that Grant's Tomb *is* (not *was*) at 122nd Street and Riverside Drive.

3. The past tense should be used in speaking of a definite past event or action.

I *heard* Dr. Camus speak when I *was* in New York.

4. The present perfect tense denotes "something happening repeatedly, continuously, or at a time not specifically mentioned."

JAMES MELVIN LEE

I *have seen* the Atlantic Ocean many times.
Helen *hasn't arrived* yet.

5. The past perfect tense denotes that the action of the verb was completed at some definite point in past time.

Before my visit to New York, I *had* never *heard* him speak.
If he *had* (not *would have*) *waited,* he would have won the prize.

Note the correct use of tense in the following sentences:

He didn't ring the bell.
He hasn't rung the bell yet.
He hadn't rung the bell when I entered the room.
I have visited most of the capitals of Europe.
I have been in America ten years.
He always has paid and always will pay the bill.
Not: He always has and always will pay the bill.

6. The future tense denotes action in the future. It consists of the auxiliary verb *shall* or *will* with the infinitive without *to.*
Shall and *will,* and *should* and *would* in simple declarative sentences:
Shall is used with the first person to denote simple futurity.

I *shall* expect to see you soon.

Shall is used with the second and third persons to denote control or compulsion on the part of the speaker.

You shall do it now, meaning *you must do it now.*
They shall not go until I tell them to.

Will is used with the first person to express determination or willingness on the part of the speaker.

I *will* come when you call.

Will is used with the second and third persons to express simple futurity.

You *will* come soon, *will* you not?
They *will* help us build the house.

Should and *would* follow the same rules as *shall* and *will*.
Should in first person expresses futurity.

If I *should* come, I *should* bring a trunk.
If you would like to have a more detailed analysis made, we *should* be glad to assist you.

Should in second and third persons expresses obligation.

He *should* do his work better.

Would in the second and third persons expresses futurity or customary action.

They *would* come every day for food. (*That is* They used to come every day for food.)

In questions, always use *shall* in the first person; in the second and third use the form expected in the answer.

Question: *Shall* I raise the window?
Question: *Will* you come with me?
Answer: Yes, I *will*.
Question: *Will* they meet us at the station?
Answer: Yes, they *will* be there.

7. The tense of the infinitive is always relative to the time of the main verb.

(1) The present infinitive denotes the same time or future time in relation to the action of the main verb. Notice that in the following sentences the present infinitive is used with verbs denoting present or past time. The time denoted by the infinitive is the same as that of the principal verb or later than that denoted by the principal verb.

I intend *to go* tomorrow.
I intended *to go* Thursday.
For several days I have been intending *to write*.
I should have liked *to do* it (not *to have done* it).

Jim would have liked *to go* with his brother last week (not *to have gone*).

I had intended *to write* the letter before breakfast (not *to have written*).

(2) The perfect infinitive denotes action that is complete at the time of the principal verb.

The Zeppelin was reported *to have been sighted* off Bermuda at noon.

8. Note the difference in meaning implied by the present and perfect infinitives in the following sentences:

His men believed Washington *to be* a great general.
We believe Washington *to have been* a great general.
The Milan Cathedral is said *to be* one of the largest in the world.
The Parthenon is said *to have been* erected in the Age of Pericles.

9. The subjunctive mood is little used today except in a few special cases:

(1) To express a wish

I wish I *were* in Europe.

(2) To express a contrary-to-fact condition

If I *were* you, I should take the position.

Kittredge and Farley's *Advanced English Grammar* states the following:

Present and past conditions may be either (1) non-committal or (2) contrary to fact.
  1. A condition is non-committal when it implies nothing as to the truth or falsity of the case supposed.
      If James is angry, I am sorry. (Perhaps James is angry, perhaps not.)
  2. A condition is contrary to fact when it implies that the supposed case is not or was not true.
      If James were angry, I should be sorry. (James is *not* angry.)
In a non-committal present condition, the *if* clause takes the present indicative; in a non-committal past condition, the past, the perfect, or the pluperfect.
  The conclusion may be in any form that the sense allows.
  Present Condition, Non-Committal:
      If this pebble is a diamond, it is valuable.
  Past Condition, Non-Committal:

If that pebble was a diamond, it was valuable.
If Tom has apologized, he has done his duty.
If John had reached home before we started, he must have made
a quick journey.

In each of these examples, the speaker declines to commit himself
as to the truth of the supposed case. Perhaps the pebble was a diamond,
perhaps not; Tom may or may not have apologized; whether or not
John had reached home, we cannot tell.

PRINCIPAL PARTS

10. The principal parts of verbs consist of the present and the past
indicative, and the past or perfect participle.

The following table shows the principal parts of many trouble-
some verbs, most of which are irregular. Illiterate and careless
errors occur most often in the use of the past tense and the past
participle; as, *has went* for *has gone, sunk* for *sank.*

Present	Past	Perfect Participle
am or be	was	been
arise	arose	arisen
awake	awoke	awaked
bear	bore	borne
beat	beat	beaten
begin	began	begun
bend	bent	bent
beseech	besought	besought
bid (card playing)	bid	bid
bid (most senses)	bade, bid	bidden, bid
bleed	bled	bled
blow	blew	blown
break	broke	broken
bring	brought	brought
broadcast	broadcast	broadcast
catch	caught	caught
choose	chose	chosen
climb	climbed	climbed
cling	clung	clung
come	came	come
dive	dived	dived
do	did	done
draw	drew	drawn

Present	Past	Perfect Participle
drink	drank	drunk
drive	drove	driven
fall	fell	fallen
fight	fought	fought
flee	fled	fled
flow	flowed	flowed
fly	flew	flown
forbid	forbade	forbidden
forget	forgot	forgotten
forsake	forsook	forsaken
freeze	froze	frozen
get	got	got
go	went	gone
grow	grew	grown
hang (most senses)	hung	hung
hang (punishment)	hanged	hanged
hide	hid	hidden
hurt	hurt	hurt
kneel	knelt, kneeled	knelt, kneeled
lay (to cause to lie)	laid	laid
lead	led	led
leap	leaped, leapt	leaped, leapt
lie (to recline)	lay	lain
lie (to tell a false-hood)	lied	lied
loose	loosed	loosed
lose	lost	lost
pay	paid	paid
plead	pleaded	pleaded
prove	proved	proved, proven
ring	rang, rung	rung
rise	rose	risen
run	ran	run
say	said	said
see	saw	seen
seek	sought	sought
set (to place)	set	set
shake	shook	shaken
shine	shone	shone
show	showed	shown, showed
shrink	shrank, shrunk	shrunk

Present	Past	Perfect Participle
sing	sang, sung	sung
sink	sank, sunk	sunk
sit (to sit down)	sat	sat
slay	slew	slain
sleep	slept	slept
speak	spoke	spoken
stay	stayed	stayed
steal	stole	stolen
stick	stuck	stuck
sting	stung	stung
stop	stopped	stopped
strive	strove	striven
swear	swore	sworn
swim	swam	swum
swing	swung	swung
take	took	taken
teach	taught	taught
tear	tore	torn
throw	threw	thrown
tread	trod	trodden, trod
wake	waked, woke	waked
wear	wore	worn
weave	wove	woven
win	won	won
wring	wrung	wrung
write	wrote	written

11. ILLUSTRATIONS OF THE CORRECT USAGE OF VERBS

Perry *began* (not *begun*) his speech early in the evening.
Ann *did* (not *done*) her work well.
Charles *drank* (not *drunk*) a glass of milk.
Father *has gone* (not *has went*) to Florida.
The criminal *was hanged* (not *hung*) at twelve.
She *lay* (not *laid*) on the beach every afternoon.
Mother *has lain* (not *laid*) down for her afternoon nap.
Helen *was lying* (not *laying*) down when I called her.
He told the dog to *lie* (not *lay*) still.
He *was lying* (not *lieing*) to you about the accident.
The patient *paid* (not *payed*) his bill promptly.
He *ran* (not *run*) to meet his mother.
I *saw* (not *seen*) Mr. Brown yesterday.

Adjectives and Adverbs

1. Adverbs, not adjectives, are used to modify verbs.

He behaved *perfectly* (not *perfect*) even in that trying situation. Will you do this for me? *Surely* (not *sure*).

Note that when the condition of the subject is described, an adjective is used.

The vegetables boiled *soft*.

But when the action of the verb is explained, an adverb is used.

The vegetables boiled *gently*.

2. The following words have the same form whether they are used as adjectives or as adverbs: *fast, first, ill*.

3. Note that *quick, slow,* and *direct* may be used as adverbs.

Correct

He drives slow.   Come quick.
He drives slowly.   Come quickly.

Orders from customers mailed direct to Boston would be shipped from Detroit.

4. A few adjectives end in *ly,* such as *cowardly, gentlemanly, leisurely, lonely, orderly*.

5. Verbs of the senses, such as *look, sound, smell, taste, feel,* and copulative verbs, such as *be, appear, seem,* take an adjective to denote a quality or condition of the subject.

Hazel looked *pretty* (not *prettily*) in her new hat.
Bells sound *clear* (not *clearly*) at dusk.
Violets smell *sweet* (not *sweetly*).
The pudding tastes *delicious* (not *deliciously*).
Robert feels *unhappy* (not *unhappily*) about his Latin.

Note that usage is divided in regard to *He feels bad* and *He feels badly*.

6. Note that the modifier should be an adjective if it denotes the condition of the object, but an adverb if it explains the action of the verb.

He kept it *firm* (not *firmly*).
She held the wheel *tight* (not *tightly*).
He looked *quietly* around.
He spoke *clearly* over the telephone.

7. *Well* may be an adverb or an adjective.

How did you sleep? *Well*, thank you. (adverb)
The work was *well* done. (adverb)

Note that *good* is not used of the state of health.

I feel *well* (not *good*). (adjective)

COMPARISON

8. The comparative degree is used in comparing two persons or things. The superlative degree is used in comparing more than two persons or things.

Henry is the *more* (not *most*) *reliable* of the two authorities.
In our club Edwin Arlington Robinson is the *most popular* poet read.

9. Adjectives of one syllable and most adjectives of two syllables form the comparative by adding *er,* and the superlative by adding *est,* to the positive.

Susie's manner was *gayer* (not *more gay*) than her sister's.
Elmer seems *wittier* (not more *witty*) than his brother.
Shakespeare is the *greatest* British dramatist.

Many adjectives of two syllables and most adjectives of more than two syllables form their comparative by prefixing *more* or *less,* and their superlative by prefixing *most* or *least.*

The recent news of the expedition seemed *more hopeful.*
As a businessman he became *most successful.*

10. Strictly, some adjectives and adverbs derived from them are incapable of comparison because they express a quality complete or perfect; as, *universal, unique, perfect, infinite, preferable.* But modern usage accepts many deviations from this rule: a *most complete* report, a *more perfect* example.

11. In comparing two things exclude the thing compared; as, Chicago is *larger* than any *other* city in Illinois.

12. In comparing more than two objects include the thing compared; as, Chicago is the *largest* city in Illinois.

NEGATIVES

13. Two negatives make an affirmative.

There aren't *any* (not *no*) books on the shelf.
He doesn't want *any* (not *no*) help.

The words *hardly, scarcely, but,* and *only* are negative in meaning and should not be used with another negative.

He *can hardly* (not *can't hardly*) hear what you say.
There was *scarcely any* (not *no*) water in the jar.
John *had but one* (not *hadn't but one*) sheet of paper.
They *had* (not *hadn't*) only one report of the meeting.

THE ARTICLE

14. "*A* is used before all consonants except silent *h* (*a history, an hour*); *an* was formerly usual before an unaccented syllable beginning with *h* (*an historical work*) . . . *A* is now usual also before vowels preceded in fact though not in appearance by the sound of *y* or *w* (*a unit, a eulogy, a one*)."
A Dictionary of Modern English Usage, H. W. FOWLER

The article should be repeated in referring to two separate persons or objects.

We engaged a typist and a stenographer (two persons).
We engaged a typist and stenographer (one person).

She has a maple and a mahogany bureau (two bureaus).
She has a maple and mahogany bureau (one bureau).

But when two or more nouns refer to the same person, the article should not be repeated.

Caesar was a general, writer, and statesman.

POSITION OF "ONLY"

15. The adverb *only* should be placed as near as possible to the word it modifies.

The bookkeeper made *only one error* (not *only made*).
He *only* nominated the president (he didn't vote for him).
He nominated *only* the president (he did not nominate anyone else).

AGREEMENT OF ADJECTIVE AND NOUN

16. *This* and *that* are singular and must be used to modify singular nouns. *These* and *those* are plural and must be used to modify plural nouns.

> *This* kind (not *these* kind) of books is instructive.
> *These* kinds (not *these* kind) of books are instructive.
> *That* sort (not *those* sort) of answer carries little weight.

Note that *kind of* (not *kind of a*) and *sort of* (not *sort of a*) are permissible although colloquial.

> That *kind of* (not *kind of a*) boy ranks high.
> That *sort of* (not *sort of a*) position is what I want.

UNNECESSARY ADVERBS

17. Unnecessary adverbs should be avoided.

> Each sheet of paper should be carefully numbered (not numbered *throughout*).
> Repeat it (not repeat it *again*).
> They returned (not returned *back*) to the hotel.
> Let us cooperate (not cooperate *together*).
> Finish the business (not finish *up* the business).
> They expect to divide (not divide *up*) the proceeds.

Prepositions

Care must be taken in the use of prepositions. A dictionary should always be consulted in case of doubt as to correct usage. The following illustrations may be helpful:

among, between
(Use *among* with more than two; *between* with two.)
The flowers were divided *among* (not *between*) the patients of the ward.
The flowers were divided *between* (not *among*) the two patients.

at, with
(*with* a person, *at* a thing)
Jane was angry *with* (not *at*) me.
The minority was angry *at* (not *with*) the resolution passed.
The lawyer was displeased *with* (not *at*) the witness.

beside, besides
(at the side of, in addition to)

George walked *beside* (not *besides*) Mary.
Besides (not *beside*) the large doors, there are several smaller ones.

back of, behind

They ran *behind* (not *back of* or *in back of*) the garage.

in, into

The boy walked *in* the room (within its walls).
The boy walked *into* (entered) the room.

of

The phrases *could of, must of,* are erroneous forms for *could have, must have.*

IDIOMATIC PREPOSITIONAL PHRASES

adapted for	The apartment is adapted for housekeeping.
adapted to	Helen soon adapted herself to her changed circumstances.
adapted from	The story is adapted from the French.
agree on	The faculty agreed on limiting the number of students.
agree to	Do you agree to this proposition?
agree with	He agrees with me on the matter.
argue about	Do not argue about the question.
argue for	They argued for the abolition of child labor.
argue with	He argued with me about prohibition.
confide in	May I confide in you?
confide to	She confided her troubles to me.
consist in	Success does not always consist in achieving wealth.
consist of	The play consists of five acts.
denounce as	Arnold was denounced as a traitor.
denounce for	The thief was denounced for his crime.
die from	They died from exposure.
die of	She died of pneumonia.
differ about	We differ about the success of coeducation.
differ from	Mary differs from her sister in appearance.
differ in	Mother and Father differ in their opinions about our summer vacation.

differ on	They usually differ on religious questions.
differ with	I differ with you in regard to the discipline of the school.
disappoint of	Bad weather often disappoints the farmers of their harvest.
disappointed in	Farmers are often disappointed in their yearly income.
enter at	Enter at the front gate.
	He entered his son at Harvard.
enter for	John has entered for the championship.
enter in	He has entered the bill in his accounts.
enter into	The Faculty entered into an agreement with the townspeople.
enter upon	He entered upon his new work with enthusiasm.
impatient at	The superintendent was impatient at the delay.
impatient with	Mother was impatient with the boys.
live at	He lives at the Hotel Astor.
live in	Helen lives in Florida.
live on	He lives on Magnolia Avenue.
prejudice against	No one is prejudiced against you.
reconcile to	He was reconciled to his father.
reconcile with	These opinions can be reconciled with hers.

NECESSARY PREPOSITIONS

Prepositions should not be omitted when they are needed to make the meaning clear. In the following sentences note the need of the italicized prepositions.

It is *of* no use to object.
Barbara will be *at* home tomorrow.
The tree was a foot *in* diameter.
Will you refrain *from* reading aloud?
His remark is unworthy *of* your notice.
They are going either to France or *to* Italy.
On this side of the river is a group of houses.
An appointment with the dentist prevented Rose *from* going to the concert.
You will find reading a comfort in youth as well as *in* later life.
The states of the East and *of* the West stood together on the question.
I had no faith *in,* or hope *for,* the movement.

UNNECESSARY PREPOSITIONS

Prepositions should be omitted when they are not needed to make the meaning clear. In the following illustrations note the unnecessary prepositions:

The girls in the school were all *about* (not *of about*) sixteen.
No one can help observing (not *from* observing) her.
Let us examine (not examine *into*) the room.
The class entered (not entered *into*) the room.
They are going home (not *to* home).
The tree is *near* (not *near to*) the garage.
The child fell *off* (not *off of*) the chair.
They sail *about* (not *on about*) the thirteenth of June.
The club disbanded *about* (not *at about*) ten.
Where has John been (not *been at*)?
Where shall we go (not *go to*)?
She does not remember (not *remember of*) any such happening.

Conjunctions

The correct use of conjunctions is sometimes confusing. Note the following suggestions which illustrate good usage:

as, as if
Do *as* (not *like*) the manager suggests.
I feel *as if* (not *like*) I need a change.

but, and
The manager believed in auditing the report, *but* (not *and*) the vice-president did not consider it necessary.

unless
Do not do it *unless* (not *without*) he gives you directions.
I cannot write a story *unless* (not *without*) I am in the proper mood.

COORDINATE CONJUNCTIONS

Correlative conjunctions, that is, conjunctions used in pairs, should be placed next to the words they connect. These words or expressions should be in the same construction.

The most common correlatives are *either–or, neither–nor, not only–but also, both–and, whereas–therefore, whether–or.*

They have read neither the book nor the magazine.
Not: They have neither read the book nor the magazine.
The work gave me both pleasure and experience.
Not: The work both gave me pleasure and experience.
We visited not only London, but also Paris, Nice, and Rome.
Not: We not only visited London, but also Paris, Nice, and Rome.

With coordinate conjunctions such as *and* and *but,* ideas must be expressed in similar construction.

He was strong in body and in mind.
Or: He was strong physically and mentally.
Not: He was strong in body and also mentally.

SUBORDINATE CONJUNCTIONS

When one idea in a sentence is dependent upon another, a subordinate conjunction is used to connect the dependent with the main thought.

Do not use *as, because, how, where* for *that* or *whether.*

He doesn't see *that* (not *as*) he ought to do it.
I don't know *whether* (not *as*) I can go.
The reason for his absence was *that* (not *because*) he felt ill.
He told them *that* (not *how*) he expected to go to South America.
I saw in the advertisement *that* (not *where*) Bankhurst became president.

Do not use *if* as a synonym for *whether* after *see, ask, learn, know, doubt,* and the like.

I don't know *whether* (not *if*) I can go.
I shall ask him *whether* (not *if*) he will do the work.

REFERENCE BOOKS

FOWLER, H. W. *A Dictionary of Modern English Usage.* Oxford and New York, Oxford University Press, 1926, etc.

GREEVER, GARLAND, and JONES, EASLEY STEPHEN. *Century Handbook of Writing.* 4th ed. New York, Appleton-Century-Crofts, 1942.

HOTCHKISS, GEORGE BURTON, and KILDUFF, EDWARD JONES. *Handbook of Business English.* 3d ed. New York, Harper and Brothers, 1945.

KIERZEK, JOHN M. *The Macmillan Handbook of English.* 3d ed. New York, The Macmillan Company, 1954.

MONRO, KATE M. *A Workbook Course in Business English.* 2d ed. New York, McGraw-Hill Book Company, Inc., 1954.

OPDYCKE, JOHN BAKER. *Harper's English Grammar.* New York, Harper & Brothers, 1941.

SMART, WALTER KAY. *English Review Grammar.* 4th ed. New York, Appleton-Century-Crofts, 1940.

Standard Handbook of Prepositions, Conjunctions, Relative Pronouns and Adverbs. By the Funk & Wagnalls Editorial Staff. New York, Funk & Wagnalls, 1953.

WOOLLEY, EDWIN C., SCOTT, FRANKLIN WILLIAM, and BRACHER, FREDERICK. *College Handbook of Composition.* 5th ed. New York, D. C. Heath and Company, 1951.

PART TWO

1. Letter Writing

Letter writing has become important, particularly in relation to business. It forms the main subject of so many texts on Business English that there is no need for extended discussion here.

As correspondence fills a large part of the secretary's day, he should know the principles of letter writing, for to write a good letter is a real accomplishment. Modern letters, whether coming from a great public organization or from a private individual, are personal and individual. Like those of the great letter writers, they reveal personality. They show due regard for the viewpoint of the reader. They are planned with care. Their language is informal but dignified; and their tone courteous and well-bred.

The cheap cordiality of some letters, particularly of the sales type, that strains to compel the reader by a too familiar colloquial tone, suggests poor taste, insincerity of purpose, and tawdriness of material. Better firms season friendliness with dignity, for they know that their clientele resents being addressed by the "hail-fellow-well-met" attitude, often too common in American business correspondence.

Dignity, however, does not mean such senseless formality as that produced by stereotyped phrases. Many expressions such as those that follow, once considered necessary to give a businesslike tone to correspondence, are fortunately disappearing from modern letters.

Yours of the 13th inst. received
We have your esteemed favor of March 20
In reply to yours of the tenth, would say
Answering yours of June 10th, would say
The favor of an answer is requested
This is to acknowledge receipt of your valued order
Awaiting your further commands
We beg to announce
We beg to call your attention

Your letter has come to hand
Your letter of recent date
Inst., ult., prox.
Replying to your letter of the 5th wish to say we have duly noted the contents
Replying to your telegram relative to, etc.
Hoping to hear from you soon, I remain
And oblige, Yours truly
Trusting to hear from you soon
Believing these considerations to be of interest, and assuring you that we shall appreciate a word in reply from you, we are, etc.
Assuring you that your past favors have been highly appreciated and anticipating a continuance of your valued patronage, we remain
Anticipating the courtesy of your favored patronage and thanking you in advance for same, I remain

Words, too new or too old, as well as trite expressions must be guarded against. If the dictionary does not vouch for the good standing of a word, the secretary should not include it in his vocabulary. The following are a few objectionable words, often unthinkingly used by even experienced secretaries:

enthuse	*for*	to be enthusiastic
humans	*for*	persons
recommend	*for*	recommendation
gotten	*for*	got
have got	*for*	have
educating	*for*	educational
anxious	*for*	desirous or eager
fulfill	*for*	fill
partake	*for*	participate

Forms for Headings

On paper containing letterheads, the typist inserts the date directly under the letterhead, or in the more conservative style to form the marginal line on the right.

The following forms illustrate correct arrangement:

May 1, 19__	April 25	April
	19__	Fourth
		19__

On paper that does not contain a letterhead, the headings should be written according to the following order: street address, name of city or town, name of state, date. (*See* pp. 41–43.)

ILLUSTRATIONS OF ATTRACTIVE LETTERHEADS

New York
247 Park Avenue
46TH TO 47TH STREETS
Boston
247 Berkeley Street
NEAR COMMONWEALTH AVE.
Providence
155 Angell Street
CHURCHILL HOUSE

Katharine Gibbs School
of Secretarial and Executive Training
for Educated Women

K.W.C.BRAND, GENERAL AGENT
FOR THE UNITED STATES AND CANADA

TELEPHONE VANDERBILT 1880
CABLE ADDRESS "PADDINGTON" NEW YORK

GREAT WESTERN RAILWAY OF ENGLAND
505 FIFTH AVENUE.
NEW YORK

HARPER & BROTHERS
PUBLISHERS
NEW YORK AND LONDON

ESTABLISHED
1817

Columbia University
in the City of New York

THE ENGLISH GRADUATE UNION
COLUMBIA UNIVERSITY
IN THE CITY OF NEW YORK
HALL OF PHILOSOPHY

HERBERT K.TWITCHELL, President
GEORGE F.CRANE, Vice President
HENRY R.TAYLOR, Vice President
WILLISTON H.BENEDICT, Secretary

RALPH H.STEVER, Cashier
FREDERICK A.CUMMINGS, Treasurer
ELMER RANG JACOBS, Asst.Treasurer
THORNTON C.THAYER, Asst.Cashier

THE SEAMEN'S BANK FOR SAVINGS
IN THE CITY OF NEW YORK
56 WALL STREET
NEW YORK

Open punctuation, except in official Government correspondence, is preferred by most authorities today for both business and social letters.

<table>
<tr><td>19 West 44 Street
New York 18, N.Y.
July 18, 19___</td><td>414 West 121 Street,
New York City,
June 30, 19___.</td></tr>
</table>

Inside Address

In a business letter the inside address, containing the name and the address of the receiver, precedes the salutation; in an official letter it is usually placed beneath the letter at the lower left-hand; in a friendly letter it is omitted.

Closed or open punctuation may be used with the indented style. Open punctuation, however, is the preferred form.

<table>
<tr><td>Mrs. George McClelland
121 Harmon Drive
Larchmont, New York</td><td>Mrs. George McClelland,
121 Harmon Drive,
Larchmont, New York.</td></tr>
</table>

It is permissible to use or to omit the ordinal endings, *st, d, nd, rd,* and *th,* after street numbers.

414 West 121st Street   *or*   414 West 121 Street

Names of avenues and streets expressed in one word should be written out, but when two or more words are needed, figures are preferred although writing in full is permissible.

456 Fifth Avenue *not* 456 5th Avenue
15 West 25 Street *or* 15 West 25th Street
or 15 West Twenty-fifth Street

Block style with open punctuation:

George Fulton, Esq.
317 Madison Avenue
New York, N. Y.

Messrs. (Abbreviation of *Messieurs*)

This title, seldom used today, is most often written in addressing professional partnerships as those composed of architects or of lawyers, one or more of whom is known to be living. *Messrs.* is not used when the word *Company, Corporation,* or *Inc.* is included in the firm name.

Correct: Messrs. Smith and Jones (a professional firm)
Incorrect: Messrs. Blank Typewriting Company
Incorrect: Messrs. American Packing Corporation
Incorrect: Messrs. Jones and Smith, Inc.
Messrs. is never used in the salutation.

Titles

In business letters it is correct to use a business title on the same line as the personal title or on the line below. The choice should depend on which arrangement would give the better balance.

> Mr. Louis R. Drake
> Treasurer, Chickering Brothers

> Dr. Daniel Jenkins, Secretary
> Wentworth Memorial Fund

> Dr. Henry Lorimer, Director
> Personnel Department

> Mr. Paul Stewart
> Secretary to the Mayor

> Dr. Kenneth Jackson
> Superintendent of Schools

Omission of Business Titles in Inside Address

When the addition of a business title, as in the following example, gives a top-heavy appearance to a letter, it should be omitted unless particularly needed for identification.

> Mr. Joseph Grant Adamson
> Advertising Manager
> Barnes Machine Tool Company
> 1200 Orange Avenue
> Orlando, Florida

The business title should not precede the name.

Incorrect methods of address:

> Secretary Henry Ernst
> Treasurer Peter Withers
> Chairman Albert Robbins

The term *Chairman* is used for officials of both sexes.

216 *The Secretary's Handbook*

A title referring to professional standing may precede the name. An addressee who has no professional title should be addressed as *Mr., Mrs.,* or *Miss* as the case may be.

President Henry Adler
Enville College

or

Dr. Henry Adler
President, Enville College

or

The President of Enville College

Dr. Janet Blake
Dean, School of Education

or

Miss Janet Blake
Dean, School of Education

or

Dean Janet Blake
School of Education

When an individual has a doctor's degree and is also entitled to the rank of professor, the address may read:

Professor John H. Livermore

or

Dr. John H. Livermore
Professor of Chemistry

or

Dr. John H. Livermore

In the case of a woman who has a doctor's degree, it is customary to write her address as follows:

Dr. Marian Baker

If she is also entitled to the rank of professor, the address should read:

Dr. Marian Baker
Professor of Fine Arts

or

Professor Marian Baker

Two titles meaning the same thing should not be used together:

> Right: Dr. Alfred Young
> Right: Alfred Young, M.D.
> Wrong: Dr. Alfred Young, M.D.

> Right: Mr. Harvey Curtis
> Right: Harvey Curtis, Esq.
> Wrong: Mr. Harvey Curtis, Esq.

An attorney is usually addressed as

> Stanley Willis, Esq.
>
> *or*
>
> Stanley Willis, Attorney
>
> *or*
>
> Mr. Stanley Willis
> Attorney at Law

In England, the title *Mr.* is not used in addressing barristers. *Esq.* following the name is the accepted form. (*See* p. 313.)

The title *Miss,* rather than *Mrs.,* is used in addressing a woman if one is uncertain what the correct title should be.

Salutation

Correct forms for business and professional letters:

Dear Sir: (*Dear Sirs* not used in America)
Dear Madam: (*Dear Madam President:*)
Gentlemen:
Mesdames or *Ladies:*
My dear Mrs. Bryan: (formal American, informal British usage)
Dear Mr. Bryan: (informal American, formal British usage)
Ladies and Gentlemen: (Committees or organizations composed of men and women).

For forms for official letters see pp. 287–331.

Gentlemen

Use this salutation when addressing a board, a committee, or a firm composed of men or of men and women or if uncertain whether the organization includes women.

Mesdames or *Ladies*

Use this salutation when addressing a board, a committee, or a firm composed exclusively of women.

BUSINESS USAGE

Whenever an individual name of a correspondent is known to the writer, it should be used rather than the title alone.

Mr. Allan Douglas, Manager

or

Mr. Allan Douglas
Manager, Lakewood Hotel

If the individual name of a correspondent is not known to the writer, he should be addressed by the correct title of the position he holds, as *chairman, director, registrar, secretary,* etc.

Addressing organizations when an individual name is not used

Associations, clubs, and societies

Address:	The Secretary Lakewood Men's Club
Salutation:	Dear Sir:
	or
Address:	The Lakewood Men's Club
Salutation:	Gentlemen:
Address:	The Secretary Lakewood Women's Club
Salutation:	Dear Madam:
	or
Address:	The Lakewood Women's Club
Salutation:	Mesdames:
	or
	Ladies:
Address:	The Lakewood Parents Association
Salutation:	Ladies and Gentlemen:
	or
	Mesdames and Gentlemen:

Address: The Lakewood Improvement Society
Salutation: Gentlemen:
                               or
                            Ladies and Gentlemen:
                               or
                            Mesdames and Gentlemen:

Boards, bureaus, departments, offices

Address: President, Board of Medical Examiners
Salutation: Dear Sir:
                               or
Address: Board of Medical Examiners
Salutation: Gentlemen:

Address: Martha Blakelock Travel Bureau
Salutation: Gentlemen:

Address: Chief, Bureau of Ordnance
Salutation: Dear Sir:
                               or
Address: Bureau of Ordnance
Salutation: Gentlemen:

Address: Chief, Police Department
Salutation: Dear Sir:
                               or
Address: Lakewood Police Department
Salutation: Gentlemen:

Address: The Postmaster
                            Lakewood Post Office
Salutation: Dear Sir:

Committees

Address: The Chairman, Building Committee
                            Lakewood Men's Club
Salutation: Dear Sir:

Address: The Building Committee
                            Lakewood Men's Club
Salutation: Gentlemen:

Address:	The Chairman, Membership Committee
	Lakewood Women's Club
Salutation:	Dear Madam:
Address:	Membership Committee
	Lakewood Women's Club
Salutation:	Mesdames:

or

Ladies:

Address:	The Program Committee
	Lakewood Community Center
Salutation:	Gentlemen:

or

Mesdames and Gentlemen:

or

Ladies and Gentlemen:

Companies

Address:	James Stone (company name)
Salutation:	Gentlemen:
Address:	Martha Wentworth (company name)
Salutation:	Gentlemen:
Address:	Messrs. Kerr and Bates (a professional partnership—as, a firm of architects or lawyers)
Salutation:	Gentlemen:
Address:	Kerr and Bates (a company or corporation name that has lost its personal significance)
Salutation:	Gentlemen:
Address:	Kerr and Bates (a professional partnership composed of women)
Salutation:	Mesdames:

or

Ladies:

| Address: | N. R. Brockman & Company |
| Salutation: | Gentlemen: |

Address:	Barbara's Dress Shop (company name)
Salutation:	Gentlemen:
Address:	Barbara's Dress Shop (firm composed of women)
Salutation:	Mesdames:

or

Ladies:

ADDRESSING PRIVATE INDIVIDUALS

Since the street, city, and state are understood to follow the name, these are omitted except in the first example; and since the same complimentary close may be used in letters to each of the following individuals, it will not be repeated. The wording of the salutations and the complimentary closes in the first example become progressively less formal.

Addressing one person

A man

Address:
Mr. Robert F. Crowell
1415 Grove Terrace
Winter Park, Florida

or

Mr. Robert F. Crowell
1415 Grove Terrace
Winter Park, Florida

Salutation:
Dear Sir:

or

Dear Mr. Crowell:

Complimentary Close:
Very truly yours,
Yours sincerely,

An unmarried woman

Address:
Salutation:
Miss Charlotte Phillips
Dear Madam:

or

Dear Miss Phillips:

A married woman

Address:
        Mrs. Harry Webster

        or

        Mrs. Edna Webster (the form generally used for a married woman separated from her husband)

Salutation:
        Dear Madam:

        or

        Dear Mrs. Webster:

Addressing more than one person

In certain instances it is preferable to address only one of the persons, indicating in the opening paragraph that the letter is also intended for the others.   *Style Manual*

Two or more men

Address:
        Messrs. Brown and Holt

        or

        Mr. Jerome Brown
        Mr. Alfred Holt

Salutation:
        Gentlemen:

        or

        Dear Mr. Brown and Mr. Holt:

Two or more men of the same name

Address:
        Messrs. Hugh and Carl Condon

        or

        The Messrs. Condon

Salutation:
        Gentlemen:

Two or more unmarried women

Address:
        The Misses Banks and Towne

        or

        Miss Laura Banks
        Miss Frances Towne

Salutation: Ladies:
                                       or
                               Mesdames:
                                       or
                               Dear Misses Banks and Towne:
                                       or
                               Dear Miss Banks and Miss Towne:

Two or more women

  Address: Mrs. Arthur Benson
                               Mrs. William Lee
                               Miss Mary Parker

  Salutation: Ladies:
                                       or
                               Mesdames

Correct order in the salutation

When the names of both men and women occur in the inside address, the individual whose name appears first should be addressed first in the salutation.

Men and women

  Address: Mr. Paul Betts
                               Mr. Horace Betts
                               Miss Janet Betts

  Salutation: Gentlemen and Dear Madam:

  Address: Miss Janet Betts
                               Mr. Horace Betts
                               Mr. Paul Betts

  Salutation: Dear Madam and Gentlemen:

  Address: Miss Janet Betts
                               Miss Irene Betts
                               Mr. Paul Betts

  Salutation: Mesdames and Dear Sir:
                                       or
                               Ladies and Dear Sir:

Address: Mr. Paul Betts
                                  Mrs. Paul Betts

Salutation: Dear Sir and Madam:
                                           or
                                  Dear Mr. and Mrs. Betts:

Punctuation of salutation

When open punctuation is used in the heading and in the inside address, either closed or open punctuation may be used after the salutation; but when closed punctuation is used in the heading, it should also be used after the salutation. (*See* pp. 41–43.)

The attention line

When the writer wishes to bring his letter to the attention of a certain official, he may do so by using the attention line. This may be written above the salutation, as it usually is in block form, or to the right of the salutation on the same line or beneath it. The name and the official position of the correspondent may follow the words, *Attention* or *Attention of;* but, if this would make the line too long, *Attention* may be omitted and the official position may be written below the name.

Placement of the attention line:

(1)

Hollywood Sportswear Corp.
1041 North Highland Avenue
Hollywood 38, California

Attention of Mr. John Doe

Gentlemen:

(2)

John Wanamaker (a company name)
Cross County Center
Yonkers, New York

Gentlemen: Attention: Miss Helen M. Blank
                                  Glove Department

(3)

The Junior Dress Shoppe
  Bay Street
    Beaufort, S.C.

Ladies: Mrs. Christopher Lawson, Manager

                    (4)

Ryan & O'Brien
  Gibbs Building
    Sarasota, Florida

Gentlemen:

                Mr. Alexander Thompson
                Sales Promotion Manager

                    (5)

The Charlotte Observer
Charlotte
North Carolina

Gentlemen:

Attention of Mr. J. H. Blank

The reference line

A reference line, containing a file number or a request that the correspondent in his answer refer to a particular person or department, is used by many organizations. Such a line should be included in the correspondent's answer.

Placement of reference line

Such a line may be placed below the date on the right, above the inside address on the left-hand margin, on a line with the salutation, or centered two lines below the salutation.

                    (1)
                [Letterhead]
                                January 2, 19___
                                File B-1728

                    (2)
                [Letterhead]
                                July 25, 19___

File C-4923
Inside address

(3)

Miss Ethel Caryl
Adelaide Avenue
Barrington, R.I.

Dear Madam: In replying, please refer to Credit Dept.

(4)

Mrs. Frank F. Gibney
  48 Green Village Road
    Madison, New Jersey

Dear Mrs. Gibney:

Your reference: N. F. Good (3–10)

The subject line

The subject line, which states briefly the topic of the letter, may be centered above or below the salutation or on a line with the salutation.

(1)

Mr. Albert Horton
P.O. Box 22
Lobeco, S.C.

The Electric Auto-Lite Company

Dear Mr. Horton:

(2)

Dr. H. J. Blank
Personnel Department
Exville College
St. Petersburg, Florida

Dear Sir: Retirement Pension

(3)

The White Insurance Company
19 West 44 Street
New York 18, N.Y.

Gentlemen:

Policy 10 954 654

Placement for data when file number, attention line, and subject line are all used may be arranged as follows:

[Letterhead]

[Date]
File G322

Ideal Electrical Company
4250 Sycamore Street
Chicago 7, Illinois

Attention: Mr. Peter Blank

Gentlemen:

Order 198675

The Body of the Letter

Block or indented form

The body of the letter may be written in indented or in block form. If the inside address is indented, the body of the letter should also be written in indented form, that is, with each paragraph beginning five spaces, or as preferred by some secretaries ten spaces, from the left-hand margin. If the inside address follows block style, the body of the letter may be either block or indented form. If block form is used, the first line of each paragraph should begin at the left-hand margin, single spacing should be used within paragraphs, double spacing between paragraphs.

Continuation pages

When a letter exceeds one page, blank pages on which letterhead does not appear or appears in abbreviated form are used. Each new page should be numbered in the center half an inch from the top or half an inch from the bottom. At the top of each continuation page with a margin to coincide with the left-hand margin of page one, the name or initials of the addressee should occur; to coincide with the right-hand margin of page one, the date should be written.

Complimentary close

The placement of the complimentary close depends somewhat on the length of the signature. It should begin to the right of the vertical center and not extend beyond the right-hand margin. It should be placed at least two spaces below the last line of the letter and in a short letter it may be placed even four spaces below the message to make an attractive letter picture.

The selection of the complimentary close depends on the nature and the tone of the letter. The following examples given here are in order of decreasing formality.

> Respectfully yours,
> Very truly yours,
> Yours very truly,
> Sincerely yours,

The complimentary close should not be preceded by a participial phrase, as, *Hoping to hear from you soon.* Punctuation following a complimentary close depends on punctuation following the salutation. If punctuation is omitted there, it should also be omitted after the complimentary close.

Signatures

Placement of signatures should correspond to the style of the heading or of the inside address.

CONTENT OF BUSINESS SIGNATURES

The signature may consist of two, three, or four lines, according to the wish of the writer or the policy of the organization. It is generally understood that the name on the first line indicates responsibility for the contents of the letter. Hence signatures of business letters usually occupy four lines, as follows:

1. typewritten name of organization
2. actual signature of writer
3. typewritten name of writer
4. typewritten official position or rank in the organization

The following illustrate correct forms of signatures:

Two-line signatures

Yours very truly,
Arlington Machine Company
William Brown (written)

Yours very truly,
William Brown, Manager
William Brown (written)

Three-line signatures

Yours very truly,
National Soap Company
John B. Williams (written)
John B. Williams, Advertising Manager

Yours very truly,
John B. Williams (written)
John B. Williams, Advertising Manager
National Soap Company

Four-line signatures

Yours very truly,
American Farms Company
Henry A. Taylor (written)
Henry A. Taylor
Credit Manager

Yours very truly,
Henry A. Taylor (written)
Henry A. Taylor
Credit Manager
American Farms Company

SIGNATURES FOR PRIVATE INDIVIDUALS

John F. Whitman
John Francis Whitman
J. F. Whitman rather than J. Whitman

Such titles as *Dr., Rev., Prof.,* should not precede signatures nor should such degrees as B.A., M.D., LL.D., follow them.

An unmarried woman should not sign herself as *Miss* Elizabeth Jones, but should place *Miss* in parentheses before her name if she thinks it necessary.

A married woman must sign her own name, as, *Vera C. Martini.* This may be preceded by *Mrs.* in parentheses or by her married name written in parentheses below the signature.

(Mrs.) Vera C. Martini

or

Vera C. Martini
(Mrs. Herbert Martini)

A widow may sign her name exactly as she did before the death of her husband.

It should be remembered in either case *Jane Morrison Ross* is her *name; Mrs. Herbert Ross* is her *title*. At present it is customary for a widow to retain her husband's title.

Some professional women prefer to keep their maiden names. In this, they follow the example of Lucy Stone, who exercised her right to use her maiden name. In such a case, *Mrs. Jane Morrison Ross* would sign her name *Jane Morrison*.

If for any reason, she should wish to indicate her married title, the signature would read as follows:

Jane Morrison

(Mrs. Herbert Ross)

A woman who is divorced has the choice of assuming her maiden name with or without *Mrs.;* as, *(Miss) Jane Morrison* or *(Mrs.) Jane Morrison*.

On the other hand, she may retain her husband's surname with *Miss* or *Mrs.;* as, *(Miss) Jane Ross* or *(Mrs.) Jane Ross*. Socially she is usually known as *Mrs. Morrison Ross*. She must not use her former title; as, *Mrs. Herbert Ross*.

On checks, a married woman usually signs her own name, not her title; as, *Jane Ross*.

In endorsing checks or signing stock certificates or other legal papers a woman should be careful to sign as the name appears in the document.

In wills and deeds, a married woman should sign her name, not her title; as, *Jane Ross,* not *Mrs. Herbert Ross*.

Usually on formal programs and announcements, a married woman prefers to use her title; as, *Mrs. Herbert Ross*.

On hotel registers she may sign as she wishes; as, *Jane Ross,* or *Mrs. Jane Ross* or the more usual form *Mrs. Herbert Ross*.

The unmarried woman may sign a hotel register with or without her title; as, *Jane Morrison* or *Miss Jane Morrison*.

Sometimes it is desirable for women in signing business or professional letters to indicate the writer's official position. In such cases after the signature the title may be written as follows:

Mary Dawson
Superintendent

or

Mary Dawson, Superintendent

Margaret Davis
President

For a private secretary

Jessie MacFarlane
Secretary to Mrs. Borden

Jessie MacFarlane
Secretary to Mr. James Brown

When the secretary signs her chief's name to a letter, she may
add her own initials or she may sign her own name adding below
it *for* with the chief's name.

Henry Newcomb
J. MacF.

or

Jessie MacFarlane

for

Henry Newcomb

Additional Data

Additional data, such as the initials of the dictator and of the
typist, are usually placed at the lower left-hand margin with a
colon between them: (*See also* p. 232.)

FCS:RG   HEA:C

When enclosures are made in the letter, that fact should be noted
in the lower left-hand corner; as, *Encl.* or *Enclosures*.

Correct Signatures for Letters Signed by Officials

Very truly yours,

[signature]

President

HKT
MW

Very sincerely yours

[signature: Leon Wieder]

Vice-President

M a y
Fourth

Sincerely yours

[signature: Katharine C. Reiley]

Katharine C. Reiley
Associate Director

KOR:C

FRED F. FRENCH COMPANIES

[signature: Fred F. French]

CHAIRMAN OF THE
BOARDS OF DIRECTORS

Sincerely yours,

[signature: Cameron Beck]

Personnel Director

CB
HEA

Sincerely yours,

[signature: Molly Blumenthal]

Secretary to Mrs. Oakley

Very truly yours,

[signature: A. Swoboda]

A. SWOBODA
TRAVEL DEPARTMENT

Letter Pictures

[Letterhead]

January 22, 19___

_____,

_____,

_____.

Gentlemen:

_____
_____
_____.

_____
_____
_____
_____
_____
_____
_____
_____
_____
_____.

_____
_____
_____
_____
_____.

Very truly yours,

_____

_____Department

___/___

[*Letterhead*]

January 18, 19___

Dear Sir:

_____
_____.

_____
_____
_____
_____
_____
_____.

_____
_____
_____
_____
_____.

_____
_____
_____.

Very truly yours,

_____

By:

_____
_____
_____

____:____

[*Letterhead*]

January 18, 19___

_____
_____
_____

Gentlemen

_____
_____
_____.

_____
_____
_____
_____
_____
_____
_____
_____.

_____
_____
_____
_____.

_____
_____.

Very truly yours

_____

By:

____:____

[*Letterhead*]

January 18, 19___

_____

_____

_____

Gentlemen:

_____

_____

_____

_____.

_____

_____

_____

_____

_____

_____

_____

_____

_____.

_____

_____

_____

_____.

_____

_____

Very truly yours,

_____

By:

___:___

Envelope Pictures

Attention:_____

ILLUSTRATIONS OF VARIOUS TYPES OF LETTERS

Order Letters

(1)

394 Maple Street
Woodsville, N. H.
December 10, 19___

Mark Cross
707 Fifth Avenue
New York 22, N. Y.

Gentlemen:

Will you please send me by parcel post the articles listed below. As the merchandise is for Christmas presents, I shall appreciate your prompt attention to my order.

1 Globe Trotter French purse, tax included	$13.75
1 sewing caddie in calfskin	8.50
1 bridge set in tan hide case	8.50
	$30.75

You will find enclosed my check for $30.75.

Yours very truly,
Mildred K. Bentley

(2)

[*Letterhead*]

June 1, 19___

Smith, Perkins and Company
15 East Avenue
Rochester, New York

Gentlemen:

In confirmation of our discussion this morning in regard to furniture for our new offices, I am sending you the order in detail. Please fill it by October 10.

8667	12	mahogany desks wood top 62″ x 34″ standard drawer subdivision	@ 675	$8,100.00
		additional for leather top	@ 35	420.00

| 8664 | 24 | mahogany arm chairs covered in top grain leather color to be determined | @ 125 | 3,000.00 |

Board Room

8666	1	mahogany board table 4' x 12' long two pedestal cored & veneered top cross-banded edge, not moulded		1,000.00
8665	2	mahogany console tables 48" x 30" rounded front corners cored & veneered top used in connection with large board table with concealed slides to support supplementary leaves	@ 400	800.00
8663	24	mahogany arm chairs top grain leather	@ 140	3,360.00

Payment will be made upon delivery and installation of the order.

Yours very truly,
James Allison

(3)
[Letterhead]

January 5, 19___

Flynn and McNamara
500 Devonshire Street
Boston, Mass.

Gentlemen:

Please deliver as soon as possible the following order for my office and charge to my account:

4 standard swivel chairs, Model 4-A @ $60	$240
6 chairs, Model 5 @ $45	270
1 bench, Model 16	100
4 steel correspondence files, Style 543 @ $75	300
2 tables, Style 30 @ $100	200
2 desks, Model 3, medium size @ $125	250
2 desks, Model 3-A, medium size @ $110	220
Total	$1,580

All the furniture, including the files, must be dark mahogany finish.

Yours very truly,
J. K. Strauss

Letters of Acknowledgment

(1)

We acknowledge with thanks your request for the following articles:

1 pr. rubber boots, size 6, price $19.95	$19.95
2 khaki cotton shirts, size 34, price $7.95	15.90
2 prs. gray worsted socks, size 9, price $3.50	7.00
	$42.85

We shall attend to this order, making sure that it will reach you before May 16. We notice, however, that you have omitted to say whether you require knee length or full length rubber boots. We have both kinds at $19.95 a pair, and we are desirous not to make a mistake in filling your order. If you will let us know at once which kind you wish to purchase, we shall forward the articles to you without delay.

(2)

The Community Center acknowledges with genuine appreciation your contribution of Three Dollars to the work of the organization for the year.

(3)

Thank you for your order of May 2. We are sending out the goods as you instructed and hope they will reach you safely.

If we can serve you further, we shall be glad to do so.

(4)

We thank you for your order of May 4. We have already made shipment by parcel post, C.O.D., of the following, which is our order No. 8235:

1 dozen best quality ladies' plain white linen handkerchiefs	$9.00
6 pairs nylon hose, medium beige, size 8½	9.00
1 dozen spools white Coats & Clark's ONT Size 50 best 6/C cotton thread	1.20
	$19.20

We hope that these goods will so please you in every detail that we shall continue to receive your orders and that we may number you among our thousands of steadily satisfied customers. We assure you of our constant personal attention and of our steadfast desire to please you.

(5)

Miss Marie Haines,
Harmon Drive,
Larchmont, New York.

Dear Madam:

Thank you for your check for $500, which we received from Miss Hathaway and which we have put to work immediately in a guaranteed first mortgage certificate maturing January 1, 1965.

As we explained to Miss Hathaway and your sister, we do not happen to have today any $500 certificate of an earlier maturity and so we have followed their suggestion in sending you this one. We firmly believe that the interest rate will drop and are recommending to all of our clients that they take as long maturities as possible, in order that they may take advantage of the present 6% guaranteed rate.

Our interest checks will be mailed to you and the certificate will be forwarded to you within ten days.

We are glad of this opportunity of investing for you. We know you will be greatly pleased with your investment and hope to have the pleasure of serving you again soon.

Yours very truly,
Florence Tyler

(6)

We acknowledge with thanks your order No. 77 for material covered by our proposal of June 30. This order has been given our prompt attention and has been entered by wire with the request that this shipment be rushed as much as possible.

Your instructions have been carefully noted. As your order does not give us any special routing or delivering railroad, we shall leave this to the factory unless you instruct us otherwise.

As soon as we receive a definite shipping date for the material on order with us, we shall write you.

(7)

Your remittance of $67.68 is acknowledged with thanks and was applied to your account with discount of $4.32.

We are enclosing our receipted statement indicating credit for the three pairs of hose which, we regret, proved unsatisfactory.

Your patronage is greatly appreciated. When we are again favored, we hope to serve you in a manner to insure your pleasure.

(8)

We acknowledge receipt of your check for $10 which has been credited to your Partial Payment account.

You are correct in your surmise that this is the fourth payment. Your account shows a credit balance, including this payment, of $40 towards the purchase of a $100 bond.

Thank you for this remittance.

(9)

We thank you for your order for six teacups and saucers in blue Old English Scenes, four supper plates, six bread and butter plates, six sauce dishes, and one small platter 10 or 12 inches.

We have ordered the six teacups and saucers desired and will ship the complete order January 20. We hope this will be satisfactory.

(10)

Thank you for your order for stationery like your sample. We hope to send it about January 28. As the paper comes 100 sheets for $3.40, we have ordered 100 sheets. Envelopes are extra.

We have no card with samples of lettering to send you. We are enclosing for your consideration samples of paper which may be had at $6.60 for 48 sheets and envelopes, including the die and stamping.

We look forward to further opportunities of serving you.

(11)

Your Sheared Raccoon Coat sent to us for storage has been placed in our vaults. It was carefully examined when received, and we are taking the liberty of submitting an estimate for work we believe would improve its condition and appearance.

#57684 Sheared Raccoon Coat—To clean fur and lining	$15.00
To repair worn edges of fronts and cuffs	20.00

If you wish us to proceed according to this estimate, kindly sign below and return this letter. Should you decide to have only part of the work done, we should be glad to have that indicated and we shall then proceed or give you a new estimate, as you may direct.

Letters Offering Charge Accounts

(1)

We've just finished the greatest year in the history of this business
. . . established more than a century ago . . . greatest not only in
volume of sales but greatest in the number of new friends we have
made—customers who have come to know our high standard of Values
and Service.

In the conduct of this business, it will be our earnest endeavor to
surpass our former achievements, both in Values and Service and in
timely offerings of dependable merchandise and styles.

We believe this is your kind of store and that you will enjoy shopping
here. We offer "More than 100 years of Service" not as an appeal to
sentiment but as proof of integrity and stability.

We should like to feel that you are going to become a regular patron
of our store and, to make your shopping easier, desire to extend to you
the convenience of a Charge Account. A signature card is enclosed for
your convenience.

(2)

Appreciation of the many conveniences of a charge account has
grown with the years, and it is to increase the pleasure of your shopping
that we offer you a charge account.

In your case, we will dispense with the usual formalities—just say
"Charge it" when sending your next purchase home, and an account
will be opened in your name. This will apply whether you purchase in
person, by mail, or by phone.

(3)

It is our endeavor to understand the desires of our customers and
to keep up with important style centers at home and abroad. From the
knowledge these studies give, we try to offer at fair prices appropriate
assortments of carefully chosen merchandise. We should like very
much to have you visit our store often because we believe we can take
good care of most of your wants.

Many of our friends feel so much at home that they frequently give
us helpful criticism about the goods we offer and the service we render.
Often they suggest new lines of merchandise and new methods of presenting them. If you would take such interest in us, we believe it would
make the task of shopping a real pleasure.

You may regard a charge account as a matter of convenience. If so,
we shall be glad to open one. No formality is required. When you make
purchases, simply tell the salesperson to charge them, and they will be
delivered to you without any further formality. We should appreciate
the return of the enclosed card.

Letters Welcoming Charge Account Customers

(1)

We hope your new account here will be both a pleasure and a convenience to you.

If you do not find in our large collections just what you want, we shall be glad to make it for you. We especially pride ourselves on our custom service.

(2)

We were pleased to learn that you used your new account last month.

Won't you come in often and give us an opportunity of proving to you how glad we are to have you for a customer?

(3)

A charge account has been opened for you, as requested, and is now available for purchases at your convenience.

Bills rendered at the first of each month are due and payable in the early part of the month following date of purchase.

We hope you will enjoy our service, which we shall endeavor to make pleasing and helpful.

(4)

It is a privilege to include you among our charge patrons.

Every possible courtesy and service will be extended to you in appreciation of your patronage.

(5)

When you opened your account with us last month, you probably felt it would save time and make shopping easier.

We should like to be sure that we are doing everything possible to carry out your wishes.

Won't you let us show you how pleased we always are to be of service to you?

Letters Refusing Charge Accounts

(1)

We are sorry to say that the data at our command are not sufficient to justify us in opening the account you wish.

It is sometimes difficult to determine just what measure of financial responsibility our friends have, and when such is the case, we are obliged to appeal to them for additional information.

If you will be good enough to call or drop us a line, we shall be glad to go into the matter further.

(2)

To our regret, we do not see our way clear, at the present time, to open a charge account for you in compliance with your recent request. We shall be very happy, however, to offer you our facilities, in the way of store service, in other directions as usual.

We appreciate your kind interest in making this inquiry.

(3)

We are sorry not to be able to pass favorably upon your application for an account.

You will doubtless appreciate that a fair knowledge must be had of a customer's responsibility and bill-paying habits, and unfortunately the data of this nature at our command are very limited.

Although we cannot be of service with a charge account, we shall always take pleasure in serving you and hope to have your permission to send your recent purchases on our regular cash terms.

(4)

In answer to your recent application for a charge account, we are sorry to say that we have been unable to secure from the usual business sources the information necessary for the establishment of an account.

We therefore regret that we shall be unable to comply with your request at this time, unless additional business or bank references are submitted, in which case we shall be pleased to give the matter further consideration.

Letters Concerning Unused Charge Accounts

(1)

As you know, your name was placed on our list of charge customers some time ago. Yet we have no record of your having used your account.

Are we to blame in any way?

We'd appreciate a frank reply and are enclosing a stamped envelope for your convenience.

Meanwhile you may be interested in glancing through the enclosed announcement of the new spring stocks now in our stores.

(2)

We have had no answer to the letter we sent you two weeks ago asking what we could do to renew your patronage with us.

As the letter has not been returned to us, we assume it has reached you.

We should like to make good whatever is wrong and hope that you will let us know how we can do so either by dropping us a line or, better still, by coming in and talking it over with us.

(3)

We like to keep in close touch with our charge customers. We notice that we have not had the pleasure of serving you for some time.

Your good-will and patronage are very highly valued, and if our service or merchandise has fallen short of the high standards we try to maintain, we shall appreciate your bringing it to our attention.

We shall be very grateful for any criticism that you may have to make.

Fund-Raising Letters

(1)

Those of us in motion pictures, on the stage and in radio are familiar with the typical story of a physically handicapped person. Almost inevitably the script has a "happy ending." But in real life, for many of the ten million crippled men and women in America today, there can be no "happy ending" without advice, vocational guidance and employment.

I have accepted the chairmanship of the special gifts committee for Federation of the Handicapped because in my frequent trips from Hollywood, I have come to know how Federation has helped and is helping thousands of these handicapped men and women become well-adjusted, self-supporting citizens.

An ever-increasing number need help desperately. But today Federation's shops and classes are filled to capacity. Without additional funds, it will be forced to close its doors to those who come seeking independence.

Six hundred dollars per year is the cost of training a handicapped person. Will you help pay for his training today so he can pay his own way tomorrow?

I know that your gift will be multiplied a thousand-fold in the assistance it gives to a handicapped person. Won't you send—today—the largest contribution you can?

(2)

(Follow-up letter)

Many of my associates in "show business" have already helped Federation of the Handicapped generously. The response was personally gratifying, as I happen to know what an uncommonly good job this very unusual organization is doing. It is composed of physically disabled men and women who work for the betterment of all who are handicapped orthopedically.

This work includes training at a self-supporting wage where useful merchandise is manufactured and sold nationally through retail stores. There are also opportunities for physical improvement, such as exercise, massage, walking and speech lessons.

Until recently no disabled person willing to try was ever turned away. In the past few months a shortage of funds has made it necessary for them to deprive hundreds of their services.

Please help them in this very worth-while work by sending your contribution today. It is urgently needed.

(3)

My specialty is writing music not letters. I'm used to drawing musical notes, not pictures. But still this is the way it seems to me.

This is the kind of summer I had as a kid—no place to cool off—no place to play—nothing to look forward to all day long but hot city streets. Hundreds of kids in New York City are facing that kind of summer.

If we—you and I—help Forest House, the kids will be able to jam Morris Playfield daily as they did last year for basketball, shuffleboard, chess, checkers, tournaments, arts and crafts, puppet shows and other activities dear to youngsters. The boys and girls most urgently in need of sunshine, country air, nourishing food and rest will be sent to camp. And for the very small fry whose mothers work all day there will be the Forest House Day Camp.

Forest House needs $5000 to do this job—only $5.15 a child!

  $2250 to send kids to camp
  $1200 to buy athletic and game equipment for the playground
  $1550 for rest period cots, hot lunches, bus trips to beaches

How about providing for 10 youngsters—or 5—or even one? Confidentially, I think once you've put your check in the enclosed envelope, you'll have a better summer yourself!

(4)

It's kind people like you—

that respond to need and manage—even in these hard days—to keep open the doors of New York's only free, non-sectarian Home for elderly gentlewomen.

There really isn't any other way to support this Home but by voluntary contributions and legacies, for I think you feel, as I do, it's sound to provide a place that requires neither entrance nor maintenance fees and extends help without regard to nationality or creed.

If you've had the impression that Peabody is heavily endowed, let me tell you it's all wrong. Because this is the only Home like it around here, free to its gallant women, we must beg that you'll keep it operating.

You understand, of course, that when we accept the elderly gentlewomen who come to Peabody we assure them of life care. That's as it should be. And I'm sure you're glad, too, that we've been far-sighted enough to be the first Home to adopt the Non-Resident Aid plan.

But I confess I'm concerned right now about our growing responsibility—it's a large one—with 50 residents and 12 non-residents dependent upon us and we dependent upon you, not to mention others anxiously awaiting acceptance.

So, this is my SOS to YOU—

please let me count on your support. Peabody's doors must continue to welcome deserving and needy women. They will if friends will help —and we need you, too.

Claim Letters

(1)

Letter of claim written by a secretary

17 East Main Street
Rochester, N. Y.
April 25, 19___

The Brown Paper Company
154 West 14th Street
New York City

Gentlemen

On Friday, April 22, Mr. Glendenning received from your firm ten dozen boxes of Grade A paper which are being returned immediately, as the quality is far below the Brown standard that we have learned to expect.

There are two noticeable errors in the engraving, which I have checked on the sheet enclosed for your inspection. One of these is the spelling of Mr. Glendenning's name.

Will you please send us a correct shipment as soon as possible? The previous order was as follows:

10 dozen boxes Grade A paper, size 8 x 10.

Very truly yours
Pearl J. Russell
Secretary to Mr. Glendenning

(2)

411 West 116 Street
New York City
May 16, 19___

Claim Department
Pennsylvania Railroad Company
Pittsburgh, Pa.

Gentlemen:

I wish to present a claim for $167.00 to cover the loss of a suitcase checked on a passenger ticket from Pittsburgh to New York on May 10.

I surrendered the suitcase in the baggage room of the Pennsylvania Station at Pittsburgh about 11:00 p.m. on May 10 to be checked to New York. I left on train No. 6 at 11:45 the same evening.

When I arrived in New York the following morning and presented myself at the baggage room, my suitcase was missing. I was told that it might come on a later train, but since that time, five days ago, I have made a daily call at the baggage room of the New York station, but have not yet obtained my bag. The check number which I hold is 8543A.

The contents of the suitcase are valued as follows:

1 Dacron and 1 Orlon dress	$80.00
1 pair pumps	18.00
2 pairs of hose	2.50
lingerie	20.00
1 negligee	15.00
toilet articles	6.00
1 pair of gloves	3.50
2 books	7.00
1 traveling clock	15.00
	$167.00

I shall gladly give you any additional information which you may need to establish the authenticity of my claim or to help you in tracing the lost baggage. If it cannot be found within a few days, I shall expect a settlement in full for my claim.

Very truly yours,
Rose Wolcott

Adjustment Letters

(1)

We are very sorry indeed that you are not pleased with the dress we made for you, and we can well appreciate your disappointment.

It sometimes happens that a made-to-order garment does not look the same made up as it does in a picture, and that the goods do not appear as they did in the piece. The same thing might happen, however, if you had a dress made in your own home by a dressmaker.

Since you yourself chose the material and style of the garment and have no complaint to make about the fit and workmanship, we must regretfully say that we cannot take back the dress. When you ordered it, we were careful to tell you that we never take back made-to-order clothing. When a garment is made to fit one person, we cannot sell it to anyone else, and thus your dress would be a total loss to us.

You will understand our position and realize we regret to make this decision.

(2)

We are sorry to know from your letter of May 12 that the radio which you ordered as a birthday gift for your husband arrived with the cabinet so badly marred that you cannot accept it.

As the Long Island Railroad Company gave us a receipt acknowledging that the radio was satisfactorily crated and in good condition when it was received, it must have been damaged in transit. Although the responsibility is really now up to the railroad company, we realize what must have been your disappointment when you found that the gift you purchased for your husband was not in good condition for his birthday. We are, therefore, sending you at once another cabinet exactly like the one you originally ordered.

If you will ask the express company to make a special delivery as soon as the radio arrives at the station, we hope that you may still receive it in time for your husband's birthday.

Please leave the damaged radio with the railroad company, and we shall ourselves enter a claim for it. You will then have no further trouble.

We thank you for notifying us promptly. We want you to know our first desire is that you should receive your order promptly in perfect condition.

(3)

In going over your account, we find that an error was made by us in connection with the tabulation of the statement rendered you on June 1. We are enclosing the corrected statement, which we request that you substitute for the previous one.

We regret the error and trust this did not inconvenience you in any way.

(4)

We regret the delay that occurred in the delivery of the chair you purchased from us. We expect to deliver this merchandise to you either today or tomorrow.

We are sorry for the annoyance and inconvenience you may have been caused by this delay.

(5)

Through an oversight, we neglected to give your account credit for your check for $16.35.

We trust you will pardon this error. We are very sorry for any annoyance our statement of January 10 may have caused you.

(6)

Upon receipt of your letter of December 22 regarding the gown sent to Miss Mary Owen, we checked our records, found that the package had been returned to us for a better address, and reshipped the merchandise to Miss Owen at 34 West 69th Street.

May we have further opportunities of serving you?

Letters of appreciation for adjustments made

(1)

Thank you for your corrected bill for the month of September. Your explanation of the error, caused by a similarity in the names of the accounts, makes it entirely excusable.

The promptness with which you rectified this matter is indeed appreciated; and now, that it has been adjusted to my entire satisfaction, I am enclosing my check for $141.50, the amount due.

(2)

I wish to thank you for your courtesy in replacing the silk hose which I recently returned to you.

This is particularly generous of you, as there is no guarantee given with silk hose. It was hardly to be expected, however, that hose of this quality should go to pieces during the first wearing. I hope I shall be more fortunate with the second pair.

In the meantime, please accept my grateful acknowledgment for your fairness and promptness in answering my complaint. The incident leaves me more convinced than ever of the expediency of trading with a firm that always stands back of its goods.

(3)

I wish to thank you for the courteous and prompt adjustment you made last week for the necklace I purchased and found imperfect.

It is pleasant to receive such considerate attention, which naturally tends to strengthen my confidence in your establishment. In the future, there will be no doubt in my mind as to the reliability and justice of your shop.

Collection Letters

(1)

May we remind you of your account for $985.25.

This amount is somewhat past due, so won't you oblige us with a check?

(2)

Did you overlook our recent reminder of your account?
The amount past due for your purchases is $985.25.
Your check at this time will be appreciated.

(3)

We must again remind you of the balance $985.25 open on your
account.
It is very much past due, and your check at this time would be
appreciated.

(4)

A balance of $490.25 is still outstanding on your account, and it
occurs to us that perhaps there are adjustments which should be made.
If so, we shall be glad to have you write us the facts, and we shall
give them immediate consideration.

(5)

The record of your account shows the outstanding balance for June
to be $11.92. Should you find any discrepancy, we shall appreciate
your informing us.
We thank you for an early remittance of this amount and enclose
an addressed envelope for your convenience when sending this.

(6)

In arranging for the settlement of outstanding accounts, it is our
custom, when they remain unpaid beyond the thirty-day period, to
send a reminder.
Our records show that your account, covering purchases made during
June and July amounting to $300.20, has not been paid. Will you
please send a check in settlement?

(7)

At this writing, our records indicate an overdue balance on your
account of $155.96.
Perhaps some necessary adjustment, of which we are not aware,
causes the delay. Should this be the case, please notify us.
Your courtesy in giving this matter your attention will be appreciated.

(8)

Previous communications having brought no response, we must
again remind you of your account for $985.25.
As this amount has been outstanding for some time, may we respectfully call attention to our terms of sale, bills due when rendered—the
first of each month.

Letters of Application

(1)

332 East 67th Street
New York City
April 19, 19___

The College of the City of New York
139th Street and Amsterdam Avenue
New York City

Gentlemen

I should like to apply for the position of stenographer, advertised in the *Times*. In answer to your requirements, I can offer the following qualifications:

Age	twenty-four years
Education	I have recently completed the two-year Secretarial Course at Columbia University and, consequently, have received thorough stenographic training.
Experience	Last summer I held a position as typist with the Indemnity Insurance Company of North America and also did some stenographic work.
Special Assets	I have studied stenography, typewriting, bookkeeping, accounting, economics, secretarial correspondence, French, and Spanish. In all of these, I have received marks of A or B. Mathematics has always been my best subject.
References	Mr. N. K. Bryant, Broadway and 116th St., New York City.
	Mr. David Grant, Indemnity Insurance Co. of North America, 122 William Street, New York City.
	Rev. Frank W. Crowder, 865 Madison Avenue, New York City.

I shall be glad to call at your office for a personal interview at any time that is convenient to you.

Very truly yours
Evelyn Gillis

(2)

Your advertisement in the *Times* appeals to me strongly, and I should like to apply for the position. As my experience has included work in the sales division of a manufacturing company and as I am a college graduate, I believe you will be interested in my application.

I am twenty-six years old, single, and a graduate of Barnard College. The various positions I have filled have made me an expert stenographer and an intelligent correspondent; they have required an understanding of office routine and the ability to assume responsibility and work on my own initiative. My experience, extending over a period of five years, has been as follows:

> Secretary to a department manager in the Columbia Graphophone Company
> Secretary to an executive in the Queens Chamber of Commerce
> Secretary to a sales manager of Pathex, Inc.

In my present position with Pathex, Inc., which I have held for the past fifteen months, I compose many of my own letters, supervise the keeping of sales records and the work of an office force.

To the position you wish to fill I can bring resourcefulness, the use of good judgment in matters for which I am responsible, the ability to meet people intelligently and to relieve you of details, as well as the desire to understand and be loyal to your interests.

I can furnish excellent personal and business references from those who know my work and who will be glad to tell you about it.

May I come to see you to explain my qualifications in greater detail?

(3)

Mr. J. A. Northcott, Associate Director of University Extension, writes me that Dr. Knox and you are looking for a secretary. Please consider me an applicant for the position.

My education has been obtained in private schools in Canada: Park School, London, Ontario, and Westbourne School, Toronto. Near the close of my last year of high school work my health became impaired, and I was obliged to give up my studies for some months. Afterwards my education was continued along general cultural lines—languages, music, nature, travel—rather than academic ones. The only degree I hold is that of Associate of the Canadian Guild of Organists.

The desire for a useful and busy life rather than an empty social one, coupled with a natural aptitude for practical things, led me to take a two-year course in English and French, bookkeeping, filing, typography, and secretarial correspondence.

As to my religious affiliations, I am a Presbyterian. I have had a little experience in social service work.

To me the prime requisite is not salary but congenial work in a cultural environment—such work as will interest me and to which I can bend all my energies.

I enclose a list of references.

If you desire any further information, I shall be pleased to furnish it. May I hear from you?

(4)

Miss Callan of the University Employment Bureau has referred me to you in the hope that you might have an opening in secretarial work. I am especially desirous of obtaining a position connected with a social service organization.

I am a graduate of Smith College from which I received my A.B. degree in June, 19___. My course there consisted of a liberal arts program—English Composition and Literature, and Sociology as my main subjects. Sociology gave me excellent theoretical knowledge. I am now taking at Columbia University the one-year secretarial course, which I shall complete this June. This course has given me a firm foundation for secretarial work. Among my subjects are typewriting, shorthand, secretarial correspondence, vocational psychology, and book-keeping, all of which provide good practical knowledge.

Although I have not had much actual secretarial work, I am familiar with business. My father is the proprietor of a large store, where I have worked for two summers as a clerk. This experience, I believe, has given me some knowledge of business principles and management helpful in any secretarial position.

The training I have received has provided a good background for the type of work I desire. Since the subject would be familiar to me and much of the business of "learning the ropes" would be done away with, I should need less supervision than the ordinary stenographer and could take up matters of an executive nature.

I am very much interested in social welfare, and I also enjoy secretarial work. I do not think I go too far in saying that you would find me willing and adaptable.

For references, I offer the following:

Professor H. E. Barnes
Smith College
Northampton, Mass.

Miss Z. Macdonald
Columbia University
New York City

I hope that I shall receive a favorable reply.

(5)

I wish to apply for the secretarial position which you advertise in the April 30th issue of the *Times*.

I am twenty-six years old and have had seven years of business experience. I am a graduate of Sharpsville High School, Sharpsville, Pa., and of Sharon College of Commerce, Sharon, Pa. I am at the present time taking the two-year secretarial course at Columbia University and expect to receive the Secretarial Certificate next August. I have had wide and varied office experience and am thoroughly familiar with business methods and routine. The details of my training and experience follow.

From April, 19___, until September, 19___, I acted as stenographer in a real estate and lumber office, the Charles S. Flower Lumber Company of Sharon, Pa. My work there included switchboard operating and assistant bookkeeping. While in this position I was also active as stenographic and clerical assistant when my employer organized the Dollar Title and Trust Company. I attended stockholders' meetings, took minutes, and wrote reports. In September, 19___, I left this position for one paying a higher salary at the freight office of the Erie Railroad Company at Farrell, Pa. There, my work consisted mainly of stenography and abstract typing.

In June, 19___, I was employed in the office of the National Malleable and Steel Castings Company at Sharon, where I was trained in the work of all departments so that I was ready to step instantly into the routine work of any absent clerk or stenographer and keep the wheels of his department running smoothly. I also did private secretarial and statistical work of a confidential nature for the treasurer, and clerical work in the payroll department.

The winter of 19___ I spent in the West. While there, I did secretarial and clerical work for the Ionaco Company of Denver, Colorado, and some sales work selling their product, an electrotherapeutic device. Not wishing to remain permanently in the West, I obtained a position in the spring of 19___ as private secretary to the sales manager of the Elf Motor Company at Cleveland, Ohio.

As I had always regretted my lack of college training, I left my position in Cleveland and came to New York for the two-year secretarial course at Columbia University. Because of my previous training and experience, I am able to shorten the course somewhat and expect to receive the Secretarial Certificate of Columbia University next August. Some of my studies at Columbia are: English composition, business administration, economics, bookkeeping, secretarial correspondence, and Spanish.

Each change in position that I have made has represented a distinct advantage. The variety of my work has given me a splendid background of valuable experience such as could never be obtained in the routine of one company.

I am eager to secure a permanent position in New York City, where I expect to continue studying in special night courses along the lines of whatever work I enter. I am looking for a position that offers a real future, and I welcome responsibility.

It is difficult to state a suitable salary with slight knowledge of the requirements and demands of the position. My last salary, however, was .... a month, and I believe that my training at Columbia warrants a considerable increase. I believe that I should receive a beginning salary of .... a month.

I should be glad to have you consult any of my former employers regarding my qualifications. I am enclosing a list of the names and addresses of the men under whom I have worked.

May I have the favor of a personal interview at your convenience?

(6)

I wish to apply for a position in the active end of your travel department, as I am very much interested in organized travel and intend to make it my occupation.

My education and experience are here briefly outlined:

Preparatory education in a military school; two years' college work at Blank University. Courses for two summers at Blank University in secretarial work, which included typing and shorthand, economics and advertising.

Four years of practical experience in travel and business. Office experience in four departments of _____ Life Insurance Company.

Traveling salesman for the _____ Electric Company of Chicago from April 19__ to 19__.

Travel experience in Canada, in the eastern states and in Mexico. Mental qualifications: a "geographical mind," apt in remembering figures, names, places; initiative; ability to meet the public.

If this should indicate to you a man who would be useful as a cruise manager or in some similar position, I should be glad of an opportunity to call at your office for an interview.

(7)

I should like to apply for the position of salesman advertised by your firm in last Sunday's *Times*.

Education:	A graduate of Adams High School, 19__
	Evening courses at New York University in advertising and salesmanship
Experience:	Salesman three years in the Men's Clothing Department of Brown and Brown; three years in the Sport Department of Brace and Company; two years as section manager of the Men's Shop, Barclay and O'Connor
Age:	Twenty-four
Nationality:	American, Irish descent

Present Salary: $4,800

| Reasons for Application: | No opportunity for advancement in present position |
| | Belief that ability and training warrant higher salary |

References:	A. B. Pickford, Personnel Manager
	Brown and Brown, 34 Street, Seventh Avenue
	Frank Blake, President
	Brace and Company
	Broadway, 80 Street
	Patrick Donnelly, Sales Manager
	Barclay and O'Connor
	11 West 57 Street

If you would grant me the privilege of an interview, I should be glad to call on Wednesday after two o'clock, my only free time.

(8)

I have learned through the Allen Teachers' Agency that there is a vacancy in the English department of your school.

May I present my qualifications with the hope that you will consider me for this position?

In 19___ I was graduated from Mount Holyoke College, where I majored in history and English. Since that time I have taught English in Biddeford High School, Biddeford, Maine, and in Newton High School, Newton, Mass. In both schools I had charge of the Dramatic Club and of the school publications.

I am now receiving a salary of $4,000; but as there is no likelihood of further advancement here, I wish to go elsewhere, particularly into a school system where there is an opportunity for executive work.

These facts may also be of interest to you:

Age	Thirty-two
Health	Excellent—no absence from school for eight years
Religion	Protestant
Nationality	American
Height	Five feet, seven inches
Weight	One hundred and forty pounds

My interest in children has always been a major one. My theories in regard to their training were published in a series of articles in *High School Education,* January to June, 19___.

If you are interested in my application, I should be glad to have you visit my classes or to grant me an interview any afternoon after two o'clock.

Letters Addressed to Reference

(1)

Miss Ida Hailparn of 1121 East Seventh Street, Brooklyn, New York, has applied to this organization for the position of private secretary and stenographer. She has given us your name as a reference, having worked with you for two years.

We should greatly appreciate a prompt reply to the following questions:

1. Is she capable in her duties as a stenographer and private secretary?
2. Is she honest and dependable?
3. What was the reason for her leaving your employ?

We are sorry to trouble you for this information, but are sure that you realize the necessity for our obtaining it.

(2)

Miss Mary E. Griffen has just applied for the stenographic position now open in our office and has given us your name as a reference.

We should very much appreciate it, therefore, if you would send us a letter giving us your opinion in regard to her ability as a stenographer while in your employ.

(3)

Miss Janette Curlenjik, 34 West 69th Street, has given me your name for reference.

I should appreciate it greatly if you would write me, giving me your opinion of her personality and business qualifications. From my short talk with her, she seems to be a very capable young woman.

(4)

Miss Joan Burdett has applied for the position of office manager in my office and has given your name as a reference. The position involves considerable responsibility and experience. The person selected must have initiative and ability to plan the work of others and maintain harmonious relationships with them.

Since I desire to secure an efficient office manager, I shall appreciate your frank opinion of Miss Burdett.

(5)

Application has been made to us by George Hunter for a position as salesman. Your name has been given as a personal reference.

We shall appreciate it if you will give us, in confidence, your opinion of the applicant's character, ability, and habits.

(6)

Mr. Arnold Wentworth desires to lease an apartment in our house and has referred us to you.

We shall appreciate it if you will write us as to his character and his ability to meet his bills promptly.

Any information you may give will be entirely confidential.

(7)

The student whose name appears below has applied to the Harvey School and has given your name as reference.

Miss Isabel Hubbard

We are attempting to select for admission those candidates who seem likely to profit most from the training offered. We have a transcript of records covering college courses. However, our experience has indicated that in addition to intellectual ability certain personal capacities are important in the successful practice of social work. Your evaluation of the student's personality equipment will, therefore, be helpful to us in gauging her fitness for admission to this School.

The following points are suggestive of the kind of evaluation that will be useful to us. We realize that your knowledge of the student may not enable you to make an exhaustive analysis of her capacities, but we shall appreciate whatever opinions you are able to offer on the basis of your contact with her.

(1) How long and in what connection have you known the candidate?

(2) Describe the candidate's personality and abilities as related to:

    sensitivity to other people's reactions
    capacity for self-expression
    capacity for assuming and discharging responsibility
    general emotional makeup (as indicated by intensity of feeling, ability to be objective, emotional control, freedom from tension)
    independence and initiative
    attitudes toward other people
    response to authority

(3) Indicate any other qualities and abilities, or limitations and disabilities which you think are important in considering this student's qualifications for social work.

A prompt reply will expedite consideration of the student's application.

Letters of Recommendation

(1)

I can sincerely recommend Miss Harriet Blake as a business secretary.

During the two years she was with me I found her work careful and accurate. In fact, I can truthfully say she is one of the best secretaries I have employed. She has a good knowledge of shorthand and typewriting, and an excellent general background, which makes her all the more valuable in an executive position. She is enthusiastic about whatever task she is performing and willing to devote as much time and energy as is necessary to have things done to perfection.

I think you will find Miss Blake a valuable helper. I myself am very sorry to lose her, but as she wished to enter a broader field, she gave up her position with me.

If I can supply any further information, I shall be glad to do so.

(2)

To whom it may concern:

Miss Jean Johnson was a student in my English class at C— College from February to June, 19___. During that time she impressed me as a student of ability interested in doing well whatever she had to do. Miss Johnson was not afraid of hard work, nor was she content to have merely a passing mark. She showed herself to be careful, painstaking, and accurate, always producing work of fine quality. When given an unusual assignment, she proved that she had read widely and appreciatively and possessed keen judgment and critical understanding.

Whatever Miss Johnson decides to do, she will, in my opinion, bring to it ability, character, and discrimination.

I am pleased to recommend her unqualifiedly.

A. B. Butler
Instructor in English

(3)

It affords me a welcome avenue for expressing my appreciation to say that I have found Miss Theresa Callan a remarkably capable secretary. She combines the qualities which one most desires of technical training and practical efficiency, good judgment, accuracy in word and action, reserve, sympathy, quick understanding, and adaptability in all contacts.

Miss Callan is gifted as a writer, and her pure diction and delightful facility of expression made the correspondence which she attended to for me an eminently satisfactory service.

She is a cultured young woman with the highest standards of honor and conduct.

(4)

It is a pleasure to say a word of recommendation in behalf of Miss Mary Burns, who has been my secretary until ill health made it impossible for me to continue the active interests which made such assistance necessary.

Miss Burns is, besides being a most efficient secretary of unusual mental and social qualities, a young woman of high character and honor, tireless and unselfish in the execution of her employer's interests, thoroughly trustworthy in her work and judgment; always tactful, able, and sympathetic as an executive.

During long absences from home, I have felt the utmost confidence and satisfaction in leaving to Miss Burns not only the manipulation of my large correspondence, accounts, etc., but also the entire oversight and direction of our household, including a large staff of servants. When I have been away, she has directed all the housekeeping for my home-keeping family and their visitors. I must stress that she has a perfect balance of knowing when to be on hand and when to withdraw, and she is never obtrusive. I think this is what one so much desires in a resident secretary.

I am always glad to give any information about one who has been a most valued secretary and friend to me.

(5)

Miss Louise Hepburn has been an invaluable secretary-housekeeper to me. She is not only thoroughly trained and experienced but she has, besides, natural gifts which particularly fit her to be of service to a busy woman with a large household who needs a sympathetic and experienced woman at her side. She is loyal and trustworthy in every way, diligent, patient and sweet-tempered, reserved, sympathetic under all circumstances, adapts herself with absolute satisfaction to the entire household. She is an excellent shopper, and on occasions when she has tutored or chaperoned for me, she has been most acceptable. Few women can fill a resident secretaryship as well as Miss Hepburn (so few that I never found anyone else who was really satisfactory) and I can think of no household, however complicated, where she would not be valued in this capacity. Her leaving me to go to New York was a matter of great regret to me.

(6)

It is my pleasure to recommend to you Miss Ethel Beekman, who has been in the employ of the Public Service Company of this city for six years. The uncle and aunt with whom she makes her home are now moving to Brooklyn. She is, therefore, striving to find work in your city.

During the six years of employment with this company, Miss Beekman has been in my own department. For accuracy in the taking of stenographic notes and for excellence in the production of a manuscript or a data sheet, we have had no one in our entire organization who has been able to measure up to the high standard which she has always maintained. She has served as reporter for many of our company meetings as well as for industry conventions and conferences. As you know, this kind of work requires unusual speed and accuracy.

Miss Beekman's resignation is, therefore, a source of very considerable regret and inconvenience to my work here. It is a matter of earnest desire on the part of a large group of company people that she be able to make a connection in New York where the same expert services will be appreciated as they have been in our office.

If I were to speak in further commendation of Miss Beekman, it would be to endorse the splendid spirit of service and faithfulness of effort which have always characterized her work. Those who have known her have regarded her as a woman of delightful personality and fine presence whether in the business office, in social and church circles, or on the tennis court or golf links.

I should be happy, indeed, if there were any place where you could fit Miss Beekman into your large organization or introduce her to some firm looking for a competent secretary or office manager. The hope that you may do this is the more readily expressed because of my certain knowledge that you would be pleased with the service which would be rendered.

(7)

Raymond Brown was employed by the City Exchange, January 10, 19___, and resigned of his own accord January 1, 19___. During the period of his employment, he served in various capacities as follows:

As a messenger, from January 10, 19___, to January 31, 19___.
As a page or assistant clerk, from January 31, 19___, to July 1, 19___.
As a tube operator from July 1, 19___, to January 1, 19___.

It is a pleasure to state that Mr. Brown's services during his period of employment with us were satisfactory. We were impressed by his worth-while character, his constant application to educational advantages, and his willingness to work. We have watched his development with a great deal of interest. It is my opinion that he would be a credit to your company.

(8)

Alexander Lewis, to the best of my knowledge and belief, has been a good student, careful and punctual in his work, well adjusted in his social relations, and honest in his financial dealings.

(9)

I am glad to write in behalf of John Smith, who is making application for a position with you.

He was a student in Blank College where his work was outstanding. As a human being he is first rate; as a scholar he is of "A" grade. I think he gets on well with his fellows.

(10)

Burton Hollis has always been interested in intellectual pursuits and is a steady worker. He would do well for a few years to be in a situation where he would have sufficient administrative oversight to acquaint him with the details of the work which he is to follow as far as items involving subject matter are concerned. In other words, I think him competent in subject matter but slightly immature in his human relations. By that I do not mean that he is ill-mannered or boorish, but merely that he is not entirely self-sufficient, sophisticated, and experienced.

(11)

Henry Brown, in his background, training, and personal achievement, presents a type of character and personality which is among the finest I know.

The applicant is intelligent, industrious, and capable of carrying on individual research which would be colored with imagination as well as characterized by thoroughness. Because of his imagination and his uncommonly good grounding in literature and artistic matters, he ought to be able to handle his field with unusual success.

(12)

In recommending James Cross for the position of director of advertising in your firm, I am glad to say that I know him to be a man of unusual ability and irreproachable character.

I have always found Cross conscientious, considerate of the men under him, industrious and imaginative in his work. As some of the finest jobs completed by our office were instigated by him, we shall have a hard time finding a competent successor.

His relations with this company have always been so cordial that we are loath to let him go. We realize, however, that a man of his ability must naturally pass on to a position of greater power and wider scope than we can give him.

(13)

I am glad to write you concerning James L. Mann of Somers High School, who is asking for a scholarship.

During the last year I have been associated with him rather closely, as he was the editor of the school literary magazine of which I am faculty adviser, and he is at present, although taking a post-graduate course, one of the editors of the school newspaper.

I have been told he does well in his studies, standing second in the class at his graduation. His work on the Publication Board, where he was editor for a year, was uniformly good and often high.

He is a fine young man, well brought up, courteous, thoughtful, and willing to work hard. I like his attitude particularly and feel sure that he will be a decidedly useful citizen.

I know nothing of his financial condition, but the fact that he has applied for a scholarship makes me believe he needs it.

If you wish any other information I can give you, I shall be glad to write you again.

(14)

Mrs. Gertrude Prince, a woman about twenty-five, has been with us for four years in the mail order and adjustment department. A high-school graduate when she came to us, she showed such unusual promise that we encouraged her to take extension courses at the University. Following her interests, she took work in sociology, economics, and social welfare.

She now feels that she has not enough to do mentally and that her salary of $4,000 is inadequate.

Mrs. Prince hopes to secure a position in survey work among women, particularly in department stores. For this, she is so well fitted that she would, I am sure, make a distinct success of it.

If you would like to talk with her in regard to a position connected with the investigations you are making, I should be glad to excuse her from her duties here for an interview at any time convenient to you. If you need an assistant, I believe it would be worth your while to see Mrs. Prince.

Requests for Letters of Introduction

(1)

[*Letterhead*]

December 2, 19___

Dear Mr. Johnson:

Last summer you told me that should I be called to London you would be good enough to introduce me to business acquaintances there. I intend to go abroad next month on a business trip and shall be in London during January and February. As it would be a great help to me to meet some of your friends, may I ask you for letters of intro-duction to men who might be interested in our products.

I assure you I shall appreciate such letters.

Yours sincerely,
Bronson T. Nichols

Mr. A. S. Johnson
7528 South Shore Drive
Chicago, Illinois

(2)

Next month I expect to start on a trip to Mexico to promote our sales there. I remember your kind offer to introduce me to some of your business friends who might be interested in knowing of our factory and its products. I should be glad to have such introductions, as they would be very useful to me and would make it much easier to break into new fields.

Letters of Introduction

(1)

605 West 115th Street
New York City
April 29, 19___

Mr. Samuel M. Jones
President, Arnold Print Works
North Adams, Mass.

Dear Mr. Jones:

This letter will introduce to you Miss Lois Littlepage, who is visiting your factory with the idea of gathering material for a survey of indus-trial relations that she is making. I believe that it would be very much to her advantage to meet you personally to learn your opinion on several subjects connected with this report.

I shall appreciate whatever assistance you give her.

Sincerely yours,
Dorothy Briggs

(2)

This will introduce to you Miss Mary E. Murray, a friend of mine, who is particularly eager to apply for the stenographic position now open in your office.

I hope that you will be able to spare a few moments of your already busy day to extend to Miss Murray the privilege of an interview.

(3)

Eleanor Bancroft, a neighbor and close friend, is leaving America next week to make a trip around the world. She expects to reach London on January third and to remain there until the twentieth and can be addressed in care of the American Express. She is a delightful person with a variety of interesting stories and experiences to relate, but not one of those bores who compel patient acquaintances to listen to dull tales of personal adventures, true or otherwise.

I am sure you will like each other and trust you will have time to get acquainted with her and enjoy hearing of the humdrum lives of your friends in America.

(4)

Mrs. Frank B. Long, whose name I am presenting for membership in the Community Club, is an unusual woman who will contribute much interest to our meetings. She is a member of the Boston Woman's University Club and of the Brookline Tennis Club. She is an officer of the Middlesex Improvement Society for the Blind and of the Child Welfare Association, and belongs to numerous other organizations of widely differing interests.

Charming, humorous, gifted, she would prove, I am sure, a most valuable club member. I consider it a real privilege to propose her name and trust that it will soon be added to our list.

(5)

The bearer of this note, Arthur F. Colby, is a teller at the First National Bank. He wants to talk with you as to prospects of finding a better paying position in some banking institution and asked me if I would write to you for an interview.

If you can give him a few minutes of your time, it will be greatly appreciated.

(6)

Richard Ames, a friend of mine, is going to Washington the week of December fourth and will stay at the Mayflower.

He is very much interested in one of the bills before Congress and has some data in regard to it that will be of interest to you. Would you be able to spare half an hour to discuss these matters with him next Wednesday afternoon? Both he and I should appreciate it if you could.

(7)

We take pleasure in introducing to you Mr. Francis Dunn of the firm of Hanley and Dunn, who is visiting New York with the idea of establishing a branch office there.

It would be a personal favor to us if you would help Mr. Dunn with advice and introduce him to other business men who could give him some practical suggestions about the opportunities for his company in New York and vicinity.

(8)

May I introduce to you a new member of the Men's League, Rodney Chalmers, who wishes to attend a session of the House while it is discussing the merits of the Copyright Bill.

Mr. Chalmers is interested in some of the phases affecting the rights of American authors whose books might be published abroad and whose rights should be protected.

May he have an appointment with you? I should appreciate it if you can find time to talk with him.

(9)

The bearer of this letter, Mr. Lee Graham, has for several years been interested in organizing camps for boys who could afford to spend only a small amount on their summer vacations. As he is considering locations for camps in Vermont, I suggested that you were the man to help him, for you know every nook and corner of the State.

I shall be happy if you can assist Mr. Graham in any way. He is a fine chap and has a most worth-while job on his hands.

(10)

This letter will be presented to you by Mr. Albert Tuttle, one of the partners in the firm of Tuttle, Mead and Brown. He is a thoroughly fine fellow and an excellent business man whom we have known for many years. He is visiting New York to form connections and open markets for his firm.

We introduce Mr. Tuttle to you, feeling sure that there is no one better able to help him meet the men in New York whom he wishes to know.

(11)

Mr. Brown and I have moved to Chicago to manage the office in that city. In making this move, however, I wanted to be sure that you would continue to receive the same personal, careful service I have always tried to give you in all matters.

Therefore, I have referred your name and all my records regarding your needs to a friend and associate whom I consider particularly well qualified, Mr. Emory Dalton.

Mr. Dalton has had a great deal of experience and you can have full confidence in his ability and recommendations. Please feel free to call on him at any time.

(12)

This letter will introduce to you Peter Bishop, a former employee of mine. He is a reliable, serious fellow of high character, devoted to his work and efficient in details. He has a fine, though not brilliant mind.

Were I still in the commercial world, I should be very glad to have him associated with me.

A Card of Introduction

Face of card

Mr. Norman McAllister

Introducing
Mr. Henry Winkelman
to
Mr. Roger Brown Peel

Reverse of card

> Dear Mr. Peel:
>   Mr. Winkelman, like yourself, is interested in first editions. May he have the pleasure of seeing yours?
>
>   Yours sincerely,
>   Norman McAllister
>
> April 15

Face of card

> *Introducing Mr. Leonard Grant*
> *to*
> *Dr. Burton Masters*
>
> **Mr. Richard Kennedy**

Reverse of card

> Mr. Grant wishes to consult you professionally. I have assured him that you will be interested in his case.
>
>   R. K.

Letters of Reminder

(1)

Dear Mr. Mitchell:

I have received your letter telling me that the convention has been extended to June fifth. May I remind you that you have a week-end engagement at Miss Smith's beginning June fourth. In case you decide to stay until the end of the convention, please let me know what word to send Miss Smith canceling the engagement.

Yours sincerely,

Catherine Rossbach, Secretary

(2)

In accordance with your request, I am writing to remind you of your promise to address the Club on April 16, on the subject of the modern novel. We are anticipating a delightful afternoon in listening to your talk.

(3)

Thank you for your gracious acceptance of our invitation to speak at the Anniversary Dinner of the Brown Club on June third. Mr. Anthony, the president of the club, will be here to receive you at seven o'clock in time to have some of our members meet you before the dinner.

We are looking forward to having you with us at that time.

(4)

129 Center Street
West Haven, Conn.
February 2, 19___

Mrs. Charles Merritt
50 Gillette Street
Hartford, Conn.

Dear Mrs. Merritt:

As I must hand my manuscript to the printer March 1, will you kindly send as soon as possible the material which you have so generously allowed me to use for illustration.

I hesitate to remind you of the nearness of the final date, for I know you have been unusually busy the last few weeks and have not had time to think of anything else but your own work.

I hope it will not inconvenience you too much to send the material very soon.

Yours sincerely,

E. P. Greenwood

A Letter of Confirmation

562 West 11 Street
New York City
May 10, 19——

Mr. Norman Walker
620 West 67 Street
New York City

Dear Sir

In regard to our conversation of yesterday afternoon, I want to make a statement, in writing, of the impression I received from it. I understood you to say that you would guarantee a rise of five per cent in the net profits from my factory if I would make a contract with your company. I understand that the service can be completed in six months at a cost of $900 a month.

Please reply telling me if I have the proposition correctly stated.

Yours very truly
Kathleen Wall

A Letter Confirming a Telephone Conversation

This is to confirm my telephone conversation with you on May 1 in regard to the second mortgage which you desire to have placed on your house located at 411 St. Clair Avenue, Buffalo.

The terms agreed upon are as follows: a mortgage of $3000, payable $150 semiannually, with interest at six per cent.

Will you please call at this office as soon as possible so that Attorney Sloane may proceed to search the title and draw up the mortgage deed.

A Letter Making a Hotel Reservation

Hotel Benjamin Franklin
Philadelphia, Pa.

Gentlemen:

Please reserve for Mr. R. M. Williams a moderately priced room with bath at your hotel for January 26 to February 28 and inform him what the rate will be.

Yours very truly,
Anne E. Burden, Secretary

A Letter Making a Steamship Reservation

The Cunard Steamship Company
25 Broadway
New York City

Gentlemen:

Please reserve for Mr. and Mrs. Nathan Keith an outside room
with bath on Deck C, cabin, on the *Mauretania* sailing September 12
for Havre.

> Yours very truly,
> Ellen A. Stevenson
> Secretary to Mr. Keith

Letters Concerning Appointments

(1)

> Chadwick Place
> Biddeford, Maine
> June 1, 19___

Dear Miss Clark:

Mrs. Marcia P. Leslie wishes me to ask whether it would be possible
for you to see her at your apartment Tuesday, June twelfth, at three
o'clock, to discuss with you an article she is writing on Tea Room
Management.

> Yours sincerely,
> Annie Perkins
> Secretary to Mrs. Leslie

Miss Grace Clark
1 Fifth Avenue
New York City

(2)

Dear Mr. Johnson:

As Mr. Roberts has suddenly been called out of town, he has asked
me to inform you that he will have to postpone the conference with
you at three o'clock. On his return he will be glad to make another
appointment with you at your convenience.

> Yours very truly,
> Josephine Gold
> Secretary to Mr. J. L. Roberts

(3)

Mr. Cooke has asked me to arrange an appointment with you during your visit in Chicago. Would it be possible for you to see him on Wednesday, December fifth, at the University Club, to discuss the matter of foreign speakers for the coming winter?

(4)

I shall be in Washington on December fifth and shall be happy to meet you at the University Club at four o'clock to discuss the matter of foreign speakers for the coming winter.

(5)

Mr. Galbraith wishes to know whether it would be possible for you to see him at your office Monday, February 15, at ten o'clock, to discuss with him important matters relating to the finances of the Western Shore Beach Club.

(6)

In answer to your letter of February 8, Mr. Hanson suggests that you call next Tuesday at twelve o'clock instead of Monday at ten.

Will you be good enough to confirm this appointment so that Mr. Hanson will definitely set aside this time to see you.

Letters of Appreciation

(1)

Iola Sanatorium
Rochester, New York

September 29, 19___

Mr. Bruce Johnson
Granite Building
Rochester, N. Y.

My dear Mr. Johnson:

Through Mr. Robert MacMurray we have just learned that you were one of the contributors to a fund which he collected for the benefit of our occupational therapy department. It is a pleasure to acknowledge your contribution and to tell you that you have done something that is of great value.

For some time Mrs. Munchow, the worker in charge of the occupational therapy department, has been asking me for material to be used by the patients in making the different articles at their bedside or in the shop. To each request I have replied, "Sometime I will be able to secure the aid you need." This time has arrived, and the money is in the bank. A conference with Mrs. Munchow has just been concluded in which I was the recipient of great thanks. These thanks I transfer to you.

Sincerely yours,
Ezra Bridge
Medical Director

(2)

Those of us who have had the privilege of knowing you rather intimately look almost with envy at what you have accomplished during your residence in this city. It is not often given to one individual to do so much for the improvement of the city as you have been able to do. Perhaps it is truer to say that it is rare to find in one person the vision to plan intelligently for the future and at the same time to interest his fellow-citizens in making the city a more permanently beautiful place in which to live. But that is exactly what we have found in you. It must give you great satisfaction to know that because you have dreamed of a better-planned and more beautiful city, others are already working to make it so.

You must also rejoice at the affectionate tribute from your fellow-citizens for your untiring service in civic improvement these many years.

As for myself, it has been a keen source of pleasure to be associated with you and to have felt the inspiring influence of your personality. May I send my hearty congratulations on this your birthday and my best wishes for many more years in which to fulfil your ideals.

(3)

I am deeply grateful for your congratulations on my seventieth birthday. I appreciate your good wishes particularly as coming from one whom I hold in special respect and affection. The opinions of my service to the city, which you and other kind friends expressed, have given me a warm glow of happiness and contentment that so many have understood and appreciated my efforts—often, to be sure, very unsuccessful—to make our community more beautiful and our fellow-countrymen more interested in the development of artistic ideals.

Such a letter as yours would gratify a man whose success has been much greater than mine. It gives me real joy to think of your sympathetic insight into the principles and ideals that have guided my long life.

(4)

I find it difficult to tell you how touched we were by your letter of congratulation on the completion of our hospital. Our gratitude goes out to you for your courageous support of the plan opposed by so many powerful and influential persons. With the strides made in medicine and psychology, the mentally ill have been given the attention they deserve. Our hospital with its beautiful location, its modern equipment, and its corps of competent nurses and doctors should be a blessing to thousands of men and women whose lives may be patched—perhaps entirely repaired.

To us who have struggled for this end, your help and encouragement have ever been a source of strength. Without the assurance of the confidence and sympathy of our friends, we could never have brought this dream to reality.

Dr. Brooks and Dr. Stone join me in sincere appreciation of your understanding of our principles and of your courage in standing by us when so many opposed the erection of the hospital on its present site.

(5)

We have learned with regret of your illness and resignation. As a pledge of our affection and esteem, your friends here in the office have deposited to your name at the Bank of New York the sum of $1500.

Please accept this in token of our appreciation of your years of long and faithful service to the firm.

That you may soon be in the best of health and able to enjoy your well-earned vacation is the earnest wish of your many friends.

(6)

It was a happy day when the book containing your lectures came. It is a splendid piece of workmanship, and I am exceedingly proud to be the owner of a copy.

The book contains a wealth of material that is interestingly set forth. It must have been a very difficult and time-consuming task to obtain this material and to express it so clearly and concisely.

I appreciate your thoughtfulness in sending me a copy, and wish you much success in your new undertaking.

(7)

The Committee wishes to thank you for your generous loan of valuable prints and etchings to the Fine Arts Exhibit held at the University in June. We believe that such exhibits have a definite place in education and do much to promote interest in representative arts.

Your own personal attitude, as shown by your contributions, should be a great incentive to other members of the alumni to make similar loans if it is in their power to do so.

Be assured we appreciate your interest in making possible such an opportunity for our students to view your collection of prints and etchings.

(8)

Before I leave for the West, I want to tell you how touched I was by your kind mention of my work in your report to the Company.

Through all these difficult months, I have appreciated your understanding of my point of view and your loyal attitude toward me.

May you find associates as appreciative of your efforts as you have been of mine.

Letters of Congratulation

To Committees

(1)

May I congratulate you on the way your committee has completed a long and difficult piece of work? The report is a masterpiece, brief but clear, accurate, and complete. It is a pleasure to find all the details in such easily digested form.

(2)

Your committee showed fine spirit and team work. Selling tickets these days is no easy matter, but evidently your committee charmed practically all our members into buying tables for the bridge. The afternoon was a huge success, and the amount of the proceeds a surprise to all.

Please accept the grateful thanks of the Club for your own hard work and extend our appreciation to your committee.

(3)

What a membership committee! Never before have we enrolled so many members or had such enthusiastic support. There is no doubt that this is due to you and your efficient committee which has worked so hard to interest the citizens of Arden in uniting to improve our township.

The officers wish to express to you and to your committee appreciation of your untiring efforts and wonderful success.

(4)

May I congratulate you on the efficient work of your committee? Every member seemed able and energetic and yet willing to cooperate with the others and with the larger organization. This showed real leadership. Evidence of your tact, foresight, and judgment made a profound impression on all who worked with you.

For all members of the Association, I wish to express grateful appreciation both to you and to your excellent committee.

On a Birthday

It was a pleasant thing for me to learn from your son of your approaching birthday as it gives me the opportunity of adding my good wishes to those of your many friends here in America. Your life has been so full of great achievements and well-earned successes that your backward glances must bring you deep and lasting satisfaction.

May you long continue to delight your American readers with your charming stories about us—stories so appreciative of our merits and so understanding of our defects that we look upon their author as one of our most discerning friends.

May freedom from sorrow, ill health, and discouragement of whatever kind you are prone to, flee far from you, leaving you able to devote yourself happily to the many notable works your readers expect from your pen.

On an Airplane Flight

The Air Club congratulates you on your successful transpolar flight. We rejoice that the thirst for adventure still inspires men to great deeds. We also extend our greetings to those who made the flight with you.

On Appointment to Office

(1)

Sincere congratulations upon your re-election. It is a splendid tribute to your efficient public service.

(2)

Please accept my heartiest congratulations upon your well-merited appointment and my best wishes for your success in your new office.

(3)

Please accept my sincere congratulations and good wishes upon your election. I hope the future will bring you still higher honors and even greater successes.

(4)

Your appointment as president is a source of great satisfaction to the alumni and friends of Arona College. At a meeting held last night to raise funds for scholarships and a new science building, I was assigned the pleasant task of sending you our joint congratulations.

We extend to you our best wishes for your happiness and success in your new work. You may count upon the support of the alumni who have watched your career and who are delighted that the College is to have as president a man of your scholarship and ideals.

On a Speech

I suppose that your mail for the past week has been crowded with letters of congratulation, and yet I cannot resist adding mine to your collection. Perhaps you are like the rest of us who enjoy a little praise now and then, but with this exception you really deserve it. Your speech at the annual dinner Thursday night was delightful. The humor was genuine, the topic of immediate interest to your audience, and the entire speech clearly and beautifully expressed. You were probably conscious of the unswerving attention of the audience, which is in itself an unusual compliment. I can only exclaim, "How do you do it!" I wish more of our speakers would emulate you.

Could you let me have a copy of the speech? That is not merely a gesture of praise. I really want a copy.

Letters of Condolence

On the Death of Business Associates

(1)

I heard with deep regret of the death of your president, James Knowlton, who has served your Company faithfully for many years. The Directors wish me to convey their sympathy to you in the loss of a great official and great citizen.

(2)

With regret we read in this morning's *Times* the death of Mr. Appleton. The officers of our firm extend to you our sympathy knowing the sorrow you must feel at the loss of so staunch a friend and so efficient a president.

(3)

The officers and staff of the Benson Company extend their sincere sympathy to the family of Mr. Alfred Benson, Jr. His loss will be felt keenly by his many associates here in the office who have long esteemed him for his integrity of character and his clear judgment in the conduct of the affairs of the company.

(4)

The officers of our company have learned with sorrow of the death of Mr. Ashley. We wish to extend to you our sincere sympathy in a loss so grave.

(5)

With sincere regret the office staff have just learned of the death of our president.

We wish to express to the officers of the Company our sympathy at their loss and our own sorrow at this time.

We are proud to have been under the direction of a man of such high integrity and of such intelligent sympathy with his employees as Mr. Everett always revealed in his relations with them.

(6)

May we express to you our deep sympathy in the death of your daughter, Mary Shipman, who, as a secretary for ten years in the Executive Office of the City Bank, commanded the respect and esteem of those she served.

Her devotion to her work and her loyal and intelligent service won for her the regard and admiration of all her associates.

To you, whose loss is irreparable, we send our sincere sympathy.

On the Death of a Mother

We were greatly shocked to hear of the death of your mother, for we had not heard of her grave illness.

You know how we all loved her for her kindness to us when we visited you. Her welcome was ever generous and sincere, and we felt we had a friend indeed in her.

We send our affectionate sympathy and love.

On the Death of a Father

Please accept my sympathy on the death of your father whose life was so bound up in the progress of the community. He will be greatly missed by all his friends and associates who admired and loved him for his high ideals of service and his deep interest in the cultural development of the city.

On the Death of a Husband

News of your husband's death brought sorrow to every member of his department.

His unfailing kindness, his delightful humor, and his keen sense of justice made work with him a rare privilege.

May we offer our sincere and heartfelt sympathy to you in your bereavement?

On the Death of a Sister

I was greatly shocked to learn of the death of your sister, as I had not even heard that she was ill. She will be sadly missed among her wide circle of friends who loved her dearly. To you the loss is the greatest, but you will have the comfort of realizing that you did all you could to make her happy and gave her much to enjoy. Please accept my sincere sympathy.

On the Death of a Brother

May I offer my deep sympathy on the death of your brother.

I admired him greatly for his fine sense of comradeship and loyal and unselfish devotion to his friends. I shall not soon see his like again.

The loss is greatest of all to you. May you bear it bravely and proudly because of the courage and ideals that your brother's life exemplified.

On the Death of a Friend

(1)

Words cannot express my deep sorrow for your loss. I first knew Mrs. Carey last year in our work at the church. Her unfailing courtesy, her sympathy, and kindly spirit endeared her to all. She was a dear friend whom I shall miss sadly.

(2)

May I offer my sympathy to you on the death of Mrs. Davis. The memories of the long years of your friendship must now return to you in all their beauty and give you happiness even in your sorrow. Such a friendship enriches life. Your unselfish devotion to her at all times will now give you peace and comfort. You have my deep sympathy and love.

Letters of Resignation

(1)

For eight years I have acted as President of the Chelsea Planning Association. Since the time has come when I must retire from active service, I ask that my resignation be accepted. It is with regret that I take this step as I have enjoyed working with a group that has contributed so much to the happiness and welfare of the community.

May I express my heartiest good wishes for the continued success of The Association and faith in its plans for further usefulness.

(2)

It is with regret that I submit my resignation as treasurer of the New England Welfare Association. The duties required are more than I can successfully fulfill at present, and I, therefore, ask to be relieved of them.

It has been a real pleasure to be associated with the organization and its valuable work, and I regret that my health will no longer permit me to share its responsibilities.

(3)

As I have decided to accept a position with Brent Brothers of Atlanta, I respectfully tender my resignation as sales manager of the Western Fruit Company. For the five years I have been employed by the company, my association has been such a happy one that I regret to sever connection with it. Only a job with greater opportunities and a higher salary would tempt me to do so.

Office Memoranda

In a large organization, interdepartmental notes are usually written on official memo paper of each office or headed by the name of the department. The name of the addressee (omitting the word *Dear*), and his department or room number when necessary should be written at the left-hand margin. No complimentary close is necessary. The signature should consist of the name, not the initials of the writer unless his identity is unmistakable. The date, placed at the upper right-hand margin or more often at the lower left-hand margin, should never be omitted. If the note is dictated, the dictator's and the stenographer's initials should occur in the usual place.

Editorial Department

Mr. Henry Thomas
Room 302

This is to confirm my telephone message of yesterday requesting that during my absence from the office you route my mail to Joseph Milam.

Philip Cumming

January 15

REFERENCE BOOKS

BUTTERFIELD, WILLIAM HENRY. *Effective Personal Letters for Business and Social Occasions.* 2d ed. rev. New York, Prentice-Hall, 1951.

HOTCHKISS, GEORGE BURTON, and others. *Advanced Business Correspondence.* 4th ed. New York, Harper & Brothers, 1947.

HUTCHINSON, LOIS IRENE. *Standard Handbook for Secretaries.* 7th ed. New York, McGraw-Hill Book Company, Inc., 1956.

OPDYCKE, JOHN BAKER. *Get It Right!* New York, Funk & Wagnalls Company, 1935.

POST, EMILY. *Etiquette.* 9th ed. New York, Funk & Wagnalls Company, 1955.

SHURTER, ROBERT LE FEVRE. *Effective Letters in Business.* 2d ed. New York, McGraw-Hill Book Company, Inc., 1954.

TAINTOR, SARAH AUGUSTA, and MONRO, KATE MARGARET. *The Handbook of Social Correspondence.* New York, The Macmillan Company, 1936.

VANDERBILT, AMY. *Complete Book of Etiquette.* New York, Doubleday & Company, 1954.

COLLECTIONS OF LETTERS

The Book of Modern Letters, compiled and edited by Sarah Augusta Taintor and Kate Margaret Monro. New York, The Macmillan Company, 1935.

The Great English Letter Writers, compiled and edited by W. J. and Coningsby Dawson. New York, Harper & Brothers, 1909.

A Letter Book, compiled and edited by George Saintsbury. London, George Bell and Sons, 1922.

Letters from Many Pens, edited by Margaret Coult. New York, The Macmillan Company, 1930.

The Literature of Letters, compiled and edited by John B. Opdycke. Chicago, Lyons and Carnahan, 1925.

Nineteenth Century Letters, edited by Byron Johnson Rees. New York, Charles Scribner's Sons, 1919.

Selected Letters, compiled and edited by Stella S. Center. New York, Charles E. Merrill Co., 1915.

LETTERS BY INDIVIDUAL AUTHORS

BELL, GERTRUDE
The Letters of Gertrude Bell, selected and edited by Lady Bell, London, Ernest Benn, 1927.
BROOKS, PHILLIPS
Letters of Travel, edited by M. F. B. New York, E. P. Dutton and Company, 1915.
BROWNING, ELIZABETH BARRETT
The Letters of Elizabeth Barrett Browning, edited with biographical additions, by Frederic G. Kenyon. New York, The Macmillan Company, 1897.
BROWNING, ELIZABETH and ROBERT
Letters of Robert and Elizabeth Barrett Browning. New York, The Macmillan Company, 1897.
CARLYLE, JANE WELSH
Letters to Her Family, edited by Leonard Huxley. Garden City, N. Y. Doubleday, Page and Company, 1924.
CARLYLE, JANE WELSH
Letters and Memorials, annotated by Thomas Carlyle and edited by Alexander Carlyle. London, John Lane, 1903.
CLEMENS, SAMUEL LANGHORNE (Mark Twain)
Mark Twain's Letters, edited by Albert Bigelow Paine. New York, Harper & Brothers, 1917.
CONRAD, JOSEPH
Conrad to a Friend. 150 selected letters from Joseph Conrad to Richard Curle, edited with an introduction and notes by Richard Curle. Garden City, N. Y., Doubleday, Doran and Company, 1927.
COWPER, WILLIAM
Letters of William Cowper, edited by the Rev. W. Benham. New York, The Macmillan Company, 1914.
DICKENS, CHARLES
Letters of Charles Dickens, edited by his sister-in-law and his eldest daughter. London, Chapman & Hall, 1882.
DODGSON, CHARLES LUTWIDGE (Lewis Carroll)
Life and Letters of Lewis Carroll, by Stuart Dodgson Collingwood. New York, The Century Company, 1899.
FITZGERALD, EDWARD
Letters of Edward Fitzgerald, edited by William Aldis Wright. New York, The Macmillan Company, 1894.
GRAY, THOMAS
Letters of Thomas Gray, edited by D. C. Tovey. London, George Bell and Sons, 1912.
HEARN, LAFCADIO
The Japanese Letters of Lafcadio Hearn, edited with notes by Elizabeth Bisland. Boston, Houghton Mifflin Company, 1911.
Life and Letters of Lafcadio Hearn, by Elizabeth Bisland. Boston, Houghton Mifflin Company, 1906.

JAMES, WILLIAM

> *Letters of William James,* edited by his son, Henry James. Boston, Little, Brown and Company, 1926.

LAMB, CHARLES

> *Letters of Charles Lamb,* newly arranged with additions, edited with Introduction and notes by Alfred Ainger. New York, The Macmillan Company, 1888.

LANE, FRANKLIN K.

> *Letters, Personal and Political.* Boston, Houghton Mifflin Company, 1922.

LOWELL, JAMES RUSSELL

> *Letters of James Russell Lowell.* New York, Harper & Brothers, 1894.

MONTAGU, LADY MARY WORTLEY

> *Letters from 1709 to 1762.* London, J. M. Dent and Company, 1906.

MOODY, WILLIAM VAUGHN

> *Letters to Harriet.* Boston, Houghton Mifflin Company, 1935.

PAGE, WALTER HINES

> *Life and Letters of Walter Hines Page,* edited by Burton J. Hendricks. Garden City, N. Y., Doubleday, Page and Company, 1922.

ROOSEVELT, THEODORE

> *Letters from Theodore Roosevelt to Anna Roosevelt Cowles,* from 1870 to 1918. New York, Charles Scribner's Sons.

SEDGWICK, ANNE DOUGLAS

> *A Portrait in Letters,* chosen and edited by Basil de Sélincourt. Boston, Houghton Mifflin Company, 1936.

SÉVIGNÉ, MADAME DE

> *Letters of Madame de Sévigné to Her Daughter and Her Friends,* edited and annotated by J. A. Harrison, selected with an introductory essay by Richard Aldington. New York, Brentano's, 1927.

STEVENSON, ROBERT LOUIS

> *Letters of Robert Louis Stevenson,* edited by Sir Sidney Colvin. New York, Charles Scribner's Sons, 1925.

THACKERAY, WILLIAM MAKEPEACE

> *A Collection of Letters by William Makepeace Thackeray.* New York, Charles Scribner's Sons, 1890.

WALPOLE, HORACE

> *The Letters of Horace Walpole,* edited by Mrs. Paget Toynbee. 16 vols. Oxford, Clarendon Press, 1903–1905.

WILSON, WOODROW

> *Life and Letters of Woodrow Wilson,* edited by Ray Stannard Baker. Garden City, N. Y., Doubleday, Doran and Company, 1927.

2. Correct Usage in Letter Parts

The forms for official usage presented in this chapter, illustrating indented style and closed punctuation, follow the practice of the Department of State; but other forms, such as those explained in Part II, Chapter I, that is, indented or block style with open punctuation, are also correct.

In letters to Government officials, the inside address, instead of appearing above the salutation, may be placed at the left-hand margin at the close of the letter. The wording and the spacing on the envelope should agree with that of the inside address.

For correct titles of American officials, see the *Congressional Directory,* the *United States Government Organization Manual,* the *Biographic Register of the Department of State,* and the Military Service registers.

Official Usage

The President of the United States

Address:
> The President,
> > The White House,
> > > Washington 25, D.C.

Salutation:
> The President:
> > *or*
> Mr. President:
> > *or*
> My dear Mr. President:

Complimentary Close:
> Respectfully submitted,
> > *or*
> Yours respectfully,
> > *or*
> Faithfully yours, (informal)

287

The Vice President of the United States

Address: The Vice President,
or
The Vice President of the United States,
or
The President of the Senate, (formal communications)
The United States Senate,
Washington 25, D.C.

Salutation: Sir:
or
My dear Mr. Vice President:

Complimentary Close: Yours respectfully,
or
Very truly yours,

Speaker of the House of Representatives

Address: The Honorable _____ _____,
The Speaker of the House of Representatives,
or
The Speaker of the House of Representatives,
Washington 25, D.C.

Salutation: Sir:
or
My dear Mr. Speaker:

Complimentary Close: Very truly yours,

Cabinet Officers

Address: The Honorable [1]
The Secretary of State,
or
The Honorable _____ _____,
Secretary of State,
Washington 25, D.C.

Salutation: (man) Sir:
or
Dear Sir:
or
My dear Mr. Secretary:

Complimentary Close: Very truly yours,

[1] With the exception of Cabinet officers and Governors of States, *The Honorable* is used only in addressing an officer by name (*Style Manual*).

Address:

> The Honorable
> The Secretary of Labor,
> > *or*
> The Honorable _____ _____,
> Secretary of Labor,
> Washington 25, D.C.

Salutation:

> Sir: *or* Madam:
> > *or*
> Dear Sir: *or* Dear Madam:
> > *or*
> My dear Mr. (Madam) Secretary:
> > *or*
> Dear Mr. (Mrs. or Miss) Doe:

Complimentary Close: Very truly yours,

Secretary to the President

Address:

> The Secretary to the President,
> > *or*
> The Honorable _____ _____,
> Secretary to the President,
> The White House,
> Washington 25, D.C.

Salutation:

> Dear Mr. Secretary:
> > *or*
> Dear Mr. Doe: (informal)

Complimentary Close: Very truly yours,

Secretary to the President with Military Rank

Address:

> Major General _____ _____,
> Secretary to the President,
> The White House,
> Washington 25, D.C.

Salutation:

> Sir:
> > *or*
> My dear General _____:

Complimentary Close: Very truly yours,

Secretary of Defense
Secretary of the Air Force
Secretary of the Army
Secretary of the Navy

Address:

> The Secretary of _____,
> > *or*
> The Honorable _____ _____,
> > Secretary of _____,
> > > Washington 25, D.C.

Salutation:

> Sir:
> > *or*
> My dear Sir:
> > *or*
> Dear Mr. Secretary:
> > *or*
> My dear Mr. Doe:
> > *or*
> Dear Mr. Doe:

Complimentary Close:

> Very truly yours,
> Yours respectfully,
> Sincerely yours,

Senator or Senator-Elect

Address:

> The Honorable _____ _____,
> > The United States Senate,
> > > Washington 25, D.C.

Salutation:

> Dear Sir *or* Dear Madam:
> > *or*
> My dear Senator:
> Dear Senator _____: (informal)
> > *or*
> My dear Mr. (Mrs., Miss) _____:

Complimentary Close:

> Very truly yours,

Representative

Address:

> The Honorable _____ _____,
> > The House of Representatives,
> > > Washington 25, D.C.

Salutation:

> Dear Sir *or* Dear Madam:
> Dear Mr. (Mrs.) _____: (informal)

Complimentary Close:

> Very truly yours,

Commissioner

Address:	The Honorable _____ _____, Chairman, Civil Service Commission, Washington 25, D.C.
Salutation:	Sir: *or* My dear Mr. Chairman: *or* Dear Mr. _____: (informal)
Complimentary Close:	Very truly yours,

In official communications to Heads of Independent Agencies the complimentary title "The Honorable" is to be used unless a Service rank or scholastic degree is used instead.

U.S. *Department of State Correspondence Handbook*

Chief Justice of the Supreme Court

Address:	The Chief Justice of the United States, *or* The Chief Justice, The Supreme Court, Washington 25, D.C.
Salutation:	Sir: *or* My dear Mr. Chief Justice:
Complimentary Close:	Very truly yours,

Associate Justice of the Supreme Court

Address:	Mr. Justice _____, The Supreme Court, Washington 25, D.C.
Salutation:	My dear Mr. Justice: *or* Dear Justice _____: (informal)
Complimentary Close:	Very truly yours,

District Judge

Address: The Honorable _____ _____,
                                      United States District Judge,
                                          Southern District of New York,
                                              New York, N.Y.
Salutation: Dear Sir:
                                          or
                                  Dear Judge _____: (informal)
Complimentary Close: Very truly yours,

Judge of State Courts

Address: The Honorable _____ _____,
                                      Chief Judge of the Court of Appeals,
                                          Albany, N.Y.
Salutation: Dear Sir:
                                          or
                                  Dear Judge _____: (informal)
Complimentary Close: Very truly yours,

Governor

Address: The Honorable
                                          or
                                  The Honorable _____ _____,
                                      The Governor of New York,
                                          Albany, New York.
Salutation: Sir:
                                          or
                                  Dear Sir:
                                          or
                                  Dear Governor _____: (informal)
Complimentary Close: Very truly yours,

Lieutenant Governor

Address: The Honorable _____ _____,
                                      Lieutenant Governor of New York,
                                          Albany, New York.
Salutation: Dear Sir:
                                          or
                                  Dear Governor _____:
Complimentary Close: Very truly yours,

State Senator

Address:

The Honorable _____ _____,
The State Senate,
Albany, New York.
or
Senator _____ _____,
The State Capitol,
Albany, New York.

Salutation:

Sir:
or
Dear Sir:
or
Dear Senator _____: (informal)

Complimentary Close: Very truly yours,

Member of Assembly

Address:

The Honorable _____ _____,
The State Capitol,
Albany, New York.

Salutation:

Dear Sir:
or
Dear Mr. _____: (informal)

Complimentary Close: Very truly yours,

Mayor

Address:

The Honorable _____ _____,
Mayor of _____,
or
The Mayor of _____,
City, State.

Salutation:

Sir *or* Madam:
or
My dear Mr. *or* Madam Mayor:
or
Dear Mayor _____: (informal)

Complimentary Close: Yours respectfully,

Women Officials

Women holding the same positions as men are addressed by the
same titles. In the address itself the given name without *Mrs.* or

Miss should be used, as, *The Honorable Helen Brown.* In the formal salutation *Madam* for both married and unmarried women is substituted for *Sir.* In an informal salutation *Mrs.* or *Miss* would be used, as, Dear Mrs. (or Miss) Brown. Socially a woman official is addressed by her personal title of *Mrs. John Brown* or *Miss Helen Brown.*

Addressing Foreign Ambassadors in Washington

In the address on the envelope and in the inside address, the name and title, if known, should be used. If this is done, the definite article *the* should be dropped in the line that follows, making it read "Ambassador of the French Republic," etc.

"The Ambassador of Great Britain" and "The Ambassador of the French Republic" are the exact and official designations, but "The British Ambassador" and "The French Ambassador" are frequently used by the general public and by writers in and outside of the Government service.

Address:	His Excellency
	    Name and title, if known,
	    Ambassador of _____
	        or
	His Excellency
	    The Ambassador of _____
	    Washington, D.C.

Salutation:	Excellency: (formal)
	        or
	Sir: (formal)
	        or
	My dear Mr. Ambassador: (informal)
	        or
	Dear Sir: (informal)
	        or
	Dear _____ _____: (title and name, in-
	    formal)

Complimentary Close:	Accept, Excellency, the (renewed) as-
	    surances of my highest consideration
	    (formal diplomatic usage)
	        or
	Very truly yours, (formal general usage)
	        or
	I am, my dear Mr. Ambassador,
	    Sincerely yours, (informal)

Ministers from Foreign Countries

Address: The Honorable _____ _____,
                    Minister of _____.
                        or
                    Envoy Extraordinary and
                    Minister Plenipotentiary from

                    _____.
                        or
                    Mr. _____ _____, (followed by the offi-
                    cial title)

Salutation: Sir:
                        or
                    My dear Mr. Minister:

Complimentary Close: Same as Ambassador's

American Ambassador (man)

Address: The Honorable _____ _____,
                    American Ambassador,
                    City, Country.

Salutation: Sir: (formal)
                        or
                    Dear Mr. Ambassador: (informal)
                    Dear Sir: (informal)
                    Dear _____ _____: (title and name in-
                    formal)

Complimentary Close: Very truly yours,
                    Sincerely yours,

Address with Naval Rank: Admiral _____ _____,
                    American Ambassador,
                    City, Country.

Salutation: Sir:
                    My dear Mr. Ambassador:
                        or
                    My dear Admiral _____: (informal)

American Ambassador (woman)

Address: The Honorable Jane Doe,
                    American Ambassador,
                    City, Country.

Salutation: Madam: (formal)
                    My dear Madam Ambassador:
                        or
                    My dear Mrs. (Miss) _____:

American Chargé d'Affaires

Address:	American Chargé d'Affaires
	or
	———— ————, Esq.,
	American Chargé d'Affaires
	City, State.
Salutation:	Dear Sir:
Complimentary Close:	Very truly yours,

Foreign Chargé d'Affaires

Address:	Baron ———— ————,
	Chargé d'Affaires,
	City, Country.
Salutation:	Dear Sir:
	or
	Sir:
Complimentary Close:	Accept, Sir, the renewed assurance of my
	high consideration,
	or
	Respectfully yours,
	or
	Very truly yours,

Consul

Address:	American Consul at ————————,
	or
	———— ————, Esq.,
	American Chargé d'Affaires
Salutation:	Dear Sir:
Complimentary Close:	Very truly yours,

EXCELLENCY

The use of the title *Excellency* in addressing American officials is not in accordance with American custom. However a few states, such as Massachusetts and New Hampshire, have officially adopted this title in addressing their governors.

According to the Department of State, "*His Excellency* is the complimentary diplomatic title in addressing foreign presidents, foreign ambassadors, foreign cabinet officers, foreign high officials, and former high officials. *His Excellency* is used in the address;

Excellency is used in the salutation and (generally) in the complimentary close; and *Your Excellency* is used in the body of the communication."

In ecclesiastical correspondence *Excellency* is used in addressing all Roman Catholic archbishops and bishops (see pp. 321–322).

HONORABLE AS USED IN AMERICA

The title *Honorable* should be used in addressing the following: ex-Presidents, President-elect, and all high ex-officials, Governors, Cabinet officers, Senators, Congressmen, American Ambassadors, American Ministers, the Secretary to the President, Under Secretaries, Assistant Secretaries of the Executive Departments, Judges (not of the Supreme Court), Heads of the Independent Boards of Commissioners, Mayors of Cities.

In formal correspondence, this title is written in full above the name. In less formal correspondence, if the length of the line permits, it is often written in full or abbreviated in the line with the name.

This title is used only when followed by initials or a first name; as, *Hon. Alexander Scott* or *Hon. A. N. Scott* not *Hon. Scott*. The word should not be abbreviated when preceded by *the*.

In certain communities *Hon.* is used with the names of city and state officials; as, Police Commissioner and Aldermen, or City Council.

Police Commissioner	Hon. James Blank Police Commissioner of _____
Alderman	Hon. John Blank
District Attorney	Hon. William Blank
Corporation Counsel	Hon. Albert Blank

ESQUIRE

Esquire is not generally used in the United States except for professional men, such as architects and attorneys. It should not be used with *Mr.* or *Honorable*. Government style advocates its use with foreign service officers below the grade of career minister, clerk of the Supreme Court of the United States, and officers of other courts.

In official American correspondence *Esquire* is written in full, but in social correspondence it is abbreviated.

Correct Usage in Addressing Invitations to City Officials and Their Wives

Mayor

The Mayor of Exville
and Mrs. Blank
or
The Honorable John Blank
and Mrs. Blank
or
The Honorable and Mrs. John Blank

Police Commissioner
or
Alderman

The Honorable John Blank
and Mrs. Blank
or
The Honorable and Mrs. John Blank
or
Mr. and Mrs. John Blank

Correct Usage in Addressing Invitations to Government Officials and Their Wives

The President
and Mrs. _____
    The White House
The Vice President
and Mrs. _____
The Secretary of State
and Mrs. _____
The Chief Justice
and Mrs. _____

Senator and Wife

Address on Envelope: The Honorable _____ _____ and Mrs.
    _____,

Address on Inside   Home Address
Envelope, as in
Wedding Invitations: Senator and Mrs. _____
His Excellency
The Ambassador of Venezuela
and Madame _____
The Minister of _____ _____
and Madame _____
The Chargé d'Affaires of _____
and Madame _____

DIPLOMATIC CORRESPONDENCE

In diplomatic notes and reports to the President, the address should appear at the lower left-hand corner of the page. In instructions and miscellaneous letters, the address should precede the salutation on the left-hand margin.

TITLES FOR MEMBERS OF THE DIPLOMATIC CORPS

As titles of the Diplomatic Corps may change, it is important to check with the *Diplomatic List* published monthly by the Department of State.

The names and titles of foreign consular officers in the United States may be found in *Foreign Consular Offices in the United States,* published quarterly by the Department of State, and also in the *Congressional Directory*.

Military and Naval Titles

Military Service Ranks

The comparative ranks of the five Services are indicated below and take precedence in the order listed:

Army [1]	Navy
(1) General of the Army	(1) Fleet Admiral
(2) General	(2) Admiral
(3) Lieutenant General	(3) Vice Admiral
(4) Major General	(4) Rear Admiral
(5) Brigadier General	(5) Commodore
(6) Colonel	(6) Captain
(7) Lieutenant Colonel	(7) Commander
(8) Major	(8) Lieutenant Commander
(9) Captain	(9) Lieutenant
(10) First Lieutenant	(10) Lieutenant (junior grade)
(11) Second Lieutenant	(11) Ensign
(12) Chief Warrant Officer	(12) Chief Warrant Officer
(13) Warrant Officer	(13) Warrant Officer
(14) First Sergeant, Master Sergeant or Master Specialist	(14) Chief Petty Officer

[1] In recent years only John J. Pershing has had the title General of the Armies.

Army

(15) Sergeant First Class or Specialist First Class
(16) Sergeant or Specialist Second Class
(17) Corporal or Specialist Third Class
(18) Private First Class
(19) Private
(20) Private

Navy

(15) Petty Officer First Class
(16) Petty Officer Second Class
(17) Petty Officer Third Class
(18) Seaman
(19) Seaman Apprentice
(20) Seaman Recruit

Marine Corps

(1) (No equivalent)
(2) General
(3) Lieutenant General
(4) Major General
(5) Brigadier General
(6) Colonel
(7) Lieutenant Colonel
(8) Major
(9) Captain
(10) First Lieutenant
(11) Second Lieutenant
(12) Chief Warrant Officer
(13) Warrant Officer
(14) Master Sergeant
(15) Technical Sergeant
(16) Staff Sergeant
(17) Sergeant
(18) Corporal
(19) Private First Class
(20) Private

Air Force

(1) General of the Air Force
(2) General
(3) Lieutenant General
(4) Major General
(5) Brigadier General
(6) Colonel
(7) Lieutenant Colonel
(8) Major
(9) Captain
(10) First Lieutenant
(11) Second Lieutenant
(12) Chief Warrant Officer
(13) Warrant Officer
(14) Master Sergeant
(15) Technical Sergeant
(16) Staff Sergeant
(17) Airman First Class
(18) Airman Second Class
(19) Airman Third Class
(20) Airman

Coast Guard

(1) (No equivalent)
(2) Admiral
(3) Vice Admiral
(4) Rear Admiral
(5) Commodore
(6) Captain
(7) Commander
(8) Lieutenant Commander
(9) Lieutenant
(10) Lieutenant (junior grade)
(11) Ensign
(12) Chief Warrant Officer
(13) Warrant Officer
(14) Chief Petty Officer
(15) Petty Officer, First Class
(16) Petty Officer, Second Class
(17) Petty Officer, Third Class
(18) Seaman
(19) Seaman Apprentice
(20) Seaman Recruit

The rank of women in the various women's services (WACS, WAVES, MARINES, SPARS, etc.) is identical with that of men of comparable rank.

U.S. Department of State Correspondence Handbook

In official and formal correspondence in the Regular Army, officers with the grade of captain and above are addressed by their titles.

In conversation and in nonofficial correspondence brigadier generals, major generals, lieutenant generals, and generals are addressed as "General"; lieutenant colonels under the same conditions are referred to and addressed as "Colonel"; fleet admirals of the Navy, full admirals, vice admirals, and rear admirals of the Navy and Coast Guard, as "Admiral."

Military Discipline, Courtesies and Customs of the Service

For correct usage in addressing in correspondence high officers of the armed services, for Secretary of Defense, Secretary of the Air Force, Secretary of the Army, Secretary of the Navy, see p. 290.

To a General

Address:	General _____ _____, U.S.A., Street, City, State.
Salutation:	Sir: (formal) My dear General _____: (informal)
Complimentary Close:	Very truly yours, (formal) Sincerely yours, (informal)

To a Major General

Address:	Major General _____ _____, U.S.A., Fort Myer, Virginia.
Salutation:	Sir: (formal) My dear General _____: (informal)
Complimentary Close:	Very truly yours, (formal) Sincerely yours, (informal)

To a Brigadier General

Address: Brigadier General _____ _____, U.S.A.,
                                 Fort Sam Houston, Texas.
Salutation: Sir: (formal)
                                 My dear General _____: (informal)
Complimentary Close: Very truly yours, (formal)
                                 Sincerely yours, (informal)

To an Admiral

Address: Admiral _____ _____, U.S.N.,
                                 Chief of Naval Operations,
                                     Department of the Navy,
                                         Washington, D.C.
Salutation: Sir: (formal)
                                 My dear Admiral _____: (informal)
Complimentary Close: Very truly yours, (formal)
                                 Sincerely yours, (informal)

To a Vice Admiral

Address: Vice Admiral _____ _____, U.S.N.
                                 U.S.S. (name of ship),
                                     San Diego, California.
Salutation: Sir: (formal)
                                 My dear Admiral _____: (informal)
Complimentary Close: Very truly yours, (formal)
                                 Sincerely yours, (informal)

In written communications officers of the Medical Department of the Army and of the Navy are addressed by their military titles regardless of rank.

Captain John Doe, Medical Corps
United States Army

Chaplains are addressed as "Chaplain" regardless of their grade.
Cadets of the United States Military Academy are addressed as "Mister" socially and in conversation, and as "Cadet" officially and in written communication.

Noncommissioned officers are addressed by their titles.

National Guard and Reserve officers on active military duty follow the customs of the Regular Army in the matter of titles and addresses.

Military Discipline, Courtesies and Customs of the Service

In official and formal communications, an officer on the active list of the Navy is addressed as follows:

Lieutenant John Doe
United States Navy

In official and formal communications, officers on the retired list are addressed as follows:

Lieutenant John Doe
United States Navy, Retired

In official and formal communications to officers of the staff, the name of the corps to which any staff officer belongs is written immediately after the name:

Lieutenant John Doe, Medical Corps
United States Navy

In official and formal communications to warrant officers, prefix the title to the name:

Boatswain John Doe
United States Navy

Chief Boatswain John Doe
United States Navy

In oral address and informal correspondence, officers of the rank of *commander* and above are always called by their rank; "male officers below the grade of commander in the Navy and captain in the Marine Corps may be addressed as 'Mister' and female officers of similar grade as 'Miss' or 'Mrs.,' except that officers of the Medical Corps and of the Dental Corps may be addressed as 'Doctor,' and officers of the Chaplain Corps as 'Chaplain.' "

U.S. Navy Regulations

"In the Army, the accepted custom is to use the military title, regardless of rank. There is one exception, which has had a steady gain in popularity in recent years, namely, that of referring to physicians whose work brings them in direct contact with patients as 'doctor' in oral communication. In administrative and field medical jobs, at official functions, and in all written communications, the military title continues as the accepted custom."

U.S. Department of the Army, Office of the Surgeon General

UNITED STATES COAST GUARD

Official communications to the officers of the United States Coast Guard follow in general the rules for the United States Navy.

> Commander J. B. Jones
> U. S. Coast Guard

A letter to the Coast Guard should be addressed to the Commandant or to the commanding officer of the unit addressed.

> The Commandant
> U. S. Coast Guard
> Washington, D. C.

> The Superintendent
> U. S. Coast Guard Academy
> New London, Conn.

> The Commanding Officer
> U. S. C. G. C. *Cayuga,*
> Boston, Mass.

UNITED STATES AIR FORCE OFFICER

Lieutenant Colonel

Address:	Lieutenant Colonel John Doe, U.S.A.F., Bolling Air Force Base, Washington 25, D.C.
Salutation:	Dear Sir: Dear Colonel Doe:
Complimentary Close:	Very truly yours, Sincerely yours,

Correct Usage in Addressing Officers and Their Wives in Social Communications

General and Mrs. John Doe
or
General John Doe and Mrs. Doe

Brigadier General and Mrs. John Doe
or
Brigadier General John Doe and Mrs. Doe

Lieutenant and Mrs. John Doe
or
Lieutenant John Doe and Mrs. Doe

FORMS OF ADDRESS USED IN CORRESPONDENCE WITH MEMBERS OF ROYALTY AND NOBILITY OF GREAT BRITAIN

American Forms

"It is only in very exceptional cases that a private individual should address a king, a queen, or other member of a royal family; in no case should a foreigner address them except through the regular diplomatic or other appropriate channel.

"American citizens, in addressing any member of the royal family or nobility, any foreign official, or anyone with whom they are not personally acquainted, may use a salutation and complimentary close in conformity with American practice."

U.S. *Department of State Correspondence Handbook.* Part III

Duke

Address:	His Grace The Duke of Rochester, (Local address)
Salutation:	Sir: (formal) My dear Duke of Rochester: (informal)
Complimentary Close:	Very truly yours, Sincerely yours,

Earl

Address:	The Right Honorable The Earl of Leicester, G.C.V.O., C.M.G., (Local address) *or* The Earl of Leicester, G.C.V.O., C.M.G., (Local address)
Salutation:	Sir: (formal) My dear Lord Leicester: (informal)
Complimentary Close:	Very truly yours, Sincerely yours,

British Forms

CORRECT USAGE IN ADDRESSING IN CORRESPONDENCE MEMBERS
OF ROYALTY AND OF THE NOBILITY OF GREAT BRITAIN

Queen

Address:	To The Queen's Most Excellent Majesty, (for formal or State documents) To Her Majesty The Queen, (otherwise)
Salutation:	Madam, *or* May it please Your Majesty,
Complimentary Close:	I have the honour to remain, Madam, Your Majesty's most obedient servant,

Queen Mother

Address:	To Her Majesty Queen Elizabeth the Queen Mother
Salutation:	Madam, *or* May it please your Majesty,
Complimentary Close:	I have the honour to remain, Madam, Your Majesty's most obedient servant,

Prince and Princess of The Blood Royal

Address:	To His (*or* Her) Royal Highness the Prince (*or* Princess) _____,
Salutation:	Sir (*or* Madam),
Complimentary Close:	I have the honour to be, Sir (*or* Madam), Your Royal Highness's most humble and obedient servant,

Dukes and Duchesses of The Blood Royal

Address:	To His (*or* Her) Royal Highness the Duke (*or* Duchess) of _____,
Salutation:	Sir (*or* Madam),
Complimentary Close:	I have the honour to be, Sir, (*or* Madam), Your Royal Highness's most humble and obedient servant,

Duke

Address:	His Grace the Duke of _____,
	or
	The Duke of _____, (informal)
Salutation:	My Lord Duke, (formal)
	or
	Dear Duke of _____, (informal)
Complimentary Close:	I remain
	Your Grace's most obedient servant,
	or
	Yours very sincerely, (informal)

Duchess

Address:	Her Grace the Duchess of _____,
	or
	The Duchess of _____, (informal)
Salutation:	Madam, (formal)
	or
	Dear Duchess of _____, (informal)
Complimentary Close:	Similar to Duke's

Duke's Eldest Son

Takes the title of Marquess (Marquis) or Earl by courtesy. (*See* Marquess and Earl, p. 308.)

Duke's Daughters and Younger Sons

Address:	The Right Honourable Lord John _____,
	The Right Honourable Lady Mary _____,
	The Lord John _____, (family name)
	The Lady Mary _____, (family name)
Salutation:	My Lord, (formal)
	My Lady, (formal)
	Dear Lord John, (informal)
	Dear Lady Mary, (informal)
Complimentary Close:	(Similar to that of Duke)

Wives of Duke's Younger Sons

The Lady John Smith (*not* Lady Smith)

Marquess

Address: The Most Honourable the Marquess
                            (Marquis) of _____,
                                      or
                            The Marquess of _____,
Salutation: My Lord Marquess,
                                      or
                            My Lord, (formal),
                                      or
Complimentary Close: Dear Lord _____, (informal)
                            Yours very truly,
                            Yours sincerely,

Marchioness

Address: The Most Honourable the Marchioness
                            of _____,
                                      or
                            The Marchioness of _____,
Salutation: My Lady Marchioness, (formal)
                                      or
                            Madam,
                                      or
                            Dear Lady _____, (informal)
Complimentary Close: Similar to Marquess's

Daughters and Younger Sons of a Marquess

Address: Lord Frederick _____, (family name)
                            Lady Helen _____, (family name)

Earl

Address: The Right Honourable the Earl of _____,
Salutation: My Lord, (formal)
                            Dear Lord _____, (informal)
Complimentary Close: I have the honour to remain,
                                Your Lordship's obedient servant,
                                (formal)
                            Sincerely yours, (informal)

Countess

Address:	The Right Honourable the Countess of _____,
Salutation:	Madam, (formal) Dear Lady _____, (informal)
Complimentary Close:	Similar to Earl's

Earl's Eldest Son

See Viscount

Earl's Younger Son

Address:	The Honourable William _____,
Salutation:	Sir, (formal) Dear Mr. _____, (informal)
Complimentary Close:	I have the honour to be, Sir, Your obedient servant, (formal) Very sincerely yours, (informal)

Earl's Daughter

Address:	The Lady Mary _____, (family name)
Salutation:	Madam, (formal) Dear Lady (Christian name), (informal)
Complimentary Close:	I have the honour to remain, Your obedient servant, (formal) Very sincerely yours, (informal)

Viscount

Address:	The Right Honourable the Viscount _____, *or* The Viscount _____,
Salutation:	Sir, (formal) Dear Lord _____, (informal)
Complimentary Close:	Believe me, my dear Lord _____, Very sincerely yours, (informal)

Viscountess

Address: The Right Honourable the Viscountess
                                     ——,
                                         or
                                 The Viscountess ——,
Salutation: Madam, (formal)
                                 Dear Lady ——, (informal)
Complimentary Close: Similar to Viscount's

Son and Daughter of Viscount

Address: The Honourable Robert ——,
                                 The Honourable Mary ——,
Salutation: Sir, [Madam,] (formal)
                                 Dear Mr. ——, (informal)
                                 Dear Miss ——, (informal)
Complimentary Close: Similar to that of Viscount

Baron

Address: The Right Honourable Lord ——,
                                     (formal)
                                         or
                                 The Lord ——, (informal)
Salutation: My Lord, (formal)
                                 Dear Lord ——, (informal)
Complimentary Close: Believe me, my dear Lord ——,
                                     Yours very sincerely, (informal)

Baroness

Address: The Right Honourable Lady ——,
                                         or
                                 The Lady ——, (informal)
Salutation: Madam, (formal)
                                 Dear Lady ——, (informal)
Complimentary Close: Similar to Baron's

Baroness in Her Own Right

Address:	The Right Honourable Baroness _____,
	or
	The Baroness _____, (informal)
Salutation:	Madam, (formal)
	Dear Lady _____, (informal)
Complimentary Close:	Believe me, my dear Lady _____,
	Yours very sincerely, (informal)

Baron's Son and Wife

Address:	The Honourable Arthur _____,
	The Honourable Mrs. _____,
Salutation:	Sir,
	Madam, (formal)
	Dear Mr. _____,
	Dear Mrs. _____, (informal)
Complimentary Close:	Believe me, Mr. (*or* Mrs.) _____
	Yours very sincerely, (informal)

Baron's Daughter

Address:	The Honourable Mary _____,
Salutation:	Madam, (formal)
	Dear Miss _____, (informal)
Married Name:	The Honourable Mrs. _____, *or*
	The Honourable Lady _____,
Complimentary Close:	Believe me,
	Very sincerely yours, (informal)

Baronet

Address:	Sir George Robinson, Bt. or Bart.,
Salutation:	Sir, (formal)
	Dear Sir George, (informal)
Complimentary Close:	Believe me, dear Sir George,
	Faithfully yours, (informal)

Wife of Baronet

Address:	Lady Robinson,
Salutation:	Madam, (formal)
	Dear Lady Robinson, (informal)
Complimentary Close:	Similar to Baronet's

Knight

Address:	Sir William _____, K.C.M.G.,
Salutation:	Sir, (formal)
	Dear Sir William, (informal)
Complimentary Close:	Believe me, dear Sir William,
	Faithfully yours, (informal)

Knight's Wife

Address:	Lady _____, (family name)
Salutation:	Madam, (formal)
	Dear Lady Mary, (informal)
Complimentary Close:	Similar to Knight's

Lady

The title "Lady" is used of all peeresses under the rank of duchess, of all daughters of the three highest ranks of the peerage, and of the wives of baronets and knights.

Titles and Forms of Address

Dame

Address:	Dame Mary Blank, D.B.E.
	(*or* G.B.E.)
Salutation:	Dear Madam, (formal)
	Dear Dame Mary Blank, (informal)

Woman Member of the House of Commons

Address:	The Rt. Honourable _____ _____, M.P.
Salutation:	If a member of the nobility, she is addressed according to her rank. If not a member of the nobility, she is addressed as *Dear Mrs. Blank,* or *Dear Miss Blank,*

HONOURABLE USED WITH BRITISH TITLES

(In correspondence used only on envelopes)

Right Honourable used with all Privy Councillors and preceding all other titles.

The Rt. Hon. _____ _____

Prime Minister

The Rt. Hon. _____ _____

Member of the House of Lords

    The Rt. Hon. the Earl of Whitby

Member of the House of Commons

    The Rt. Hon. _____ _____, M.P. (without *Mr.* or *Esq.*)
    The Rt. Hon. Lady Astor, M.P.

Knight

    The Rt. Hon. Sir John _____

Baronet

    The Rt. Hon. Sir Arthur _____, Bart.

Younger Son of a Duke or Marquess

    The Rt. Hon. Lord _____ _____

Honourable

    The title *Honourable* is given to children of Peers, maids of honor, and judges of the High Court of Justice.

MILITARY TITLES

    Military titles precede all other titles.

        Admiral Sir _____ _____
        Field Marshall The Lord (or other title) _____ _____
        Captain the Hon. _____ _____, R.N.

ESQUIRE (BRITISH USAGE)

    The almost universal use of this title for every man who cannot claim a higher one persists in spite of protests and objections from those who are really entitled to it. The practice has established itself that it is considered positively rude to address an envelope to anyone above the rank of working man as Mr.

Titles and Forms of Address

Examples of correct British usage

Robert Hill, Esq.
Thomas Brown, Esq., **M.D.**

Henry Jameson, Esq.,
H.B.M.'s Consul

Style of Address in Correspondence with French Officials as Advocated by the United States Department of State

It is the more common practice for Americans in general to use the English language and appropriate American forms.

COMPLIMENTARY TITLES

The complimentary titles "Monsieur," "Madame," and "Mademoiselle" are to be written in full in all correspondence.

OFFICIALS

The complimentary title "Excellence" is used in addressing the President of the French Republic, high officials of the Republic, and foreign ambassadors. The forms of salutation, of complimentary close, and of appellation in the body of a communication naturally vary according to the official or social positions of the person addressed and the writer.

The following forms of address, salutation, and complimentary close may be used:

President

Address: (always formal)	Son Excellence Monsieur le Président de la République, Paris, France.
Salutation:	Monsieur le Président de la République:
Complimentary Close:	Je vous prie d'agréer, Monsieur le Président, les assurances de ma très haute considération,

President of the Council

Address: (always formal)	Son Excellence Monsieur le Président du Conseil, Paris, France.
Salutation:	Monsieur le Président du Conseil:
Complimentary Close:	Je vous prie d'agréer, Monsieur le Président du Conseil, les assurances de ma très haute considération,

Mayor

Address:	Monsieur le Maire de Nantes, (Local address)
Salutation:	Monsieur le Maire:
Complimentary Close:	Veuillez agréer, Monsieur le Maire, les assurances de ma considération la plus distinguée,

The United Nations

The United Nations is an organization of sovereign states. It functions through six principal branches, called *organs* in the language of the Charter, as follows:

> The General Assembly
> The Security Council
> The Economic and Social Council
> The Trusteeship Council
> The International Court of Justice
> The Secretariat

There is considerable variation in the titles of the different representatives. That the title accorded a representative is determined by the position which he holds in his Government's service is generally correct; but his title is to some extent also dependent upon the nature of his position vis-à-vis the United Nations.

Executive Office of the Secretary General

The following examples are taken from U.S. *Department of State Correspondence Handbook*. Part III.

The Secretary General of the United Nations

Address:	His Excellency [1]
	John Doe,
	    Secretary General of the United Nations,
	        United Nations, New York.

Salutation:	Excellency: (formal) My dear Mr. Secretary General: (informal preferred) *or* My dear Mr. Doe:

[1] For use of Excellency see pp. 296–297.

Complimentary Close: Accept, Excellency, the (renewed) [1] as-
                        surances of my highest considera-
                        tion, (formal diplomatic usage)
                        Sincerely yours, (informal)

The Assistant Secretary General of the United Nations

Address: The Honorable _____ _____,
                            Assistant Secretary General of the
                            United Nations,
                                United Nations, New York.
Salutation: Sir: (formal)
                        My dear Mr. _____: (informal)
Complimentary Close: Very truly yours, (formal)
                        Sincerely yours, (informal)

A Foreign Representative to the United Nations with the Personal Rank of Ambassador

Address: His Excellency
                        John Doe,
                            Representative of (country) to the
                            United Nations,
                                (City, State or Country)
Salutation: Excellency: (formal)
                        My dear Mr. Ambassador: (informal)
Complimentary Close: Accept, Excellency, the (renewed) [1] as-
                        surances of my highest considera-
                        tion, (formal diplomatic usage)
                        Yours sincerely, (informal)

The United States Representative to the United Nations

Address: The Honorable
                        John Doe,
                            United States Representative (or
                            Acting United States Representa-
                            tive) to the United Nations,
                                New York 16, New York.
Salutation: Sir: (formal)
                        My dear Mr. Doe: (informal)
Complimentary Close: Very truly yours, (formal)
                        Sincerely yours, (informal)

[1] This word is used only in second and subsequent communications.

The United States Representative on the Economic and Social Council

Address:

> The Honorable
> John Doe,
>> United States Representative on the Economic and Social Council,

The United States Representative on the Trusteeship Council

Address:

> The Honorable
> John Doe,
>> United States Representative on the Trusteeship Council,

The Senior Representative of the United States to the General Assembly of the United Nations

Address:

> The Honorable
> John Doe,
>> Senior Representative of the United States to the General Assembly of the United Nations,

Salutation and Complimentary Close:

The Secretariat of the United Nations employs the English usage, not the American, as regards titles, spelling, and phraseology in formal communications written in the English language. In formal letters, therefore, the salutation is "Sir:" the complimentary close is

> I have the honour to be, Sir,
> Your obedient Servant,

The private individual might use any of the following expressions, depending on the tone of the letter:

Salutation:
> Sir:
> My dear Sir:
> Dear Sir:
> Dear _____ _____: (title and name)

Complimentary Close:
> Very truly yours,
> Yours very truly,
> Yours respectfully,
> Sincerely yours,

Canadian Officials

Governor General

Address:

If the governor general of a Dominion or Colony is a member of the royal family or of the nobility, he is addressed according to his rank, i.e., duke, earl, viscount, etc., preceded by the title *His Excellency;* if without rank of nobility, his name is preceded by *His Excellency The Right Honourable.* If the governor general has a military title, it must precede other titles.

His Excellency
  Field Marshal The Right Honourable
    The Earl of _____, G.C.M.G.
      Governor General of Canada,
        Ottawa, Canada.

Salutation:

Excellency:
      or
Sir:
      or
My dear Governor General:
      or
My dear Mr. _____: (*or* title)

Complimentary Close:

I have the honour to be
  Your Excellency's obedient servant,
      (formal)
Believe me, my dear Governor General,
  Sincerely yours, (informal)

Prime Minister

Address:

The Right Honourable
  Full name with initials of decorations or orders, if any.
    Prime Minister of the Dominion of Canada.
      Ottawa, Canada.

Salutation: Sir:
                                          or
                           Dear Sir:
                                          or
                           My dear Mr. Prime Minister:
                                          or
                           My dear Mr. _____:

Complimentary Close: I am, my dear Mr. Prime Minister, (*or*
                                Mr. _____,)
                                Respectfully yours,
                                Sincerely yours,

Correct Ecclesiastical Usage for Officials of the Anglican Church

Archbishop

Address: The Most Reverend His Grace
                                The Lord Archbishop of _____,

Salutation: My Lord Archbishop: (formal)
                           My dear Archbishop: (informal)

Complimentary Close: I have the honour to be, my Lord Arch-
                                bishop,
                                Your Grace's most obedient and
                                humble servant,

Bishop [1]

Address:
(American style)   The Right Reverend
                                The Bishop of Washington,
                                          or
                           The Right Reverend
                                John Doe, D.D., LL.D.,
                                Bishop of Washington,
                                (Local address)

(British style)   The Right Reverend the Lord
                                Bishop of _____,
                                          or
                           The Lord Bishop of _____,

[1] The Presiding Bishop of the Protestant Episcopal Church in America is addressed as "The Most Reverend."

Salutation:
(American style)

Right Reverend Sir: (formal)
My dear Bishop _____:

or

My dear Bishop: (informal)
(British style)   My Lord,

or

My Lord Bishop, (formal)

or

Dear Bishop _____, (informal)

Complimentary Close:
(American style)
(British style)

Respectfully yours,
Sincerely yours,
I have the honour to remain your Lordship's obedient servant, (formal)
I have the honour to remain, my dear Lord Bishop, faithfully yours, (informal)

Dean

Address: The Very Reverend the Dean of _____,
Salutation: Very Reverend Sir: (formal)
                           Dear Dean _____: (informal)
Complimentary Close: Faithfully yours,

Archdeacon

Address: The Venerable the Archdeacon of _____,
Salutation: Venerable Sir: (formal)
                           Dear Archdeacon _____: (informal)
Complimentary Close: Faithfully yours,
                           Respectfully yours,

Canon

Address: The Reverend Canon _____,
Salutation: Reverend Sir:
                           Dear Canon _____: (informal)
Complimentary Close: Yours faithfully,
                           Yours respectfully,

Correct Ecclesiastical Usage for Officials of the Roman Catholic Church

The Pope

Address:	His Holiness Pope ____ ____,
	or
	His Holiness the Pope,
Salutation:	Your Holiness:
	or
	Most Holy Father:
Complimentary Close:	Your dutiful son (or daughter),
	or
	Respectfully yours,

Cardinal

Address:	His Eminence
	The Most Reverend
	John Cardinal Doe,
	Archbishop of ____,
Salutation:	Your Eminence: (ecclesiastical usage)
	Most Reverend Sir: (formal)
	My dear Cardinal Doe: (informal)
Complimentary Close:	Respectfully yours,

Archbishop

Address:	His Excellency, the Archbishop of ____,
	or
	The Most Reverend Archbishop of ____,
	or
	The Most Reverend
	John Doe, S.T.D.,
	Archbishop of ____,
Salutation:	Your Excellency:
	or
	Most Reverend Archbishop:
	or
	Dear Archbishop ____: (informal)
Complimentary Close:	Respectfully yours,

Bishop [1]

Address:	His Excellency,
	The Most Reverend
	John Doe, S.T.D.,
	Bishop of Baltimore,
	(Local address)
Salutation:	Your Excellency:
	Most Reverend Sir:
	Dear Bishop _____: (informal)
Complimentary Close:	Respectfully yours,
	Sincerely yours,

Member of the Papal Household
Monsignor (Domestic Prelate)

Address:	The Very Reverend Monsignor _____,
	The Right Reverend Monsignor _____,
Salutation:	Monsignor: (formal)
	My dear Monsignor Doe: (informal)
Complimentary Close:	Respectfully yours,

Priest

Address:	The Reverend Father Brown,
	or
	Rev. J. B. Brown,
Salutation:	Dear Father Brown:
	or
	Dear Reverend Father:
	or
	Dear Father:
Complimentary Close:	Respectfully yours,
	or
	Sincerely yours,

[1] A bishop of the Roman Catholic Church is addressed in America and in Ireland as The *Most* Reverend; in England and in Scotland as The *Right* Reverend. In England the addition of D.D. or the prefixing of Doctor or Dr. to the names of Roman Catholic bishops is not in conformity with the best usage.—U.S. *Department of State Correspondence Handbook.*

Correct Ecclesiastical Usage for Protestant and Jewish Clergy in America

Protestant Episcopal Bishop

Address:	The Right Reverend _____ _____, Bishop of New York, *or* The Right Reverend John Doe, D.D., LL.D., Bishop of Washington, (Local address)
Salutation:	Right Reverend Sir: (formal) *or* Dear Bishop _____: (informal)
Complimentary Close:	Sincerely yours,

Dean

Address:	Dean _____ _____, *or* The Very Rev. John Doe,
Salutation:	Very Reverend Sir: (formal) Dear Dean _____: (informal)
Complimentary Close:	Yours respectfully, *or* Sincerely yours, *or* Cordially yours, (informal)

Methodist Bishop

Address:	The Reverend John Doe, D.D., Methodist Bishop, (Local address)
Salutation:	Reverend Sir: (formal) Dear Bishop: (informal) *or* Dear Bishop _____:
Complimentary Close:	Sincerely yours, *or* Respectfully yours,

Other Clergymen

Address:	The Reverend ____ ____,
	or
	Rev. Dr. ____ ____, (if entitled to a degree)
	or
	Rev. ____ ____, D.D.
Salutation:	Dear Sir:
	or
	Dear Mr. ____: (informal)
	or
	Dear Dr. ____: (if entitled to a degree)
Complimentary Close:	Yours respectfully,
	or
	Yours sincerely,

Jewish Rabbi

Address:	Rabbi ____ ____,
Salutation:	Dear Sir:
	or
	My dear Dr. ____:
	Dear Rabbi ____:
Complimentary Close:	Yours respectfully,

Correct Usage for Members of Religious Institutions

Superior of a Sisterhood

Address:	Reverend Mother, (followed by initials designating order, if desired)
	or
	Reverend Mother Superior, (without initials of order)
Salutation:	Reverend Mother:
	or
	Dear Reverend Mother: (informal)
	or
	My dear Reverend Mother: (name added if desired)
Complimentary Close:	Yours respectfully,

Member of a Sisterhood

Address:	Sister Mary Angela, (followed by initials of order, if desired)
	or
	Sister Mary Angela, O.S.D. (Order of St. Dominic)
Salutation:	Dear Sister:
	or
	Dear Sister Angela:
	or
	My dear Sister Angela:
Complimentary Close:	Yours sincerely,

Superior of a Brotherhood (Roman Catholic)

Address:	Brother James, F.S.C., Superior, St. John's College, (Local address)
Salutation:	My dear Brother James:
Complimentary Close:	Sincerely yours,

Superior of a Brotherhood (Protestant)

Address:	John Doe, S.B.B., Superior, St. Joseph's College, (Local address)
Salutation:	My dear Brother Doe:
Complimentary Close:	Sincerely yours,

The address for the superior of a brotherhood depends upon his church affiliation and upon whether or not he is a priest or has a title other than *Superior*. A Roman Catholic brother is usually addressed by his Christian name; a Protestant brother is usually addressed by his surname.

U.S. *Department of State Correspondence Handbook*

Correct Usage for Officials in Universities and Colleges

President of a Theological Seminary

Address:	The Reverend President _____ _____,
Salutation:	Dear President _____:
	or
	Dear Dr. _____: (if preferred)
Complimentary Close:	Yours respectfully,
	or
	Yours sincerely,

Professor in a Theological Seminary

Address:	The Reverend Professor ____ ____,
	or
	Rev. ____ ____,
	or
	Professor ____ ____,
Salutation:	Dear Professor ____:
	or
	Dear Dr. ____:
Complimentary Close:	Yours respectfully,
	or
	Yours sincerely,

President of a University

Address:	*(Full name followed by initials for degree or degrees),*
	President of Columbia University,
	or
	President ____ ____,
	Columbia University, New York.
Salutation:	Dear Sir:
	Dear President ____:
Complimentary Close:	Respectfully yours,
	Sincerely yours,

College or University Professor

Address:	Professor ____ ____,
	or
	____ ____, Ph.D.
Salutation:	Dear Professor ____:
	Dear Dr. ____:
Complimentary Close:	Sincerely yours,
	Very truly yours,

Dean of a College

Address:	Dean ____ ____,
	or
	Dr. ____ ____,
Salutation:	Dear Dean ____:
	Dear Dr. ____:
	Dear Miss *or* Mr. ____, (informal)
Complimentary Close:	Sincerely yours,
	Very truly yours,

Usage in Addressing Foreigners (Private Individuals)

The following forms are correct if the body of the letter is written in a foreign language, but if the letter is worded in English it is more common practice for Americans to use the appropriate American forms.

FRENCH USAGE

Gentleman

Address:	Monsieur _____ _____,
Salutation:	Monsieur:
Complimentary Close:	Veuillez agréer, Monsieur, l'assurance de ma considération distinguée,

Married or Unmarried woman

Address:	Madame _____ _____,
	or
	Mademoiselle _____ _____,
Salutation:	Madame:
	or
	Mademoiselle:
Complimentary Close:	Veuillez agréer, Madame *or* Mademoiselle, mes respectueux hommages (when letter is written by a man to a woman).

A woman writing to a woman she knows slightly may address her as: Chère Madame and close thus: Veuillez agréer, chère Madame, l'expression de mes sentiments distingués *or* distingués les meilleurs.

SPANISH USAGE

The forms here given may be used in addressing persons in any Spanish-speaking country.

Firm Name or Organization

Address:	Señores (Sres.) González Hermanos,
Salutation:	Muy señores nuestros:
Complimentary Close:	Muy attos. y s.s., s.s.,

Gentleman

Address:	Señor (Sr.) González
	or
	Señor (Sr.) Don Rafael González
Salutation:	Muy señor mío:
Complimentary Close:	Muy atentamente,

Married Woman

Address:	Señora (Sra.) González *or*
	Señora (Sra.) Doña (Da.) María
	González,
Salutation:	Mi estimada señora:
Complimentary Close:	Soy de Vd. s.s.,

Unmarried Woman

Address:	Señorita (Srta.) *or*
	Señorita (Srta.) Doña (Da.) María
	González,
Salutation:	Mi distinguida señorita:
Complimentary Close:	De Vd. afma. amiga,

In Spanish when Christian names or initials are used with the surname, the title *Don* follows *Señor* and *Doña* follows *Señora.* These titles, *Don* and *Doña,* are not used when Christian names are omitted.

GERMAN USAGE

Firm or Organization

Address:	Name, _____ _____
Salutation:	Geehrte Herren:
Complimentary Close:	Mit dem Ausdruck vorzüglicher Hoch-
	achtung *or* Hochachtungsvoll,

Gentleman

Address:	Herrn _____ _____
Salutation:	Sehr geehrter Herr: (formal)
Complimentary Close:	Mit dem Ausdruck vorzüglicher Hoch-
	achtung *or* Hochachtungsvoll,

Married Woman

Address:	Frau ____ ____
Salutation:	Meine liebe Frau ____: (semi-formal)
	Sehr geehrte Frau ____: (formal)
Complimentary Close:	In Erwartung Ihrer freundlichen Antwort bin ich Ihre Ergebenste,

Unmarried Woman

Address:	Fräulein ____ ____
Salutation:	Mein liebes Fräulein! (cordial)
	Sehr geehrtes Fräulein ____: (formal)
Complimentary Close:	Mit Grüssen an Sie und Ihre Freundin,

ITALIAN USAGE

Firm Name or Organization

Address:	Spettabile Ditta ____,
Salutation:	Spettabile Ditta:
Complimentary Close:	Di voi Obbligatissimo, (*also:* Con rispettosa osservanza,)

Gentleman

Address:	Gentilissimo Signor ____,
Salutation:	Gentilissimo Signore:
Complimentary Close:	Cordialmente vostro, (*also:* Distintamente vostro,)

Married Woman

Address:	Distinta Signora ____,
Salutation:	Distinta Signora:
Complimentary Close:	Vostro devotissimo,

Unmarried Woman

Address:	Esimia Signorina ____ ____,
Salutation:	Esimia Signorina:
Complimentary Close:	Devotamente vostro,

BRAZILIAN USAGE

Business Organization

Inside Address:

Ilustrissimos Senhores (Il^{mos} Srs.)
A.B. & Cia. Ltda.
Rua _____, número _____
Rio de Janeiro
Brasil

Salutation: Prezados Senhores,

Complimentary Close: Apresento a Vossas Senhorias os protestos de minha distinta consideração,

Gentleman

Inside Address:

Excelentíssimo Senhor (Exm^o Sr.)

Rua _____, número _____
Rio de Janeiro
Brasil

Salutation: Prezado Senhor,

Complimentary close: Apresento a Vossa Senhoria os protestos de minha cordial estima e elevado aprêço,

Married Woman

Inside Address:

Excelentíssima Senhora (Exm^a Sra.)

Rua _____, número _____
Rio de Janeiro
Brasil

Salutation: Prezada Senhora,

Complimentary close: Apresento-lhe os meus respeitosos cumprimentos,

Unmarried Woman

Inside Address:

Excelentíssima Senhorita (Exm^a Srta.)

Rua _____, número _____
Rio de Janeiro
Brasil

Salutation: Prezada Senhorita,

Complimentary close: Apresento-lhe os meus cordiais cumprimentos,

REFERENCE BOOKS

BURKE, SIR JOHN BERNARD. *Genealogical and Heraldic History of the Peerage and Baronetage, the Privy Council and Knightage.*

Kelly's Handbook to the Titled, Landed, and Official Classes.

MEASURES, HOWARD. *Styles of Address, A Manual of Usage in Writing and in Speech.* New York, Thomas Y. Crowell.

Titles and Forms of Address: Guide to Their Correct Use. 9th ed., 1956. London, Adam & Charles Black, and New York, The Macmillan Company.

United States. Department of State. *Diplomatic List.* Washington (issued monthly).

Webster's New International Dictionary.

Whitaker's Peerage, Baronetage, Knightage and Companionage.

3. Invitations

Formal Invitations

INVITATIONS TO DINNER

(1)

The pleasure of your company is requested
at a dinner
in honor of
Thomas Gray Lawrence
President of the National Company
to be held at the
Hotel New Yorker
on Wednesday the twelfth of October
at seven o'clock
Tickets Five Dollars   Informal

(2)

The Edgar Allan Poe Club
cordially invites you and your friends to subscribe to a dinner
in celebration of
The One Hundred and Fiftieth Anniversary of the Birth of
Edgar Allan Poe
Friday evening January nineteenth
The Ballroom
Benjamin Franklin Hotel
Philadelphia
seven-thirty o'clock
Speakers include: [Listed]
R.S.V.P.

The City of Norwich will celebrate on July 1st, 2nd, 3rd & 4th 19_, the one hundred and fiftieth anniversary of the incorporation of the City and the two hundred and seventy fifth anniversary of the founding of the Town.

It is the desire of the Committee that as many as possible of the former residents of the City return to their old home town to aid in this celebration and to this end we extend to you a most cordial invitation to visit your old home, or the home of your ancestors and to help us make this a great event, which will last long in your memory.

The Invitation Committee
Roy D. Judd · Chairman

(3)

The Netherland-America Foundation
and
The Chamber of Commerce
of the State of New York
cordially invite you to attend
a dinner in honor of
Ambassador Carl Schurmann
of the Permanent Mission
of the Netherlands
to the United Nations
Wednesday, the twenty-second of January
seven thirty o'clock
The Waldorf-Astoria
Speakers
Ambassador Schurmann
Rev. Robert I. Gannon, S.J.

(4)

To commemorate the One Hundredth Anniversary
of the Consecration
of the present edifice of Trinity Church
The Rector, Churchwardens and Vestrymen of
Trinity Church in the City of New York
request the pleasure of your company
as a member of Trinity Parish
at a Parish Dinner
on Thursday, the sixteenth of May
at seven o'clock
at the Hotel Astor
Broadway and 44th Street, New York

Informal dress

Please make your reservations on the enclosed blank and
return it with your remittance, not later than May first

INVITATIONS TO AN AT HOME

(1)

Doctor and Mrs. Ernest Clark
at Home
on Tuesday, November the tenth
from four until seven o'clock

320 Riverside Drive

(2)

To meet Mrs. Edward Howard
(Written)

Mrs. John Richard Thornton
(Engraved)

Four to seven o'clock
Tuesday, November the twelfth *(Written)*

INVITATIONS TO RECEPTIONS

(1)

In honor of
The Vice President of the United States
and
Mrs. _____
The Congressional Club
requests the pleasure of your company
at a reception
on Sunday the thirty-first of March
at four o'clock in the afternoon
2001 New Hampshire Avenue

Two Guests

(2)

Governor and Mrs. _____
request the pleasure of your company
on
at   o'clock

Governor's Mansion
Tallahassee, Florida

(3)

To meet
Mrs. Edward Howard

Mrs. John Richard Thornton
requests the pleasure of your company
On Friday afternoon, the twelfth of April
from four until seven o'clock
at 7 Lenox Drive

INVITATION TO A RECEPTION AT WHICH A DAUGHTER IS INTRODUCED

Mrs. John Richard Thornton
Miss Helen Louise Thornton
At home
on Wednesday afternoon, the fifth of April
from four until seven o'clock
7 Lenox Drive

INVITATION TO A RECEPTION AND TEA

(1)

Mrs. Andrew Lent and women members of the
Federation Executive Committee
cordially invite you to a
Reception and Tea
In honor of
Mrs. James Lockwood
at the Hotel Ambassador
on Thursday afternoon, September the fourth
from four to six o'clock

Please reply to
Miss Ellen Barnes
500 Riverside Drive

(2)

Honoring

President and Mrs. Robert Gordon Sproul
Provost and Mrs. Monroe E. Deutsch

The Honor Students Society
requests the pleasure of your company
at a Reception and Tea
on Tuesday, the thirteenth of May
from three until five o'clock
Women's Club Room, Stephens Union
University of California

Please respond
Box 8, Wheeler Hall

(3)

Honoring

Mrs. Garold A. Leach

Delta Zeta
requests the pleasure of your company
at Tea
on Thursday, the first of May
from three thirty until five o'clock
Twenty-seven twenty-eight Durant Avenue
Berkeley, California

Please respond

(4)

You are cordially invited
to the President's reception
honoring New Faculty members,
arranged by the Faculty Women's Club
Memorial Building
Thursday, December 12, 19___

Reception 8–10   Dancing 10–12

(5)

The Medical and Surgical Staff
and
The Board of Directors
of
The Children's Hospital Association
cordially invite you to attend
the Anniversary Day Tea
Wednesday, the seventeenth of February
three to five o'clock
Nineteenth Avenue at Downing

INVITATION TO A DANCE

Mr. and Mrs. John Richard Thornton
Miss Helen Louise Thornton
Mr. Harold Thornton
request the pleasure of your company
at a dance
on Wednesday evening, the tenth of February
at ten o'clock
at 7 Lenox Drive

The favor of a reply is requested.

INVITATION TO A DANCE AT WHICH A DAUGHTER IS TO BE INTRODUCED

Mr. and Mrs. John Richard Thornton
request the pleasure of your company
at a dance in honor of their daughter
Miss Helen Louise Thornton
on Thursday evening, the fifteenth of March
at half after ten o'clock
at The Riverside Country Club

INVITATIONS TO A SUBSCRIPTION DANCE

(1)

The pleasure of your company
is requested at the
Second Annual Subscription Dance
on Thursday evening, the tenth of October
at half after ten o'clock
at the Susquehanna Valley Hunt Club

Subscription Tickets, $5.
Please respond to
Mrs. Frank Stevenson
410 College Road

(2)

Mu Zeta
of
Lambda Chi Alpha
requests the pleasure of your company
at a Spring Formal
on Friday, the second of May
at half after eight o'clock
Orinda Country Club

R. s. v. p. $10 per couple

Invitation to a Luncheon Given in Honor of a Guest

Mrs. Thomson would be glad if Miss Varney would take luncheon with her quite informally, at half after twelve o'clock, on Saturday, January fifteenth, at the City Club, 55 West 44th Street, to meet Miss Monteith.

Philosophy Hall
January 9, 19___

Wedding Invitations

(1)

Mr. and Mrs. Robert Lawrence
request the honour of your presence
at the marriage of their daughter
Dorothy Anne
to
Mr. James Eaton
on Friday evening, the ninth of April
nineteen hundred and _____
at six o'clock
at the Huguenot Memorial Church
Pelham Manor, New York

Reception
immediately following the ceremony
Brae Burn Country Club
Pelham, New York

The favour of a reply is requested
495 Rochelle Terrace
Pelham, New York

(2)

When a widow remarries, her Christian name instead of that of her former husband is preferred in the invitation.

The honour of your presence is requested
at the marriage of
Mrs. Ann Gray Green
to
etc.

Issued by remarried mother

Mr. and Mrs. Colin Gordon III
request the honour of your presence
at the marriage of Mrs. Gordon's daughter
Stephanie Wentworth
to
Mr. John Philip Powell
on Saturday, the twenty-sixth of January
at half after four o'clock
Chapel of the Beloved Disciple
Church of the Heavenly Rest
New York City

WEDDING ANNOUNCEMENTS

Issued by parents

Mr. and Mrs. Ira Whittier Wentworth
announce the marriage of their daughter
Amy Constance
to
Mr. Philip Edward Strong
on Friday, the first of January
One thousand nine hundred and _____ _____
Edgewood, Rhode Island

Issued by the bride

A bride may send out a wedding announcement when she has
no relative or friend to make the announcement.

(1)

Miss Margaret Mary Barnes
and
Mr. James Randall Dunham
announce their marriage
on Monday, the sixth of September
nineteen hundred and _____ _____
Whippany, New Jersey

(2)

When a widow remarries, her Christian name instead of that of her former husband is preferred in the announcement.

Mrs. Ellen Gray Farrar
and
Dr. Eliott Shannon
have the honour to announce their marriage
etc.

The wedding of a widowed daughter

The Reverend and Mrs. Ward Grayson
have the honour of
announcing the marriage of their daughter
Mary Grayson Birch
to
etc.

From a widowed mother

Mrs. Alexander Cushman
announces the marriage of her daughter
Katherine
to
Dr. Donald Morris
on Saturday the fourteenth of November
Arlington Street Church
Boston, Massachusetts

INVITATIONS TO WEDDING ANNIVERSARIES

Golden Weddings

(1)

Mr. and Mrs. Alexander Johnson
request the pleasure of your company
at the fiftieth anniversary of their marriage
on Thursday the third of April
at nine o'clock
Ten Cedar Drive
The favor of an answer is requested

(2)

The Pollock Family
request the pleasure of
(name written in)
company at the Fiftieth Anniversary
of the marriage of their parents
Mr. and Mrs. William Pollock
on Saturday, the twenty-fourth of June
at seven o'clock
Hotel Langford

Kindly reply to
Mr. Andrew Pollock
423 Mayfield Avenue

(3)

Mr. and Mrs. Hilary Holt
request the pleasure of your company
at the celebration of their
Golden Wedding
on July fourth
Nineteen hundred and _____ _____
seven o'clock in the evening
at the
Terrace Club Room
Hotel St. Moritz
50 Central Park South
New York, N. Y.

R. S. V. P.
40 East Tenth Street
New York 11, N. Y.

A Club At Home

The Women's Faculty Club
of Columbia University
At Home
on Monday, the ninth of February
from four to six and eight to ten o'clock
at the Club Rooms in Johnson Hall
Four Hundred and Ten West One Hundred and Seventeenth Street
New York City
Afternoon, from four to six, Open House
Greetings   Miss Gunther
Lighting the hearthfire   Miss Nutting
Reminiscences   Miss Goodsell, Miss Carney
Music   Mrs. Cowl, piano, Mr. Rosanoff, cello
Evening, from eight to ten, Reception
Honorary Guests (Listed)

Invitations to Exhibitions

(1)

THE PRESIDENT AND GOVERNORS OF
THE NATIONAL ARTS CLUB
INVITE YOU TO BE PRESENT
AT THE OPENING AND PRIVATE VIEW
OF THE
TWENTY-FIRST ANNUAL EXHIBITION
BY
THE SOCIETY OF AMERICAN ETCHERS, Inc.
(formerly The Brooklyn Society of Etchers)
IN THE CLUB GALLERIES
FIFTEEN GRAMERCY PARK
TUESDAY EVENING, NOVEMBER 24
AT 8:30

(2)

YOU ARE CORDIALLY INVITED TO ATTEND
AN EXHIBIT OF BOOKS FOR YOUNG PEOPLE AT
THE NEW YORK PUBLIC LIBRARY
OFFICE OF THE SUPERINTENDENT OF SCHOOL WORK
121 EAST 58TH STREET
ON SATURDAY, JANUARY 16TH
FROM 10 A.M. TO 6 P.M.

Tea will be served from 3 to 6 p.m.

(3)

THE CONNECTICUT TERCENTENARY COMMISSION
AND
THE TRUSTEES OF THE WADSWORTH ATHENEUM
REQUEST THE HONOR OF YOUR PRESENCE
AT THE OPENING OF THE
TERCENTENARY EXHIBITION OF CONNECTICUT
FURNITURE
IN THE MORGAN MEMORIAL
590 MAIN ST., HARTFORD
ON SATURDAY, JUNE 15TH
FROM ONE TO FIVE O'CLOCK

(4)

*The President and Trustees of The Museum of Modern
Art request the honor of your presence at the private
opening of a comprehensive exhibition of the works of*
PABLO PICASSO
*prepared in collaboration with The Art Institute of
Chicago, on Tuesday Evening, March seventeenth,
from nine to twelve o'clock, 11 West 53 Street, New York.*

THIS INVITATION WILL ADMIT TWO

(5)

THE PRESIDENT OF
THE BROOKLYN INSTITUTE OF ARTS AND SCIENCES
AND THE
GOVERNING COMMITTEE OF THE
BROOKLYN MUSEUM
REQUEST THE HONOR OF YOUR PRESENCE
AT THE MUSEUM
FOR
A PRIVATE VIEW OF AN EXHIBITION
OF
EUROPEAN ART, 1450–1500
ASSEMBLED BY
THE ROCKEFELLER FOUNDATION INTERNES
OF THE BROOKLYN MUSEUM
ON THE EVENING OF FRIDAY THE EIGHTH OF MAY
AT HALF AFTER EIGHT O'CLOCK

(6)

The President and the Patrons of
The Studio Guild
cordially invite you to
A Special Exhibition of Water Colors
and Sepia-Tone Reproductions
by Edwin H. Denby
Architect
from April thirteenth to May eighth
ten to six o'clock
730 Fifth Avenue
New York

(7)

The President and the Trustees of the Museum of Modern Art,
11 West 53rd Street, New York, invite you to attend a preview of three
exhibitions on Tuesday, January the fourteenth, from two until six
o'clock.

Posters by Cassandre
The Architecture of H. H. Richardson
Modern Paintings and Drawings
    The Gift of Mrs. John D. Rockefeller, Jr.

(8)

The Newark Museum cordially invites you to attend the opening of a
loan exhibit, *Pictures by Children,* on Wednesday, January the twenty-
ninth, from two to five thirty o'clock.
At three o'clock, Miss Carolyn Heller of the Museum staff will talk
about the paintings, drawings and the methods used in the thirty
museums represented in this exhibit.

January 29 through March 15

The Newark Museum, Washington Park West
Newark, New Jersey

INVITATIONS TO RECITALS

(1)

THE DEPARTMENT OF MUSIC
NEW JERSEY COLLEGE FOR WOMEN
CORDIALLY INVITES YOU TO ATTEND
A RECITAL BY
CATHERINE KNOOP, ORGANIST
PUPIL OF RAYMOND EARL RUDY
ON SUNDAY AFTERNOON, MAY THE THIRD
AT FOUR-THIRTY O'CLOCK
THE ELIZABETH RODMAN VOORHEES CHAPEL
NEW BRUNSWICK, NEW JERSEY

(2)

THE COMMUNITY HOUSE
of
ST. BARTHOLOMEW'S CHURCH
Park Avenue and 50th Street
New York

□

An Evening of Music
Wednesday, March 17, 19___
at nine o'clock

Mrs. H. H. A. Beach
Miss Katherine Platt Gunn
Mr. George E. Rasely
Mr. David McK. Williams

(3)

Members of the Patrons of Art and Music
at the
California Palace of the Legion of Honor
are cordially invited to attend a Recital by

_____ _____

Soprano of the
Metropolitan Opera Company
to be held in the Little Theatre of the Museum
eight-thirty o'clock on Monday evening
April twenty-second

Applications for tickets will be
filled in order of their receipt.

RSVP, Skyline 2-2189
Tickets, non-members $2.50

INVITATIONS TO ACADEMIC FUNCTIONS

(1)

The Corporation and Faculty
of
Brown University
cordially invite all holders of Brown Degrees,
all former students of the University,
and all friends of the University
to attend the public exercises
of Commencement Week
so far as limitations of space permit

(2)

THE PRESIDENT AND TRUSTEES
OF ROLLINS COLLEGE
INVITE YOU TO BECOME A
PATRON OF THE COLLEGE
FOR THIS ACADEMIC YEAR
AND
REQUEST THE HONOR OF YOUR PRESENCE
AT
THE FOUNDERS' WEEK DINNER
TO BE HELD ON
SATURDAY, THE TWENTY-FIFTH OF FEBRUARY
NINETEEN HUNDRED AND _____ _____
AT SEVEN O'CLOCK
SAN JUAN HOTEL, ORLANDO

PLEASE REPLY ON
THE ENCLOSED
RESERVATION CARD.   BLACK TIE

(3)

[SEAL]

THE PRESIDENT AND TRUSTEES
OF COLUMBIA UNIVERSITY
REQUEST THE HONOR OF YOUR PRESENCE
AT A SPECIAL CONVOCATION
IN OBSERVANCE OF THE
FIVE HUNDREDTH ANNIVERSARY OF THE
INVENTION OF PRINTING

LOW MEMORIAL LIBRARY
FRIDAY, JANUARY 19, __ __
8:15 P.M.

(4)

*The President and Fellows
of Harvard College
request the honor of the company of*
. . . .
*at the exercises on
Commencement Day
June . . . . .19 . .*

Please reply to
The University Marshal
Wadsworth House
Cambridge, Mass.

(5)

THE ELMIRA AND UNION COLLEGE CLUBS
OF NEW YORK CITY
Cordially invite you to attend a Concert given by the
ELMIRA-UNION GLEE CLUBS
*at the Starlight Roof of the Waldorf-Astoria Hotel
Friday Evening, February 19th,
at 8:30 o'clock*

(6)

THE ALUMNI COUNCIL OF AMHERST COLLEGE
REQUESTS THE HONOR OF YOUR PRESENCE
ON SATURDAY, NOVEMBER 17, AT 10.00 O'CLOCK
IN COLLEGE HALL

_____ _____, LL.D.
PRESIDENT OF WILLIAMS COLLEGE
WILL DELIVER THE ADDRESS

(7)

THE UNIVERSITY OF BUFFALO
cordially invites the members of the
NEW YORK STATE ASSOCIATION OF DEANS
to be its guests during the meetings of the Association
on
N O V E M B E R   1 3 t h   a n d   1 4 t h
●
The session on Friday afternoon will be held in Norton Hall,
on the University campus. Tea will be served.

(8)

The Officers and Cadets
of the
Staunton Military Academy
request the honor of your presence
during the
Seventy-fourth Commencement Exercises
June third to fifth
Nineteen hundred and _____ _____
Staunton, Virginia

(9)

Headmaster and Mrs. _____ _____
request the honor of your company at a
Reception and Dance for the Senior Class
from half past eight until twelve o'clock
on Saturday evening, June the sixth
Milford Academy Gymnasium

(10)

THE CLASS OF JANUARY _____ OF THE
BLANK HIGH SCHOOL
invites you to the
SENIOR DANCE
to be held at
HOTEL STATLER
Friday Evening, January Tenth,
at eight o'clock

INVITATIONS TO ANNIVERSARIES

(1)

Commemorating the
One hundred and twenty-ninth Anniversary
of the Founding of

THE NEW-YORK HISTORICAL SOCIETY

The President, Officers and Executive Committee
request the honor of your presence
at the awarding of the Society's gold medal to

MR. DeWITT McCLELLAN LOCKMAN

in recognition of his painting for the Society
a series of portraits of distinguished contemporary Americans
With an address
by
MR. LÉON DABO
and a special showing of the portraits
in the Assembly Hall
on Monday evening, November the 20th, at eight-thirty o'clock

R. S. V. P.
170 Central Park West

(2)

THE AMERICAN ACADEMY OF ARTS AND LETTERS
AND
THE NATIONAL INSTITUTE OF ARTS AND LETTERS
REQUEST THE HONOR OF YOUR PRESENCE
AT THE ACADEMY AUDITORIUM
632 West 156th Street, New York
FOR
LITERARY EXERCISES
AT THREE O'CLOCK
ON THE AFTERNOON OF NOVEMBER 14
TO COMMEMORATE
THE CENTENARY OF
SAMUEL LANGHORNE CLEMENS
AND FOR
AN ORCHESTRAL CONCERT
AT NINE-FIFTEEN O'CLOCK
ON THE EVENING OF NOVEMBER 15

Please reply to
The Assistant to the President,
633 West 155th Street, New York

INVITATIONS TO DEDICATIONS

(1)

The President and Trustees
of
The American Museum of Natural History
Seventy-seventh Street and Central Park West
New York, N. Y.
Cordially invite you to be their guest
at the Museum on the
Eighth Annual
Members' Visiting Day
and
Dedication of Akeley Memorial African Hall
Tuesday, May Nineteenth
Nineteen Hundred and _____ _____
From three until six o'clock

(2)

The Governor of Mississippi
and the
Davis-George Statues Commission
request the honor of your presence
at the ceremonies attending the
unveiling of a Statue of
Jefferson Davis
Officer in the Army of the United States, Secretary of War
of the United States, United States Senator and
President of the Confederate States,
and the unveiling of a Statue of
James Z. George
Soldier, Lawyer and United States Senator
on the afternoon of June second
at three o'clock
in Statuary Hall
in the Capitol of the United States

(3)

The Governor of California
and the
California Commission Representation
National Statuary Hall
request the honor of your presence
at the ceremonies attending the
unveiling of the Statues of
Junípero Serra
Thomas Starr King
on the afternoon of March first
at three o'clock
in Statuary Hall
in the Capitol of the United States
Members of the California Commission Representation
National Statuary Hall
Hon. John F. Davis, Past Grand President
Native Sons of the Golden West
Mrs. Frank A. Gibson
California Federation of Women's Clubs
Herbert E. Bolton, Ph.D., LL.D.,
University of California
Miss Mabel R. Gillis
State Librarian
Miss Grace S. Stoermer, Past Grand President
Native Daughters of the Golden West

(4)

THE AMERICAN SCENIC AND HISTORIC
PRESERVATION SOCIETY
cordially invites you and your guests to be present
at
Hamilton Grange, home of Alexander Hamilton
287 Convent Avenue, Washington Heights, New York City
at four o'clock on Monday afternoon
October nineteenth
for
The dedication of the bronze statue of Alexander Hamilton, the work
of William Ordway Partridge, to be presented to the Society
by the Crescent-Hamilton Club of Brooklyn
and
The awarding of the Cornelius Amory Pugsley Medals for Park Service
in the United States. The recipients are Mr. Howard B. Bloomer of
Detroit, Mr. John McLaren of San Francisco, and Mr. Will O.
Doolittle of Tulsa.

R. S. V. P.
LeRoy E. Kimball, President
Hamilton Grange, 287 Convent Avenue
New York City

(5)

THE REGENTS OF THE UNIVERSITY
OF MICHIGAN
AND
THE FACULTY OF THE LAW SCHOOL
HAVE THE HONOR TO INVITE

TO BE PRESENT
ON FRIDAY, THE FIFTEENTH OF JUNE,
NINETEEN HUNDRED AND _____ _____,
AT THE
DEDICATION OF THE LAW QUADRANGLE
PRESENTED TO THE UNIVERSITY BY THE LATE
WILLIAM WILSON COOK

THE FAVOR OF A REPLY TO THE
DEAN OF THE LAW SCHOOL IS REQUESTED

INVITATION TO A PRESS REVIEW

You are cordially invited to attend
A Press Preview
of
The Hayden Planetarium
at 5 o'clock P.M. Wednesday, September 25th
upon which occasion
Admiral _____ _____
will be the Guest of Honor

Please address your reply to:
Hans Christian Adamson
American Museum of Natural History
On acceptance two admission cards
will be forwarded for your use.

INVITATIONS TO OPENING OF A BUILDING

(1)

THE DIRECTORS AND OFFICERS OF
BLANK TRUST COMPANY
INVITE YOU TO ATTEND
THE FORMAL OPENING OF THE BANK ADDITION
EIGHT FIFTY SEVEN TENTH AVENUE
WEDNESDAY EVENING, JANUARY FIFTEENTH

(2)

You are invited to inspect the new
MEDICAL CHAMBERS
140 EAST FIFTY-FOURTH STREET
at its formal opening, Saturday afternoon
February sixth, from four until six

INVITATIONS TO LECTURES

(1)

THE GIRLS SERVICE LEAGUE
requests the pleasure of your company at its Annual Meeting
in the Ballroom of
THE PIERRE
Fifth Avenue and Sixty-first Street
Tuesday, December eighth
at three-thirty o'clock

SUBJECT

"YOUTH'S NEED TODAY"

Speakers

DR. JOSEPH R. SIZOO
President of New Brunswick Theological Seminary
MISS ANNE FRANCES HODGKINS
Mrs. Alexander M. Hadden will preside

Please reply
138 East Nineteenth Street   Kindly present this card

(2)

THE NORTHERN SECTION OF THE ACADEMIC SENATE OF THE
UNIVERSITY OF CALIFORNIA INVITES YOU TO ATTEND THE
TWENTY-THIRD ANNUAL FACULTY RESEARCH LECTURE TO BE
GIVEN BY JOEL H. HILDEBRAND, PROFESSOR OF CHEMISTRY, ON
WEDNESDAY EVENING, MARCH EIGHTEENTH, AT EIGHT O'CLOCK,
IN THE AUDITORIUM OF BENJAMIN IDE WHEELER HALL

(3)

THE DECORATORS CLUB
*has the honor of presenting
a series of symposia*
on

THE THEATER . . .

MR. LEE SIMONSON
MISS RACHEL CROTHERS
MR. JOSEPH WOOD KRUTCH

THE FINE ARTS . . .

MR. DONALD CARRICK
MISS HILDRETH MEIERE
MR. WILLIAM ZORACH
MRS. MILLICENT C. MC INTOSH
at the
COSMOPOLITAN CLUB
129 EAST 65TH STREET

(4)

The American Woman's Association
REQUESTS THE PLEASURE OF YOUR COMPANY
ON Wednesday EVENING, October THE TWENTY-SECOND
AT EIGHT-FIFTEEN O'CLOCK
TO MEET AND HEAR
The AWA Woman of the month for October

WINIFRED FISHER

Executive Director, New York Adult Education Council
Recipient of the George Arents Medal
AND THE Metropolitan Award
FOR OUTSTANDING ACHIEVEMENT IN ADULT EDUCATION,
WHO WILL SPEAK ON

WISE WOMEN KNOW
THAT WISE WOMEN GROW—NOT HAPPEN

IN THE American Woman's Association Clubrooms
The Barclay
One Hundred and eleven East Forty-eighth Street
New York City

R.S.V.P.
Members may request guest privileges.

Formal Acceptances

Answers to invitations follow the form of the invitations. A formal invitation is answered in the third person with lines properly spaced as in the invitation; an answer to an informal invitation follows the form for informal social notes.

No answer is required to an invitation to a church wedding unless the invitation includes a reception or unless a reply is requested.

Formerly, no answer was expected to an At Home invitation. Today, however, as such receptions are so often held at hotels or clubs, where it is necessary to know the number of guests likely to be present, an answer is often requested.

Usually invitations, other than those for weddings and At Homes, should be answered.

Both the formal and the informal answers must always be written by hand, never engraved.

Of a Wedding Invitation

When a reply is requested to a formal wedding invitation, the note of acceptance may be worded as follows:

Mr. and Mrs. David Bronson
accept with pleasure the kind invitation
of Mr. and Mrs. Richard Burton
to the marriage of their daughter
and Mr. William Kent
on Wednesday, the third of June
at half past three o'clock

A response must be made to an invitation to a church wedding if a breakfast, a luncheon, or a reception card is included.

Mr. and Mrs. Joseph Bidwell
accept with pleasure
Mr. and Mrs. Henry Long's
kind invitation to be present at the
marriage of their daughter
Gertrude Anne
to
Mr. Patrick Stone
on Thursday the tenth of May
at twelve o'clock
and afterward at the wedding breakfast

For a Wedding Anniversary

Mrs. George Frame
accepts with pleasure
the kind invitation of
Mr. and Mrs. Thomas O'Leary
to be present at the
Twenty Fifth Anniversary of their marriage

Of an Invitation for Dinner

Mr. and Mrs. Arthur Wilson
accept with pleasure
Mr. and Mrs. Everett A. Arnold's
kind invitation to dine
on the evening of December the fifth
at 15 Pondfield Road

Of an Invitation to a Luncheon

(1)

Mrs. Eliot Prescott
accepts with pleasure
the invitation of Mrs. Hastings
to luncheon and to meet Mrs. Burke

(2)

Mrs. Howard Ames
accepts with pleasure
Mrs. Charles Allen Brown's
kind invitation
for Wednesday the tenth of June
in honor of
Mrs. Harold Lane Rigby
and
Mrs. Norman Hill Langton

FORMAL REGRETS

To an Invitation for Dinner

Mr. Walter Huntington
regrets extremely that a previous engagement
prevents his accepting
Mr. and Mrs. Ashburton's
kind invitation for dinner
on Tuesday the second of January

Miss Mary Appleton
regrets that she is unable to accept
Mr. and Mrs. Frank Grafton's
kind invitation for dinner
on Wednesday the fifth of March

To an Invitation for a Dinner or for a Dance

Mr. and Mrs. Arthur Wright Cogswell
regret that a previous engagement
prevents their accepting
Mrs. Henry Beekman's
kind invitation for
Friday the eleventh of February

To an Invitation for a Dance

Judge and Mrs. Allan Williams
regret that they are unable to accept
the kind invitation of
Mr. and Mrs. G. Hamilton Crane
to be present at the dance
in honor of their daughter
on Tuesday evening the fourth of June

To a Wedding Invitation

When a reply is requested to a formal wedding invitation, the note of regret may be worded as follows:

Miss Anna Langley
regrets that by reason of absence from town
she will be unable to attend the wedding reception
of Miss Esther Blake
and Mr. Thomas Livingston
on Wednesday, the third of June
at four o'clock

To a Wedding Invitation and a Wedding Breakfast

Mr. and Mrs. James Thompson
regret exceedingly that they
are unable to accept
Mr. and Mrs. Ernest Molloy's
kind invitation to be present at the
marriage of their daughter
Marie Louise
to
Mr. Frank Bartley
on Thursday the tenth of May
at twelve o'clock
and afterward at the wedding breakfast

or

Mr. and Mrs. James Thompson
regret that they are unable to accept
Mr. and Mrs. Ernest Molloy's
kind invitation for
Thursday the tenth of May

To an Invitation for a Luncheon

Mr. Robert Bliss
regrets that he is unable to accept
Mr. Moore's kind invitation to luncheon
in honor of Mr. Alexander Graham
on Friday, the twentieth of November

Notes Recalling Invitations

Notes canceling or postponing social functions may be handwritten or, in connection with affairs to which many invitations have been issued, they may be printed. In an emergency when it is necessary to postpone or cancel an invitation, there is no time to have notes engraved.

(1)

Owing to the sudden death of their son
Mr. and Mrs. Robert Jackson
recall the invitations issued for
the marriage of their daughter
Catherine Mary
on Tuesday the tenth of June

(2)

The Reverend and Mrs. Philip Moore
announce that the marriage of their daughter
Susan Estelle
to
Mr. Albert Waverly, Jr.
will not take place

(3)

Owing to the sudden illness of their son
Mr. and Mrs. Stephen Bishop
are obliged to recall their invitations
for Tuesday, the tenth of June

(4)

Mr. and Mrs. Nathan Macdonnell
regret exceedingly
that illness in the family
prevents their receiving their
friends at dinner
on Friday the third of October

For Social Occasions

(1)

45 West 119th Street
July the fifth

Dear Mrs. Holmes,

Will you and Mr. Holmes give us the pleasure of dining with us on Friday, July the twelfth, at seven o'clock? We shall be very glad if you are able to come.

Sincerely yours,
Mary R. Fox

(2)

Dear Mrs. Patterson,

Mr. Bradley and I shall be greatly pleased if you and Mr. Patterson can dine with us at the Montclair Hotel on June fifteenth at seven o'clock and attend the theater with us afterwards. We hope you have no other engagements for that evening.

Sincerely yours,
Alice Bradley

24 East 76th Street
June tenth

(3)

[*Letterhead*]

February 15, 19___

Dear Mrs. Appleton:

Mrs. Francis Randolph, of the Faculty Advisory Committee of the Women's Club, would be pleased if you would take luncheon with her on Saturday, March first, and afterwards attend, as her guest, the matinee of "My Fair Lady."

The luncheon will take place at one o'clock at Mrs. Randolph's apartment, 40 Morningside Drive.

Will you please send your answer directly to her.

Yours sincerely,
Frances Kelway
Secretary

Mrs. Richard Appleton
116 West 60 Street
New York City

INVITATIONS TO MAKE ADDRESSES

(1)

University House
Philadelphia, Pa.
May 2, 19___

Dear Judge Bartley:

On June 30 we are to lay the cornerstone of our new college library. If it had not been for your enthusiastic support in arousing the interest of the alumni in the raising of funds, we should probably not be laying the cornerstone this June.

We want you to make the principal address for the occasion as no one else could speak so effectively or so acceptably to both students and alumni.

Will you do us the honor to be present and to speak at that time?

Yours sincerely,
George P. Canfield

Hon. Arthur H. Bartley
Annapolis
Maryland

(2)

530 West 122 Street
New York City
March 2, 19___

Dear Mr. Greenfield:

Remembering your kind hospitality to the Scandinavian students of International House at Christmas time, I should like to ask you on behalf of the whole Scandinavian Group if you will be our guest of honor at our National Night to be presented at the International House on Friday, March 27, at eight-thirty.

We shall all be very glad if you can be with us at this celebration and give an informal talk on your experiences in Norway and Sweden last summer.

Yours sincerely,
Elsa Jensen

Mr. Harold Greenfield
125 West 12 Street
New York City

INFORMAL ACCEPTANCES

(1)

Dear Mrs. Fox,
 Mr. Holmes and I are delighted to accept your very kind invitation to dine with you on Friday, July the twelfth, at seven o'clock, and are looking forward to that evening with great pleasure.

Sincerely yours,
Elizabeth Holmes

52 West Thirteenth Street
June fifth

(2)

Dear Mrs. Bradley,
 There is nothing we should like to do more on Thursday the fifteenth than to dine with you and Mr. Bradley at the Montclair at seven and attend the play with you later. We are delighted to accept your very kind invitation.

Sincerely yours,
Emily Patterson

52 West Thirteenth Street
June fifth

(3)

Middlebury, Vermont
January 7, 19___

Dear Professor Haines:
 If it is possible, as I hope it will be, for me to escape from official duties on January twelfth, I shall be delighted to be present at the recital given in the college chapel.
 I appreciate your kindness in sending me the tickets and shall look forward to hearing the music and to meeting your friends.

Yours sincerely,
Alfred Dunmore

Professor Arthur Haines
 Clinton
  Vermont

INFORMAL REGRETS

(1)

Dear Mrs. Fox,

We are sorry that we are unable to accept your very delightful invitation for dinner on Friday, July the twelfth, as unfortunately we have another engagement for that evening.

Sincerely yours,
Elizabeth Holmes

52 West 13th Street,
  July the tenth

(2)

52 West 13th Street
New York City
July 10, 19___

Dear Mrs. Fox,

Mr. Holmes and I regret exceedingly that we shall be unable to dine with you on Friday the twelfth, as we have accepted another invitation for that evening.

Yours sincerely,
Elizabeth Holmes

(3)

Dear Mrs. Garrett,

I am so sorry that pressure of engagements will prevent my being present at your At Home on Thursday afternoon next, but if you will allow me I shall take another opportunity of calling upon you.

With kindest regards,

Yours sincerely,
James Moore

Mrs. Alexander Garrett,
  7, King's Bench Walk,
    Temple, E.C.4.

(4)

Dear Mrs. Andrews,
Indeed we wish we could accept your delightful invitation for dinner and the theater on the fifteenth, but unfortunately we have another invitation for that evening which we have already accepted. We regret that we cannot be in both places at the same time!

Very sincerely yours,
Anne Broughton

14 Willard Street
October fifth

(5)

65 Broadway
New York, N. Y.
January 3, 19___

Dear Mr. Newman:
Mr. Bryant regrets that, as he has been unexpectedly called out of town, it will be impossible for him to return in time to act as toastmaster at the dinner given by the Horseshoe Club in honor of Mr. Allan Burns.

Yours sincerely,
Louise Spencer
Secretary to Mr. Bryant

Mr. Wallace Newman
Evergreen Avenue
Larchmont, N. Y.

(6)

2 Wall Street
New York, N. Y.
March 10, 19___

Dear Mr. Hume:
Mr. Little is grateful to you for your kind invitation of April tenth. He is to be in the Middle West on April twelfth and, therefore, cannot accept your invitation to speak at the Club. His calendar for the present is so full that he is under the necessity of declining any engagements for the rest of the year.

Sincerely yours,
Susan Lambert
Secretary to Mr. Little

(7)

Cuthbert Hall
Springfield, Mass.
April 4, 19___

Dear Dr. Gray-Lawrence:

Unfortunately I have a business appointment in Philadelphia on May tenth and therefore cannot accept the invitation of the Appleton Club to be present at its Annual Dinner. Please convey to the members my sincere appreciation of the honor of being asked to address them and my keen regret at not being able to do so.

Sincerely yours,
John L. Martin

(8)

Noroton, Conn.
January 10, 19___

Dear Mr. Horton:

I regret that my engagements are such that it will be impossible for me to be with you next Wednesday evening. The pressure of work at this office is so heavy that it is difficult for me to be absent long enough to make the trip to Atlanta.

I am sincerely sorry that I cannot join you and renew acquaintance with the members of the Board.

Yours sincerely,
Frank Burbank

Hon. James L. Horton
Peach Tree Street
Atlanta, Georgia

(9)

140 Broadway
New York City
October 14, 19___

Dear Mr. Hanson:

On returning from a business trip yesterday, I found your kind invitation to lunch on Wednesday waiting for me. So much work has piled up during my absence that I shall not be able to leave the office this week even for a noon recess. I shall eat my lunch off a tray and keep my secretary's typewriter clicking.

I shall think of you dining with your Southern guests and shall, indeed, envy you.

Yours sincerely,
Alfred Downing

(10)

Washington Street
Boston, Mass.
March 6, 19___

Rev. Archibald Kent
8 Center Street
Winter Hill, Mass.

Dear Mr. Kent:

I regret that I cannot accept the invitation of your committee to speak at the dinner in honor of Mr. Dalton on February twenty-fourth. Just at present I am so overwhelmed with meetings, both day and evening, that I find it impossible to accept invitations for this month, no matter how tempting they may be.

It is, indeed, with regret that I decline this particular invitation as I have the greatest respect and liking for Mr. Dalton and should enjoy meeting the members of the Association again.

Yours sincerely,
Walter K. Morris

(11)

Wellesley Hills, Mass.
June 15, 19___

Dear Dr. Stanley:

Thank you for asking me to the reunion at the Roosevelt on October twenty-fourth. I regret exceedingly that as I have already made an engagement for that evening, it will be impossible for me to be with you. I shall want to hear of the program and of the interesting reminiscences of the speakers, both formal and informal.

Yours sincerely,
Anthony Warren

(12)

3276 Southern Avenue
South Gate, California
January 3, 19___

Mr. John P. McAlpine
834 Terrace Avenue
Fresno, California

Dear Mr. McAlpine:

I am sorry that it will not be possible for me to be present at the luncheon on January tenth, as the firm is sending me to Chicago on that date to attend a business conference.

Please convey my regrets to the Committee.

Yours sincerely,
Joseph Brent Foster

(13)

Beechmont, New York,
December 24, 19___.

Dear Mr. Flynn:

I appreciate your courtesy in asking me to be present at the luncheon in honor of Professor Caldwell. I regret that as it is impossible for me to get away from official duties on January fifth, I shall not be able to attend the luncheon.

Yours sincerely,
Allan Benson

Mr. M. P. Flynn
Lockwood Avenue
New Rochelle, New York

REFERENCE BOOKS

POST, EMILY. *Etiquette.* 9th ed. New York, Funk & Wagnalls Company, 1955.

VANDERBILT, AMY. *Complete Book of Etiquette.* New York, Doubleday & Company, 195].

4. Business Announcements

Of Change in Firm Name

ON JANUARY 2, 19___
THE FIRM NAME OF
FANNING, BURKE & CO.
WILL BE CHANGED TO
BURKE, MANSFIELD & CO.
New York   Chicago

Of the Formation of a Company

(1)

We desire to announce the formation
of the firm of
Brown and O'Donnell
Stationers
with offices located at
275 Main Street
New Rochelle
August First   Telephone _____

(2)

We wish to announce the formation of
the Rigby Company
for the transaction of a
General Investment Business with offices at
150 Broadway, New York
John David Rigby
Telephone _____   Samuel P. Lynch

369

Of an Election to Office

We take pleasure in announcing
the election of
MR. ELIOT RAMSAY FOOTE
as a Vice-President of this Company
HUNTER & CO. INC.
40 Exchange Place, New York
January 1, 19___

Of Admission of New Members

(1)

HAROLD SHERMAN & CO.
We take pleasure in announcing that
ROBERT ANDERSON JR.
has this day been admitted to general partnership
in our firm
December 31, 19___

(2)

WE ARE PLEASED TO ANNOUNCE THAT
THE FOLLOWING MEMBERS OF OUR STAFF
MR. CHARLES CANFIELD
MR. JOSEPH BROWN
MR. HENRY GRANT
WILL BE ADMITTED TO OUR FIRM AS GENERAL
PARTNERS, AS OF JANUARY 1st, 19___
MR. ERNEST R. DUNN and MR. GEORGE STANTON
RETIRE AS PARTNERS, BUT CONTINUE
IN AN ADVISORY CAPACITY
L. R. DEAN & CO.
1819 Broadway   New York, N. Y.
December 31, 19___

(3)

THE MEMBERS OF THE FIRM OF OGDEN & DAVENPORT
ANNOUNCE THAT THEY HAVE THIS DAY FORMED A NEW
PARTNERSHIP FOR THE GENERAL PRACTICE OF THE LAW
WITH JAMES C. LAWRENCE, ESQ., UNDER THE NAME OF
LAWRENCE, OGDEN, & DAVENPORT

UPTOWN OFFICES	DOWNTOWN OFFICES
230 PARK AVENUE	120 BROADWAY
NEW YORK CITY	NEW YORK CITY

(4)

WE TAKE PLEASURE IN ANNOUNCING THAT
MR. ABRAHAM HALPERN
HAS BECOME ASSOCIATED WITH US
AS SALES MANAGER

COHEN and ROSENBERG
NEW HAVEN, CONN.

November 1, 19___

(5)

MR. PETER VAN ALLEN
ANNOUNCES HIS ASSOCIATION WITH
BOYD AND LANGDON
FOR THE GENERAL PRACTICE OF LAW
330 MAIN STREET
POUGHKEEPSIE, N. Y.

March 15, 19___

(6)

WE TAKE PLEASURE IN ANNOUNCING THAT
MR. ERNEST P. WARREN
FORMERLY PARTNER OF
NEWCOMB AND DUNN, BOSTON
HAS BECOME ASSOCIATED WITH OUR FIRM
AS BOSTON REPRESENTATIVE
FIRST NATIONAL BANK BUILDING
TELEPHONE _____
GRAVES AND HILTON, INC.
MANAGERS OF INVESTMENT FUNDS

(7)

Grant and Holland
100 East Avenue

We take pleasure in announcing that
Mr. Frank C. Stevenson
and
Mr. Wilbur Jurist
formerly of Benson Company are now
associated with us at our Branch Office
221 West Main Street

(8)

WE TAKE PLEASURE IN ANNOUNCING THAT
MR. GORDON STOCKTON
HAS BEEN ADMITTED AS A GENERAL PARTNER
IN OUR FIRM AS OF JANUARY 1, 19___
MURPHY, O'BRIEN & CO.

165 Broadway   New York

(9)

WE TAKE PLEASURE IN ANNOUNCING THAT
MR. VAN R. BURCHARD
HAS THIS DAY BEEN ADMITTED TO OUR FIRM
AS A GENERAL PARTNER
CONNOR, BLAKE & CO.
50 Broadway, New York

January 1, 19___

Of Opening an Office

(1)

DR. JOSEPH STERNBACH, JR.
ANNOUNCES
THE OPENING OF OFFICES AT
4500 OLIVE STREET
LISTER BUILDING

January 15, 19___

(2)

Dr. Henry Conklin
Surgeon Dentist
announces the opening of his uptown office
at
Professional Building
Two East Fifty-fourth Street

X-Rays   WIckersham 2-8040

Of Change of Address

(1)

FREEMAN and BETTS
ANNOUNCE THE REMOVAL OF THEIR OFFICES
TO THE TWENTY-SECOND FLOOR OF THE
EMPIRE STATE BUILDING
350 FIFTH AVENUE
NEW YORK

October 1, 19___   Telephone _____

(2)

DANIEL GODDARD
WISHES TO ANNOUNCE THAT ON AND AFTER
APRIL 10, 19___
HIS OFFICES FOR THE PRACTICE OF LAW
WILL BE LOCATED IN
THE HILTON BUILDING
FLUSHING, N. Y.

(3)

BROWN, SMITH and COMPANY
INSURANCE
ANNOUNCE THE REMOVAL OF THEIR OFFICE TO
THE LINCOLN BUILDING
60 EAST 42 STREET
NEW YORK

MURRAY HILL 2-8130

(4)

ALEXANDER FOWLER ANNOUNCES
THE REMOVAL OF HIS OFFICES
FROM THE BLAKE BUILDING TO
21 MAIN STREET, NORWALK, WHERE
HE WILL CONTINUE THE GENERAL
PRACTICE OF LAW.

October twenty-third   Telephone _____

(5)

DR. PETER SLETSON
WISHES TO ANNOUNCE
THAT HIS OFFICE IS NOW LOCATED AT
784 PARK AVENUE

Telephone
BUtterfield 8-3451

Hours
By Appointment

(6)

ANTHONY LOOMIS, M.D.
ANNOUNCES THE REMOVAL OF HIS OFFICE TO
116 WEST 68 STREET
NEW YORK CITY

Hours:
1–2, 5–7 p.m.
by Appointment

Telephone
_____ _____

Of Retirement

We announce the retirement from active
participation in Company business of Mr.
Arnold Redfern, for many years Secretary
of the Company.

B. R. Fenton & Company
35 East Wacker Drive
Chicago, Illinois

Of Death of a Member of a Firm

(1)

It is with great sorrow that we announce
the death of our President
Mr. Horace Fulton
on Saturday the twelfth of May
Nineteen hundred and _____ _____

Nichols Carpet Company

(2)

The Everett Cement Company
announces with deep sorrow
the death of its Secretary
Mr. Carlton Reese
on Wednesday the second of May
nineteen hundred and _____ _____
725 Riverside Drive
New York City

Of Exhibitions and Openings

(1)

Allen Brockton and Company
invites you
to an exhibition of
distinguished table settings
in its Table Linen Salon
from the third to the twenty-fourth
of November

(2)

The Delph Shoppe
announces the Formal Opening of its
Salon de Luxe
where patrons may examine at their leisure the beautiful
Mexican Embroideries and Pottery
now on display
521 Madison Avenue
New York City

5. Telegrams and Cablegrams

Telegrams

Telegrams are classed as follows:

1. Fast Telegrams
2. Day Letters
3. Night Letters
4. Telemeter

1. Fast Telegrams are sent at any time of the day or night and represent the fastest service that is available. The rate on such messages is based on fifteen words. Words in excess of fifteen are charged at a reduced rate.

2. Day Letters are messages deferred in service at lower rates than those of regular Fast Telegrams. The charge for a Day Letter is approximately one and one-third times that of a fifteen-word Fast Telegram. The minimum charge is for fifty words.

3. Night Letters are sent at reduced rates to be delivered the following day. They are accepted at any time of the day or night up to 2 A.M. Social Night Letters are delivered the following day. Business Night Letters are delivered on the ensuing business day. (The charge for the first fifty words or less is substantially lower than the charge for a fifteen-word Fast Telegram.)

4. Telemeter provides a fast and flexible service for concerns or individuals having occasion for the exchange of a considerable volume of communication with each other. The service is charged for according to the number of words exchanged. The minimum monthly charge is for 25,000 words, the rate for words in excess of 25,000 words decreasing progressively.

PREPARATION OF TELEGRAMS

How to Write a Telegram

Every telegram consists of a number of parts, each of which has been given a name and serves some particular purpose, either in handling the message or in conveying information to the addressee. To minimize errors and facilitate handling, all telegrams should be clearly and legibly written, and when typed, should be double-spaced, regardless of their length. Code words are desirably typed in capital letters.

The Place From or Point of Origin

The place from is the city and state where a telegram originates.

The Date

Each telegram should bear the month and the date on which it is written.

The Addressee

The addressee is the name of the person, firm or corporation to whom a telegram is to be delivered.

The Address

The address contains the name of the street and the street number or other information necessary to locate the addressee at the place of destination. No charge is made for whatever information is necessary to help the company to locate the addressee quickly.

In certain cases, extra words in the addresses are charged for. If, for instance, a telegram is addressed to "Henry Smith or Harry Brown, 220 Fifth Ave., Chicago, Ill.," the words "Or Harry Brown" are extra chargeable words. When telegrams are addressed to two persons at different addresses in the same city, the telegram is sent to each, and each telegram is charged for separately.

A complete street address facilitates the delivery of telegrams and should always be given if known. If a transient is involved, give the name of the person in whose care the telegram is sent.

Code addresses may not be used in domestic telegrams.

The practice of addressing telegrams in care of "some hotel" or "try hotels" should be avoided as far as possible, because of the delays involved while the addressee is being located. In the case of telegraphic replies to transients for whom no street address can be given, delivery will be facilitated by writing in the address the words "answer date," or "answer" followed by a figure indicating the date if it is a reply to a telegram of an earlier date, and addressing the answer in care of the office or branch office from which the original telegram was sent, as indicated by the office call, consisting of one or two letters, which appear immediately preceding the "place from" in the date line. The identifying number of the message being answered should also be included in the address.

Indicating Class of Service Desired, and Whether "Paid" or "Collect"

In preparing a telegram, care should be exercised to indicate not only the class of service desired but also whether it is to be sent "paid" or "collect." This latter is done by writing one of those words at the upper right-hand corner in the space provided. When a telegram is to be charged to an account, the name of the account, if different from the message signature, should be shown in the space provided.

Reports of Delivery

If a report of the delivery of any telegram is wanted, the words "Report Delivery" should be written conspicuously at the top of the telegram blank. This instruction, which is charged for, will be wired to destination and a report stating to whom and when the telegram was delivered will be wired back to the sender. The report will be in the form of a collect telegram to sender.

Telegrams Repeated Back

Occasionally patrons desire to have their telegrams repeated back as a guard against inaccuracies. In such cases the telegram is repeated back from receiving operator to sending operator for comparison at each stage of its transmission. An extra charge equal to fifty per cent of the regular tolls is made, in addition to the cost of the two extra words, "repeat back," in the original telegram.

The Destination

The destination is the name of the city and state to which a telegram is directed. The name of the city should be spelled out in full and the name of the state abbreviated.

The Body or Text

The body of a telegram embodies the information which the sender desires to convey to the addressee. Terseness is desirable, but should not be carried to a point where the meaning is obscured. The parts of speech most often used in telegrams are nouns, verbs, adjectives, and adverbs. If possible, do without pronouns, prepositions, articles, and copulative verbs. Use simple sentences, rather than complex or compound. If more than one sentence is needed, use the same form or the same order of words.

In telegrams within the United States and between points in the United States and points in Canada, Mexico, and St. Pierre-Miquelon Islands, punctuation marks are transmitted without charge. The use of the word "Stop" is not necessary or desirable and, if used, it is counted as a word.

Because of the low word cost of domestic telegrams, code language, which is useful principally for condensing purposes, is not usually employed in such messages. The saving in tolls is hardly commensurate with the labor involved in the coding and decoding processes. The use of code serves to delay correspondence and substitutes the stilted language of the code for the free expression that is so desirable. However, the use of code is permitted in all classes of domestic telegrams.

The Signature

The signature is that portion of a telegram which identifies the sender. If a telegram is not to bear a signature, there should be written in place of the signature the word "Unsigned." When the name is not written in full, or if the sender is not well known at the telegraph office, his local street and telephone number should be written at the bottom of the form for reference in case there should be occasion to communicate with him.

Count of Chargeable Words in Domestic Messages

Domestic messages are messages between points within the United States, and between points in the United States and points in Canada, Mexico, and St. Pierre-Miquelon Islands.

Dictionary words in the English, German, French, Dutch, Italian, Portuguese, Spanish, and Latin languages are counted as one word each, irrespective of length.

Combinations of two or more dictionary words of the eight authorized languages are counted according to the number of words of which they are composed.

All groups of letters which are not dictionary words of the eight authorized languages or combinations of such words, or proper names, are counted at the rate of one word for every five letters. This includes dictionary or non-dictionary words in languages not authorized, initials, abbreviations, mutilated dictionary words, and trade names which are not dictionary words of the authorized languages.

Punctuation marks (period, comma, colon, semicolon, hyphen or dash, question mark, apostrophe, quotation marks, and parentheses) are not counted, regardless of where they appear in the message. A decimal point in a group of figures is considered as a period. Words such as stop, comma, period, and quote used in lieu of punctuation marks are counted as one word each.

All proper names from any language are counted according to the number of separate words, or separate words and separate initials, which they contain.

Initials in any proper name, or as an abbreviation for a proper name, may be written together without space between, and when so written are counted as a letter group at the rate of one word for every five letters. Periods may be inserted and are not counted. If initials are separated by spaces each initial is counted as one word. Examples:

Van Dorne .... 2 words
DeWitt .... 1 word
St. Louis .... 2 words
J. L. R. Smith (space between initials) .... 4 words
J.L.R. Smith (without space between initials) 2 words

The characters \$ / & # ′ (indicating feet or minutes) and ″ (inches or seconds) are the only characters that can be accepted in messages in addition to the letters of the English alphabet, Arabic numerals, and the punctuation marks enumerated in Paragraph 5. Any other character not mentioned in this paragraph cannot be accepted and must be expressed by the use of acceptable characters. For example, the percent sign % is replaced in transmission by the characters 0/0, and if a percent sign appears with a group of figures such as 100%, it is transmitted with the percent sign linked to the group of figures by a hyphen or dash: 100–0/0.

Groups of figures, other characters enumerated in Paragraph 7, and mixed groups composed of any combination of figures, other characters, and letters are counted as follows:

In messages between points within the United States, and between points in the United States and points in Alaska and Mexico, the charge is at the rate of one word for each five figures, other characters, or letters. Examples:

5	1 word
12345	1 word
123456	2 words
B.D/A:C (period and colon are punctuation)	1 word
AB12CD	2 words
12-3/4 (hyphen is punctuation)	1 word
12¾ (transmitted as 12 3/4)	2 words
B&O (without spacing)	1 word
B & O (spaced)	3 words
10&20 (without spacing)	1 word
10 & 20 (spaced)	3 words
$20.25 (decimal is punctuation)	1 word

In messages from, to, or between points in the United States and points in Canada and St. Pierre-Miquelon Islands each figure and other character is counted as one word and each uninterrupted sequence of letters appearing in a combination group is counted at the rate of one word for each five letters. Examples:

12345	5 words
B.D/A:C	3 words
(B.D. is letter sequence; / is other character; A:C is letter sequence; period and colon are punctuation.)	
B&O (letter, other character, and letter)	3 words
$20.25	5 words
(Other character and 4 figures; decimal is punctuation.)	

Ordinary addresses of messages, and signatures, are not charged for.

The title of an official or the name of a department, branch, or division, or the name of an individual when added to the signature of a firm or organization is not charged for. However, when the name of more than one individual, or the name of an individual and of a department, branch, or division, or the name of an individual and a title, or the names of more than one department, branch, or division are added to the signature, only the first added name will be carried free; the remainder will be counted and charged for. Examples:

John R. Smith, President (no extra charge)
Standard Can Co., Sales Dept. (no extra charge)
Standard Can Co., John R. Smith, President (President is one extra word, charged for).
Standard Can Co., Sales Dept., Retail Division (Retail Division are extra words, charged for).

Family signatures such as Mother and Father, John and Mary, and H. A. Brown and Family are treated as a single signature, and there is no charge for extra words.

"Answer by Western Union," "Wire by Western Union," and similar phrases occurring in messages are charged for.

How to Send Telegrams

When a telegram is ready it may be handed to Western Union over the counter at any one of the numerous branch offices maintained to facilitate receipt of messages for transmission; or it may be given from a business office or home telephone, or from any coin-operated public telephone. Expert typists are employed for the accurate and speedy reception over the telephone of telegrams. Ask for "Western Union." On a dial telephone, dial "Operator" and ask for Western Union, or in certain cases call by number.

By telephone it will be found helpful, in the case of uncommon words, unusual names, code or cipher words, foreign words, and initials which are not easily understood, to pronounce each letter and follow it with an identifying word. For example, if the word "Sioux" cannot be understood, say "S as in Sugar, I as in Ida, O as in Ocean, U as in Union, X as in X-ray." The following code is designed for this purpose:

A as in Adams
B as in Boston
C as in Chicago
D as in Denver
E as in Edward
F as in Frank
G as in George
H as in Henry
I as in Ida

J as in John
K as in King
L as in Lincoln
M as in Mary
N as in Ned
O as in Ocean
P as in Peter
Q as in Queen
R as in Robert

S as in Sugar
T as in Thomas
U as in Union
V as in Victory
W as in William
X as in X-ray
Y as in Young
Z as in Zero

File Copies

The original copies of telegrams telephoned, and carbon copies of all others, should be filed away. This will facilitate checking monthly bills.

CONGRATULATIONS

The Western Union suggests the following telegrams as illustrations of acceptable messages. The Company is prepared to offer forms for many other occasions.

On anniversaries

My best wishes and love to you both on your anniversary. May you enjoy every happiness for many years to come.

Wish we could be there to propose a toast to you both for many more happy years together.

Congratulations on your anniversary. May the years to come be as happy as those that have passed.

Our warmest congratulations to one of the most happily married couples in the world.

Best wishes to the husband, best wishes to the wife, for many years together of blissful married life.

May this and many other wedding anniversaries be filled with happiness and contentment.

Love and best wishes to you both. May you always have fair weather and clear sailing.

Congratulations and best wishes for a long life, prosperity, health and happiness.

On engagements

Your engagement is wonderful news. Love and happiness to you both and best wishes for a future full of joy.

May your engagement be filled with a joy surpassed only by the happiness of your married life.

Wonderful news. May your future together be filled with all possible happiness and joy.

Delighted to hear the good news and wish you great happiness.

On making a speech

Congratulations on a fine speech. I am confident it has won many new friends and supporters to your cause.

Congratulations on a fearless, fighting speech. On a platform so clearly for the common good, you are sure to win.

Your speech was truly inspirational. It has given us a great lift. Congratulations and good luck.

On Public Service

Our respect and admiration go out to you as a great public servant. We all applaud your right and straightforward action.

Congratulations on a fine and courageous job. Americans everywhere are proud of your accomplishments.

It's men like you who are helping to make this country a better place to live in. Congratulations.

On a promotion

Happy to hear of your promotion. Hope it is just one of many more to come. Sincere congratulations.

Hearty congratulations on your promotion. No one ever deserved it more. Good luck and the best of everything.

Delighted to hear the good news. Please add my congratulations to the many you are receiving.

On election to office

Overjoyed that you won. Predict great success in your new office. Congratulations.

You fully deserve the honor of your new office. Congratulations and the best of everything.

On opening a store

Congratulations on the opening of your new store. Best wishes for a prosperous future.

With all good wishes for the grand opening and a success for your store that exceeds your expectations.

CONDOLENCES

Words are inadequate to express my (our) sorrow at the news of your great affliction. My (Our) love and sympathy to you all.

I (We) have just heard of your great loss. Please accept my (our) heartfelt sympathy.

Our hearts are with you in love and sympathy. May happy memories bring a measure of comfort and peace.

I (We) share your sorrow, for I (we) have lost a good friend. All love and sympathy to you and yours.

Cablegrams

CLASSES OF CABLE SERVICE

Ordinaries or Full-Rates

The "ordinary" or full-rate cablegram is the standard plain-language or secret language (code or cipher) cable service, and the rates charged therefor constitute the base from which other cable rates are derived.

Cable Letter Telegrams

Cable Letter Telegram Service is an overnight service designed primarily for plain-language business and social communications of some length which are not of sufficient urgency to warrant payment under the higher-priced classification. The necessary prefix for this service is LT, which is placed before the name-to and is counted and charged for as one word. Code is not permitted in the text of cable Letter Telegrams, but registered (code) addresses may be used. The LT rate is one-half the ordinary rate, with a minimum charge for twenty-two words.

PREPARATION OF CABLEGRAMS

Cablegrams are constructed similarly to domestic telegrams, except that registered (abbreviated code) addresses are customarily employed to save tolls and code language is largely used. In cablegrams each word in the address (other than the country of destination and routing indicators), text, and signature is counted and charged for.

Plain language is that which represents an intelligible meaning in any language that can be expressed in Roman letters, each word and each expression having the meaning normally assigned to it in the language to which it belongs. In plain-language messages each dictionary word not exceeding 15 letters is counted as a single word.

Commercial marks composed of figure and letter groups are counted at the rate of one word for each five characters or fraction thereof.

A stroke in a group of figures counts as a figure and not as a separate word. The same is true of fraction bars, periods, commas, and other decimal points grouped with figures. Punctuation marks, hyphens, parentheses, dashes, underlines, and apostrophes are not transmitted, except when expressly requested, and then are charged for as one word each. A dollar sign or pound sterling mark cannot be transmitted and should be replaced by the word "dollars" or "pounds," or by an abbreviation.

Addresses

The name of the city and country of destination is required. However, when it is necessary to use the name of the state, country, or other geographical subdivision, it should be combined with the office (city, town, or place) of destination, both written together as one word, which will be counted and charged for as one word regardless of the number of letters it contains. The country of destination, which is neither counted nor charged for, should be enclosed in parentheses. Experienced cable clerks will often be able to identify unnecessary words in addresses, and assistance in preparing cablegrams will be gladly given by the telegraph company's employees. Addresses that are not in code and registered should not be unduly shortened, since correct and sufficient addresses are necessary in making delivery.

While the names of the place of destination and of the state or county are counted as one word each, irrespective of how composed, the names of streets and of persons in addresses are counted at fifteen letters or fraction thereof to a word.

Cablegrams for places where there is no telegraph office should bear the name of the nearest office as the last word of the address and the word "post" as the first word. These two words are counted and charged for.

6. The Framing of Petitions

The writing of petitions should be characterized by clearness of expression, by an orderly marshaling of ideas, by forceful presentation of material, and by dignified, respectful tone.

Petitions are usually expressed in a conventional form based on one of the following plans:

1. The reasons arranged in order of their importance followed by the request, each reason being preceded by *In view of the fact that* or by *Inasmuch as*.

2. The explanation of who is making the request, as, *We, the Members of the New Rochelle Woman's Club,* or *We, the Undersigned Citizens of* ...., or, *We, the Residents of* ...., followed by the request itself and the reasons for such a request.

Petition for Local Improvement

New York,

To (Name of Borough President)
President of the Borough of
The subscribers, whose names are written underneath, respectfully petition you and the Local Board of the
District for a certain local improvement, to wit:

Regulate, reregulate, grade, regrade, curb, recurb, lay or relay sidewalk and pave with a permanent (type of pavement—granite, sheet asphalt, etc.) on a concrete foundation avenue from   street to street, together with all work incidental thereto

and they hereby request that you appoint a time for a meeting of the said Local Board, and that you submit this petition to said Board and do all such other acts as may be required of you by law, in order that the local improvement above described may be initiated and obtained or constructed:

Names   Addresses   Description of property owned

DEAR SIR:

The subscribers whose names are written underneath, being owners of property directly affected, respectfully petition you and the Local Board of ....
for the laying out on the map of The City of New York ....
....
....
in accordance with accompanying sketch.

And we hereby request that you appoint a time for a meeting of the said Local Board, and that you submit this petition to said Board, and do all such other acts as may be required of you by law in order that the above described lay-out may be obtained and become a part of the map of The City of New York.

NAME OF OWNER	ADDRESS	FRONTAGE ON IM-PROVEMENT	LOT NUMBER	BLOCK NUMBER

Reprinted by permission.

Petition for a Road

To the Board of   of   County

The undersigned ask that a public highway, commencing at and running thence north and terminating at
be established [or vacated, or altered, as the case may be].

Names   Addresses

Petition for a Church

We, the undersigned, do hereby petition
Presbytery to appoint a Commission to organize a Presbyterian church
in   , South Carolina, and in testimony that we desire to become charter members of said church, we have hereunder affixed our signatures.

Signed:

Petition to the Governor

The undersigned residents of the State of New York respectfully call to your attention the fact that the Highlands of the Hudson, which are generally regarded as one of the chief beauty spots of America, are being seriously damaged by the operations of the Hudson River Stone Corporation, which is quarrying and operating a crushing plant on Mount Taurus, just opposite the great Military Academy at West Point.

It has been the practice of the State, for many years, to create parks and reservations at the principal points of beauty and interest. We venture the assertion that there is no point of greater scenic or historic interest in New York than the particular point at which this stone quarry is operating. This quarry has already cut a deep gash in the mountain and has made an enormous pile of debris in the river itself. Moreover, it is rapidly blasting out and shipping away the projection in the river known as "Little Stony Point."

With due respect, we most urgently request that the State of New York take immediate steps to secure this property and put an end to the irreparable and rapidly increasing damage now being done at that point.

Used by permission of THE AMERICAN
SCENIC AND HISTORIC PRESERVATION SOCIETY

Withdrawal of Signatures

We, the undersigned, having signed a petition for
in the city of   , state of   , which petition
is on file with you, do hereby request that our names be taken from
such a petition filed with you on the
day of   . 19___.

Names   Addresses

7. The Writing of Minutes

Minutes are records of meetings and of the action taken in them. They should, therefore, be written accurately, clearly, and concisely, for they are often referred to in confirmation of an action, as a source of information, or as records.

The language is formal and follows traditional lines. Generally, definite forms are used which are to be observed strictly. Minutes often conform to the following order, although not all organizations make use of the complete list given below.

(*a*) Name of body holding meeting
(*b*) Type of meeting (regular, annual, special, etc.)
(*c*) Time, date, and place
(*d*) Name of presiding officer
(*e*) Names or number of those present
(*f*) Approval of previous minutes
(*g*) Unfinished business and reports of committees of investigation
(*h*) Action taken on unfinished business; digest of business pending
(*i*) New business, such as motions both lost and approved. Those withdrawn without vote may be omitted. Names of the proposers of all main motions should be given.
(*j*) Date of next meeting
(*k*) Adjournment and time of adjournment
(*l*) Approval and signature of minutes

Because keeping the minutes of an organization is so important, full notes should be made by the recording secretary of all business transactions of a meeting, omitting matters on which no action was taken and references to reports not given. An objective tone should be kept; and personal opinions, such as an "interesting" meeting, an "inspiring" address, a "delightful" hour, should not be inserted. Before being read, the notes should be written in the minute book in permanent form, so that they may be presented to the organization for approval. After the minutes have been read to the assembly, corrections may be suggested. If these are accepted they should be inserted in red ink. When this is done and the minutes have been approved, they should never be changed or rewritten. The secretary should then sign her name, followed on the same line or on the line below by the word *Secretary*. The expression *Respectfully submitted* is not used today. The word *Approved,* with the date, should be written at the left margin on the line below the signature, followed by the secretary's name and also by that of the president if the organization requires it.

The Secretary's Signature

An unmarried woman should sign the minutes by her given name and her surname, preceded by *Miss* in parentheses if she thinks it necessary. *Dorothy Anne Gordon* or *Dorothy A. Gordon* is considered better form for a woman than *D. A. Gordon*.

A married woman should not sign her name as *Mrs. Burton Lane*. She should sign her given name with her maiden name or initial and her husband's surname, as *Jane Powell Chambers*. Occasionally it may be desirable for her to give her married name. If so, it should be written in parentheses below her signature.

Recording Motions

The name of the person making a motion should be given in the minutes, but that of the seconder is usually omitted. Whether the motion was carried, lost, referred to a committee, or laid on the table should be recorded. However, if a motion is not seconded no record is made of it. In some cases it may be advisable to tell how the motion was voted upon, that is, by show of hands, by standing, by voice, by ballot, or by roll call. If the vote was by ballot or by roll call, the number voting, the number for the affirmative, and the number for the negative should be stated.

Committee Reports

Committee reports may be entered in the minutes in one of the following ways, depending on the importance of the subject or upon the wish of the organization:

1. A summary of the report with the name of the chairman
2. A copy of the entire report as submitted by the chairman
3. Reference to the subject of the report when the entire report is filed separately and therefore available in the files

When a resolution contained in a report has been adopted by an organization, it should be included in the minutes exactly as it was worded.

Types of Meetings

The following types of meetings will be found recorded in minutes of organizations: regular, special, annual, and possibly adjournments of one or more of these. The examples given illustrate the form and phraseology that may be used in the minutes of such meetings.

Regular Meetings

(1)

The regular meeting of the Pleasant Valley Civic Association was called to order by Andrew Nash, president, at 2:30 on February 20, 19___, at the Chamber of Commerce, 43 members being present.

Following the roll call, the minutes of the meeting of January 24 were read. Mrs. Lewis Rankin called attention to the fact that the name of the speaker was Amelia Howe, not Amelia Howell. The minutes were approved as corrected.

The report of the treasurer, showing a balance of $495.55, was read and placed on file.

Mr. White, chairman of the Hospital Beautification Committee, reported that a plan of landscaping the hospital grounds had been submitted on February 6 by John Briggs, of the Greenway Landscape Company. This plan called for the planting of 10 trees and 8 shrubs at a cost of $325. Mr. White then asked for an appropriation from the association to cover the cost of this project. Alexander Lawson moved that the sum of $325 be appropriated. The motion was seconded and carried.

It was moved by Miss Alice Graham, and duly seconded, that a committee be appointed to work with the City Commissioners on City Planning. Action on the motion was postponed until the next meeting.

Mr. Hadley moved that the association go on record as opposed to the annexation of Goodwin Estates to the city of Pleasant Valley. The motion was seconded. A voice vote was taken, resulting in 6 affirmative, 37 negative. The motion was declared lost.

Mr. Horace Blake, city manager, addressed the meeting on "The Importance of City Planning." He was accorded a vote of thanks for his presentation of the subject.

There being no further business, the meeting was adjourned at 4:15 P.M.

HARRIET JACKSON
Secretary

Approved March 20, 19___

HARRIET JACKSON
Secretary

(2)

At the first meeting of the English Graduate Union, some eighty charter members being present, the association was called to order by Ernest Hunter Wright, who acted as temporary Chairman and who requested Mildred Loxton de Barritt to serve as temporary Secretary.

For the information of the members, the Chairman spoke at some length of the purposes and prospects of the Union. In record of the state of the association as of March 1, he reported a membership of 186, of whom 121 were resident members and 65 non-resident; and of whom 40 were life-members, 28 being resident and 12 non-resident. He further reported subscriptions already pledged to the Endowment as totaling $1719.00, and to current expenses as totaling $188.00.

In behalf of the Committee of Organization, the Chairman then read a copy of the Constitution for the Union as drawn and offered with a view to the proximate incorporation of the association under the laws of the State of New York. Upon motion of Dudley Howe Miles, seconded by William Haller, the Constitution was unanimously adopted, and ordered printed and distributed to members.

As a first act under the Constitution, Charles Sears Baldwin, in behalf of the Committee of Organization who had so far acted as the Council of the Union, moved the election to honorary membership of Brander Matthews, Emeritus Professor of Dramatic Literature, and of William Peterfield Trent, Emeritus Professor of English Literature. The motion was seconded in a speech of reminiscence by Arthur H. Nason, and was carried by a rising vote.

The next business under the Constitution was the election of officers for the remainder of the current year. Dorothy McSparran Arnold, Chairman of the Nominating Committee, presented the following slate:

President:
    Ernest Hunter Wright
Secretary:
    Mildred Loxton de Barritt
Treasurer:
    Hoxie Neale Fairchild

Members of the Council:
    Harry Morgan Ayres
    Arthur E. Christy
    Dwight L. Durling
    Ruth Mohl

At the request of the Chairman, Mr. Nason took the chair. After a call for further nominations, it was moved by William A. S. Dollard that the nominating ballot become the elected ballot. The motion was seconded and carried, and the officers were declared elected as follows:

[offices and names of officers repeated]

After brief congratulations, in prose and verse respectively, by Blanche Colton Williams and by Harry Morgan Ayres, the Union adjourned.

MILDRED LOXTON DE BARRITT
Secretary

Special Meeting

A special meeting of the Pleasant Valley Civic Association was held at the Chamber of Commerce at 2:30 P.M. on March 10, 19___, with Andrew Nash, president, in the chair. Fifty-six members were present.

Mr. Nash reported that the following notice in accordance with the bylaw requirements had been mailed to every member of the Association on March 5: "Notice is hereby given that a meeting of all members of the association will be held on March 10 at 2:30 at the Chamber of Commerce for the purpose of determining what action the assembly wishes to take regarding the proposed recreation center on the plot of land between Magnolia Avenue on the east, Lakeview Road on the west, Glencoe Street on the north, and French Boulevard on the south."

Mrs. Albert Wentworth read the following resolution and moved its adoption:

WHEREAS, converting the plot of land between Magnolia Avenue on the east, Lakeview Road on the west, Glencoe Street on the north, and French Boulevard on the south, would depreciate the property in the neighborhood, and

WHEREAS, land bordering on a busy thoroughfare, such as French Boulevard, is not suitable or safe for a recreation center, therefore

RESOLVED, That it is the sense of the Pleasant Valley Civic Association that this plot of land shall not be converted into a recreation center, and

BE IT FURTHER RESOLVED, That this resolution be spread upon the minutes of the association and a copy be sent to the Mayor.

The motion was seconded and carried.

On motion of Mrs. Miles Merrill the meeting was adjourned at 3:10 P.M.

HARRIET JACKSON, Secretary

Annual Meetings

(1)

The annual meeting of the Pleasant Valley Civic Association was called to order at the Chamber of Commerce at 2:30 P.M. on April 5, 19__, by President Andrew Nash, 56 members being present.

The minutes of the previous meeting were approved as read.

Mr. Nash expressed his appreciation of the officers and the committees for their cooperation in carrying out the work of the association during the year.

Reports of officers and committees were read.

The vice president took the chair while the president read his annual report.

The president then called on Richard Stanley, Chairman, for the report of the Nominating Committee. The following slate of officers was presented:

> President: Peter Collins
> Vice President: Mrs. Lawrence Doane
> Treasurer: Philip Maxwell
> Secretary: Miss Elizabeth Fulton

There being no other nominations, the nominations were declared closed.

The Chair appointed Messrs. Hall, Betts, and Cole as tellers. They distributed the ballots. The meeting was in recess during the voting. After the chairman of the tellers had handed his report to the president, Mr. Nash declared that 55 votes had been cast in favor of each candidate and that the following officers were therefore elected: President, Peter Collins; Vice President, Mrs. Lawrence Doane; Treasurer, Philip Maxwell; Secretary, Miss Elizabeth Fulton.

President Nash then handed the gavel to the President-elect, who closed the meeting with an expression of appreciation for the honor the association had conferred upon him.

There being no further business, the meeting was adjourned at 4:15 P.M.

HARRIET JACKSON, Secretary

(2)

The Thirty-fifth Annual Meeting of the Association for the Protection of the Adirondacks was held in the office of Mr. George Welwood Murray, First Vice President, at No. 15 Broad Street, New York City, on Monday, April 13, 19__, at 3 P.M.

The Acting President, Mr. George Welwood Murray, presided. Others present were Messrs. Ernest T. Carter, Henry L. de Forest, Morris Douw Ferris, Karl T. Frederick, E. Hubert Litchfield, Robert Marshall, Ellwood M. Rabenold, Francis Louis Slade, Eric P. Swenson, and Frederick K. Vreeland.

The minutes of the Thirty-fourth Annual Meeting of the Association, held May 3, 19___, were approved.

The Acting President stated that the Annual Report of the President would be completed after the adjournment of the Legislature, and printed and distributed to the members of the Association. This was approved.

The Annual Report of the Treasurer, Mr. Morris Douw Ferris, audited and approved by Riddle & Camp, Certified Public Accountants, was presented and approved and ordered on file. The report is appended to these minutes.

The report of the Nominating Committee, appointed at the January meeting of the Board, to name Trustees to be elected in the Class of 19___, was presented on behalf of the Chairman, Mr. Ottomar H. Van Norden, the other members, Messrs. Litchfield, Marshall, Hayes and Chace, having concurred. The Committee recommended the re-election of all the Trustees in the Class of 19___, whose terms were then expiring.

The Acting President asked whether there were any other nominations. As there were none, he declared the nominations closed. Mr. Ferris moved that the slate as presented by the Nominating Committee be declared elected. The motion was seconded, voted upon, and carried. The Acting President declared the following officers were elected. [Offices and officers listed.]

There being no other business, the meeting adjourned.

RAYMOND H. TORREY
Secretary

Reprinted by permission.

Minutes of Stockholders' Meeting

The Minutes of a Stockholders' Meeting generally include the following: the names of those present, how many shares they hold, which are represented in person and which by proxy, an alphabetical list of stockholders, proof of mailing of notice-of-the-meeting with affidavit duly acknowledged before notary, copy of proxy, oath of inspectors, nomination of officers, report of inspectors on votes cast, announcement of elections, approval of preceding minutes, all in great detail and formal order. These minutes are usually written by the Company attorney.

The following illustrates in detail the minutes of such a meeting:

> The annual meeting of the stockholders of The Greene Company, a Maine corporation, was held at the office of the Company, 240 Park Avenue, in the Borough of Manhattan, City, County and State of New York, on Monday, February 27, 19___, at 4:00 o'clock in the afternoon, pursuant to adjournment.

Mr. John Greene, President of the Company, called the meeting to order and Mr. W. A. Sands, its Assistant Secretary, kept the minutes.

The Secretary presented the alphabetical list, required by statute, of the stockholders entitled to vote at the meeting and, after comparing the list with the proxies presented and after ascertaining the stockholders present in person, reported that the following stockholders whose stock had not been transferred on the books of the Company within twenty (20) days next preceding the meeting, holding the number and kinds of shares indicated opposite their respective names and aggregating a total of 3,326 shares out of a total of 5,422 shares entitled to vote at this meeting, were present in person or represented by proxy and entitled to vote.

STOCKHOLDERS PRESENT IN PERSON

Name of Stockholder	1st Pref.	Sec. Pref.	Common
(Names)	(Number of shares held by each)		

STOCKHOLDERS REPRESENTED BY PROXY

Name	Name of Proxy	No. of Shares		
		1st Pref.	Sec. Pref.	Common

The alphabetical list of stockholders referred to above is attached.

The Chairman thereupon announced that a quorum was in attendance at the meeting.

The Secretary presented and read a copy of the notice-of-the-meeting together with proof of the due mailing thereof to each stockholder of the Company at least ten (10) days before the meeting, as required by the bylaws.

On motion, it was unanimously

RESOLVED, That the original affidavit of mailing notice of this meeting together with the copy of said notice, the form of proxy and the list of stockholders thereto annexed, be kept among the records of the Company and that copies thereof be incorporated in the minutes of this meeting.

Following are copies of said affidavit of mailing, said notice of this meeting, said form of proxy and said list of stockholders.

THE GREENE COMPANY

Affidavit of Mailing Notice

of

ANNUAL MEETING OF STOCKHOLDERS

STATE OF NEW YORK } ss.:
COUNTY OF NEW YORK }

VIRGINIA WHYTE, being duly sworn, deposes and says that she is over the age of twenty-one years.

That on February 9th, 19___, at about 11:45 A.M., she placed in a mail-chute maintained by the United States Post Office, at No. 420 Park Avenue, in the Borough of Manhattan, City, County and State of New York, securely sealed, post-paid envelopes addressed to the persons and at the addresses set forth upon the annexed "List of Stockholders"; that each of said envelopes contained a copy of the "Notice of Annual Meeting of Stockholders," of which another copy is hereto annexed.

                                   Virginia Whyte

Sworn to before me this
9th day of February, 19___

            Mary Heald
              Notary Public,
            New York County Clerk's No. 483
            New York County Register's No. 8262
            Commission expires March 30th, 19___

(Mary Heald   )
(Notary Public   )
(New York, N. Y.)

THE GREENE COMPANY
NOTICE OF ANNUAL MEETING
of
STOCKHOLDERS

TO THE STOCKHOLDERS OF THE GREENE
COMPANY

NOTICE IS HEREBY GIVEN pursuant to the bylaws of The Greene Company (a Maine Corporation) that the annual meeting of its stockholders will be held at the office of the Corporation at No. 240 Park Avenue, New York, N. Y., on Monday, February 27th, 19___, at 11:00 o'clock in the forenoon.

1. To elect a Board of Directors;
2. To ratify, approve and confirm previous action of the stockholders, the Board of Directors and the officers of the Corporation and act on any reports of the officers made on said meeting;
3. To take action on any other matters that may properly come before the meeting.

W. A. SANDS
Assistant Secretary

New York, N. Y.
February 9, 19___.

If you do not expect to be present in person, please sign the accompanying proxy and return it at once.

THE GREENE COMPANY

PROXY

First Preferred Shares........
Second Preferred Shares......
Common Shares ....
Total ....

KNOW ALL MEN BY THESE PRESENTS that the undersigned stockholder of THE GREENE COMPANY, a Maine Corporation, does hereby constitute and appoint attorneys, agents and proxies, and each of them attorney, agent and proxy, for the undersigned and in the name, place and stead of the undersigned, with full power of substitution and revocation, to vote upon and act as proxy of the undersigned in respect of all preferred stock and all common stock, or either, of THE GREENE COMPANY held by or standing in the name of the undersigned (hereby revoking any proxy or proxies heretofore given by the undersigned in respect of such stock or any thereof), at the annual meeting of stockholders of said Corporation to be held at its office, No. 240 Park Avenue, New York, N. Y., on February 27th, 19___, at eleven o'clock in the forenoon, and at any and all adjournments thereof, upon all matters that may come before said meeting, including the election of a Board of Directors and the ratification, approval and confirming of all previous action of the Board of Directors and officers of said Corporation, according to the number of votes the undersigned would be entitled to vote if then personally present. A majority of such of said attorneys, agents, and proxies as shall be present at the meeting (or, if only one be present, then that one) shall have and may exercise all the powers of all of them hereunder.

February , 19___

_____(L.S.)
Stockholder's Signature

WITNESS:

_____

LIST OF STOCKHOLDERS OF THE GREENE COMPANY TO WHOM NOTICE OF ANNUAL MEETING OF STOCKHOLDERS WAS SENT ON 2/9/___

Names   *Addresses*

The Chairman announced that the next business before the meeting was the election of directors to hold office until the next annual meeting of the stockholders and until the election and qualification of their respective successors.

Miss Edna Payne and Mr. A. F. McMillan (neither of them being a candidate for the office of director) were appointed inspectors of election and took the oath required by law, of which the following is a copy:

THE GREENE COMPANY
Oath of Inspectors of Election

STATE OF NEW YORK   }
COUNTY OF NEW YORK } ss.:

EDNA PAYNE and A. F. McMILLAN, being duly sworn upon their respective oaths, do severally promise and swear that they will faithfully, honestly and impartially perform the duties of inspectors of election for all votes that may be cast at the annual meeting of stockholders of The Greene Company, held on February 27, 19___, at the office of the Company, No. 240 Park Avenue, in the Borough of Manhattan, City, County and State of New York, and make true reports of said votes.

EDNA PAYNE
A. F. McMILLAN

Subscribed and
sworn to before me
this 27th day of
February, 19___.

MARY HEALD
Notary Public
New York County Clerk's No. 483
New York County Register's No. 8262
Commission expires March 30th, 19___

(Mary Heald   )
(Notary Public   )
(New York County)

   Thereupon, the following were duly nominated as directors to serve until the next annual election and until the election and qualification of their respective successors.

John Greene
F. G. Huyler
L. D. Louis
A. P. McLaren
R. T. Porter
E. O. Reynolds
W. A. Sands

   The nominations having been closed, the polls were opened and the stockholders prepared their ballots and delivered them to the inspectors. Thereupon the polls were closed.

   The inspectors having canvassed the votes for directors, prepared a report in writing of which the following is a copy:

THE GREENE COMPANY
Report of Inspectors

   We, the subscribers, inspectors of election, appointed by the stockholders of The Greene Company, at the annual meeting of said stockholders, held this day at the office of said Company at No. 240 Park Avenue, in the Borough of Manhattan, City, County and State of New York, do report that, having taken an oath impartially to conduct the election of directors and all other votes at said meeting, we did receive the votes of the stockholders by ballot.

We report that 3,326 votes were cast and that the following persons received the number of votes set opposite their respective names:

John Greene	3,326
F. G. Huyler	"
L. D. Louis	"
A. P. McLaren	"
R. T. Porter	"
E. O. Reynolds	"
W. A. Sands	"

all of which is respectfully submitted, this 27th day of February, 19____, at New York, N. Y.

> Edna Payne
> A. F. McMillan
> Inspectors

The Chairman then announced that Messrs. John Greene, F. G. Huyler, L. D. Louis, A. P. McLaren, R. T. Porter, E. O. Reynolds and W. A. Sands had been elected directors of the Company to serve until the next annual election and until the election and qualification of their respective successors.

There being no further business, the meeting, thereupon, on motion, adjourned.

_____
                                                  Secretary

_____
             Chairman

Order of Business for a Directors' Meeting

ROLL CALL

MINUTES OF LAST MEETING

REPORT OF THE PRESIDENT

REPORT OF THE TREASURER (or FINANCE COMMITTEE)

UNFINISHED BUSINESS (Under this are put items which are left over from preceding meetings; progress reports from committees appointed or their final reports, etc.)

NEW BUSINESS (any new business matters coming up since the last meeting)

ADJOURNMENT

In general the matters coming up at the Board meeting are those involving large capital expenditures affecting the policies of the company.

Report of the President. This usually gives a résumé of the outstanding events of the past month, including amount of business done, outlook for the next month or the next quarter, and any recommendations the president may wish to make in regard to these matters.

Report of the Treasurer. This gives the financial position of the company in cash and securities, and reports on any new investments made. It also gives any figures on earnings and expense required with statistics showing comparison with previous year or years.

> MINUTES OF A MEETING OF THE BOARD OF DIRECTORS OF THE BLANK COMPANY HELD AT THE OFFICES OF THE COMPANY, 240 PARK AVENUE, NEW YORK, N. Y., ON MONDAY, MARCH 26, 19___, AT 9:30 A.M.

The following directors were present: Messrs. Black, Greene, Reade, Sands, and White. Mr. Sands acted as Chairman and Mr. Greene as Secretary.

The secretary presented a notice of the meeting that had been mailed to all directors on March 12.

The minutes of the meeting of Friday, March 23, were read and approved on motion duly made, seconded, and unanimously carried. The Secretary reported that at the meeting of the stockholders on February 27 the following directors had been elected for the ensuing year: F. H. Greene, W. A. Sands, B. L. Thomas, H. O. Vance, G. F. White, L. K. Wilde, and J. S. Zimmerman. The Chair then announced that the first business of the meeting was to elect officers, and the following nominations were duly made and seconded:

President—W. A. Sands
Vice President—L. K. Wilde
Vice President—J. S. Zimmerman
Secretary—F. H. Greene
Treasurer—B. L. Thomas
Assistant Secretary—R. P. Mitchell

There being no further nominations it was moved, seconded, and unanimously carried that the nominations be closed and the above officers be declared duly elected to serve until their successors be duly elected and qualified.

The President then read a report which was accepted and filed with the minutes of the meeting.

It was moved by Mr. Greene and seconded by Mr. Thomas and unanimously carried that the thanks of the Board be expressed to Mr. Vance for his services to the Company as Vice President during the several years of his occupancy of that office.

There then followed a discussion of several of the matters covered in the President's report without formal action.

It was moved by Mr. Thomas and seconded by Mr. Wilde and unanimously carried that a regular dividend of $6.00 per share and an extra dividend of $1.50 per share upon the Common Stock of the company be declared for the second quarter of the calendar year 19___ payable in equal monthly payments to Common stockholders of record on the last day of each month.

There being no further business, on motion duly made, seconded, and unanimously carried the meeting adjourned at 10:30 A.M.

F. H. Greene
Secretary of the Meeting

For Reference Books see p. 433.

8. The Framing of Resolutions

Resolution writing generally follows conventional lines. It is usually a formal expression, couched in almost legal phrasing, consisting of two parts: the reasons for the resolution, preceded by *Whereas,* and the resolution itself, preceded by *Resolved,* in case of more than one resolution, *Resolved further.*

The first word following *Whereas* in resolutions, contracts, etc., is not capitalized; the first word following an enacting or resolving clause is capitalized.

A more informal type, increasingly used in modern writing, is a straightforward statement of the occasion for taking action, followed by the action taken, without the use of *Whereas* or *Resolved.* This form is particularly suitable for resolutions to be passed by an organization which wishes to indicate its stand on certain subjects. It also seems appropriate on the death of a prominent citizen, as it offers a wide scope for individual expression of appreciation. Such resolutions are characterized by dignity, simplicity, and sincerity.

Resolutions are framed for various purposes, some of which are:

1. To express appreciation for courtesies received
2. To do honor to one who has achieved distinction
3. To commemorate a distinguished service
4. To indicate action taken by an association
5. To express regret at the resignation of an official
6. To offer congratulations on the promotion of an individual
7. To express appreciation of the life of a prominent citizen who has recently died, and to extend sympathy to his family
8. To present a program carried out by an organization

Resolutions Passed by the General Federation of Women's Clubs

(1)

Redwood Mountain Area of Big Trees

WHEREAS, the so-called Redwood Mountain Grove of Big Trees lying between Sequoia and General Grant National Park, California, is regarded by many tree authorities and renowned botanists as one of the finest and largest redwood groves in existence, containing the best examples of young and middle-growth sequoias to be found anywhere, and

WHEREAS, John Muir, an eminent authority, spoke of this area as being the only place where big trees are growing on top of a mountain and may be seen silhouetted against the sky, and

WHEREAS, this grove is now privately owned, and the owners are willing to sell at a reasonable price, desiring that the trees be preserved for park purposes, and

WHEREAS, these trees are in imminent danger of being cut, the fallen timber already being cut for posts and rough lumber; therefore

RESOLVED, That the General Federation of Women's Clubs in convention assembled, June 19___, proposes that the Redwood Mountain Grove of Big Trees be acquired through purchase by the United States Government, or the State of California, or otherwise for park purposes, to be preserved unspoiled in perpetuity as a wilderness area.

(2)

Prevention—Control—Cure of Diseases

WHEREAS, the General Federation of Women's Clubs has been carrying on intensive educational work in various fields of public health, and

WHEREAS, it is estimated that 40,000,000 persons are without adequate full-time local public health service, which is basic to the promotion of better health and the prevention of disease, and

WHEREAS, the United States Public Health Service reports that the application of present scientific knowledge could substantially reduce the serious toll being taken by cancer, mental illness, tuberculosis, venereal, and heart diseases; therefore

RESOLVED, That the General Federation of Women's Clubs urges State Federations and individual clubs to encourage the establishment of full-time local health services where none exist and the strengthening of existing services; to cooperate with state agencies in securing necessary hospitals and health centers; to assist health departments and voluntary agencies in working for the prevention, control and cure of cancer, mental illness, tuberculosis, venereal, and heart diseases; and to maintain vigilance in holding the gains made in communicable diseases and environmental sanitation.

(3)

Fire Prevention

RESOLVED, That the General Federation of Women's Clubs in convention assembled, June 19___, continues to promote a program of education and activity for the protection of life and property from fire hazards in homes, hotels and places of public assembly; and further

RESOLVED, That the General Federation urges the respective states and municipalities to provide adequate fire inspection laws and other laws necessary to protect hotels and places of public gathering against fire hazards; and administer strict enforcement of such laws.

(4)

Naturalization

WHEREAS, a great many immigrants from foreign countries have come to and made their homes within the United States for long periods of years and have not become naturalized citizens, and

WHEREAS, it is advisable that every person who resides within the boundaries of these United States or its territorial possessions should feel a sense of obligation and duty toward the United States; therefore

RESOLVED, That the General Federation of Women's Clubs in convention assembled, June 19___, recommends to the Congress of the United States that an Act be passed making it mandatory that any person not a citizen of the United States, who enters this country or its territorial possessions from any foreign country, and resides in said country for five years or more, shall immediately, at the expiration of five years, make a declaration of his intention to become a citizen of the United States and proceed to a final Decree of Naturalization within the required time; and further

RESOLVED, That those persons who do not apply for naturalization within the legal time limit and those who do not qualify for naturalization be deported; and further

RESOLVED, That the provisions of this Act should not apply to duly accredited representatives of friendly foreign governments nor to representatives of approved foreign business enterprises.

(5)

Education Reference Section of the Library of Congress

WHEREAS, the Library of Congress is the principal library of the United States, the custodian of many of the principal national treasures, and the recognized head of the American library system, and

WHEREAS, the use of its facilities is not widely available; therefore

RESOLVED, That the General Federation of Women's Clubs goes on record as approving the establishment of an Education Reference Section in the General Reference and Bibliography Division of the Library of Congress to be available to individuals, libraries and other groups interested in education and research throughout the country; and that this action become an immediate objective of the Federation.

Reprinted by permission of the General Federation of Women's Clubs.

Formal Resolutions Adopted by Members of the American Council of Learned Societies

Sociological Society

As an expression of the appreciation felt by our members at a generous contribution toward an enterprise of scholarship the following resolution was unanimously passed:

The American Sociological Society in its nineteenth annual meeting assembled desires to express its enthusiastic appreciation of the munificence and rare wisdom displayed by Mr. Adolph S. Ochs and The New York Times Company in underwriting to the extent of five hundred thousand dollars the authoritative work on American biography projected by the American Council of Learned Societies.

E. W. BURGESS, Secretary

Political Science Association

As Secretary of the American Political Science Association, I take pleasure in forwarding to you the following copy of a resolution unanimously adopted at the recent meeting of the association in Washington. Permit me to say, personally, that your benefaction is deeply appreciated by scholars in the field of political science, as indeed in all branches of learning.

Upon being informed of the gift of $500,000 by The New York Times Company to promote the preparation of a Dictionary of American Biography under the auspices of the American Council of Learned Societies, devoted to Humanistic studies, the Political Science Association, in session in Washington, D.C., Dec. 29, 19___, adopted the following by unanimous vote:

Whereas, in the opinion of the members of this association the projected dictionary is a much-needed work of reference; and

Whereas, it is imperative that the dictionary be prepared under such direction as will guarantee its high scholarly character; be it

Resolved, That the American Political Science Association take note of the benefaction of Mr. Adolph S. Ochs and The New York Times Company and express alike its appreciation of so signal an act of generosity toward an enterprise of scholarship and its endorsement of the plan whereby the preparation of the manuscript of the dictionary will be under the control of the societies represented in the American Council.

Resolved further, That the Secretary be instructed to send a copy of these resolutions to Mr. Ochs personally, as well as to The New York Times Company and also to Dr. J. Franklin Jameson, Chairman of the council committee in charge of editorial and publishing arrangements.

FREDERIC A. OGG, Secretary

A Letter Containing a Resolution of Appreciation

Passed at a meeting of an Executive Committee of the Charity Organization Society of the City of New York.

Dear Miss Burrows:

At a very well attended meeting of the Executive Committee I presented your resignation and there were expressions of regard for you on the part of a number of those present who are acquainted with you. The Executive Committee thereupon adopted a resolution and the minutes will read as follows:

The Secretary reported that in her fortieth year of service Miss Sarah F. Burrows has resigned from the service of the Society and that in announcing her retirement to the district secretaries and heads of bureaus he had sent the following notice:

"In her fortieth year of faithful service to the Charity Organization Society, Miss Sarah F. Burrows has retired and carries with her the affectionate good will of all those who have known her.

"Miss Burrows has filled almost every place in the family work department of the Society, having been for many years district secretary, and for years assistant to the director. During all these years of service Miss Burrows brought to the Society the affection of many persons, young and old, whom she served and the affection and esteem of many for whom she acted as almoner.

"For many years the Society was an Institutional Member of the

Red Cross and in that capacity and on its own behalf it was first in the field when any disaster occurred of fire, flood or shipwreck. In some of these cases Miss Burrows did the major part of the work and in most of them she played an important part. When the great fire took place in San Francisco and Dr. Devine directed the activities of the Red Cross, at a moment's notice Miss Burrows went to San Francisco and served the people in distress with intelligence and sympathy. It was a hard service faithfully performed."

It was thereupon resolved that this record be spread upon the minutes and that the Executive Committee thereby records its appreciation of the service rendered by Miss Burrows and its hope that she may long enjoy such activities as may be congenial and helpful to others.

Sincerely yours,
LAWSON PURDY
Secretary

Reprinted by permission of the Charity Organization Society.

Resolutions Passed by the State Charities Aid Association in Praise of the Fund for the Hundred Neediest Cases

George F. Canfield, president of the State Charities Aid Association, forwarded resolutions adopted by the board of managers of the Association, as follows:

Whereas, *The New York Times,* at the beginning of the Christmas season, by editorial comment and news articles and by publication of the tragedies and problems of one hundred families and individuals in dire need of help from their fellow-citizens, has stirred to action the generous impulses of a large number of persons, and

Whereas, *The New York Times,* in so doing, has widened public understanding of the problems and needs of those who, by reason of sickness and misfortune, must rely upon the generosity of others, and

Whereas, the public has responded wholeheartedly to the peculiar needs of each case and has also, by its generous contributions, endorsed the wise and kindly method by which the appeal is carried out,

Resolved, That the Board of Managers of the State Charities Aid Association warmly commends this call for aid to the Hundred Neediest Cases, both because of its direct and vital help to the sick and poor in distress, and because of its great benefit to the community, and expresses to *The New York Times* its deep gratitude for the insight and skill with which this human and personal appeal has been directed, wisely assuring the greatest good to those who, at this season of good-will, most desperately need succor from their more fortunate brothers.

From the Annual Report of the City Library Association of Springfield, Massachusetts

In Memoriam

George Walter Vincent Smith

It was the happy lot of our late associate, George Walter Vincent Smith, to make for himself a fortunate life, and to be given the satisfaction of knowing that the ample fruits of his labors were to remain for the enrichment of this community. Over years far beyond the scriptural span of life, Mr. Smith was permitted the joy that lay in his unselfish quest after objects of high artistic merit. It was a service rich in results for education and craftsmanship in the present and the future. How surpassing was his spiritual and cultural achievement is revealed by the treasures in the Art Museum, as is the thoughtfulness of his generosity by the fund provided for their care. Fitly placed under his direction, these fine possessions are to be studied and enjoyed to the profit of our people, whose gratitude, it is pleasant to remember, was often expressed during the life of the giver.

Impressive in its suggestiveness to the men and women who seek enduring ways of serving their fellows, was our friend's exceptional accomplishment. The City Library Association of Springfield has been fortunate in its appeal to wisely generous benefactors, and never more so than in this conspicuous instance. The members of the Board of Directors pledge themselves and their successors to constant and sympathetic nurture of this noble gift, by which Mr. and Mrs. Smith are to benefit the public to an extent beyond reckoning.

Adopted by the Board of Directors, April 17, 19___.

Reprinted by permission of the City Library Association of Springfield, Mass.

In Memoriam

Samuel Bowles, 3d

With profound sorrow, the Directors of the City Library Association record the death of one of its most earnest and zealous friends—Samuel Bowles, 3d. Mr. Bowles, succeeding his father in 1878, was for thirty-seven years a member of the Association, during twenty-four of which he was active in its Board of Directors. In the Springfield which he so loved and served, the City Library Association in a peculiar degree claimed his interest and support. He was ever ready to advance its usefulness by material contributions toward its buildings, as well as by wise counsel and enthusiasm for its aims. His high conception of the mission of public library and museums in enlightening and safeguarding a democratic community was not only felt in this city, but through the columns of the *Springfield Republican* became of far-reaching influence.

With the sense of community-loss is mingled deep sympathy for the members of his family.

Adopted by the Board of Directors, March 27, 19___.

Reprinted by permission of the City Library Association of Springfield, Mass.

Resolutions Passed on the Death of Prominent Citizens

Resolution passed by the Vocational Guidance Association at Boston on the death of Mr. Frederick J. Allen.

In recognition of the long and untiring services of Frederick J. Allen in the field of vocational guidance, the National Vocational Guidance Association at its annual meeting in Dallas, Texas, on February 25, 19___, wishes to express its sense of personal loss in the death of Mr. Allen, and its appreciation of his services as a member and officer of the Association.

From the earliest beginnings of vocational guidance in the United States, Mr. Allen has been identified with constructive research in educational and vocational guidance. At the time of his death he was the only member of the Association who had worked intimately with Frank A. Parsons, the father of vocational guidance in the United States.

Perhaps his most distinguished service to the Association was his work as Editor of *The Vocational Guidance Magazine,* which was brought by his unusual vision and diligence from a modest and occasional publication to its present high standard of editorial and mechanical perfection.

Be it therefore resolved, That this expression of appreciation be sent to the family of Mr. Allen and to Harvard University, also that it be spread upon the minutes of this meeting.

Reprinted from *The Vocational Guidance Magazine.*

Resolution included in a letter.

January 9, 19___.

My dear Professor Seager:

I have the honor of informing you that the following resolution was passed at the Annual Meeting of the Archæological Institute of America at Ithaca, New York, on December 29, 19___:

On the death of Richard Berry Seager, by Stephen B. Luce:

In the sudden and untimely death of Richard Berry Seager, at Candia, Crete, on May 12, 19___, America has lost one of her foremost archæologists. His success in scientific excavation won for him the respect, and his warm heart and enduring qualities the affection, of all that knew him. This is proved by the fact that the citizens of Candia tendered him a public funeral, a distinction offered to the memory of only the most distinguished citizens. Seager's name will always be identified with Crete, as one of the pioneers in the opening to the world of the marvelous civilization of the Minoan Age. His first work was done for the University of Pennsylvania, when he was associated with Mrs. Harriet Boyd Hawes at Gournia; and most of his subsequent excavations were conducted under the same auspices. His name is also associated with the American School at Athens, in connection with his excavations on the island of Mochlos. His residence at Pachyammos, in Eastern Crete, was always open to the stranger, and his hospitality there unbounded. During the World War, he served with great distinction as an officer in the Red Cross, in Italy and Greece. As long as archæology is studied, so long will his monographs on Vasiliki (in the volume on Gournia), Pseira, and Mochlos be indispensable to the student.

The Council of the Archæological Institute of America desires to spread upon its records its keen sense of personal loss in Seager's untimely death, and the feeling that professionally this loss can never be replaced or made good. With every prospect of a life of continued usefulness and brilliance before him, he was taken away from us before his forty-third year had ended. To such as he there is no successor.

Yours very truly,

_____ _____

Recorder

Resolution adopted by the New York Academy of Medicine on the death of Dr. George David Stewart.

In his death we have lost a forceful leader and teacher, a wise counselor, a kindly man and a dear friend. The Academy desires to express its great appreciation of these qualities and enter upon the minutes this testimony to the memory of one we can ill afford to lose.

With his magnetic personality, his rare gift of humorous expression and his wisdom acquired through wide experience, he was a dominant figure among his fellows.

Dr. Stewart was unusually well endowed to become such a figure. Untiring energy applied to the enlargement of this endowment made of him a man of great insight, rare force, fine tact, and a lover of culture and the beautiful. His leadership was kindly and his followers found it easy to become his disciples.

It is known that he was influenced by a strong religious feeling and he brought to every decision a sense of fairness which made his counsel much sought. As a surgeon and teacher he has left the world his debtor. His writings testify to the breadth of his training and he exerted great influence in keeping the rôle of general surgery equally broad.

Dr. Stewart was elected to fellowship in 1895 and for nearly forty years devoted much of his effort and abundant energy to furthering the interests of the Academy. In 1916 he became vice-president and three years later was elected to the presidency. He received the unusual honor of being asked to hold his office for three successive terms until 1925, as the Academy refused to relieve him from leadership at that critical time.

It was during this period that the long-considered plans for the new Academy building were brought to completion, and to no one belongs greater credit for this accomplishment than to George Stewart. His broad vision made it easy for him to grasp the great opportunity for unusual service which lay before us were we provided with adequate facilities. His power of persuasion was a chief factor in convincing our many benefactors that we should be accorded their support.

His active interest in and his work for the Academy were not lessened by his retirement from the presidency. He continued as a trustee until the time of his death and devoted much thought to the work of the committee on public health relations.

Minute adopted by the Board of Directors of The Fifth Avenue Bank of New York on the death of Algernon Sydney Frissell.

The passing of Algernon S. Frissell brings to a close the life of one of the most interesting and inspiring men of our city. Born in a Dutchess County village, the son of a clergyman, the small banking activities of a country merchant attracted his attention as a boy and he determined to make banking his life work. It was characteristic of the man that he never deviated from this purpose. As soon as he was old enough he sought a position in a Poughkeepsie bank, from there he went to a bank in Washington, D.C., and from thence to the old Importers and Traders National Bank of this city, where in 1875 he occupied the position of Loan Clerk. In that year The Fifth Avenue Bank was organized uptown and Mr. Frissell was made Cashier. He was then thirty years of age. He recognized at once that his opportunity had come. He put every other ambition behind him and from that time to the day of his death he devoted himself to the upbuilding of The Fifth Avenue Bank. In a very real sense the history of the bank is the history of his life. In 1885 he became its president.

Mr. Frissell brought to the bank a sound training in correct banking principles, but above and beyond this he possessed a most unusual character. Combined with the most uncompromising honesty and the highest moral character he had a genial, helpful manner of dealing with the bank's customers. He built up a new kind of friendly relationship between bank and customer. Many a successful business man of later years has spoken of the friendly advice and encouragement received from Mr. Frissell in those early days.

Another side of his management of the bank to which he gave the most careful attention was the selection and training of his clerks. Nothing received more care. Many of them were young country boys like himself, and once enrolled they became "members of the family." They were taught to regard the work of the bank as their life work. They entered as messengers at the bottom of the ladder and were trained through all of the departments of the bank. He put great trust in these young men and gave them heavy responsibilities. They did not disappoint him. To these methods the subsequent success of the bank may largely be traced.

While The Fifth Avenue Bank was the main occupation of his life, Mr. Frissell found time to be interested in many other things. He was a wide reader; he was fond of the society of cultured people and he was deeply interested in religion and philanthropy. He had a strong sense of civic duty and responsibility. All of his life a large part of his income was devoted to charity. He was treasurer of the Emergency Fund to give relief by work in the dark days of 1893. He was especially interested in the welfare of the colored race. He never sought public office, but after the panic of 1907 he became a member of the Commission to revise the banking laws and later he became a member of the Board of Education of the City of New York. He was modest to the point of diffidence. He was most genial in his social contacts, but no one could be more indignant at wrong-doing or error. There was nothing of the "happy-go-lucky" in his nature. He reflected long before reaching a conclusion and reviewed and reviewed the subject to be sure he was right. In his business relations he was inflexibly straightforward and entirely free from guile. He never tried to get an advantage by being smart or clever. He was conscientious to a fault. He always kept his old-fashioned idea of thrift and abhorrence of personal debt.

As few men have been able to do, he lived out his life according to his own plan. From a country boyhood, without the advantage of wealth or position, he succeeded in the most remarkable way by force of character and ability in working out the plan of his life to complete fulfillment. His life was an inspiration to those who served with him on this Board of Directors, to the great number of young men who were trained under him in The Fifth Avenue Bank, as well as to the larger number of those who had business and social relations with him during the many years of his active life.

A life such as his cannot end even at his advanced age without a sense of loss to those who had been associated with him, but in a very real sense he had so far completed his work that it might truly be said of him that he had fought the good fight and finished his course.

His memory will remain as a choice possession for his children and for a multitude of friends who knew him and loved him.

THEODORE HETZLER, President
GEORGE ACHESON, Secretary of the Board

Joint resolution passed by the New York Legislature, on the death of Elihu Root.

Whereas, we have learned with deep sorrow of the death of the Honorable Elihu Root, former United States Senator from the State of New York, former Secretary of War and former Secretary of State; and,

Whereas, in his services as Secretary of War under President McKinley and later as Secretary of State under President Theodore Roosevelt, as a member of the Permanent Court of Arbitration at The Hague in 1910, as recipient of the Nobel Peace Prize for 1912, as "Spiritual Father of the World Court," as one of the American Commissioners at the Washington Conference on the Limitation of Armament in 1921, as recipient of the award of the Woodrow Wilson Foundation in 1926, and as honorary president of the Carnegie Endowment for International Peace, Mr. Root has done more for international peace and justice than any American of the present century; and,

Whereas, by great courage, by clear wisdom, by remarkable patience, by unusual thoroughness and conscientiousness, and by a mighty intellect he has established a record of achievement which will be a source of inspiration to all generations to come; and,

Whereas, in his passing, not alone the community where he was born and which he called "home," not alone the State of New York, not alone the United States of America, but the whole world has suffered an irreparable loss; therefore, be it

Resolved (if the Senate concur), That when the Legislature adjourns this day, it do so out of respect to the memory of the Hon. Elihu Root; and be it further

Resolved, That as a final tribute to this very great American, when the Legislature shall convene tomorrow, February 9, at eleven o'clock in the morning, it shall immediately stand in recess for one hour during the period of his funeral services; and be it further

Resolved, That a copy of this resolution, suitably engrossed, be transmitted to the family of the deceased.

Reprinted by permission of the *New York Herald Tribune*.

Resolution passed by the American Council of Learned Societies in memory of Dr. Allen Johnson.

The sudden and premature death of Dr. Allen Johnson on February 17, which on personal grounds has brought sorrow to the hearts of a multitude of friends, is to the American Council of Learned Societies an inestimable loss. The Council gratefully recognizes that his wise, skillful and vigorous conduct of one of its chief enterprises has conferred distinction upon the Council and has done much to establish all its future work in public regard.

When the plan for a Dictionary of American Biography of superior quality had been formed, and by the generosity of Adolph Ochs the means for adequate preparation of it had been provided, it was natural, in view of the intelligence, firmness, and efficiency with which Dr. Johnson had lately carried to a successful conclusion the editing of a large historical series, that the committee of management would ask him to be the editor-in-chief of the proposed dictionary.

He undertook the long task with enthusiasm, and brought to it a well-furnished and cultivated mind, large knowledge of American history and biography, experience, ripe judgment, literary taste and a fixed determination that the highest practicable standards of accuracy, truthfulness and just portraiture should be maintained. The praises which, from all quarters, have been bestowed upon the five volumes thus far published, show how well his ambitions for the dictionary have been realized. His conduct of it has fairly surpassed the expectations of those who chose him to its charge. With all the scholarship he brought to it from the academic world in which his life had hitherto been spent, he brought also a broad appreciation, not usual among academics, of the forces which have been at work in the American world at large and of the varied characters, often unknown to literature, which have made that world what it is.

Catholicity and discrimination in composing the list of names and in the selecting of writers for each, and good judgment in the apportionment of space, marked his work from the beginning. He resisted with firmness all pressure toward favoritism, ancestor-worship, or bias in such arrangements. He applied to the manuscripts of contributions an alert and resourceful mind, checking excess or conventional eulogy, criticizing with severity and skill, insisting on solid and accurate workmanship.

Yet despite the unsparing vigor with which he strove to ensure to the dictionary the highest possible quality, his correspondence with contributors abounded in appreciation, sympathy and helpfulness, while his relations with his staff, as with all his friends, were made happy by constant kindness and generous and affectionate consideration. The Council gratefully records its sense of obligation and of bereavement.

Resolution passed by the National Press Club on the death of Richard V. Oulahan.

In Memoriam of Richard V. Oulahan

RESOLVED, That in behalf of the entire membership of the National Press Club the Board of Governors adopts these resolutions in tribute to the memory of our late fellow-member and distinguished colleague, Richard V. Oulahan.

The National Press Club has lost by death many distinguished and beloved members. None are more genuinely mourned by its rank and file in the sense of a personal loss to such an extent as is Mr. Oulahan.

By his death we have lost a beloved associate whose outstanding character as a journalist reflected high honor upon our profession and whose memory is a worthy inspiration for all time.

It is fitting that we should record Mr. Oulahan's personal qualities as they were revealed to the members of this club in our daily contact. His was a sterling character. Its genuineness was reflected in his gentlemanly demeanor at all times, his high-minded sense of duty to his profession and to the public, his unselfishness, his kindness, his understanding and his wholesome good-fellowship.

The best expression of our feeling is found in the words of Kipling's "Dedication," where it was said that

> He scarce had need to doff his pride or
> slough the dross of earth—
> E'en as he trod that day to God so walked
> he from his birth
> In simpleness and gentleness and honour
> and clean mirth.

Resolved further, That a copy of these resolutions be spread upon the official minutes of the Board of Governors and that a copy be transmitted to Mrs. Oulahan that we may extend to her and to the members of the family an expression of our sincere sympathy and our heartfelt condolence.

Attest:
OLIVER B. LERCH   EUGENE S. LEGGETT
Secretary   President

Resolution passed by the Henry Street Settlement on the death of one of its benefactors.

The Board of Directors of the Henry Street Settlement has learned of the passing away of Mrs. Jacob H. Schiff with a deep sense of personal loss. Since the inception of the Visiting Nurse Service forty years ago, Mrs. Schiff has been a constant friend who has given most generously of her time and her means. The social activities of the settlement have likewise been the object of her great generosity and her unflagging interest.

We extend to the members of her family this expression of heartfelt sympathy in the great loss that they, in common with the community, have suffered through her death.

LILLIAN D. WALD,
Chairman Executive Committee

A Letter Containing a Formal Resolution of Appreciation

My dear Miss Jacopraro:

It gives me great pleasure to inform you that at the last meeting of the Board of Directors of the Woman's Roosevelt Memorial Association the following resolution was unanimously passed:

"WHEREAS, the co-operation of the principals and teachers of the public schools of Greater New York having made possible the success of the meeting of Affiliated Roosevelt Clubs at Town Hall on the sixty-seventh anniversary of Theodore Roosevelt's birth, be it

"RESOLVED, That the Board of Directors of the Woman's Roosevelt Memorial Association take this means of expressing their thankfulness to the aforesaid principals and teachers and members of the Affiliated Roosevelt Clubs for their generous co-operation."

Sincerely yours,
Ellen C. Lambert
(Mrs. Alexander Lambert)
Secretary

Resolutions Presented to Congress

Resolution presented to Congress, January 25, 1929, to express gratitude to heroes of the S.S. *America,* in saving the crew of the S.S. *Florida.*

Whereas, The world is again thrilled by the heroic rescue of the entire crew of the Italian freighter, S.S. *Florida,* by Captain George Fried, Chief Officer Henry Manning and eight members of the crew of the United States Lines ship *America;* and

Whereas, In that rescue these eight sailors, under the doughty Chief Officer Manning, risked death in darkness and mountainous seas; and

Whereas, A grateful nation remembers the rescue three years ago of the crew of the British freighter *Antinoe* by the same Captain George Fried, then commanding the S.S. *President Roosevelt* of the United States Lines; now,

Therefore, Be it resolved by the House of Representatives (Senate concurring) that in gratitude for the precious intrepidity, unblanching courage and splendid seamanship of these valiant officers and men, the thanks of Congress be expressed to the said Captain George Fried, Chief Officer Manning and the eight members of the crew.

Resolution on Highways presented to Congress, by a Civic Association.

WHEREAS, The Lincoln Civic Association has been deeply concerned over the growing hazards to traffic on our highways and, also, for the need to protect the natural scenic beauty of our roadsides; therefore

RESOLVED, That the Association urges Congress to develop standards for the adequate protection for the safety and beauty of highways as a requirement of government cooperative effort with the states in building highways.

Resolutions Passed at the Twenty-eighth Annual Conference of the Indiana Library Trustees' Association

WHEREAS, This Twenty-eighth Annual Conference of the Indiana Library Trustees' Association has proved to be one of unusual benefit, inspiration and entertainment, with a fine spirit of friendliness and understanding prevailing; and

WHEREAS, This result has been attained by the concerted efforts of those who planned the program and those who participated therein; therefore, be it

Resolved, That this Association express its grateful appreciation to the officers and all participants in the program, and especially to:

Miss Hazel Warren, of the State Library, whose service to the libraries throughout the state means more than can be expressed in mere words;

The management of Hotel Lincoln for the provision made for the comfort of our delegates, courteous service, and facilities offered for this meeting;

The Convention Bureau of the Indianapolis Chamber of Commerce for the valuable and helpful service rendered in connection with registration;

L. S. Ayres & Co. for the encouragement to the library cause expressed by their gift of the printed programs;

Bobbs, Merrill Co. for the display of James C. Wilson's book, *Three Wheeling Through Africa;*

Otto K. Jensen of the State Board of Accounts, for his time and excellent advice and information to trustees relating to the budget;

James C. Wilson, author and lecturer, who provided, with the assistance of his wife, a most delightful evening's entertainment, illustrated with colored slides and moving pictures of his trip across Africa, about which he has written the book *Three Wheeling Through Africa;*

Victoria Montani, harpist, who provided most delightful music at the dinner meeting;

The officers and various committees of the Association for their efficient management and wise planning during the past year, and particularly to Mrs. George R. Bridwell, the retiring secretary-treasurer, who has for five years so faithfully and efficiently discharged the arduous duties of that office; and

WHEREAS, During the past year death has taken Mrs. J. B. Wilson, Bloomington; Mrs. A. L. Ulrey, North Manchester; Charles C. Cassell, Connersville, and Claud R. Stoops, Nappanee, all of whom have served the Indiana Library Trustees' Association in some official capacity and given of their time and talents to library work in their own communities; therefore, be it

Resolved, That the library cause has suffered a great loss in the passing of these friends of libraries, and that expressions of sympathy and of our loss be sent to the relatives of the deceased; and

WHEREAS, in the departure of Louis J. Bailey from the State Library to another field of service the libraries of Indiana have lost one who has for many years been a source of very great help and inspiration; therefore, be it

Resolved, That the Indiana Library Trustees' Association express to him in writing the deep appreciation of its members for what he has done for this Association and these trustees, their sense of great loss in his departure, and their congratulations on his well deserved advance in the library profession; and be it further

Resolved, That the interests of libraries in Indiana must be looked after and guarded during the coming session of the state legislature, and that every trustee shall recognize his own responsibility to promote the interests and safety of the public library by presenting the situation of the library and its needs to his senator and representative whenever legislation affecting libraries is proposed. We urge all trustees to become alert to the dangers that lurk at our doors, and to double their interest and take more seriously their responsibilities.

In submitting this report your committee recommends its adoption. It further recommends that these resolutions be spread upon the minutes of the Association, and that the Secretary send letters of appreciation and sympathy respectively to the individuals and groups mentioned herein.

_____ _____, *Chairman*

Reprinted by permission of the Indiana Library Trustees' Association.

Reference Books, see p. 433.

9. Constitutions, Bylaws, and Standing Rules

All organizations that operate under a governing body need regulations so that they may function smoothly and efficiently. The document that sets forth these regulations must be so worded that there is no question as to its meaning or its interpretation. Its style should be formal; its structure should have little variety; its material, though differing in details to suit the individual requirements of an organization, will embody similar subjects, such as name, object, membership, duties of officers and committees, time of meetings, and method of amendment.

The document of an organization that is federated must not be in conflict with the charter of the parent organization; but whether it is bound by a charter or not, it will also require its own rules to meet its particular needs. These may be set forth in a constitution that gives the fundamental regulations, supplemented by bylaws containing rules subordinate to those of the constitution with details that amplify the constitution. However, it is more usual today for all rules to be combined in one document called bylaws. In this, each subject, such as name, purpose, membership, names and duties of officers and committees, time of meetings, and the method of amendment, with full explanation, is placed under an article divided into sections when necessary. In *Parliamentary Law*, Robert explains that unless it is more difficult to amend the constitution than to amend the bylaws, there is no advantage in having these separated.

Standing Rules

As an organization grows it often finds it advisable to make specific rules that apply to special occasions or problems, such as guest privileges at certain functions, fines for absence or lateness, the length of time a member may speak at one time. These rules are usually temporary and can be annulled or repealed by a majority vote when no longer needed.

An organization with a constitution and bylaws

An organization that decided to have a constitution supplemented by bylaws would follow more or less the outline here presented:

CONSTITUTION

ARTICLE I
Name

ARTICLE II
Purpose (unless given in a preamble)

ARTICLE III
Membership (general requirements)

ARTICLE IV
Officers (list of offices)

ARTICLE V
Provision for Executive Board, or Committee

ARTICLE VI
List of other Committees

ARTICLE VII
Meetings (time for regular and annual meetings and provision for calling special meetings)

ARTICLE VIII
Amendment (method of amending)

BYLAWS

ARTICLE I
Membership
Section 1. Methods of admission
Section 2. Rules for resignation
Section 3. Rules for suspension
Section 4. Classes of membership

ARTICLE II
Fees and Dues
Section 1. Amount
Section 2. Provision for special assessments
Section 3. Time of payment

ARTICLE III
Executive Committee, or Board
Section 1. Time of meeting
Section 2. Powers
Section 3. Duties

ARTICLE IV
Committees
Section 1. Method of appointment
Section 2. Kinds (program, hospitality, membership, etc.)
Section 3. Duties

ARTICLE V
Officers
Section 1. Method of election
Section 2. Term of office
Section 3. Duties

ARTICLE VI
Meetings
Section 1. Detailed provisions for calling meetings
Section 2. Conduct of meetings (order of business)

ARTICLE VII
Parliamentary Authority

ARTICLE VIII
Number Constituting a Quorum

ARTICLE IX
Amendment of Bylaws

Order of Business

The Order of Business an organization observes at its regular meetings may be given in the bylaws. If not specifically stated, the following order is the one generally adopted:

1. Reading of minutes of the previous meeting, their correction, and approval
2. Report of treasurer
3. Reports of standing committees
4. Reports of special committees
5. Unfinished business
6. Announcements
7. New business
8. Adjournment

Bylaws

For an organization that does not separate its rules into a constitution and bylaws, but combines them under bylaws, the following outline sets forth a working plan:

BYLAWS

ARTICLE I
Name

ARTICLE II
Object or Purpose

ARTICLE III
Membership
Section 1. Classes
Section 2. Admission
Section 3. Fees and dues

ARTICLE IV
Officers
Section 1. List
Section 2. Method of election
Section 3. Terms of office
Section 4. Duties

ARTICLE V
Meetings
Section 1. Time of regular and annual meetings
Section 2. Provision for special meetings
Section 3. Number constituting a quorum

ARTICLE VI
Board of Directors or Executive Committee
Section 1. Composition
Section 2. Powers and duties
Section 3. Time of regular meetings and provision for special
        meetings

ARTICLE VII
Committees
Section 1. Kinds
Section 2. Methods of appointment
Section 3. Number in each
Section 4. Duties

ARTICLE VIII
Departments

Section 1. Kinds
Section 2. Regulations
Section 3. Meetings

ARTICLE IX
Parliamentary Authority

ARTICLE X
Amendment of Bylaws

Example of a Constitution and Bylaws

VOCATIONAL GUIDANCE ASSOCIATION OF NEW YORK CITY

CONSTITUTION

ARTICLE I

Name

Section 1. The name of this association shall be the VOCATIONAL GUIDANCE ASSOCIATION OF NEW YORK CITY.
Section 2. This association is organized as a constituent local organization of the Vocational Guidance Association of the United States.

ARTICLE II

Objects

Section 1. The objects of the Association shall be:

    a—To unite in one local organization those persons who are engaged or interested in any phase of vocational guidance in New York City and vicinity.

    b—To correlate closely the vocational guidance work being performed by public and private agencies in New York City and vicinity.

    c—To act as a central agency through which will clear information relating to the vocational guidance work being conducted in New York City and vicinity.

    d—To formulate standards and principles for vocational guidance work in New York City and vicinity.

    e—To encourage legislation and public support of vocational guidance in New York City and vicinity.

ARTICLE III

MEMBERS—*Qualifications and Admission*

Section 1. Any person engaged or interested in vocational guidance in New York City or vicinity may apply for membership.

Section 2. Any person may become a member of the Association *whose name has been approved by the committee on membership* and on the payment of the annual dues of the local Association, together with those of the Vocational Guidance Association of the United States, to the treasurer of the organization.

ARTICLE IV

Officers, Trustees, and Annual Meeting

Section 1. The officers of this association shall be:

> President
> First Vice President
> Second Vice President
> Secretary
> Treasurer

all of whom shall be members in good standing in the local organization.

Section 2. The Board of Trustees shall consist of the president, vice presidents, secretary and treasurer and nine other members.

ARTICLE V

Election of Officers and Trustees

Officers and Trustees shall be elected at the annual meeting of the Association.

In the case of a vacancy of office, the board of trustees shall have power to fill the same until the next annual meeting.

ARTICLE VI

Amendments

Amendments to the constitution or the bylaws of this Association shall be made only at a regular meeting thereof, by a two-thirds vote of the members present. No proposition to amend shall be acted upon unless written notice thereof has been given to the secretary at least thirty days prior to the meeting. A copy of such a proposition shall be embodied in the call for the next regular meeting, and a copy sent to every member of the Association at least ten days before the date of the next regular meeting at which the amendment is to be voted upon.

BYLAWS

ARTICLE I

OFFICERS

****

President

Section 1. It shall be the duty of the president to preside at all meetings and to enforce all laws and regulations relating to the administration of the Association.

Section 2. He shall call meetings of the Association or board of trustees when he deems it necessary, or when requested so to do by the executive committee, or upon written request of at least one-fourth of the constituent societies for a meeting of the Association, or one-fourth of the trustees for a meeting of the board of trustees.

He shall appoint all standing committees.

Vice President

Section 3. In the absence of the president, one of the vice presidents named by the president, or failing this, designated by the board of trustees, shall have all the powers and prerogatives of the president, provided that if the president be absent from the annual meeting of the Association the chairman shall be appointed from the vice presidents by the board of trustees.

Chairman Pro Tempore

Section 4. In the event of the absence of the president and vice presidents from any meetings of the Association or board of trustees, one of the members present shall preside.

Secretary

Section 5. All resolutions and proceedings of meetings, whether of the Association or of the board of trustees, shall be entered in proper books by the secretary. The secretary shall conduct all correspondence relating to the Association, shall issue all notices of meetings, and shall perform all duties pertaining to the office of secretary. The secretary shall keep a register of the members of the Association.

Treasurer

Section 6. All moneys payable to the Association shall be paid to the treasurer of the Association. All moneys payable by the Association shall be paid by checks signed by the treasurer.

He shall report at each meeting of the Association the condition of the treasury.

Board of Trustees

Section 7. It shall be the duty of the board of trustees to take the initiative in determining the policies of the Association. They shall also be responsible for the relations of the local branch to the National Vocational Guidance Association.

It shall be their duty to take charge, control and manage all the property belonging to the Association.

They shall keep a record of their proceedings and make a report thereof in writing to the Association at the annual meeting.

The board of trustees shall appoint an executive committee consisting of the president of the Association as chairman, the secretary, the treasurer, and the chairmen of the program and membership committees. It shall be the duty of this committee to supervise the finances of the Association and audit all bills prior to the payment thereof.

Section 8. The office of a member of the board of trustees may be vacated by his absence from two consecutive meetings of the board without good and sufficient reason satisfactory to the board of trustees.

Committees

Section 9. There shall be three standing committees of the Association:

The Program Committee shall make all plans and arrangements for the regular meetings of the Association.

The Membership Committee shall receive applications for membership, pass on such applications and make recommendations of the Association.

The Nominating Committee shall prepare a slate of officers for the succeeding year.

Committee chairmen shall attend all trustees' meetings.

ARTICLE II

Meetings of the Association—Regular

Section 1. The annual meeting of the Association shall take place on the third Tuesday of May of each year. There shall also be at least four other regular meetings from September to May at times to be set by the Program Committee. Notices of meeting shall be sent out ten days prior to such meeting direct to each member. The place at which meeting shall be held shall be determined by the Program Committee.

Special Meetings

Section 2. Special meetings may be called at any time with the approval of the president of the Association.

Board of Trustees Meetings

Section 3. There shall be two regular meetings of the board of trustees to take place in May and October of each year. Other meetings may be called by the president.

Ten days' notice of a meeting of the board of trustees shall be given to each member, mailed to him at his usual or last known address, and such notice shall, as far as practicable, contain a statement of the business to be transacted at such meeting.

Committee Meetings

Section 4. All committees shall be subject to the call of their respective chairmen.

Quorum

Section 5. A representation of a majority of the members of this Association shall constitute a quorum authorized to transact any business duly presented at any meeting of the Association.

Seven trustees shall constitute a quorum of the board of trustees; a majority of any and all committees shall constitute a quorum of such committees.

ARTICLE III

Representation at Meetings of Vocational Guidance Association of the United States

Section 1. Delegates and alternates to the annual meeting of the Vocational Guidance Association shall be elected prior to such meeting, the number to be in proportion to the membership of the New York Association.

ARTICLE IV

Nomination and Election of Officers and Delegates

Section 1. The Nominating Committee shall present a slate at the annual meeting for the following officers:

President	Secretary
First Vice President	Treasurer, and
Second Vice President	Nine trustees

except as otherwise provided in Section 2.

Any member of the Association may make additional nominations from the floor.

Section 2. At the first election under these laws three of the nine trustees referred to in the preceding section shall be elected for one year, three for two years each, and three of them for three years each. At every succeeding annual meeting thereafter three trustees shall be elected for a term of three years each.

Section 3. Election shall be by ballot when necessary. A chairman and two tellers shall be appointed to receive the ballots for each officer and trustee. They shall canvass the ballots so cast and announce the result to the presiding officer, who thereupon shall declare the members receiving the majority of the votes cast elected to the respective offices.

Section 4. In case of no choice on the first ballot for any one or more officers or trustees, a new election shall take place at once for the particular case or cases in which there had been no choice, until a choice be made.

ARTICLE V

Initiation Fees and Dues

Section 1. The dues for each fiscal year ending December 31, shall be two dollars and a half ($2.50), one dollar and a half ($1.50) of which shall be paid to the treasurer of the Vocational Guidance Association of the United States.

Section 2. Such dues shall be due and payable annually in advance of November 30 of each year, or at the date of a member's election or admission to membership, and until such payment thereof, no certificate of membership shall be issued.

ARTICLE VI

Rules of Order

Section 1. The rules of parliamentary procedure as laid down in *Robert's Rules of Order* shall govern all meetings of the Association.

Reprinted by permission of the Vocational Guidance Association of New York City.

REFERENCE BOOKS

Fox, EMMA A. *Parliamentary Usage,* 4th ed. Detroit, Maurice W. Fox.

HALL, ALTA B., and STURGIS, ALICE F. *Textbook on Parliamentary Law.* New York, The Macmillan Company, 1956.

ROBERT, HENRY M. *Parliamentary Law.* New York, Appleton-Century, 1929. A more detailed book than the author's *Rules of Order Revised.*

ROBERT, HENRY M. *Robert's Rules of Order Revised.* Chicago, Scott, Foresman and Company, 1956. The standard authority on parliamentary law.

10. The Writing of Reports

Reports may be defined as "careful and accurate presentations of facts or statistics compiled, or conditions or operations studied, for the purpose of informing those desiring such information."

The purpose in writing a report is to present matter clearly and impersonally and to make such explanation as is necessary for a complete understanding of the subject.

Perhaps the most important principle of writing which the report writer should observe is that formed in Herbert Spencer's famous dictum of style in his essay *The Philosophy of Style:*

The reader has at each moment but a limited amount of mental power. To study the economy of words, of sentences, of figures of speech, of suggestion, of association, is to have the means of writing positively, directly, and vigorously. The more simple and the better arranged in parts, the greater will be the effect produced.

A report writer follows this suggestion "of economizing the reader's attention." He views his material in a right perspective. He knows how to present his points in their true proportion and finds the best possible arrangement. To effect this, he must adhere to a form that is clear, logical, and easily grasped. To that end, he should insert and number heads and sideheads to show the relation between main topics and subtopics; he should underline key words to make them arresting; he should include maps, charts, tables, and other visual devices to present facts graphically.

Because the scope, and hence the form, of a report depends upon its purpose, the readers for whom it is intended, and the organization whose work it presents, no plan can be given that will fit every requirement; but the outline here suggested may be adapted as a working basis.

Outline for Making a Report

1. Title page
2. Introduction through letter of transmittal or foreword

3. Acknowledgments
4. Table of contents
5. Summary or synopsis
6. Body of the report (the text or discussion)
7. Conclusion
8. Recommendations
9. Appendix
10. Bibliography
11. Index

Title page

The title page is often omitted from short, informal reports, the title appearing as a heading on page one. On long, formal reports the title, when inadequate, may be supplemented by a subtitle in smaller type. That is followed by the name of the compiler—that is, an individual with his position, a commission, a board of directors, or an organization. The name of the company for which the report is made, and its address with the date when the report was submitted, occur at the bottom of the page.

The introduction

The introduction may be formal or informal. It should state clearly the nature of the report, the scope, the purpose and, if necessary, the circumstances under which it has been made.

The letter of transmittal

Such an introduction is often embodied in a formal letter of transmittal preceding the report, illustrations of which follow:

(1)

MR. _____ _____, *Chairman,*
Committee of Arrangements,
New York Stock Exchange.

Dear Sir:

In the accompanying report of the Personnel Department for 19__ an effort has been made to present as concisely as possible the "Human Relationship Policy" of the Stock Exchange. Observations made in many sections of the country lead me to believe that the public in general looks upon our institution simply as a great organization whose sole interest is concerned with finance.

It is hoped that this report may be a means of conveying to the members of the Exchange an adequate conception of the scope of the work, as evidenced by the interest of the management in the individual employee.

The hearty cooperation of many governors and other members of the Exchange and leaders in the financial world in appearing as special lecturers before our Institute has been of material assistance in the advancement of our educational program.

During the past year the members of the Exchange have taken to their offices an increasing number of our employees—an indication of their high regard for the character and intelligence of the youth in our employ.

The Personnel Department wishes to acknowledge its appreciation to the President, the Committee of Arrangements, and the members of the Exchange and to the officers and employees for their cooperation during the past year.

———— ————

Personnel Director

Reprinted by permission of the Personnel Department of The New York Stock Exchange.

(2)

WEST VIRGINIA UNIVERSITY
MORGANTOWN

OFFICE OF THE PRESIDENT

September 15, 19__

TO THE PRESIDENT AND MEMBERS
OF THE BOARD OF GOVERNORS
OF WEST VIRGINIA UNIVERSITY

Gentlemen:

Supplementing the detailed reports already in your hands, I have the privilege of submitting the following general report of University operations for the fiscal year July 1, 19__, to June 30, 19__.

———— ————

President

(3)

THE COMMONWEALTH OF MASSACHUSETTS

State Planning Board,
11 Beacon Street, Boston 8, December 4, 19__.

To the Honorable Senate and House of Representatives.

In compliance with General Laws, chapter 30, section 33, as amended, I have the honor to submit herewith, on behalf of the State

Planning Board and by its direction, such portions of its annual report as involve recommendations for legislative action, together with drafts of bills embodying the legislation recommended. These drafts have been seasonably submitted to the Counsel to the House of Representatives for advice and assistance as to form thereof.

ELISABETH M. HERLIHY
Chairman, State Planning Board

(4)

Hon. _____ _____
Mayor of the City of _____

Dear Sir:

The City Planning Board submits herewith its annual report containing a statement of its activities and of receipts and expenditures for the year ending December 31, 19___.

The membership of the Board remained unchanged during the year, Mr. John Brown having been reappointed for the term ending March 30, 19___.

During the year twenty formal meetings and ten special sessions were held, together with many informal conferences.

In order to facilitate the work of the Board, the following committees have been reappointed: [listed, with their members]

In the report that follows, various problems studied during the past year are presented in some detail for purposes of record. They have been arranged in groups under appropriate headings, while the maps, plans, statistics are on file at the office of the Board, Room _____, City Hall.

[Concluded with the reports of studies and surveys under several headings.]

(5)

NEW HAVEN
CHAMBER OF COMMERCE

OFFICE OF THE PRESIDENT
February 28, 19___

To the Members of the
New Haven Chamber of Commerce:

People make the news. In this report for the fiscal year ending February 28, 19___, Mr. Johnson shows in striking fashion how many people conduct the activities of your Chamber.

People make the nation. In this broader field, your influence can shape the destinies of the nation if you make your influence heard and seen and felt in places of political representation and power.

People make the Chamber. It is *your* Chamber of Commerce. It is what *you* make it. It thrives upon your interest, your enthusiasm, your support. Work for it, think of it and talk for it. With your help it can continue to do great things for New Haven.

Your directors, officers and staff appreciate the interest and support you are giving, and they look forward to a year of unremitting effort and accelerated progress for our City.

Yours very sincerely,
NEW HAVEN CHAMBER OF COMMERCE
————— ——————, President

Printed by permission.

Foreword

Sometimes in place of the formal letter of transmittal, a Foreword, which serves the same purpose, precedes the text. Four illustrations follow.

(1)

The University of Chicago Settlement is a monument to the devotion and energy of Mary McDowell. To her magnetic personality is due the growth of the institution from the restrictions of a small flat "Back of the Yards" to its quadrangle of buildings on the avenue which now bears Miss McDowell's name, and Camp Farr, on forty acres of land near Chesterton, Indiana.

The Settlement is not under the jurisdiction of the University of Chicago, but was established by the faculty of the University, and continues to draw its financial support and volunteer service from the University community. The President of the University, the Dean of Rockefeller Chapel, members of the Faculties, and representatives of the Board of Social Service and Religion, the University of Chicago Settlement League, and of student and alumni organizations are members of its Board of Directors.

Through the generosity of its friends, the Settlement has been repeatedly improved and enlarged to meet the growing demands made upon it by the expanding services to its community. "But," as one of our board members put it, "why describe the buildings—it's the people and their activities which make a Settlement—not the buildings!"

(2)

Foreword to a bulletin published by The Women's Municipal League of Boston:

What is the significance to the practical work of the League of the ideas of municipal housekeeping and municipal homemaking which it embodies, and which the City Institute will develop actively in the different neighborhoods?

1. Cleanliness is essential in every home.

 The Department of Streets and Alleys and Waste Disposal is accomplishing visible results in cleaning the city through the co-operation of the housewives, the expert engineer and the public officials.

2. Decent Housing Conditions are necessary for any home.

 The Department of Housing has already effected important ameliorations in the housing conditions of the city, but in order to secure radical and permanent improvement, an aroused public opinion is needed which shall put an end to this disgrace of Boston,—twenty thousand of *us* living in houses unfit for human habitation—in *our* home. A conservative estimate.

3. Public Health means personal health in the home.

 The Department of Public Health has incorporated into its work the Habit Clinics for Children of Pre-School Age. Clinics for adults who are supposedly well are being carried on at the Blossom Street Health Unit in cooperation, by the Department, the League and the city.

4. The Foreign Born are our guests; we must make them our friends in our home.

 The Department of the Foreign Born and the Community House at North Brighton have been largely helpful in many different ways in making the strangers who come to live here feel at home in our house.

5. The Service of Trained Women is needful in every home.

 The Training School for Women in Public Service is focusing and organizing the public opinion of women to demand that they be allowed the opportunity to render their trained service to the community as police women to prevent evil before it becomes crime, as school attendance officers to care for the children, and as sanitary inspectors to help the housewives.

6. The Upbringing of the Children is the responsibility of every home.

 The Children's City Club is being organized by the League in close cooperation with the teachers of the public schools, and at their request, in order that the women of the community, with the teachers, may share the responsibility of leading the children to understand the obligations and duties, as well as the pleasures and privileges of their great home, the city. The Vacant Lot Gardens and the work in the Playgrounds during the summer have brought to the children a little of the beauty and vital stimulation that should come to all children in their own homes.

(3)

The number of requests that have come to the Exchange regarding policies, methods, and procedure in the handling of personnel problems has been increasing. In this report we have explained in detail our method of handling these problems now confronting others with the thought that our own experience may be of value to many. We are confident that our threefold approach to the employee; namely, in his daily work, in his mental training, and in his play, together with the encouragement given to our program by the management of the Exchange, has been in no small measure the reason for any success we have obtained in the handling of personnel problems.[1]

(4)

Foreword from an Annual Report of The Charity Organization Society:

In making public this fifty-third Annual Report of The Charity Organization Society I should like to thank the committee members, volunteers, contributors and staff who have worked together in the Society to make possible the activities for human welfare herein described.

This report marks the close of the first year during which the family work of the Society has been carried on under the new name, Institute of Family Service. The use of this name by the Society's district offices has proved its value in making clear to the community that our service is intended for all who have family and personal problems and in removing any barrier which the word "charity" might present.

From its experience with the manifold problems with which families are confronted, problems that are inevitable in any walk of life, the Society is acquiring knowledge which sheds light on many of the larger social questions of the day. Many of these social problems are but the extreme forms of the problems of ordinary family life. It is while these problems are still within the family circle and susceptible of treatment, that the Society seeks to deal with them.

The increasing enrollment of the New York School of Social Work is encouraging evidence of the recognition of adequate preparation for the field of social work. It is significant for the future efficiency of public welfare programs that many of the School's graduates are accepting positions in public service.

[1] Reprinted by permission of the Personnel Department of The New York Stock Exchange.

To understand the part The Charity Organization Society is playing in the world of today I recommend the careful reading of this fifty-third Annual Report.[1]

——— —— ———
President

Acknowledgments

Acknowledgments often precede the report. They may be included in the letter of transmittal or follow it as a separate part.

As Chairman of the Board, it is my privilege to acknowledge with sincere appreciation the services of those who selected, submitted, compiled or reproduced the matter within these pages. Particularly do I wish to record indebtedness of the Society to public officials and advertisers without whose assistance the publication would not have been possible. That it may serve the purpose for which it has been envisioned and prove of mutual advantage to reader and advertiser alike is the hope of your Board of Editors.

Frederick H. Zurmuhlen
Editor-in-Chief

From a Yearbook of the New York State Society of Professional Engineers, Inc. Reprinted by permission.

Table of Contents

In long reports a Table of Contents is often included. This is a guide to what follows. It contains the principal subjects or the names of the chapters, if divided into chapters. Main subjects are usually preceded by Roman numerals followed by subtopics indented from the beginning of the line. Page numbers to these subjects or chapters are written in Arabic numerals.

Summary or synopsis

A brief summary, following the Letter of Transmittal or the Foreword, often precedes the report. It contains a digest of the main points, including the results of the investigation and the recommendation made for the benefit of the reader who does not have the time to read the whole.

Body of the report (text or discussion)

The body of a report presents the carefully outlined study of the subject logically organized and concisely expressed. Headings, subheads, and every other device that will make the subject clear,

[1] Reprinted by permission.

show relationship of parts, emphasize the main points, or give an outlined view of the whole, should be inserted.

Conclusion

The conclusion of a report ordinarily consists of a brief summary of results obtained, or of points presented, or of recommendations made, in the light of data studied.

An illustration of a general summary follows, taken from a Report of the Westchester County Park Commission:

The projects herein recommended will provide the following:

Suitable areas for not less than 4 public golf courses, one of which is already partly developed.

Space for scores of baseball fields, playgrounds, tennis courts and other field and water sports.

Wide areas of picturesque lands for picnicking and general park use.

Several thousand acres in the northerly part of the County for individual and group camps and general reforestation purposes.

The protection of important municipal water supplies, so vitally necessary to our built-up communities.

The opening up of the Sprain Valleys and securing therein large recreation areas at moderate cost. These valleys are now almost inaccessible, and the increase in value following the proposed improvements will stimulate development that will shortly pay the cost of the improvements.

Secondary cross-county and diagonal connections between valleys and main parkways.

Then follows a schedule of the projects recommended.

The report is concluded by the following:

The Commission respectfully requests favorable consideration from your Honorable Board of the projects recommended herein.

WESTCHESTER COUNTY PARK COMMISSION

By _____ _____,
President

Sometimes in order to make conclusions emphatic, important points are arranged in an original way, as in the report of the Women's Municipal League Bulletin of Boston, which sums up the ideals of the League.

WHAT WE ALL WANT!

Clean Streets
Decent Houses
Mutual Understanding among
All Races

Work and Recreation for Health
and Happiness
The Best Interests of the Children

The League is trying to make these things possible for every member of our great family, and especially for the children.

BECAUSE

We all TOGETHER owe to each child the opportunity for healthy and happy development.

JOIN THE LEAGUE!

LET US WORK TOGETHER!

Recommendations by the Citizen's Committee on Children of New York City, Inc., in their report *Citizens Look at Their Schools,* following a discussion of the question, Can the Bureau of Attendance become more efficient in solving the basic problems of truancy?

WE RECOMMEND:

A. That truancy cases be sifted and minor cases handled by teacher or teacher-counsellors and school social workers.
B. That part of the in-service program be concerned with this problem.
C. That attendance officers have more mental hygiene and social work training.
D. That more time be allowed by schools for study of truancy cases, which would prevent court action for children who could respond to other treatment.
E. That the Attendance Bureau and the Child Guidance Bureau be more closely integrated. Further study may reveal that the Attendance Bureau should be a unit of the Child Guidance Bureau.
F. That wherever court action is deemed necessary in truancy cases, it should be handled in the Children's Part of the Domestic Relations Court and not in a specially labeled Truancy Court.
G. That consideration be given to the possibility of a real school census as an aid to improving attendance.

The Appendix

The appendix, found only in long, formal reports, contains supplementary material—such as bibliographies, maps, charts, graphs, and other visual devices and references—fortifying the statements in the text but too lengthy or digressive or of too general interest to be included in the main discussion.

The Index

The index also is found only in long, formal reports. It resembles the index of a book, being an alphabetical arrangement of important words in the text with paging to enable a reader to find particular material easily and quickly.

Report in Letter Form

Some reports, such as those to Boards of Trustees, to the President of a University, or to Stockholders, are often made in letter form. The introduction is brief and formal, admitting of little variation.

The body of the report in letter form is organized in much the same manner as that of other reports. It presents the chief features in narration or exposition without too much detail.

The letter report is concluded by appropriate remarks and signed by the writer with his official position.

Report of National Committee of Award, Theodore N. Vail Medals.

May 7, 19___

To the Trustees,
      Theodore N. Vail Memorial Fund

In the reports of the fifty-four Theodore N. Vail bronze medal awards made by Committees of Award of the Bell System Associated Companies for 19___, and the many other cases considered by these Committees, this Committee finds inspiring evidence that the men and women of the Bell System are carrying out the high ideals which Mr. Vail held as to public service and that they cheerfully accept special responsibilities in times of emergency.

The Committee feels that to be selected for National Vail Medal recognition an act must have for its objective the accomplishment of something of real value in the public interest through the medium of Bell System facilities, organization, training or experience, and must reveal to a high degree many, if not all, of the positive qualities of intelligence, initiative and resourcefulness, and usually courage, endurance and fortitude. The Committee believes that in making its selections it has recognized acts which meet these requirements.

During the year the Mississippi Valley was inundated by one of the worst floods in its history and extensive sections of the telephone plant operated by the Southwestern Bell Telephone Company, the Southern Bell Telephone and Telegraph Company and the Long Lines were not only crippled but rendered almost inaccessible for days and in some cases for weeks. Throughout this emergency the entire organizations of these companies in the affected areas, together with many others called from different sections, rendered conspicuously outstanding public service in maintaining and restoring telephone service under well-nigh impossible conditions.

The Committee welcomes this opportunity to commend in the most unqualified terms the initiative and resourcefulness, loyalty and devotion, courage and endurance displayed by these great groups of telephone men and telephone women in the manner in which they carried on throughout this distressing period.

This outstanding service was essentially the result of group organization and effort and accordingly does not offer the opportunity for individual awards as did the New England flood where, although the group performance was equally noteworthy and outstanding, the suddenness of the onset made emergency individual action vital before group action could be organized.

The National Awards for the year follow: [1]

Outlines of Less Formal Reports

(1)

Outline of the Annual Report of the Music School of the Henry Street Settlement, New York:

Introduction

The _____ year of the Music School has seen its highest development as a professional school and as a neighborhood school, where the young artist ready for a Town Hall debut and a child learning to "match" tones are equal partners in a common enterprise.

TOPICS DISCUSSED

Expansion	Broadcasts
New Courses	Parents' Organizations
New Faculty	Finances
Students	Improvement of Equipment
Scholarships	The Outlook
Concerts	

[1] Reprinted by permission.

(2)

Outline of report by the Federal Security Agency, U.S. Public Health Service:

Introduction

Medical science has made great strides in recent years, and rapid progress has taken place in the field of public health. Accomplishments since the turn of the century show that a high level of national health can be achieved—and in a short span of time.

TOPICS DISCUSSED

Death Rate Decreased
Gains in Disease Control
Extending Public Health Services
Advances in Research
Proposal of a Six-Point National Health Program
Comprehensive Health Services

(3)

Outline of the Report of The Montclair Dental Health Project:

Who started this?
How did they embark on this project?
What has been done this year?
What are the figures as of September 1, 19__?
What are the aims of the project?
What will this cost?
What other dental clinic facilities are available?
A list of the Social Agencies that prepared the report with their representatives.

Three of the Annual Reports of a Woman's Club

REPORT OF THE CORRESPONDING SECRETARY

Madam President and Members of the Club:

In accordance with the prescribed duties of the Corresponding Secretary, the following communications have been sent out during the past fiscal year:

2985 monthly program and reservation cards
  37 thank-you letters
  16 notes of sympathy

19 acknowledgments of resignations
16 miscellaneous letters

3073 communications
1088 envelopes addressed for the Scholarship and the Fashion Committees

The cooperation of the President and the Board members has been most helpful and is greatly appreciated.

REPORT OF THE THIRD VICE PRESIDENT

Responsibility for the programs throughout the club year has been the duty of the third vice president of the _____ Woman's Club. As the Club has two meetings a week, one regular business meeting followed by a program, and one program meeting, this sounds like a monumental task. However, the facts are quite different, because I, as chairman of the program committee, have had a group of department chairmen who have responded with such good will and enthusiasm that my greatest responsibility for these programs has been the one of getting the notices to the printer at the right time.

Mrs. _____ _____, chairman of the art department, has not only arranged delightful programs, but also made possible the various exhibits which have given us so much pleasure throughout the year.

Mrs. _____ _____, the chairman of the American home department, has brought us information on many phases of home life. We are especially grateful to her, as she took over the chairmanship after the beginning of the year at the resignation of Mrs. _____ _____.

Miss _____ _____, chairman of the international relations department, has kept us on our mental toes with outstanding speakers on problems of the day. In these times of international stress it is fitting and important that great emphasis be placed on this particular department. Miss _____ has done a remarkable piece of work in this field.

Music is such an important part of our lives and means so much to a great many of our members that I am sure that the work of Mrs. _____ _____, chairman of the music department, in bringing so many talented artists before us is much appreciated.

The Club has been fortunate in having Mrs. _____ _____ as chairman of literature and drama. The programs she has sponsored have been noteworthy and enjoyable.

Our first vice president, Mrs. _____ _____, has been in charge of our social activities, a most important feature of our club life. The program chairmen are indebted to her committee for their excellent work in connection with the various meetings. The program chairmen have tried to suit all tastes and, I might add, all ages, not always an easy task. We hope we have succeeded.

I should like to express my personal appreciation for the privilege of working with this group of women. I have realized as never before how delightful it can be to be associated with people who are spending so much of their time in service to the community.

REPORT OF THE RECORDING SECRETARY

During the last club year, March 19___ to March 19___, forty-nine regular program meetings, eleven meetings of the board of directors, and one meeting of the executive committee have been held.

In accordance with the prescribed duties of the recording secretary, a faithful and accurate record of all regular and special meetings has been kept and a copy of each sent to the president. Lists of the department chairmen and of all standing committees have been kept for ready reference, and all reports have been received and filed, properly dated and signed.

I wish to express my appreciation of the capable leadership of our president. It has been a pleasure to be of service to her, to the board of directors, and to the other members of the club.

Illustration of a Complete Report

The following represents a long, formal report, including its parts and contents, the charts, graphs and bibliography alone being omitted.

STUDENT'S REPORT ON MARKETING MADE BY MARIE KONZELMAN,
COLUMBIA UNIVERSITY, 19___

CONTENTS

I. *Introduction*
    A. Synopsis of Report
    B. Foreword
II. *Text*
    A. Purpose of Report
    B. Discussion
        Part One: Marketing Functions
        Part Two: The Development of Retailing
        Part Three: The Middleman
        Part Four: Marketing Problems
        Part Five: Conclusion
III. *Appendix*
    A. Charts
    B. Graphs
    C. Bibliography
    D. Outline of Report

I. INTRODUCTION

A. SYNOPSIS

The report on "Marketing" which is submitted below is divided into four general discussions. Under the heading of "Marketing Functions" the general services performed by marketing agencies are outlined. In the second section the development of the various forms of retailing organizations is traced. A discussion of the general, specialty, department, and chain stores and of the mail-order house is included. Another section deals with the four most common forms of middlemen. The marketing problems of the manufacturer are outlined in the final section, as well as the present trends in the solution of these problems.

B. FOREWORD

In recent years more emphasis has been placed upon the importance of marketing than formerly, and it is because of this widespread interest that the investigation resulting in the report which follows was undertaken.

The standardization of production within the past two decades has enabled the manufacturer to turn his attention toward the problem of distribution and, as a result, marketing has become the outstanding problem. The present report is concerned with this problem, as it affects the business organization. The purpose of the investigation has been to trace the development of marketing.

As a result of this investigation, some general recommendations concerning the future of marketing are embodied in the conclusion of the report.

II. TEXT OF REPORT

A. PURPOSE OF REPORT

The aim of this investigation and of the presentation of this report has been primarily to indicate the nature of the marketing problems which confront the modern business organization. A discussion of the development of the various branches of the modern distributing mechanism has been given. The secondary purpose has been to show present trends toward a solution of these various problems.

B. DISCUSSION

PART ONE: MARKETING FUNCTIONS

Assembling
and
Grading

The primary function of marketing is the assembling and grading of merchandise preparatory to its distribution to the consuming public.

Assembling is of two general types. Its aim may be either the concentration in one central locality of great quantities of one particular commodity or the concentration of a sufficient variety of commodities to effect the most economical distribution. The specialty store is an example of the former type while the department store possesses the characteristics of the latter. Both these types are common not only in the retailing field, but also in the field of the jobber and of other wholesale agencies.

Grading is a function of marketing that has developed more fully in recent years. It has tended to enlarge markets by making sales by description possible and it has tended to reduce the cost of marketing by lowering the percentage of spoilage and of unsalable goods.

Grading is based upon a large variety of characteristics, varying with the type of product and the demand of the consumer. Such factors as quality, size, quantity, variety and packing methods are among the more common bases of distinction.

Storing

The storing function is one which is present in all branches of marketing. There are a great many products which are not immediately consumed and for which, therefore, storage facilities must be provided. This function is performed by one or more of the following, according to the special requirements of the product concerned: the producer, the middleman and the consumer.

In the case of some products, especially those of an agricultural nature, the supply is seasonal, i.e., production is limited to certain periods of the year. For this reason, some adequate method of storage must be provided to cover these seasonal inequalities. In still other cases there is sectional inequality of production.

As a result of these types of inequality, the storage function in marketing has developed. Storage not only adjusts the supply of commodities and broadens markets, but it also reduces waste and thereby increases profits.

Transportation

The function of transportation is also present in all stages of marketing. In the manufacturing field raw material must be transferred to the plant and the finished product shipped to the distributing agency employed. The jobber must, in turn, transfer the goods to dealers; and, finally, the retail delivery to the consumer must be made.

Transportation costs have a direct effect upon the extent of the producing area and upon the size of the potential market. Rail, highway, and water transportation play an important part in distribution.

The transportation problem which confronts the manufacturer is essentially that of developing an efficient traffic department. The retailer's problem is concerned chiefly with the choice of that type of transportation which provides adequate service for the consumer.

Financing and Risk Taking

The importance of the financing function in marketing varies directly with the length of the period of time between production and consumption. The ordinary methods used in connection with marketing are bank loans and deferred payments. Manufacturers, middlemen, retailers and consumers take advantage of these methods of financing.

Risks are either covered by insurance or by price margins. Definite risks such as those of a physical nature are usually provided for by resort to insurance, while those of an indefinite nature, such as the possible losses attendant upon the carrying of style goods, are taken care of in the price margin.

Creation of Demand

Demand is of three general types: seasonal, class, and sectional. The function of creating a demand is largely that of the producer and of the retailer. By the use of demonstrations, premiums, special sales, etc., the producer can appeal directly to the consumer. The retailer appeals to the consumer through price policies and the rendering of services. The most effective demand creation is that based upon a knowledge of buying motives and an effective utilization of this knowledge.

Advertising plays an important part in the creation of demand. By this means an attempt is made to fix the product firmly in the mind of the buying public and to arouse an active demand. The effectiveness of demand creation depends to a large extent upon the choice of advertising copy and media.

Merchan-
dising

Merchandising is complementary to the creation of demand. It consists of the transferring of the title of goods
from the manufacturer, the jobber, or the retailer, to
the customer. The methods employed vary with the
article since some commodities "sell themselves" while
others, such as services, are intangible and therefore
require a distinct merchandising plan.

One aid to the merchandising of products is display.
This method is usually employed by the retailer. The
latter also resorts to demonstrations. The manufacturer,
on the other hand, makes use of samples and premiums
in an effort to promote sales.

Another part of the merchandising function is stock-
keeping and inventory. The manufacturer keeps his
record in the form of a control on material and supplies,
while the retailer or wholesaler keeps the record as an
indication of stock turnover.

PART TWO: THE DEVELOPMENT OF RETAILING

Commodity distribution originally took the form of direct barter. It
was not until the time of the Civil War that retailing ceased to be a
system of bargaining. Then a new system developed. The department
store, the chain store, and the mail-order house sprang up as remedies
for the inefficiency of the prevailing system.

Specialization founded on either need or service has greatly increased
and the present tendency is toward a still greater increase in retailing
types.

The
General
Store

The present tendency is toward a decline in the number
of general stores. The decline of this type is due to defec-
tive management rather than to any essential inefficiency
as a means of distribution. The proprietor of the general
store usually knows nothing of purchasing plans or of
the importance of stock turnover.

The chief competitor of the general store is the mail-
order house on the one hand, and the larger stores of
the adjacent communities made accessible by the use of
automobiles.

The
Specialty
Store

The specialty store was the first improvement of the
general store. Merchandising in this type is confined to
one or a few lines. The term is applied to both the small
neighborhood store and to the small exclusive, city store.

The buying problem of the specialty store is particularly difficult since, in most cases, merchandise must be better than, or at least as good as, that carried by the department store.

The tendency, at present, is toward an increase in the numbers of the specialty store.

The
Department
Store

The department store is one form of large-scale merchandising. It is the result of an attempt to supply the principles of large-scale production to retail selling problems.

The general purchasing policy of the department store is to buy directly from the manufacturer in large quantities, taking advantage of the discounts for cash payment.

The advertising of the department store is generally based on a definite price policy with emphasis on the effectiveness of display.

The functions of the department store are highly specialized since each function is under the management of a specialist. In addition to buying and selling, the chief functions are accounting and finance and personnel management. The latter is subdivided into problems of employment, training and relations with employees.

The
Chain
Store

The chain store movement began after the close of the Civil War. The number of chain stores has increased rapidly in recent years. The chain store is an example of standardization in retailing. The application of standardization to all of its activities enables this type of organization to undersell its competitors.

The chief advantage of the chain store over the individual proprietor store is its ability to undersell competitors due to the economies it effects through standardization.

Its great disadvantage lies in the fact that there is a great loss due to the fact that employees are in charge of branches and for this reason the personal contact with customers, which plays such an important part in the individual store, is usually lacking.

The
Mail-Order
House

The mail-order house is another illustration of the tendency shown by all large-scale retailers. In addition to utilizing the economies made possible by large-scale buying and selling, it has introduced the instalment plan of payment for its customers. It has also developed the use of the mails for selling purposes to their highest extent.

Developing its own private brands as an advertisement is another step taken by the mail-order house.

The rapid expansion of railroads and the introduction of the parcel post system were largely responsible for the development of the mail-order system of retailing.

PART THREE: THE MIDDLEMAN

The Jobber   The jobber assumes for the manufacturer the problems of assembling, grading, financing and distribution to the dealers. Manufacturing costs are relatively higher than distributing costs, and for this reason the manufacturer concentrates his efforts on a reduction in producing costs, leaving the problem of distribution to some outside agency.

Jobbers are of various types. There is the agent who deals in a variety of lines, the agent who specializes in one line, and also the agent who is a manufacturer as well as a distributor.

The jobber usually maintains a warehouse for storing products in time of slack demand. In this way he assists in stabilizing production.

Advertising by a jobber is a difficult problem, since he does not come in direct contact with the consumer. When, however, he makes use of the private brand, he indulges in one form of advertisement. His chief means of creating demand is through dealers' catalogues.

The Broker   In some lines of business, the jobber has not completely satisfied the need for a specialist in distribution. Thus, the broker has arisen in answer to a definite need. "Brokers as middlemen may be divided into three groups:

"1. The broker who functions between the producer and other middlemen.

"2. The broker connected with one phase of a particular business.

"3. The broker on the organized exchange."

All classes of brokers merely act in the name of a principal. The broker does not possess goods but deals in orders. He has no discretionary power in making sales. Brokers usually specialize either in selling or in buying.

There has been some discussion as to the necessity of the broker's existence. Despite the fact that a large amount of the work formerly done by brokers has been taken over by cooperative marketing agencies, the broker still exists in large numbers. This fact seems to justify his position in the economic field.

Organized Exchanges

An organized exchange is an association of those who deal in a certain type of commodity. These concentrate in a specified locality and function according to set regulations.

Sales on an organized exchange are made either by sample or by the use of a standard system of grading. The organized exchange is a development of the market place. It is merely a specialization of the original form.

In order to establish an organized exchange certain conditions must be met. The volume of potential business must be large enough to justify the adoption of regulations and the commodity, itself, must be suitable.

"Brokers as middlemen may be divided roughly into three groups:

"1. The broker who stands between producer and other middlemen, commonly called the merchandise broker. He is active in lines of business where there is a large number of small producers and widely extended markets, such as textiles, canned goods, fruits, etc.

"2. The broker who has come into existence because of the peculiar circumstances connected with the trade channels of a particular line of business. He deals in a highly specialized commodity, such as insurance, foreign exchange, or real estate.

"3. The broker on the organized exchange who deals in stocks and bonds and in grain, cotton, sugar and other commodities." [1]

The article should be a staple, capable of being graded and not highly perishable. The exchange is justified economically despite the fact that certain defects in its organization and operation still require correction.

The chief cause for complaint on the part of the public lies in the fact that it exists chiefly for speculation and consequently disturbs prices.

[1] White, Percival, and Walter S. Hayward, *Marketing Practice,* p. 176.

Cooperative Marketing

Cooperation in marketing is effected for the purpose of securing for small units the advantages of large-scale selling. The cooperative organization assumes the functions of the more common types of middlemen. It limits its operation, however, to the primary market.

The modern movements are organized on the basis of product rather than locality. Short-term contracts are made with small producers to turn over their total production capacity to the cooperative organization. This organization assumes all the functions of marketing. It establishes standards and grades; it finances the producer and it creates demand through advertising.

The cooperative marketing movement has developed rapidly in recent years and has been particularly successful in Denmark. The agricultural industries in California have also been organized on this basis.

PART FOUR: MARKETING PROBLEMS

Market Analysis

Market analysis deals with the product, the market and the means of bringing them together. In general, it may be said that market analysis is the application of the principles of research to marketing. It has had a recent development simultaneous with that of scientific management in industry. Market analysis is conducted either by a research department within the organization or by an outside agency, specializing in that type of work.

The procedure in making an analysis includes first of all a study of the product to be marketed with special consideration of its uses. A survey of the potential market is also made by means of interviews and questionnaires. The purpose of this survey is to determine what the line of appeal should be and how to adjust it to various sections and classes of the consuming public.

Sales Planning and Promotion by the Manufacturer

Planning in its application to the many branches of business was the most important contribution of the scientific management movement. The planning of sales is based upon market research, and coordinated with production schedules. Its object is to predict sales possibilities and to coordinate the various branches of an organization with reference to its research.

Sales promotion connects sales planning and advertising. It is really the carrying out of sales plans. An important part of this work is obtaining the proper momentum for sales campaigns.

Sales Management

The importance of salesmanship in marketing is so great that a great deal of emphasis is placed upon the function of sales management. The first step in sales management is the choice of a sales organization suitable to the type of product manufactured and to the character of the potential market. Sales may be controlled either centrally through one large organization or territorially by means of district branches.

Problems growing out of this primary choice are the selection and training of salesmen, the assignment of territory to each individual, and developing a system of reports for the purpose of maintaining contact with the sales force. Upon the proper coordination of these matters of sales policy with the character of the product and market depends the success of the organization.

The Advertising Campaign

The primary purpose of the advertising campaign is to increase the demand for a product. The secondary purpose is to familiarize the consumer with the name of the organization manufacturing that product.

The advertising campaign is based upon a market analysis the purpose of which is to determine in what sections and among what classes the potential market lies. Advertising copy is then adapted to the character of the market. The choice of media is the result of a careful analysis of the probable effectiveness of each of the available forms.

The advertising agency is of great importance to the average organization since only the largest companies can effectively finance an advertising department. The agency has developed from a broker of space to an organization equipped to take over the entire management of a client's campaign. Today's advertising methods and policies have evolved during the past twenty years.

PART FIVE: CONCLUSION

The direct effect of marketing policies upon other branches of an industrial organization, as shown in the foregoing discussion, is so great that marketing has become, within the past two decades, the most important problem confronting the modern business institution.

In his search for more economical methods of distribution, the business man will undoubtedly bring about a standardization of marketing similar to that effected in the field of production. This cannot, however, be achieved until certain obstacles are overcome. Foremost among these is the apparent duplication of effort prevailing in many of the distributing functions.

The tendency seems to be toward standardization but it is doubtful whether the degree of standardization in marketing will reach that attained in production.

OUTLINE OF REPORT

I. *Introduction*
    A. Synopsis of Report
    B. Foreword

II. *Text of Report*
    A. Purpose of Report
    B. Discussion
        1. Marketing Functions
           a. Assembling and grading
           b. Storing
           c. Transportation
           d. Financing and risk taking
           e. Creation of demand
           f. Merchandising
        2. The Development of Retailing
           a. The general store
           b. The specialty store
           c. The department store
           d. The chain store
           e. The mail-order house
        3. The Middleman
           a. The jobber
           b. The broker
           c. Organized exchanges
           d. Cooperative marketing
        4. The Marketing Problems of the Manufacturer
           a. Market analysis
           b. Sales planning and promotion
           c. Sales management
           d. The advertising campaign
        5. Conclusion

III. *Appendix*
    A. Charts
    B. Graphs
    C. Bibliography

REFERENCE BOOKS

BALL, JOHN, and WILLIAMS, C. B. *Report Writing.* New York, The Ronald Press Company, 1955.

DOUGLASS, PAUL. *Communication Through Reports.* Englewood Cliffs, N. J., Prentice-Hall, Inc., 1957.

GAUM, CARL G., GRAVES, HAROLD F., and HOFFMAN, LYNE S. S. *Report Writing,* 4th ed. Englewood Cliffs, N. J., Prentice-Hall, Inc., 1950.

HOTCHKISS, GEORGE BURTON, and others. *Advanced Business Correspondence.* New York, Harper & Brothers, 1947.

LINTON, CALVIN D. *How To Write Reports.* New York, Harper & Brothers, 1954.

NELSON, J. RALEIGH. *Writing the Technical Report,* 3rd ed. New York, McGraw-Hill Book Company, Inc., 1952.

TURABIAN, KATE L. *Manual for the Writers of Term Papers, Theses and Dissertations,* rev. ed. Chicago, University of Chicago Press, 1955.

11. Preparation of Manuscript

1. Typewrite manuscript to be sent to a publisher or printer. It will present a better appearance and will be easier to read. Type in double-space.

2. Leave margins as follows: one and a half inches at the top, one and a half inches at the left, one at the right, and one at the bottom.

3. If possible keep the number of lines on each sheet the same. This will enable the printer to estimate the amount of space the copy will take.

4. Use good bond paper, eight and a half by eleven inches. Typewrite on one side of paper only.

5. Number all sheets consecutively, not separately by chapters.

6. If you wish to include additional pages, note on the margin of the page after which the insert is to be made, the number of pages to be inserted; as, *Insert 8a-8c,* and write on the following pages. *8a, 8b, 8c.*

7. Do not pin inserts to a sheet, but paste them carefully in their proper places.

8. Fasten the sheets of a manuscript by clips or pins. Do not sew or tie them together, as they are likely to be torn.

9. Begin new chapters at the top of a sheet. Clip all pages together belonging to a chapter.

10. Footnotes should be placed directly below that part of the text to which they refer. They should be typed in single-space and should have lines drawn across the page above and below them.

11. Write in the text after the punctuation mark (if any), a superior figure to correspond with the figure preceding the footnote.

12. Number footnotes consecutively throughout a chapter or an article. If there are several footnotes to appear on one page, write them one below the other, so that they will read down.

13. Spell out in full all references to periodicals. When more than one reference to the same work is made, abbreviations may be used after the first one.

14. Number chapters, charts, plates, and graphs consecutively throughout. Most writers use Roman numerals.

15. The development of the subject matter by sections, parts, chapters, topics, etc., should be clearly shown.

16. Make the index after the page proof has been returned from the printer. (*See* p. 474.)

17. Do not roll manuscript. Send it flat in a box or a strong envelope. Mark on the outside the author's name and return address. It is best to insure the manuscript or register it if sent by mail.

18. Read a manuscript through carefully before submitting it to anyone for consideration. Edit it critically to be certain that it contains no incorrect usage and no inexact punctuation. Be sure that each sentence conforms to the best rhetorical principles, that the paragraphing is clear and defined, and that the manuscript contains no errors. Uniformity in spelling, punctuation, and abbreviations is to be desired.

19. Always send the original copy to the publisher, as it is clearer in type than a carbon. Retain a carbon copy for reference and as protection against loss of the original.

A Glossary of Terms

The following list of definitions of terms commonly used in bookmaking and publishing is adapted through the courtesy of *Publishers' Weekly* from a longer glossary published serially by that journal through the months of July and August, 1924.

bastard title. The name of a book standing by itself on the leaf preceding the title-page. Also known as *"fly title"*—not to be confused with *"half title."*

book sizes.

Size	Approximate dimensions in inches
Atlas folio	16 x 25
Elephant folio	14 x 20
Folio	12 x 15
4to (quarto)	9 x 12
8vo (octavo)	6 x 9
12mo (duodecimo)	5 x 7½
16mo	4½ x 6¾
18mo	4 x 6¼
24mo	3½ x 6
32mo	3½ x 5
48mo	2½ x 4
64mo	2 x 3

The common book-trade designation of sizes was based originally on their relation to a sheet of paper measuring 19 x 25. When folded to 8 leaves and trimmed, each 6 x 9 inches, it is the standard dimension of an 8vo. When folded to make 16 leaves it is a 16mo. With the present infinite variety of paper sizes all dimensions are approximate.

bulk. The thickness of a book without its covers.

cancel. A leaf reprinted and inserted in consequence of an error or defect on the leaf replaced.

caption. A heading, as of a chapter, table, etc. Caption is sometimes used to designate the title of an illustration or the brief description printed immediately below it. *See* LEGEND.

colophon. An emblem, usually a device assumed by the publishing house, placed on the title page.

cut. A term commonly used to mean either a half-tone engraving or zinc etching. Also the block or plate from which it is printed.

cut-in side note. A note set into the side of a page of printed matter.

dummy. Unprinted paper, folded, trimmed or untrimmed, bound or unbound, to show size, bulk, and general appearance of a projected publication.

electrotypes. Facsimile plates for use in printing made by taking an impression in wax or other substance, depositing in this mold a thin shell of copper or other metal by an electrotyping process, and backing it with type metal. Electrotypes are made for books which are to have a large printing or a second printing. The plates will stand more wear than the original type and can be more easily stored. Moreover, new electrotypes can be made from "molders" (electrotypes used as patterns only) or from type kept standing.

end papers. Strong sheets, sometimes decorated, pasted on the interior of the cover.

flyleaves. Unprinted leaves at front and back of books, between the lining papers and body of book.

format. The general make-up of a book as to size of page, margin, binding, etc.

front matter. The pages preceding the first chapter of a book, known as "front matter," include the following, frequently in the order named:

Bastard title
Frontispiece (facing title-page)
Title-page
Copyright notice and printer's imprint
Dedication
Preface (or foreword)
Table of contents
List of illustrations
Introduction
Half title

Each to begin on a right-hand or odd-numbered page, excepting the frontispiece, which faces the title-page, and the copyright, which appears on the verso of the title-page.

frontispiece. A picture or plate facing the title-page.

half title. A brief title standing alone on a separate page, preceding the text or a section of the text of a book.

head margin. The blank space above the first line on the page. Usually planned at half the width of the bottom margin. *See* MARGINS.

initial letter. A large capital or decorated letter sometimes used to begin a chapter or section of a book.

inserts or insets. Illustrations, maps, or other material not part of the printed sheets, included when binding a pamphlet or book.

jacket. The printed or unprinted paper placed around a bound book. Sometimes called the wrapper.

layout. Practically, the working diagram for the printer to follow. Usually marked to show the general grouping of a job, and specifying the sizes and kinds of type to be used.

leaders. Dots or dashes set in succession so as to lead the eye, as in the table of contents.

leading. The space between lines in order to provide a more open space and make the matter easier to read.

legend. The title or short description printed under an illustration, not to be confused with *caption* (q. v.).

list price, or published price. The price to the individual consumer as set by the publisher.

margins. The proportional width of the margins is a very important element in a properly balanced book page. A good ratio is: top margin, 2; outside, 3; bottom, 4; inside, 1½.

net; net price. "Not subject to discount or reduction."

plates. Illustrations printed on special paper and inserted separately in the binding of a book. *See also* INSERTS; ELECTROTYPES.

reprints. A new printing of a book.

royalties. A compensation paid by a publisher to the owner of a copyright for the right to act under it.

running head; running title. The line which appears across the top of a printed page. Usually the title of the book is run on the left-hand page while the chapter title is on the right-hand page.

sheets; "in sheets." Printed pages of a book, either flat or folded, but unbound. English term is "In Quires."

subtitle. An additional or second title to a book; an undertitle. For example, "Fundamentals of Pedagogy: *A Textbook for Teachers.*"

tail piece. An ornament at the bottom of a page or at the end of a chapter.

title-page. A page at the beginning of a book always on the right, giving its title, its author, if acknowledged, and its publisher, with place and date of publication. *See* FRONT MATTER.

type sizes.

This is 4½ point, old name "Diamond"
This is 5 point, old name "Pearl"
This is 5½ point, old name "Agate"
This is 6 point, old name "Nonpareil"
This is 7 point, old name "Minion"
This is 8 point, old name "Brevier"
This is 9 point, old name "Bourgeois"
This is 10 point, old name "Long Primer"
This is 11 point, old name "Small Pica"
This is 12 point, old name "Pica"
This is 14 point, old name "English"
This is 18 point, old name "Great Primer"

REFERENCE BOOKS

THE UNIVERSITY OF CHICAGO PRESS. *A Manual of Style with Specimens of Type,* 11th ed. The University of Chicago Press, 1949.

UNITED STATES GOVERNMENT PRINTING OFFICE. *Style Manual of the United States Government Printing Office.* Washington, 1953.

12. Compiling a Bibliography

A bibliography is a list of books or parts of books, pamphlets, periodicals, or articles in periodicals by a given author or relating to a given subject. A bibliography may be simple or elaborate according to its purpose.

There are various kinds of bibliographies: subject, author, and trade bibliographies. The subject type deals with titles on one subject; the author type with titles by one author; while the trade bibliography is made up for the book trade and is not confined to one subject or to one author.

Although the forms used in the making of a bibliography differ in details, such as capitalization and punctuation of titles and of authors' names, the data recorded, however, are for the most part uniform. These consist of author's name, title of book, and facts of publication—place, publisher, and date, or, in the case of periodical articles, the name, date, and paging of magazine.

Author. Enter author under last name followed by first and second names or initials; as, Clapp, John Mantle, or Clapp, J. M. When there is only one forename, it is usually written out; as, Anderson, Sherwood. Titles and degrees should be omitted. If there are two authors, use both names connected by *and;* as, Hotchkiss, George Burton, and Kilduff, Edward Jones, or Hotchkiss, G. B., and Kilduff, E. J.

If there are three or more authors, use first name mentioned on title page followed by words *and others;* as, Commons, John Rogers, and others.

When listing more than one work by the same author, do not repeat the name, but use a long dash (three-em dash) to represent it as follows:

KRAPP, GEORGE PHILIP. *A Comprehensive Guide to Good English.* Chicago, Rand, McNally & Co., 1927.

—————. "Is American English Archaic?" *Southwest Rev.,* xii. 292–303.

When a reference to the same work is repeated immediately, use the abbreviation *ibid.* (*ibidem,* in the same place) as follows:

NOYES, ALFRED. *The New Morning.* "Victory," p. 10. New York, Frederick A. Stokes Company, 1919.
Ibid., "The Lost Battle," pp. 94–95.

Collections. Compilations of plays, stories, essays, or poems by several authors should be entered under the name of the editor or compiler; as, Tinker, H. L., comp.

Official Publications. Books issued by an association or reports of a business firm should be entered under the name of the association or firm responsible for the publication.

American Association for Adult Education. *Handbook of Adult Education in the United States.*
Columbia University. University Extension. *Annual Report of the Director.*

Books issued by a department of a government should be entered under the name of the country, followed by the name of the department issuing such material; as, United States Government Printing Office. *Manual of Foreign Languages.*

Title Entries. Books such as encyclopedias, yearbooks, and anonymous classics are entered under their titles.

Encyclopædia Britannica
Who's Who in America
Arabian Nights

Title. Enter the title exactly as it occurs on the title-page except for the introductory articles, *a, an,* and *the,* which are usually omitted; as, *Secretary's Handbook.*

Capitalization of Titles. The chief words in titles may be capitalized; as, *Doing Business by Letter; a Complete Guide.* Library usage, however, advocates lower case for all but the first word of the title page except in the case of proper nouns.

Doing business by letter; a complete guide
American Catholic who's who

Editions. If editions other than the first have been consulted, this information should be stated; as, *Advanced Business Correspondence,* 3d ed. rev.

Place, Publisher, and Date. This information may be given in various ways.

Full form—Boston, Mass., Houghton Mifflin Company, 19__
Shortened form—Boston: Houghton Mifflin, 19__
Abbreviated form—Place omitted, Houghton, 19__

Paging. In a complete and exact bibliography, the number of pages in the volume, or in the case of more than one volume, the number of volumes, should be stated. This information follows the date.

CROBAUGH, C. J. *Handbook of Insurance.* New York, Prentice-Hall, 1931. 1413 p.

U.S. Bureau of Foreign and Domestic Commerce. *Commercial and Industrial Handbooks.* Washington, Government Printing Office, 1920–31. 20v. il., maps.

Paging follows date in citations of parts of books.

OPDYCKE, J. B. *The Literature of Letters: Famous Literary Letters, as Related to Life, to the History of Literature, and to the Art of Literature.* New York, Lyons and Carnahan, 1925. pp. 206–245.

Punctuation. Place a period after the name of the author. If the names of two authors occur, place a comma after names of the first author; as, Rosenkampff, Arthur Henry, and Wallace, William Carroll. Place a period after the title of the publication. After the place of publication, most authorities prefer a comma although some permit the use of the colon. Place a comma after the name of the publisher. Place a period after the date.

When referring to articles in magazines use quotation marks around the name of the article and write the name of the periodical in italics. Date follows paging in periodical references.

LOWELL, ABBOTT LAWRENCE. "Self-Education in College." *Forum,* 79, No. 4, pp. 519–526, April, 1928.

Price. If the price is considered a necessary addition, it should be the last item written.

CHISHOLM, G. G. *Handbook of Commercial Geography,* 12th ed. rev. Longmans, 1932. 825 p. $6.50.

13. Proofreading

Proofreading requires accuracy, alertness, and judgment. Errors should be carefully sought out and corrected in the first reading.

Writers and their secretaries should be familiar with commonly accepted marks of proofreading and with their actual use on proofs.

Kinds of Proofs

Galley Proofs, about the length of a newspaper column, are the first proofs made by the printer. They are usually revised and cleared of all apparent errors before being sent to the author.

An author's proofs are those corrected and revised from the first Galley Proof and sent to him for correction.

Page Proofs are those made from the Galley Proofs as they are to appear in regular page form. These should be corrected with great care, as any changes are at additional cost. The proofreader should observe closely the headings, subheads, numbering of pages, footnotes, and all other parts of the page to be sure that all are correct.

After corrections have been made by the author on the Page Proof, the pages are then locked up for the press.

The plate proof is the final proof furnished to the publisher, but not usually sent to the author.

SIGNS USED IN CORRECTING PROOFS

♉	Push down the lead which is showing with the type.
ℒ	Delete; take out.
℘	Turn inverted letter right side up.
stet	} Let it remain; change made was wrong.
☐	Indent one *em*.
⊙	A period.
‖	The type line is uneven at the side of the page; straighten it.
✕	A broken letter.
=	A hyphen.
ital.	Use italics.
⌒	Join together; take out the space.
℘	Take out letter and close up.
center	Put in middle of page or line.
≡	Straighten lines.
⩒	Insert an apostrophe.
⋀	Insert a comma.
⌐¬	Raise the word or letter.
⌊⌋	Lower the word or letter.
⊏	Bring matter to the left.
⊐	Bring matter to the right.
#	Make a space.
lead	A thin metal strip used to widen the space between the lines.
space out	Spread words farther apart.
¶	Make a paragraph.
no ¶	Run on without a paragraph.

cap.	Use a capital.
l.c.	Use the lower case (small type), *i.e.* not capitals.
s.c.	Small capitals.
w.f.	Wrong font — size or style.
font	Kind of type.
tr.	Transpose.
rom.	Use roman letter.
overrun	Carry over to next line.
∧	Indicates where an insertion is to be made.
Qy. or (?)	Doubt as to spelling, etc.
≡	Indicates CAPITAL letters.
=	Indicates SMALL CAPITAL letters.
——	Indicates *italic* letters.
～～～	Indicates **black-type** letters.

GENERAL DIRECTIONS FOR PROOFREADING

1. Read all proofs slowly, letter by letter, in order to detect every error.

2. Read through the proof several times with a definite point in view. Consider carefully punctuation, correct usage, typographical errors, general alignment, spacing, general effect.

3. Make all corrections in ink of a color contrasting with that used by the professional proofreader.

4. Put all corrections in the margin near the word marked. If several are made, place them in the order of their appearance with a slanting line between them; as, *w.f./tr./s.c./*.

5. Do not erase a correction made which you have found unnecessary. Draw a line through the correction and

write *stet,* which means *Let it stand.* If necessary, re-write a correction.

6. Underline three times a word or words to be written in large capitals and write "caps" in the margin; underline twice to indicate small capitals and write "s.c." in margin.

7. When a word is incorrectly capitalized, draw a line through the letter and write "l.c." in the margin to indicate "lower case."

8. Underline a word once to indicate that it is to be italicized, and write "ital." in the margin.

9. Place a circle in the margin around a period or colon to be inserted. To indicate a comma write ,/or ⩓ ; to indicate an apostrophe write ᐯ ; to indicate quotation marks write ᐯ ᐯ.

10. To indicate that a word or expression should be removed draw a line through the word or expression and write in the margin the sign ℐ (dele), which means *Take out.*

11. Write in the margin all new material to be inserted and indicate by caret (⩓) where it is to be placed.

12. Write in the margin a double (=) to show that a hyphen is to be placed where indicated by a caret sign.

13. Use the sign # to indicate that more space is needed where indicated by the caret.

14. Use the sign ⊃ to indicate that space between letters of words is to be eliminated.

15. Answer all queries made by the printer's proofreader. To indicate your approval, cross out the question mark and allow the correction to stand. To show disapproval of the correction suggested, cross out the question or answer it in full.

PROOF SHOWING CORRECTIONS

cap. ADDRESS AT GETTYSBURG

Fourscore and, seven years ago our fathers brought
forth on this continent a new nation, conceived in
liberty, and dedicated to the proposition that all
men are created equal. Now we are engaged in a
great civil war, testing whether that nation or any
nation so conceived and so dedicated, can long
endure. We are met on a great battlefield of that
war. We have come to pedicate a portion of that
field as a final resting-place for those who here here
gave their lives that that Nation might live. it is
altogether fitting and proper that we *should* do this.
But, in a larger sense we cannot dedicate —
we cannot consecrate — we cannot hallow this
ground The brave men, living and dead, who
struggled here, have consecrateditfarabove our
poor power to add or detract. The world will
little note nor long remember what we here say,
but it can never forget what they did here.
It is for us, the living, rather, to be deddicated
here to the unfinished work which they who fought

(Address at the dedication of the Gettysburg National Ceme-
tery, Nov. 19, 1863. Reprinted, by permission of The Macmillan
Company, from Abraham Lincoln, the Man the People, by
Norman Hapgood.)

CORRECTED PROOF
ADDRESS AT GETTYSBURG

Fourscore and seven years ago our fathers brought forth on this continent a new nation, conceived in liberty, and dedicated to the proposition that all men are created equal.

Now we are engaged in a great civil war, testing whether that nation, or any nation so conceived and so dedicated, can long endure. We are met on a great battlefield of that war. We have come to dedicate a portion of that field as a final resting-place for those who here gave their lives that that nation might live. It is altogether fitting and proper that we should do this.

But, in a larger sense, we cannot dedicate — we cannot consecrate — we cannot hallow — this ground. The brave men, living and dead, who struggled here, have consecrated it far above our poor power to add or detract. The world will little note nor long remember what we say here, but it can never forget what they did here. It is for us, the living, rather, to be dedicated here to the unfinished work which they who fought here

(Address at the dedication of the Gettysburg National Cemetery, Nov. 19, 1863. Reprinted, by permission of THE MACMILLAN COMPANY, from "Abraham Lincoln, the Man of the People," by Norman Hapgood.)

14. Making an Index

The purpose of an index is to present a means of ready reference. An index should offer to the reader an opportunity to find
quickly what he wishes without reading more than is necessary.
It is essential, then, for an indexer to know what the average reader
may want to refer to and under what headings he will naturally
look. One or two may not be enough.

Chapter headings, subheads, subjects, and even minor subjects
may be included in the index. Cross references should be made
wherever possible. The indexer should list topics under as many
headings as he thinks necessary.

There are several typographical forms for indexing. If a given
form is not required by a publisher, an author may select a type
which he considers suitable to the content or nature of his work.

In the form selected, he should observe the capitalization, spacing, indention, punctuation, and phrasing of topics, and follow
that form rigidly.

The making of an index begins with the receipt of the page proofs
from the printer. In order to be sure that all important subjects are
indexed, it would be well to start at the beginning and read through
all pages consecutively, writing on separate cards each subject or
name important enough to be indexed. One main subject only
should be written on a card. Subentries, indented a few spaces to the
right, alphabetically arranged, may be included on the same card.
If more subentries are to be indexed than there is space for, the
main subject is repeated on a new card with the word *Continued*
following it. Often it is necessary to make subentries under subentries. This is done by double indention.

When all subjects are completely and carefully indexed and cross
references made under suitable headings, the cards should be
alphabetized. From these the index, a complete list of all entries
on the cards, may then be made in its final draft.

Every reference should be checked to see whether the index reference corresponds to the page quoted. This is most important, as errors frequently creep in, particularly in the proof.

Suggestions for Indexing Names

In indexing proper names write the last name first, followed by a comma, then the Christian or given name, followed by a comma and page number.

> Carlyle, Jane, 20
> Conrad, Joseph, 116

The following illustrate ways often observed in making an index: by column form with indention and subindention; by paragraph form for all topics; by the use of main entries only; by the use of the dash to indicate subentries.

Index with indention and subindention:

> Secretary, the business training of, 8
>   cultural training of, 5–7
>   definition of, 2–3
>   duties of, 3
>   efficient, the, 61–62
>   from point of view of employment
>   managers, 57–60
>   of man, 64
>   of woman, 65
>   general qualities of, 17–18
>   history of, 72–81
>   hundred per cent secretaries, 65–66
>   From *Training for Secretarial Practice*

Paragraph form for extensive index:

> Subjects, of letters, accept-
> ance, 225; accident, 368;
> advice, 218; arrest, 353;
> art, 388; authorship, 231;
> autobiography, 34, 56,
> 106, 435, 457; bank, 290;
> biography, 372, 432; busi-
> ness, 402–411
>   From *The Literature of Letters*

Index for main entries:

File clerk, duties of 178
File clerk, promotion of 177–178
File clerk service 177
File clerk service, importance of 177
File clerk, training and experience required 178
Filing methods, importance of 33
Financial advice and information 47
Financial reports 56
Folders, special tabs 37
Freight shipments 84

From *Secretarial Studies*

The use of the dash to indicate subentries:

Tables, open (without rules):

—blanks, leaders in, 314; except "Remarks," 317

—bookkeeping, 319; balance, 319; "Brought forward," "Carried forward," supplied, in italics, 319

—captions for, 310

—column heads in, 310

—of contents, 314

—leaders, 9-unit, 314

—list of illustrations, 314

—primary heads, 140

—subheads, 140

15. Rules for Alphabetical Filing Used in Business Offices

General Directions

1. Entries of names of individuals, on cards, lists, etc., should always be placed in the following order:

1. Surname
2. Comma
3. Christian name (or first initial)
4. Middle name or initial
5. Title (in parentheses) Stewart, George D. (Dr.)

2. Many names are pronounced exactly alike but spelled differently:

(1) File exactly as spelled.
(2) When spelling differs only at the end of the word, no cross reference is necessary, since one spelling would follow immediately after another:

Smith	Conner
Smithe	Connor

When spelling differs in the beginning of a word, make blanket cross reference from one form of name (surname only) to the other:

Monroe ....*See also* Munroe
Munroe ....*See also* Monroe
Conolly ....*See also* Connolly
Connolly ....*See also* Conolly

Illustration of Alphabetic Divisions Found on Filing Guides

25 Divisions	*40 Divisions*	*60 Divisions*
A	A	AA-AM
BA-BL	BA	AN-AZ
BO-BY	BE-BI	BA
CA-CL	BL-BO	BE
CO-CZ	BR-BY	BI-BL
D	CA-CE	BO
E	CH-CL	BR
F	CO-CZ	BU-BY
G	DA-DE	CA-CE
HA-HE	DI-DY	CH-CL
HI-HY	E	COA-COP
I-J	FA-FL	COR-COZ-CR-CZ
K	FO-FY	DA-DE
L	GA-GL	DI-DO
MA-MC	GO-GY	DR-DY-EA-EK
ME-MY	HA	EL-EZ-FA
N-O	HE-HI	FE-FL
P-Q	HO-HY	FO-FY
R	I-J	GA-GE
SA-SE	KA-KI	GI-GO
SH-SO	KL-KY	GR-GY
SP-SY	L	HAA-HAP
T-U-V	MA	HAR-HAZ-HEA-HEK
WA-WH	MC	HEL-HEZ-HI
WI-WY-X-Y-Z	ME-MI	HO
	MO-MY	HU-HY-I
	N-O	J
	PA-PH	KA-KE
	PI-PY-Q	KI-KY
	RA-RI	LA
	RO-RY	LE-LI
	SA-SC	LO-LY
	SE-SK	MAA-MAN
	SL-SQ	MAR-MAY
	ST-SY	MC
	T	ME
	U-V	MI-MOA-MOO
	WA-WE	MOR-MOZ-MU-MY
	WH-WI	N
	WO-WY-X-Y-Z	O

25 Divisions	40 Divisions	60 Divisions
		PA-PEA-PEM
		PEN-PEZ-PF-PH-PI
		PL-PY-Q
		RA-RE
		RH-RI-ROA-ROG
		ROH-ROZ-RU-RY
		SA
		SC
		SE-SH
		SI-SM
		SN-SQ-STA
		STE-STY
		SU-SY-TA-TE
		TH-TY
		U-V
		WA
		WE
		WH
		WI
		WO-WY-X-Y-Z

3. For ease and quickness both in filing and in research, *Mac* and *Mc* may be filed as though the prefix were spelled *Mac*. This method is used in libraries and in many business houses.

Mackey, Thelma	McMahon, Agnes
McKinney, Louis	McNab, Robert
McLain, Alice	Macnamara, Henry
MacLaren, Frank	McNaughton, Mary
MacLean, Samuel	Macnutt, Albert

Note that the telephone directory and some organizations file names beginning with *Mac* before those beginning with *Mc*:

MacBride, Roy
MacDonald, Peter
McBride, Roy
McDonald, Peter

4. When filing a group of one surname, alphabetic order, bear the following in mind:

(1) Nothing stands before something.
(2) Initials always precede names beginning with the same letter.

> Lord, (Mrs.)
> Lord, A. F.
> Lord, A. Frances
> Lord, Augustus

5. Hyphenated surnames of individuals should be indexed under the surname as a whole and, when necessary, a cross reference made from the second part:

> Thoburn-Arzt, James
> Quiller-Couch, Arthur T.

Cross references:

> Arzt, James Thoburn—*See* Thoburn-Arzt, James
> Couch, Arthur T. Quiller—*See* Quiller-Couch, Arthur T.

Foreign Names

6. Foreign names commencing with *D', da, de, della, di, du, la, le, van, von,* etc., are filed alphabetically as they are spelled. The prefix is considered as part of the name, not separately.

> Da Costa, Carl
> D'Agnostina, Albert
> De Kosa, L. A.
> D'Elia, Louis J.
> Della Fazia, Anielo
> De Stefano, Adolfo
> Des Verney, Kenneth
> De Takacs, Maria
>
> Du Bois, Paul
> La Barre, Emily
> La Bell, W.
> Le Blanc, Jean
> Van Loon, Hendrik
> Van Ness, George
> Von Bremen, Fritz
> Von Burg, Karl

7. When names beginning with *La* or *Le* are family names (as *Le Roy, Le Bolt,* etc.) they follow the foregoing rule. When *La* or *Le* is used in place of *the,* index as written.

> La Barre Realty Corp.,
> Le Barton Mfg. Co.,

When *El* stands in place of *the,* index as written: El Caso Apartments.

8. Foreign titles are indexed strictly according to title. Make as many cross references as may be necessary for identification:

> La Société Anonyme des Cycles Peugeot
> Make cross reference under *Peugeot*.

Company Names

9. If a *company* is a customer, enter under the company's title, with name of officer following:

> Best & Co.,
>   Strickland, W., Manager
> Stetson Shops, Inc.,
>   Interman, K. M.

If the *officer* himself is the customer, enter under his name in care of the company:

> Brown, Joseph A.,
>   Credit Manager, Stewart & Co.

10. If a company name contains a Christian name under which it is commonly known, it should be filed under the familiar form:

> John Hancock Mutual Life Insurance Company
> Marshall Field & Company

But more often company names containing Christian names are known by the surnames and should be so filed:

> Crowell, Thomas Y., Company
> Heath, D. C., and Company

11. Arrange all material in A Z sequence of letters to the last letter of the word, considering each word separately. Consider the second words only, when the first words are identical:

> Amer, Walter
> Amerest Baking Co.
> American Can Co.
> American Car Co.
> Americana Art Co.
> Amerman, A.
> Ames, E. C.

12. Names that begin with numbers should be indexed as if spelled out.

> File
> > 1st National Bank, as
> > First National Bank
>
> File
> > 3d Presbyterian Church, as
> > Third Presbyterian Church
>
> File
> > 14th Street Curiosity Shop, as
> > Fourteenth Street Curiosity Shop

13. Company names which do not embody full names of individuals should be alphabetized under the first name and the names following in strict alphabetic order, with cross reference from the second name when necessary:

> Canadian Pacific Railway Company
> Cross reference
> > Pacific Railway Company, Canadian

14. When there are a large number of titles of the same name, these should be alphabetized according to names of towns in the address:

> American Can Company, Allentown, Pa.
> American Can Company, Memphis, Tenn.

15. Companies with initials or Christian names should be filed (1) by surname, (2) by Christian name or initial, (3) by remainder of title (& Co., Bros., etc.). Small words, like *and, for, of,* etc., should be disregarded in filing.

Ryan, A.	Ryan & Co.
Ryan, B. C.	Ryan, Edward, & Bros.
Ryan, Bernard	Ryan, Henry, & Son

16. When companies of one name are followed by the words *Bros., Co., Inc., Sons,* etc., the titles are filed as though they were Christian names:

Patton, Abner	Patton, Co.
Patton Bros.	Patton, Inc.

17. Apostrophe s (*'s*) or s apostrophe (*s'*) is not considered in filing. Strict alphabetical order should be followed.

> Stark, Edward
> Stark's Grocery Store
> Starks, Louise
> Starks' Moving Company
> Stark's Service Station
> Starks, William
> Starks Woodyard

Miscellaneous Names

18. When filing material pertaining to a state, county, or city, file under name of state, county, or city; subdivide by department or bureau:

> Washington Assurance Corporation
> "   Candy Corporation
> "   , City of
> "   Public Health, Bureau of
> "   Coffee Co., G. (cross reference)
> "   , County of
> "   Heights Battery Service
> "   , Martha, Hotel Co. (cross reference)
> "   Pipe and Foundry Co.
> "   Square Book Shop
> "   , State of
> "   Education, Board of

19. Titles beginning with *Mt., New, Pan, Rock, St., Saint, San, Santa,* etc., are alphabetized as distinct names. Abbreviations are filed as though spelled in full:

Mt. Carmel	St. Agnes Day Nursery
Mt. Vesuvius Lumber Co.	Saint Joseph's Union
Mt. Zion Cemetery	St. Mary's Church
New Lenox Market	Saintsbury, George
New Life Co.	San Francisco Chronicle
Newark Refining Co.	San Joseph, Harold
Pan American Society of U.S.	Sanka Coffee House
Pancoast Co.	Santa Fé Co.
Rock Island R.R.	Santangelo Bros.
Rockefeller, John D.	

20. Churches are filed as the name appears.

> Cathedral of St. John the Divine
> Cross reference
> St. John the Divine, Cathedral of

Corporate Titles

21. Institutions or societies beginning with a Christian name should be filed under the surname, with a cross reference from the Christian name when necessary:

> Delgado, Isaac, Museum
> Ringling, John and Mable, Museum

But they should be filed under the Christian name if that is the generally recognized form:

> George Washington University
> John Crerar Library
> Sarah Lawrence College

22. When titles are composed of two or more names joined by *and,* the & is disregarded.

> American & Canadian Flour Corporation
> American-Canadian Property Corporation
> American-Russian Chamber of Commerce

23. When points of the compass are part of the name, index under *north, south,* etc.

> North Chicago, Ill.
> South Boston, Mass.

Northwest, Northwestern, etc., spelled as one word, are so alphabetized:

> North River Savings Bank
> Northwest Paper Company
> Northwestern Chemical Company

24. Titles beginning with descriptive words should be inverted, so that the main entry will come first.

Trustees of Cornell University
should be
Cornell University, Trustees of
Estate of Chauncey M. Depew
should be
Depew, Chauncey M., Estate of

REFERENCE BOOKS

BASSETT, ERNEST DICKEY, and AGNEW, P. L. *Business Filing,* 2d ed. Cincinnati, South-Western Publishing Company, Inc., 1955.

WEEKS, BERTHA M. *How to File and Index,* rev. ed. New York, The Ronald Press Company, 1951.

WHEELER, MARTHA THORNE. *Indexing; Principles, Rules and Examples.* 4th ed. New York State Library, 1942.

16. Sources of Information

Secretaries can best familiarize themselves with many of the following books by consulting them in libraries. Because dates of publication of many reference books are subject to change, these have been omitted from many of the following items. Additional reference books will also be found at end of chapters.

American Authors: 1600–1900, by S. J. Kunitz and Howard Haycraft. 1320 biographies and 400 portraits.

American Catholic Who's Who. A biographical dictionary of prominent Catholics of the higher rank of the priesthood and those distinguished in some particular line of work, as author, scientist, missionary.

Biography Index; a cumulative index to biographical material in books and magazines. First published in 1946. This gives no biographies but lists sources from which such information may be obtained.

British Authors Before 1800. A biographical dictionary complete in one volume with 650 biographies and 220 portraits, by S. J. Kunitz and Howard Haycraft.

British Authors of the Nineteenth Century, by S. J. Kunitz and Howard Haycraft. One thousand biographies and 350 portraits of authors of the British Empire, including Canada, Australia, South Africa, and New Zealand.

Current Biography. Since 1940 this publication has given sketches with portraits of people prominent in news of the day. Monthly with yearly cumulations.

Dictionary of American Biography. An important set in twenty volumes and supplements which contains authoritative accounts of noteworthy Americans no longer living.

Dictionary of National Biography. The source, in twenty-two volumes and supplements, for lives of prominent persons of the British Empire exclusive of those living. Also, in one volume, the *Concise Dictionary of National Biography.*

Directory of American Scholars, edited by Jaques Cattell. Sketches of leaders in the humanities and in the social sciences.

International Who's Who. Biographical data about well-known people of Europe, North and South America, Asia, Australia, etc.

The New Century Cyclopedia of Names, in three volumes. Comprehensive dictionary of proper names, table of world history, list of rulers and other notables by country.

Twentieth Century Authors, compiled by S. J. Kunitz and Howard Haycraft. In addition to biographies this contains many portraits. Also *First Supplement,* by S. J. Kunitz.

Webster's Biographical Dictionary. A comprehensive guide, in one volume, to dates, nationality, and activities of prominent persons from earliest times.

Who Was Who in America, 1897–1942; volume 2, 1943–1950. A biographical dictionary of persons whose names formerly appeared in *Who's Who in America,* but whose deaths occurred within the dates given.

Who's Who. A biographical dictionary issued annually, devoted mainly to people of note in Great Britain.

Who's Who in America. A biographical dictionary of contemporary men and women of note in America, with addresses, lists of works of authors, pronunciation of difficult names, educational statistics, and geographical index. Continued by monthly supplements. *Who's Who* is also published for sections of the United States under the titles of *Who's Who in the Midwest, Who's Who in the South and Southwest, Who's Who in the West.*

Who's Who in Art. A biographical dictionary of contemporary artists.

Who's Who in Canada. A biographical record of persons of note in the Dominion of Canada.

Who's Who in Commerce and Industry. Brief biographies of people prominent in business.

Who's Who in Engineering. A biographical dictionary of those prominent in engineering.

Who's Who in Latin America. A biographical dictionary of the outstanding living men and women of Spanish America and Brazil. Biennial.

Who's Who in the Theatre. A British biographical record of the contemporary stage, containing some American names; contains a list of leading dramatic critics of London and New York, a list of hereditary theatrical families, and a list of notable productions and revivals.

SOCIAL DIRECTORIES

Social Register. Directories containing names of men and women of social rank and prominence with names of all members of the family, city and country addresses, names of colleges attended, and club memberships. Published for twelve cities of the United States.

FORMS OF ADDRESS

Measures, Howard. *Styles of Address.* New York, Thomas Y. Crowell Company. Forms of address used in speech as well as in writing for formal and informal style for Great Britain, the United States, France, Germany, India, Italy, etc.

Titles and Forms of Address. London, Adam & Charles Black (New York, The Macmillan Company). A manual containing concise information about the orders of nobility in England, the clergy, the army, the navy, the law, the universities, and government services, with manner of addressing them, order of precedence, etc.

DIRECTORIES AND HANDBOOKS

Official Congressional Directory for the Use of the United States Congress. Authoritative information on all legislative, judicial, and executive departments at Washington; lists of foreign diplomatic and consular officers in the United States, and of ranking diplomatic and consular officers in the foreign service of the United States. Revised semiannually.

U.S. Civil Service Commission. *Official Register of the United States.* List of persons occupying administrative and supervisory positions in the legislative, executive, and judicial branches of the Federal Government.

EDUCATIONAL

Good, Carter Victor. *A Guide to Colleges, Universities, and Professional Schools in the United States.*

Lovejoy, Clarence Earle. *Lovejoy's College Guide;* a complete reference book to 2,049 American colleges and universities.

Patterson's American Educational Directory. Published annually.

U.S. Office of Education. *Educational Directory.* Lists of national and state educational officials, county, town, and district superintendents, college presidents, professors and superintendents in training schools, educational boards, and federations of women's clubs, officers of education in foreign countries, etc. Published annually.

RELIGIOUS

Official Catholic Directory. A directory and compilation of statistical information concerning the clergy, churches, religious orders, etc., of the Catholic Church in the United States and its possessions, in Great Britain, Canada, and other parts of British America, in Cuba, and in Mexico. Published annually.

U.S. Bureau of the Census. *Religious Bodies.* Statistical information of the church membership, building, Sunday schools, missionary activities, etc.

Yearbook of American Churches. A book of current statistical and directory information compiled for the Federal Council of the Churches of Christ in America.

BUSINESS, PROFESSIONS AND FOUNDATIONS

Kelly's Directory of Merchants, Manufacturers, and Shippers of the World. A guide to the export, import, shipping, and manufacturing interests. Contains official lists, consuls, glossaries of foreign trade terms with English equivalents. Published annually.

Poor's Register of Directors and Executives. A guide to directorates held by prominent financiers in the United States and in Canada.

Thomas' Register of American Manufacturers. Entered by products of state and city with names of manufacturers. Contains trade names, boards of trade. Annual.

American Medical Directory. Lists physicians in the United States and Canada, hospitals, medical societies, colleges giving degrees in medicine, etc.

Martindale-Hubbell Law Directory. Lists members of the bar of the United States and Canada with law digests.

Rand McNally International Bankers Directory. Facts and statistics on individual banks of the world.

American Foundations for Social Welfare. A directory of approximately five hundred foundations.

American Foundations and Their Fields. Foundations listed under each state, with appendices showing samples of legal documents used by foundations, and indexes by field and by foundation names.

HOTELS

Official Hotel Red Book and Directory. A list of hotels. Published annually by the American Hotel Association Directory Corporation for the American Hotel Association of the United States and Canada.

YEARBOOKS

Canada Year Book. Official information on Canada's social, industrial and economic development.

Information Please Almanac, edited by Dan Golenpaul Associates. Statistics on sports, literature, theater, education, government, etc.

New International Year Book; a compendium of the year's progress in scientific, educational, cultural and political fields.

Statesman's Year-Book (published in England). Concise and authoritative information about the governments of the world. Information given about the ruler, constitution, government, population, religion, finance, industry, commerce, money and credit, diplomatic representatives, etc.

Whitaker's Almanack. Statistical information relating to Great Britain particularly.

World Almanac and Book of Facts. A comprehensive American almanac. Contains statistics of industry, politics, governments, finance, religion, education, etc.

FINANCIAL SERVICES

Dun and Bradstreet, Inc. Reports on financial standing of individuals and companies. Available to subscribers only.

The following groups offer basic and current information on corporations, stocks, and bonds: Fitch Publishing Company, Moody's Investors Service, Standard and Poor's Corporation.

GUIDES AND INDEXES TO BOOKS AND PERIODICALS

Ayer & Son's Directory of Newspapers and Periodicals. Alphabetical by state and city. Annual.

Cumulative Book Index. A cumulative index issued monthly except August, containing names of all publications of the year in English and forming a supplement to the *United States Catalog.*

Industrial Arts Index. An index to a selected list of engineering and trade journals.

New York Times Index. An index appearing monthly of references to articles and names appearing in *The New York Times,* with date, page number, and column.

Public Affairs Information Service. The combination of a subject index to the current literature in its field: books, documents, pamphlets, articles in periodicals, multigraphed material, etc., and a digest of recent events and developments in the fields of sociology, political science, and economics, particularly the practical side of these subjects.

Publishers' Weekly. American book-trade journal containing lists of books announced for publication and the new publications for the week.

Readers' Guide to Periodical Literature. An index to cultural and scientific articles found in a selected list of periodicals.

Ulrich's Periodicals Directory: A Classified Guide to a Selected List of Current Periodicals, Foreign and Domestic. Edited by E. C. Graves.

United States Catalog. An index of all books in print in the United States in 1928, with author's name, short title, edition, date, publisher, price, and paging.

SYNONYMS AND ANTONYMS

Allen, F. Sturges. *Allen's Synonyms and Antonyms.*

Crabb, George. *Crabb's English Synonyms.*

Fernald, James Champlin. *Funk & Wagnalls Standard Handbook of Synonyms, Antonyms and Prepositions.* Completely rev. ed.

Roget, Peter Mark. *Thesaurus of English Words and Phrases.* Arranged according to ideas rather than by alphabet. Helpful in finding exact words or expression for a given idea, together with idiomatic combinations peculiar to it.

Webster's Dictionary of Synonyms.

Style Books

Ives, George B. *Text, Type and Style: A Compendium of Atlantic Usage.*
U.S. Government Printing Office. *Manual of Foreign Languages for the Use of Printers and Translators.*
U.S. Government Printing Office Style Manual.
University of Chicago Press. *A Manual of Style.*

Transportation Guides

Official Airline Guide. Timetables for the airlines.
Official Guide of the Railways and Steam Navigation Lines of the United States, Puerto Rico, Canada, Mexico, and Cuba; also timetables of railroads in Central America and air-line schedules. National Railway Publication Company. Issued monthly.
Russell's Official National Motor Coach Guide. Bus schedules for the United States.

Postal Guides

Bullinger's Postal and Shippers Guide. Comprehensive guide for the United States and Canada, listing post offices, railroad stations, and steamer landings; domestic and foreign postage and parcel post rates.
Canada. Post Office Department. *Canadian Official Postal Guide.* Alphabetical list of post offices in Canada with postage rates.
U.S. Post Office Department. *Directory of Post Offices.* Issued in loose-leaf binder with monthly supplements. Lists post offices by state, with branch offices and stations. This replaces Part I of the former *United States Official Postal Guide.*

Atlases and Gazetteers

Columbia Lippincott Gazetteer of the World.
Encyclopædia Britannica Atlas.
The Macmillan World Gazetteer and Geographical Dictionary.
Rand McNally Commercial Atlas and Marketing Guide.
Rand McNally Cosmopolitan World Atlas.
Webster's Geographical Dictionary.

GOVERNMENT PUBLICATIONS

U.S. Bureau of Foreign and Domestic Commerce. *Statistical Abstract of the United States.* An annual publication giving statistics about commerce, manufactures, mining, population, agriculture, etc.

United States Government Manual. A useful outline of the functions of the various bureaus and agencies of the Federal Government.

ETIQUETTE

Post, Emily Price. *Etiquette—The Blue Book of Social Usage.*
Vanderbilt, Amy. *Complete Book of Etiquette.*

LAW AND TECHNICAL SUBJECTS

Ballentine, James Arthur. *Law Dictionary with Pronunciation.* Lawyers Co-operative Publishing Company.

Black, Henry Campbell. *Law Dictionary.* West Publishing Company.

Crispin, Frederic S. *Dictionary of Technical Terms.* Terms used in architecture, building, electrical, and metal working trades, chemistry, etc. 8th ed. rev. Bruce Publishing Company.

QUOTATIONS

Bartlett, John. *Familiar Quotations.* Arranged by authors chronologically.

Stevenson, Burton Egbert. *The Home Book of Quotations, Classical and Modern.* Arranged alphabetically by subject.

BROADCASTING, TELEVISION, MOTION PICTURES

Broadcasting Yearbook. Washington, D.C. Broadcasting Publications, Inc. Supplement to *Broadcasting Telecasting* magazine.

International Motion Picture Almanac. New York, Quigley Publishing Company.

International Television Almanac. New York, Quigley Publishing Company.

Telecasting Yearbook. Washington, D.C. Broadcasting Publications, Inc. Supplement to *Broadcasting Telecasting* magazine.

17. Citations

Citations made by Columbia University in conferring honorary degrees:

John St. Loe Strachey—

Trained, broadened and deepened at Balliol College under the guidance of the powerful personality of Benjamin Jowett; scholar, historian, man of letters and journalist; conducting for a full generation, under the shadow of the names of Addison and Steele, the most noteworthy journal of opinion in the English-speaking world; careful and sympathetic student of American history, institutions and life; and interpreter of them with insight and understanding to all who use the speech of Shakespeare and Milton, of Franklin and Lincoln, I gladly admit you to the degree of Doctor of Letters in this University and confer upon you all the rights and privileges which belong thereto. In token whereof I hand you this diploma.

Alfred Emanuel Smith—

Born on Manhattan Island and trained in the hard school of its many-sided cosmopolitan life; since manhood a constant and eager public servant in posts of steadily growing importance and authority; sometime Speaker of the Assembly, member of the Constitutional Convention of 1915, three times chosen by the people of a truly imperial State to be their Governor; alert, effective, public-spirited and courageous, constantly speaking the true voice of the people; on this one hundredth anniversary of the Commencement at which your great predecessor, DeWitt Clinton, received like honor, I gladly admit you to the degree of Doctor of Laws in this University, and confer upon you all the rights and privileges which belong thereto. In token whereof I hand you this diploma.

The Rt. Hon. and Rt. Rev. Arthur Foley Winnington-Ingram—

Lord Bishop of London, Dean of the Chapels Royal, and Prelate of the Order of the British Empire; fortunately trained, with high honors, at Marlborough College and at Keble College, Oxford; passing steadily and quickly from one post to another of ecclesiastical usefulness, in-

494

fluence and distinctions; now administering the vast work of the
Church of England in the capital city of the British Commonwealth of
Nations; eager in service, constant in labor, guided always and everywhere by deep insight into human nature and keen sympathy with the
inspiration and activities of youth, I gladly admit you to the degree of
Doctor of Sacred Theology in this University, and confer upon you
all the rights and privileges which belong thereto. In token whereof I
hand you this diploma.

John Bassett Moore—

Native of Delaware, graduated at the University of Virginia with
the Class of 1880; quickly entering the public service in the Department of State and serving there until appointed Hamilton Fish Professor
of International Law and Diplomacy in 1891; called from time to time
by the Government to serve either in high and responsible office in
the Department of State or as special envoy or as delegate to numerous international conferences; signally honored in many lands; first of
living authorities on international law and procedure; profound in
scholarship and unwearied in industry; member of the Permanent
Court of Arbitration at the Hague since 1913 and Judge of the Permanent Court of International Justice since 1921, I gladly admit you
to the degree of Doctor of Laws in this University and confer upon
you all the rights and privileges which belong thereto. In token whereof
I hand you this diploma.

Reprinted by permission.

A citation made by President Thomas of Rutgers University in
conferring the degree of LL.D. upon Dr. James C. Egbert.

James Chidester Egbert,

Alumnus and Doctor of Philosophy of Columbia University; distinguished scholar and teacher in the field of Roman Archæology and
sometime President of the Archæological Institute of America;
    builder of the outstanding Summer Session of American Universities;
    director of the world's greatest enterprise in adult education, through
whose leadership the privileges of learning have been extended to many
thousands whose educational needs and possibilities had been unnoticed, whereby the institutions of higher learning in America have
been brought to a new and inspiring realization of their responsibilities
in a democracy;
    Rutgers University, Columbia's next of kin, confers upon you the
degree of Doctor of Laws.

Reprinted by permission.

Citation made by President Clothier of Rutgers University in conferring the degree of LL.D. upon Franklin D. Roosevelt.

FRANKLIN DELANO ROOSEVELT:

First citizen of this Commonwealth, one who has dedicated his life to the service of his countrymen;

Politician whose conception of public life is that of lofty public service;

Statesman who has proved that friendship and candor are more effective in international diplomacy than subtlety and strategy;

You have been called to the Presidency of this nation in order that by courage and imagination and initiative, you might lead your fellow countrymen out of the shadows which have encompassed them into the light of a new and better day.

We welcome you to the fellowship of the Dutch tradition in which this University was founded. In testimony of that fellowship and in evidence of the admiration and confidence in which the nation holds you, I confer upon you the degree, honoris causa, of DOCTOR OF LAWS.

Reprinted by permission.

Honorary degree of LL.D. conferred upon Herbert Hoover by Princeton University. The following citation was made by Dean West in introducing Mr. Hoover.

HERBERT CLARK HOOVER, geologist and engineer, student and writer on mining; developer and director of large enterprises in Australia, China, Burma and Siberia, our first authority on the history and economics of mining; at the outbreak of the war relieving the stranded hordes of Americans in London with swift succor; then head of the Commission for Relief of Belgium and there fighting a hard fight to shelter the homeless, to cover the naked and "to deal bread to the hungry"; chief master of the problem of producing, dividing and using our national food supply to feed all who need it; a true son of the people, a youth in heart, a giant in vast achievement; swift, sleepless and resistless, bending all to one great purpose—to save and not to destroy.

Reprinted by permission.

Citation made by President Lemuel H. Murlin of Boston University, in conferring the degree of LL.D. on behalf of the Trustees on Mrs. Calvin Coolidge:

Student, university graduate, teacher; daughter, wife, mother; in every station exemplifying the finer qualities of mind and heart we most admire in women; your own works praise you; you have gained the confidence, admiration and love of the American people. Upon the recommendation of the University Council, I have been authorized by the Board of Trustees of Boston University to admit you to the degree of Doctor of Laws.

Reprinted by permission.

Citations made by President Daniel L. Marsh of Boston University.

CLARENCE WALKER BARON, editor, publisher, spokesman of industrial America to the investing public of the United States, promulgator of the doctrine that the laws of happiness are the laws of service, by the authority vested in me, I admit you to the degree of Doctor of Commercial Science of Boston University and to all the rights, privileges and distinction belonging thereto, and in testimony thereof I present to you this diploma bearing the seal of the University and the inscriptions of its proper officers.

HAMILTON HOLT, President of Rollins College, educator, publicist, constructive advocate of international good-will and world-peace, foe of war and by the same token friend of humanity, by the authority vested in me, I admit you to the degree of Doctor of Humanities of Boston University and to all the rights, privileges and distinction belonging thereto, and in testimony thereof I present to you this diploma bearing the seal of the University and the inscriptions of its proper officers.

Reprinted by permission.

Citations made by Princeton University in conferring honorary degrees:

Bernard Mannes Baruch—

For over thirty years he has devoted himself without stint to public service, first as the friend and adviser of President Woodrow Wilson and thereafter through successive administrations, serving with distinction both here and abroad in many and diverse fields and an amazing variety of undertakings. He has brought to these important undertakings a keen and well-trained mind, a wide knowledge of men and affairs, a passion for facts as the only sound basis for decisions, and the courage to make and uphold those decisions. In brief, a wise counselor and patriotic American citizen who has given expression to his love of country by continued and devoted labors in the nation's service.

Frank Diehl Fackenthal—

Educator and skilled administrator, who has dedicated his life with singleness of purpose and rare devotion to the welfare of his famous alma mater. Becoming provost in 1937, he served as the trusted and able lieutenant of his illustrious predecessor, and with self-effacing efficiency conducted the day-to-day operations of that far-flung organization with smoothness and ease of execution. Upon the retirement of Dr. [Nicholas Murray] Butler, he became acting president, without disruption or dissent, without commotion or loss of motion, and with the complete confidence and friendly support of trustees, faculty and undergraduates. Such a result could only have been achieved through qualities of fairness, modesty, thoughtful consideration, courage and best type of constructive leadership. In his own quiet way he has made an outstanding contribution, not only to Columbia, but to American education.

Thomas Stearns Eliot—

Critic and poet of distinction, whose work has affected the course of literature and exerted a strong influence upon all contemporary writing. As a critic he has made possible by his perceptions a new and more coordinated view of the whole of literature. As a poet he has widened the scope of the art to include the everyday life of the average man. Keenly aware of the trends of the time, he has become the literary conscience of an era.

Charles Franklin Kettering—

Engineer, inventive genius extraordinary, possessed of a restless curiosity combined with a driving persistency which never admits the possibility of defeat, he, with the aid of his associates, has provided an incredible succession of creative achievements which contributed to the comfort and well-being of millions and heightened the joy of their living. His active mind, with its passion for productive research tempered by canny common sense, penetrates widely varied fields of human interest and leaves each the richer for its presence.

Chester William Nimitz—

An admiral in the best tradition of the United States Navy. Called to the command of the Pacific Fleet in its darkest hour after the disaster at Pearl Harbor, this son of Texas took up his difficult task with quiet and assured determination. Reconstructing his shattered command with amazing results, he turned at the first possible moment from defensive to offensive warfare and by daring leadership and brilliant strategy achieved a succession of victories which culminated in one of the greatest triumphs in naval history. In this accomplishment his personal qualities played an important part. Modest, resolute and wise, firm but human, his faith in his officers and men was reflected in their confidence and enthusiastic loyalty to him. His decisions were dictated by unerring judgment and a sturdy common sense which won whole-hearted support and were executed with skill and vigor. Today in well-merited recognition of his achievements, he is commanding our Navy in its adjustments to new responsibilities in a troubled world.

Citation made by President Meader of Russell Sage College in conferring the degree of Doctor of Humane Letters upon Mrs. Franklin Roosevelt, 1929.

Anna Eleanor Roosevelt

Anna Eleanor Roosevelt, native of the State of New York, niece of the twenty-sixth President of the United States of America; teacher, educational administrator, director of industry; guiding spirit of many civic and legislative organizations, active associate in many public and private philanthropic movements; First Lady of the Empire State, Russell Sage College considers you one of the ablest, most energetic and most versatile women in public life today. One of the purposes of this College is to send out into the world women who have the desire and the ability to produce something which society needs, to carry on some constructive, up-building activity, to participate creatively in the work of the world. Our College aims not at leisure but leadership, and stresses the importance of dedicating one's self to service in the interests of one's home, one's community, one's state and one's nation. We have chosen to honor you today because we feel that you exemplify with distinction these ideals for which our College stands. As the wife of our Governor, as the mother of four sons and one daughter, as a teacher of youth and as an enthusiastic and capable worker in the interests of the general welfare of this Commonwealth, we feel that you are participating creatively in the work of the world, and that you are producing many things for which society in this present-day world of ours has great need.

By the authority vested in me as President of Russell Sage College, I now admit you to the degree of Doctor of Humane Letters, in token of which I present you with this diploma, cause the appropriate hood to be placed upon your shoulders, and request that your name be inscribed upon the list of honorable alumnae of the College.

Reprinted by permission.

Citations for honorary degrees made at Yale University.

Robert Moses, M.A.

Professor Phelps:

Born in New Haven but moved to New York at the age of nine. When sixteen years old, he illustrated the return of the native by entering Yale College, taking his B.A. in 1909, a member of Phi Beta Kappa. Then he studied at Oxford, achieving amphibious renown, being the first American to become President of the Oxford Union while also Captain of the swimming and water-polo teams. In 1911 he took his B.A. at Oxford, and in 1913 M.A. at Oxford, and Ph.D. at Columbia, in 1914.

His career has been devoted to the public welfare, unselfishness matched with efficiency. He began as Chief of Staff of the New York Reconstruction Commission, was Adviser to Governor Smith in extending the activities of the State Government for the benefit of the people. In 1922 he planned and was solely responsible for the creation of the State Council of Parks; in 1924 he was appointed by Governor Smith President of the Long Island State Park Commission and was elected Chairman of the State Council of Parks and still holds both these offices.

In 1927 he became Secretary of State in New York. In 1929 appointed by Lieut. Governor Lehman Commissioner to investigate the banking department of the State of New York. Then came a succession of appointments to important positions, every one of which he adorned. In 1934 he was appointed by Mayor LaGuardia Commissioner of Parks. He has reorganized the whole Park System. Instead of leading the people into or through the wilderness, Mr. Moses has changed the wilderness into a park; the desert blossoms like the rose; and we can say in the words of Pope,

'Pan to Moses lends his pagan horn.'

For Mr. Moses combines the love of battle with the love of beauty. Everything he has done he has done well.

He might now be Governor of New York if he were not a Republican. It is certain that some day the people will say, 'Friend, go up higher.'

President Angell:

With clear vision, indomitable courage and single-minded purpose you have devotedly given your remarkable powers to promoting the enduring interests of your State and City. Your Alma Mater is proud to have had some part in training you for these outstanding public services and in recognition thereof gladly confers upon you the degree of Master of Arts, admitting you to all its rights and privileges.

William McFee, M.A.

Professor Phelps:

Born an Englishman, now an American citizen, and a resident of Connecticut. Engineer, sailor, novelist, critic. Seven cities claimed to be the birthplace of Homer, but there are only two places that have put in a claim for this man. One of them is the largest city in the world and the other is the ocean; according to the best authority, his mother, he was born at sea on the three-masted square-rigger *Erin's Isle,* June 15, 1881. His father was designer, builder, owner, and master of the ship. Five uncles were sea-captains.

His childhood was spent near London, and later he went to a public school at Bury St. Edmunds. He was apprenticed to an engineering firm, and spent his spare time reading good literature, and began at an early age to collect books. During the war he was a lieutenant in the British Navy; after the war he was Chief Engineer of the vessels of the United Fruit Co., plying between New York and the Spanish Main. This temperamental officer had charge of what has been called the most temperamental of fruits; he had to control the engines, the crew, and the bananas; one of his biographers says he had such problems as keeping bananas at an even temperature of 54 degrees, whether in tropical or in below-zero weather, yet he managed to do a vast amount of reading and writing. On one voyage he read Sallust, Livy, Gibbon, Horace, Shakespeare, Balzac, Tolstoi, Whitman, Goethe and Emerson.

He has taken the highest possible position concerning the responsibility of ship's officers for the safety of passengers at sea; here he is as uncompromising as he is in literary standards; for he has in mind the sanctity of human life and the austere law of the sea.

Mr. McFee has written verse, novels, essays, and is an honest, discerning and fearless literary critic.

One of the privileges of a great university is to recognize officially not merely research scholarship but creative writers and artists.

President Angell:

Distinguished and versatile man of letters, poet, novelist, essayist and critic, creator of authentic and absorbing portraits of sailors and their ships, able and ardent advocate of better laws more honestly administered to safeguard life at sea, Yale University is proud to count you among her sons and confers upon you the degree of Master of Arts, admitting you to all its rights and privileges.

James Francis Byrnes—

Grateful for your conduct of the foreign affairs of the nation and for your capacity to unify public opinion in a critical period that called for strength of leadership as well as diplomatic skill, Yale University confers upon you the degree of Doctor of Laws.

John Hersey—

Appreciative of the quality of your service, combining the finest of literary skill with the keenest understanding of human beings as they contend with catastrophe, your alma mater proudly confers upon you the degree of Master of Arts.

Citations made by the University of Buffalo in conferring honorary degrees:

Robert Houghwout Jackson—

Interpreter of the law and through the law of man's dignity and his moral aspirations; member of the nation's highest tribunal; authentic spokesman of America's unchanging principles and noblest purposes; the University of Buffalo confers upon you the degree of Doctor of Laws.

Vannevar Bush—

Physicist, engineer and administrator, imaginative mobilizer of the nation's scientific forces for the creation of new weapons of offense and defense in the hour of America's greatest need, civilian architect of victory, the University of Buffalo confers upon you the degree of Doctor of Laws.

Mildred McAfee Horton—

Social scientist and administrator; president of one of the nation's most famous colleges for women; organizer and wartime commander of the Women's Reserve of the United States Navy; in recognition of your eminent contributions both to education and to America's military achievement, the University of Buffalo confers upon you the degree of Doctor of Laws.

Citations made by the University of Wisconsin in conferring honorary degrees:

John Hasbrouck Van Vleck—

Born to a great tradition of outstanding scholarship; indefatigable worker in widening the boundaries of human knowledge and its applications to human problems; renowned authority in the field of mathematical physics recognized at home and abroad; the University of Wisconsin is confident you will add to the luster of your scientific achievements in the quarter-century of active service still ahead, and is happy to confer upon you today the honorary degree, Doctor of Science.

George Ives Haight—

Distinguished son of Wisconsin and alumnus of this University, whom we are glad to welcome back today to scenes long since built into many happy memories; illustrious member of the legal profession, who has brought the wealth of his abilities and experience to the service of his clients, both private and public; loyal alumnus whose helpful counsel is always welcome and whose generous cooperation is most inspiring; the University of Wisconsin has both pride and pleasure in conferring upon you today the degree of Doctor of Laws.

The citation of General Dwight D. Eisenhower that accompanied the Gold Medal of Achievement presented by the Poor Richard Club.

To an American possessed of a rare combination of talents who has risen by his own efforts to a place of great eminence; who in serving his country in armed conflict proved himself a far-sighted planner, a superb tactician and a courageous and inspiring leader; who in his outstanding contribution to the winning of World War II won also the confidence, respect and admiration of millions of fighting men and freedom-loving people everywhere.—

To the Supreme Commander of the Allied Expeditionary Force and General of the Army whose brilliant record fills his fellow citizens with pride, and whose modest bearing and generous sharing of his honors assure him a warm place in their hearts—

To General Dwight D. Eisenhower, affectionately known to all who served in the ranks under his skilled direction as "General Ike"—

The Poor Richard Club of Philadelphia, in the name of Benjamin Franklin, Scientist, Philosopher, Statesman and Patriot, herewith presents a token of its esteem reserved for the most deserving of contemporary American citizens, the Gold Medal of Achievement.

In testimony whereof, the Poor Richard Club of Philadelphia has hereunto affixed its corporate seal.

Harry L. Hawkins, president; James J. D. Spillan, first vice president; Harold S. LeDuc, second vice president; Andrew C. Kunkel, secretary; Robert P. Lukens, treasurer.

Citations made by Hermann Hagedorn for the Roosevelt Memorial Association in conferring the Roosevelt Medal for Distinguished Service.

(1)

For the medal for distinguished service in the administration of public office and in the development of public and international law,

I have the honor, Mr. President, to present the name of one who has served the nation in many capacities, and always served her well; a public investigator, clear-minded and relentless, a governor, upright and brave; a brilliant judge; an advocate, eloquent in defense and attack; a statesman in the field of foreign affairs who has won the admiration of the world by his resourcefulness, his courage, his intellectual power, the nobility of his vision, the determination and the enthusiasm of his pursuit. His country is richer by his life and a world-peace is nearer because of his labors.

Charles Evans Hughes

(2)

For the medal for distinguished service in the promotion of the study of natural history, Mr. President, I have the honor to present a name which is beloved wherever in America, in school or home, the birds are permitted to come down from the treetops to be the companions of men; a writer and lecturer of persuasive charm, who has taught a nation to see, to know, to love and to protect the entrancing and forever mysterious familiars of its daily life; a creative innovator in methods of exhibition and of ornithological research; a scientist, wise and unsatisfied, whose laboratory is a wilderness of Andean peaks, where fluttering wings betray to him things secret since the beginning of time—

Frank Chapman

Citation read by Miss Mary Vail Andress on the presentation by the American Woman's Association to Dean Virginia C. Gildersleeve of Barnard College of a gold medal awarded for outstanding achievement in her own field by a woman in the New York metropolitan area during the year 1936.

Virginia Crocheron Gildersleeve, Bachelor of Arts, Master of Arts, Doctor of Philosophy, Doctor of Literature, Doctor of Laws: It is my high privilege, in the name of the American Woman's Association Achievement Awards Committee, to present to you this medal as a recognition of the wise and generous use you have made of your eminent abilities.

We recognize you as a gifted scholar in varied fields of English and Latin literature, but we honor you still more for your vision which has broadened the scope of women's opportunities.

We recognize you as a thinker who moves eagerly in the higher reaches of the mind; a speaker of precision and charm, with a persuasiveness that results in action; a teacher who develops in her students the ardor of literary creation; an executive who achieves her goal through cooperative enthusiasm; but we honor you still more for the example you have set in the personal sense of responsibility in society.

With this medal we bestow upon you our affections and through it we express tangibly our pride in the high quality of citizenship which you so completely represent.

Citations made by the American Telephone and Telegraph Company in conferring the Theodore N. Vail Medal.

Fred F. Brown   Foreman
The Connecticut Valley Telephone   Bradford, Vermont

Citation

For courage, initiative and resourcefulness in restoring vital telephone service in a serious emergency, in the face of grave personal danger.

When the unprecedented rains in Northern Vermont in early November had turned the rivers into torrents of destruction which paralyzed activities in that section of the state, Foreman Brown and two fellow-employees set out on November 5 to clear at least one toll line into Montpelier, the capital city, which had been isolated.

After driving twenty miles over back roads and high ground, they found that the lines were crossed where the Wells River had washed out a pole and left the tie wires tangled in the toll circuits. The cross could not be shaken out and, although the river was a rushing torrent filled with logs, trees and other debris, and a fall would have meant almost certain death, Brown hooked his safety strap over the four wires and rode out on what was then a two hundred and sixty foot span, untangled the ties which caused the cross and, when one wire broke as he started back, rode the remaining three back to the pole in safety.

The circuit which he restored was immediately put in service for official use of the state authorities and was of vital importance in the organization of the relief work and in giving accurate news to the outside world.

Patrick B. McCormick   Agent
New England Telephone and   Becket, Mass.
Telegraph Company

Citation

For fortitude, initiative and devotion to public service despite grave personal danger.

Unprecedented rains in Western Massachusetts early in November had swelled the rivers and streams to torrents and it was feared that the dams in the vicinity of Becket would go out and cause great destruction. About four o'clock in the morning of November 4, when McCormick was notified that the nearest dam a mile above the town would doubtless fail, he notified every subscriber in the valley, warned them to leave, and asked them to notify those who had no telephones. He sent his own family to safety in the hills and, realizing that some of the residents would remain despite his earlier warning, stayed at the switchboard in his home, in constant telephone communication with people at the dam, to receive and transmit the final warning.

The dam went out at six o'clock, and after notifying all who had remained, he started warning all the towns in the path of the danger. This task completed, his escape was cut off and he was forced to remain, while houses and trees were torn up and carried past, and his own home was flooded and the switchboard put out of order.

As soon as the water began to recede he climbed a pole, cut in on the toll line with his test set, and gave to the outside world the first call for relief.

Reprinted by permission.

Citation by Boston University

Nathan Marsh Pusey, president of Harvard University . . . LL.D

You have an abiding faith in the life of the mind. You possess the courage to state your convictions. You reveal a vital concern for the effectiveness of religion in these confusing days.

Citation by Columbia University

Senator H. Alexander Smith . . . LL.D

A lawyer, a man of the people, a master of the science of politics and government, his varied career has found him always busy, ever generous, constructive in works and in philosophy, never dismayed by foreboding events.

Citation by New York University

Jonas Edward Salk . . . Sc.D

Discoverer of the vaccine for the prevention of poliomyelitis, that scourge which has caused dread in the hearts of every family, not only in America, but throughout the world; his is the name that will go down in history and will be spoken amongst men in words of wonder and gratitude.

Citation by Rollins College

Charles DuBois Hurrey—

Charles DuBois Hurrey, ambassador of good will to many nations on three continents, you have won the affection and admiration of all the Rollins family who have been privileged to know you. A public speaker of great fluency, you have for many years made a lasting impression, particularly upon the youth in the educational institutions of many lands.

Many of your students have risen to places of power and responsibility, one to become President of the General Assembly of the United Nations. Through them your influence for friendly relations and international good will has been multiplied.

Your talents have been freely given to many good causes. Here at Rollins for several years you have worked diligently with the Inter-American Department, advising, encouraging and inspiring our students from the other American Republics.

But it is not for your achievements, great as they are, that we are today bestowing upon you the Algernon Sydney Sullivan Award. It is rather in the words of the donors, "for those enduring qualities of mind and spirit; reverence, human understanding, good will, courage and unselfish devotion to others." These you have exemplified in large measure. A modest demeanor and a gracious personality are but the setting in which these gems of the spirit shine forth.

18. Inscriptions

On the Post Office at Washington, D.C.

Carrier of news and knowledge, instrument of trade and industry, promoter of mutual acquaintance, of peace and goodwill among men and nations.

Messenger of sympathy and love, servant of parted friends, consoler of the lonely, bond of the scattered family, enlarger of common life.

On the Post Office, Eighth Avenue and Thirty-third Street, New York City.

Neither snow nor rain nor heat nor gloom of night stays these couriers from the swift completion of their appointed rounds.

On the Union Station, Washington, D.C.

He that would bring home the wealth of the Indies must carry the wealth of the Indies with him. So it is in travelling—a man must carry knowledge with him if he would bring home knowledge.

A frieze of inscriptions in the Detroit Public Library.

Books are the most enduring monuments of man's achievement. Through them, civilization becomes cumulative.

Read not to contradict and confute, nor to believe and take for granted, but to weigh and consider.

Through seas of knowledge we our course advance, discovering still new worlds of ignorance.

To promote self-development by ample facilities for wide reading in an atmosphere of freedom and morality.

Inscriptions at the north and south ends of Detroit Public Library, respectively.

Consider what nation it is whereof ye are; a nation not slow and dull, but of a quick, ingenious and piercing spirit, acute to invent, subtle and sinuous to discourse, not beyond the reach of any point the highest that human capacity can soar to.

Reading, trying all things, assenting to the force of reason and convincement; what wants there to such towardly and pregnant soil, but wise and faithful laborers to make a knowing people, a nation of prophets, of sages, and of worthies.

Inscription on No. 1 Broadway, New York City.

ADJOINING THIS SITE WAS THE FIRST DUTCH FORT ON MANHATTAN ISLAND KNOWN AS FORT NEW AMSTERDAM. THE FIRST HOUSE WAS ERECTED HERE BEFORE 1664. IN 1771 CAPTAIN ARCHIBALD KENNEDY BUILT HERE HIS RESIDENCE WHICH WAS USED IN 1776 BY GENERAL WASHINGTON AS HIS HEADQUARTERS AND LATER BY GENERAL HOWE DURING THE BRITISH OCCUPATION. IT WAS LATER USED AS A HOTEL. TORN DOWN IN 1882, IT WAS REPLACED BY THE WASHINGTON BUILDING WHICH WAS TRANSFORMED IN 1920–21 INTO THIS BUILDING FOR OCCUPANCY BY ITS OWNERS THE INTERNATIONAL MERCANTILE MARINE COMPANY AND KNOWN AS
NO. 1 BROADWAY

Inscription in a room entered through the east portal of the Amphitheater at Arlington near the tomb of the Unknown Soldier. Taken from the oration of President Harding delivered at the dedication.

THE NAME OF HIM WHOSE BODY LIES HERE TOOK FLIGHT WITH HIS IMPERISHABLE SOUL. WE KNOW NOT WHENCE HE CAME, BUT ONLY THAT HIS DEATH MARKS HIM WITH THE EVERLASTING GLORY OF AN AMERICAN WHO DIED FOR HIS COUNTRY. WE DO NOT KNOW THE EMINENCE OF HIS BIRTH, BUT WE DO KNOW THE GLORY OF HIS DEATH. HE DIED FOR HIS COUNTRY, AND GREATER DEVOTION HATH NO MAN THAN THIS. HE DIED UNQUESTIONING, UNCOMPLAINING WITH FAITH IN HIS HEART AND HOPE ON HIS LIPS THAT HIS COUNTRY SHOULD TRIUMPH AND ITS CIVILIZATION SURVIVE.

Inscription on tomb of Unknown Soldier in Westminster Abbey, London.

Beneath this stone rests the body of a British Warrior
Unknown by name or rank
Brought from France to lie among
The most illustrious of the land
And buried here on Armistice Day
November 11th, 1920, in the presence of
His Majesty, King George V,
Ministers of State,
The chiefs of the forces,
And a vast number of the nation.
Thus are commemorated the many
Multitudes who during the Great War
of 1914–1918 gave the most that
Man can give, life itself,
For God
For King and country,
To loved ones, home, and empire,
To the sacred cause of justice, and
The freedom of the world.
They buried him among the kings
Because he had done good toward God
And toward His house.

Inscription within Lincoln Memorial, Washington.

IN THIS TEMPLE
AS IN THE HEARTS OF THE PEOPLE
FOR WHOM HE SAVED THE UNION
THE MEMORY OF ABRAHAM LINCOLN
IS ENSHRINED FOREVER

Panels in the Northeast Pavilion of the Library of Congress contain the following inscriptions:

On Treasury and State Seals

'TIS OUR TRUE POLICY TO STEER CLEAR OF PERMANENT ALLIANCES WITH ANY PORTIONS OF THE FOREIGN WORLD.

—Washington

LET OUR OBJECT BE OUR COUNTRY, OUR WHOLE COUNTRY, AND NOTHING BUT OUR COUNTRY.

—Webster

On War and Navy Seals

THE GREATEST HAPPINESS OF SOCIETY IS, OR OUGHT TO BE, THE END OF ALL GOVERNMENT.
TO BE PREPARED FOR WAR IS ONE OF THE MOST EFFECTUAL MEANS OF PRESERVING PEACE.

—Washington

On Agriculture and Interior Seals

THE AGRICULTURAL INTEREST OF THE COUNTRY IS CONNECTED WITH EVERY OTHER, AND SUPERIOR IN IMPORTANCE TO THEM ALL.

—Jackson

LET US HAVE PEACE.*—Grant*

On Justice and Post Office Seals

EQUAL AND EXACT JUSTICE TO ALL MEN, OF WHAT-EVER STATE OR PERSUASION, RELIGIOUS, OR POLITICAL; PEACE, COMMERCE, AND HONEST FRIENDSHIP WITH ALL NATIONS, ENTANGLING ALLIANCES WITH NONE.

—Jefferson

Inscription in the ceiling encircling the Great Seal of the United States.

THAT THIS NATION, UNDER GOD, SHALL HAVE A NEW BIRTH OF FREEDOM, AND THAT GOVERNMENT OF THE PEOPLE, BY THE PEOPLE, FOR THE PEOPLE, SHALL NOT PERISH FROM THE EARTH.

—Lincoln

Inscriptions encircling the dome in the National Academy of Sciences, Washington.

AGES AND CYCLES OF NATURE
IN CEASELESS SEQUENCES MOVING
TO SCIENCE, PILOT OF INDUSTRY, CONQUEROR OF DISEASE, MULTIPLIER OF THE HARVEST, EXPLORER OF THE UNIVERSE, REVEALER OF GOD'S LAWS, ETERNAL GUIDE TO TRUTH.

Inscriptions in the Reading Room of the Library of Congress.

Religion

WHAT DOTH THE LORD REQUIRE OF THEE, BUT TO DO JUSTLY, TO LOVE MERCY, AND TO WALK HUMBLY WITH THY GOD?—*Micah* VI:8.

Commerce

WE TAKE THE SPICES OF ARABIA, YET NEVER FEEL THE SCORCHING SUN, WHICH BRINGS THEM FORTH. *Considerations on East India Trade.*

History

ONE GOD, ONE LAW, ONE ELEMENT,
AND ONE FAR-OFF DIVINE EVENT,
TO WHICH THE WHOLE CREATION MOVES.
　　　　　　　　　　—Tennyson

Art

AS ONE LAMP LIGHTS ANOTHER, NOR GROWS LESS, SO NOBLENESS ENKINDLETH NOBLENESS.
　　　　　　　　　　—Lowell

Philosophy

THE INQUIRY, KNOWLEDGE AND BELIEF OF TRUTH IS THE SOVEREIGN GOOD OF HUMAN NATURE.
　　　　　　　　　　—Bacon

Poetry

HITHER, AS TO THEIR FOUNTAIN, OTHER STARS REPAIRING, IN THEIR GOLDEN URNS, DRAW LIGHT
　　　　　　　　　　—Milton

Law

OF LAW THERE CAN BE NO LESS ACKNOWLEDGED THAN THAT HER VOICE IS THE HARMONY OF THE WORLD.
　　　　　　　　　　—Hooker

Science

THE HEAVENS DECLARE THE GLORY OF GOD AND THE FIRMAMENT SHOWETH HIS HANDIWORK.
　　　　　　　　　　—Psalms XIX

Inscriptions on the walls of the Union Station, Washington. Selected by President Eliot of Harvard University.

In the Waiting Room
WELCOME THE COMING
SPEED THE PARTING GUEST.

VIRTUE ALONE IS SWEET SOCIETY
IT KEEPS THE KEY TO ALL
HEROIC HEARTS AND OPENS YOU
A WELCOME IN THEM ALL

Over the State Entrance
LET ALL THINGS THOU AIMEST AT BE
THY COUNTRY'S—GOD'S AND TRUTH'S.

BE NOBLE AND THE NOBLENESS THAT
LIES IN OTHER MEN—SLEEPING, BUT
NEVER DEAD—WILL RISE IN MAJESTY TO
MEET THINE OWN.

Plaque accompanying the dedication of an organ

TO THE GLORY OF GOD IN GRATEFUL RECOGNITION OF MANY YEARS OF DEVOTED SERVICE, THIS ORGAN IS GIVEN TO CATHEDRAL SCHOOL IN HONOR OF EDITH ROBINSON MASSEY, PRINCIPAL EMERITUS, DEDICATED MAY 28, 1957.

Dedicatory Inscriptions for the Chimes of Bells in Mitchell Tower, University of Chicago, in Memory of Alice Freeman Palmer.

Bronze Tablet
JOYFULLY TO RECALL
ALICE FREEMAN PALMER
DEAN OF WOMEN IN THE UNIVERSITY
1892–1895
THESE BELLS MAKE MUSIC

Lines on Individual Bells
A GRACIOUS WOMAN RETAINING HONOR

.   .   .   .

EASY TO BE ENTREATED

.   .   .   .

ALWAYS REJOICING

MAKING THE LAME TO WALK AND THE BLIND TO SEE

GREAT IN COUNCIL AND MIGHTY IN WORK

ROOTED AND GROUNDED IN LOVE

FERVENT IN SPIRIT

GIVEN TO HOSPITALITY

THE SWEETNESS OF HER LIPS INCREASES LEARNING

IN GOD'S LAW MEDITATING DAY AND NIGHT

Inscription on the East Wall of the Reynolds Club Theater, University of Chicago.

MEN MUST KNOW THAT IN THIS THEATER OF MAN'S LIFE IT IS RESERVED FOR GOD AND ANGELS TO BE LOOKERS-ON.

Inscription on the West Wall of the Reynolds Club Theater.

THUS WE PLAY THE FOOLS WITH THE TIME AND THE SPIRITS OF THE WISE SIT IN THE CLOUDS AND MOCK US. GOD GAVE US WISDOM THAT HAVE IT; AND THOSE THAT ARE FOOLS, LET THEM USE THEIR TALENTS.

Inscription on Tablet to President Harper, University of Chicago.

TO HONOR THE MEMORY OF
WILLIAM RAINEY HARPER
FIRST PRESIDENT OF THE UNIVERSITY OF
CHICAGO
Born 1856   Died 1906
THIS BUILDING WAS ERECTED
BY GIFTS OF THE FOUNDER OF THE UNIVERSITY
MEMBERS OF THE BOARD OF TRUSTEES
AND FACULTIES

A Dedicatory Inscription on the Wall of the Frank Dickinson Bartlett Gymnasium, University of Chicago.

To
THE ADVANCEMENT
OF PHYSICAL EDUCATION
AND THE GLORY OF MANLY SPORTS
THIS GYMNASIUM IS DEDICATED
TO THE MEMORY OF
FRANK DICKINSON BARTLETT
A. D. 1880–1900

Inscriptions carved on exterior of Boston Public Library.

On the Dartmouth Street side
THE PUBLIC LIBRARY OF THE CITY OF BOSTON.
BUILT BY THE PEOPLE AND DEDICATED TO
THE ADVANCEMENT OF LEARNING
A. D. MDCCCLXXXVIII.

On the Boylston Street side
THE COMMONWEALTH REQUIRES THE EDUCATION OF
THE PEOPLE AS THE SAFEGUARD OF ORDER AND LIBERTY.

On the Blagden Street side
MDCCCLII. FOUNDED THROUGH THE MUNIFI-
CENCE AND PUBLIC SPIRIT OF CITIZENS

Inscription over the Dexter Memorial Gate, Harvard University.

ENTER TO GROW IN WISDOM
DEPART TO SERVE BETTER THY COUNTRY AND
THY KIND

Inscription on the Library of Columbia University.

KING'S COLLEGE FOUNDED IN THE PROVINCE OF NEW
YORK—BY ROYAL CHARTER IN THE REIGN OF GEORGE II
—PERPETUATED AS COLUMBIA COLLEGE BY THE PEOPLE
OF THE STATE OF NEW YORK—WHEN THEY BECAME FREE
AND INDEPENDENT—MAINTAINED AND CHERISHED
FROM GENERATION TO GENERATION—FOR THE AD-
VANCEMENT OF THE PUBLIC GOOD AND THE GLORY OF
ALMIGHTY GOD

Inscription at the entrance of Reading Room, New York Public Library.

A GOOD BOOK IS THE PRECIOUS LIFE-BLOOD OF A MASTER SPIRIT, IMBALM'D AND TREASUR'D UP ON PURPOSE TO A LIFE BEYOND LIFE.

Inscription on a Tablet to John Pierpont Morgan in the Metropolitan Museum of Art, New York.

ERECTED BY THE MUSEUM

IN GRATEFUL MEMORY OF

JOHN

PIERPONT

MORGAN

From 1871 to 1913

As Trustee, Benefactor and President

He · was · in · all · respects

A · great · citizen · · He

helped ·.to · make · New · York

The · True · Metropolis

of · America · · His · interest

In · art · was · lifelong

His · generous · devotion

To · it · commanded

Wide · appreciation

His · munificent · gifts · to

The · museum · are · among

Its · choicest · treasures

Vita · plena

laboris

M C M X X

Inscription on St. Louis Public Library.

SPEAK LOW, TREAD SOFTLY, THROUGH THESE HALLS:
HERE GENIUS LIES ENSHRINED;
HERE SLEEP IN SILENT MAJESTY
THE MONARCHS OF THE MIND.

Inscription on a Tablet of the Young Men's Christian Association Memorial Building, New York.

YOUNG MEN'S CHRISTIAN ASSOCIATION
OF THE
CITY OF NEW YORK
WILLIAM SLOANE MEMORIAL BUILDING
To Honor the Memory
of
WILLIAM SLOANE

and to be of service to young men, especially our soldiers and sailors to whom he gave his life in unselfish devotion.

Chairman, National War Work Council of the Young Men's Christian Associations from 1917 to 1921; Vice-Chairman International Committee from 1910 to 1919; Chairman Army and Navy Department of the International Committee from 1901 to 1917.

Born 1873   Died 1922

Inscription for the Walter Camp Memorial, Yale University.

GIVEN BY
AMERICAN COLLEGES
AND SCHOOLS
UNITED WITH GRADUATES OF YALE
TO HONOR
WALTER CAMP
AND THE TRADITIONS
OF
AMERICAN COLLEGE SPORTS
WHICH HE EXEMPLIFIED

19. Programs

Founders' Day Convocation

ROLLINS COLLEGE
FOUNDERS' DAY CONVOCATION
February 23, 19___

*

10:00 A.M.

KNOWLES MEMORIAL CHAPEL
President Hamilton Holt, *Presiding*

Processional: March of the Priests,
     from "Athalie" ....*Mendelssohn*
               Herman F. Siewert, *Organist*

Invocation — Dean Theodore Stanley Darrah

Rollins Chapel Song ....*Hamilton Holt*
               The Chapel Choir
          Christopher O. Honaas, *Choirmaster*

Address: The Nuremberg Principle — Thomas J. Dodd

Anthem: The Heavens Are Telling,
     from "The Creation" ....*Haydn*
               The Chapel Choir

Address: My Experiences in the Pacific War
                    General Jonathan Mayhew Wainwright

Conferring of Honorary Degrees by the President
    Public Orators: Arthur D. Enyart
                Donald A. Cheney
                Marian van B. Cleveland
                Wendell C. Stone
                Angela Palomo Campbell
                Nathan C. Starr

Awarding of the Algernon Sydney Sullivan Medallion
    Public Orator: Theodore S. Darrah

Alma Mater

Benediction — Dean Darrah

Recessional: March Pomposo ....*Kindler*

        The audience is asked to remain standing
        until the procession has left the Chapel

Inauguration of College President

PRESIDING

RAYMOND E. SALVATI

President of the Board of Governors

ORGAN PRELUDE

PROCESSIONAL

INVOCATION
REV. CHARLES W. SYDNOR,
Rector of St. Paul's Episcopal Church, Petersburg, Va.

ADDRESS
THE UNIVERSITY AND THE STATE
DR. JAMES BRYANT CONANT, *President of Harvard University*

INDUCTION OF THE PRESIDENT
RAYMOND E. SALVATI,
President of the Board of Governors

INAUGURAL ADDRESS
THE TASK OF THE UNIVERSITY
DR. IRVIN STEWART, *President of the University*

CONFERRING OF HONORARY DEGREES

BENEDICTION
REV. CHARLES W. SYDNOR

Reprinted by permission of West Virginia University, Morgantown.

Commencement and Graduation

(1)

ORGAN PRELUDE ....CHARLES E. BILLINGS, JR.
  "All Glory Be to God on High" ....*Johann Sebastian Bach*
  Prelude and Fugue in E Minor ....*Johann Sebastian Bach*
  Pastorale ....*Leo Sowerby*
  Symphonic Suite: "L'Ascension" ....*Olivier Messaien*
      I. The majesty of Christ praying for glory
     II. Prayer from Christ ascending toward his Father
  Toccata on an Easter Hymn Tune ....*Francis W. Snow*

ACADEMIC PROCESSION OF THE GRADUATES
  Marche Triomphale ....*Sigfried Karg-Elert*

ACADEMIC PROCESSION OF THE GUESTS OF HONOR, THE
  CORPORATION, THE CLASS OF 1897, THE CLASS OFFI-
  CERS OF 1922, AND THE FACULTY
  Processional March ....*John Weigand*

STAR-SPANGLED BANNER ....*Francis Scott Key*

INVOCATION
  DOCTOR SIDNEY LOVETT
  Chaplain of Yale University

ADDRESS
  THE HONORABLE WARREN ROBINSON AUSTIN
  United States Delegate to the United Nations General Assembly

ORGAN INTERLUDE
  Chorale from "A Modern Fantasia" ....*Henry Lasker*

PRESENTATION OF DEGREES AND ANNOUNCEMENTS OF
  HONORS
  DOCTOR KARL TAYLOR COMPTON
  President

ADDRESS TO THE GRADUATES
  DOCTOR KARL TAYLOR COMPTON

ACADEMIC PROCESSION OF THE ASSEMBLY
  Pomp and Circumstance ....*Sir Edward Elgar*

  Reprinted by permission of Massachusetts Institute of Technology, Cambridge, Mass.

(2)

Academic Procession—TRUMPET VOLUNTARY IN D ....*Purcell*

Invocation ....THE REVEREND THOMAS WALTON TALKINGTON
Hattiesburg, Mississippi

Commencement Address ....OLIVER CROMWELL CARMICHAEL
President, The Carnegie Foundation for the Advancement of Teaching

Address to Graduates and Conferring of Degrees
RUFUS CARROLLTON HARRIS
President of the University

Presentation of Candidates for Degrees, The College of
Engineering
James Marshall Robert, Dean

Presentation of Candidates for Degrees, The College of Law
Paul Brosman, Dean

Presentation of Candidates for Degrees, The School of Medicine
Maxwell Edward Lapham, Dean

Presentation of Candidates for Degrees, The School of Social Work
Elizabeth Wisner, Dean

Presentation of Candidates for Degrees, The Graduate School
Roger Philip McCutcheon, Dean

Presentation of Candidates for University Honors
Ernest Carroll Faust, Chairman, Committee on University Honors

Greetings from the Alumni Association ..AMBROSE HOWELL STORCK

Music—ALMA MATER ....*Williams and Ruebush*

Benediction ....THE REVEREND THOMAS WALTON TALKINGTON

Recessional—TRUMPET TUNE IN C ....*Purcell*
Wesley Day, Organist

Reprinted by permission of The Tulane University of Louisiana, New
Orleans.

(3)

The Academic Procession

Entrance March from Karelia ....*Sibelius*

Presiding
 PRESIDENT ROBERT ERNEST DOHERTY, B.S., M.S., LL.D.

Presentation of Colors

Star-Spangled Banner ....*Francis Scott Key*
  (The audience will remain standing until after the invocation)

Invocation
         THE REVEREND THOMAS F. COAKLEY, D.D.
              Rector of Sacred Heart Church

Two Russian Nocturnes ....*Nikolai Lopatnikoff*
              ORCHESTRA, DEPARTMENT OF MUSIC
              FREDERICK DORIAN, PH.D., *Conductor*

Presentation by Howard N. Eavenson, President, Bituminous Coal
  Research, Inc., in behalf of Bituminous Coal Institute of Washington, D.C.

Prelude to Die Meistersinger ....*Richard Wagner*
              ORCHESTRA, DEPARTMENT OF MUSIC

Announcements

Conferring of Degrees
    (The audience will refrain from applause until entire class
                  has received diplomas.)

America ....*Samuel Francis Smith*

Retiring of Colors

Recessional
       Triumphal March from Sigurd Jorsalfar ....*Edvard Grieg*

Reprinted by permission of Carnegie Institute of Technology, Pittsburgh.

(4)

PROGRAM

10:45 A. M.

ORGAN PRELUDE
   Grand Chorus ....*Dubois*
   Valse, Opus 18 ....*Chopin*
   La Fille aux Cheveux de Lin ....*Debussy*
                    Walter Kenneth Sprague '47

11:00 A. M.

ACADEMIC PROCESSIONAL—Pomp and Circumstance ....*Elgar*
                    Alfred M. Masonheimer

INVOCATION
         The Reverend Powell H. Norton, *School Pastor*

HYMN 221

SCRIPTURE READING—Romans 12
              The Reverend Paul M. Humphreys
                    First Baptist Church

PRAYER
              The Reverend David B. Watermulder
                    First Presbyterian Church

THE COMMENCEMENT ADDRESS
              Benjamin M. Johnson, Jr. '47

PRESENTATION OF DIPLOMAS
              The Honorable Horace Roberson
              President of the Board of Corporators

INITIATION OF SECOND GROUP, CUM LAUDE
              Everett L. Swift, *President*
              William S. Litterick, *Secretary*

AWARD OF PRIZES
         Doctor Wilbour E. Saunders, *Headmaster*
              William Fairhurst '11
              J. Walter Reeves

BENEDICTION
              The Headmaster

PEDDIE—TO THEE

RECESSIONAL—Petite Marche ....*Dubois*
              Alfred M. Masonheimer

(5)

1. Processional: *War March of the Priests*—Athalie—
   Mendelssohn ....The Orchestra

2. *The Star-Spangled Banner* ....The Audience

3. Scripture: *Proverbs* 24:1–14 ....William Pitus

4. *Clarinet Duet*—Volckmar
   Eli Butensky and Bernard Lieberman
5. Valedictory ....Seymour Singer

6. *Overture Excerpts*—Arr. by Sanders ....The Orchestra

7. Address ....Harrison C. Thomas
   Assistant Superintendent, High School Division

8. Trombone Solo—*Serenade*—Victor Herbert ....Earl Alexander

9. Announcement of Honors ....Alphonse Lafon

10. Tenor Saxophone Solo—*Blues*—Don Byas ....Bert Kosow

11. *Tales from the Vienna Woods Waltz*—Strauss ....The Orchestra

12. Presentation of Diplomas .....Arthur Franzen—Philip J. Pinkus
    Principal   Head of
    Aviation Annex

13. School Song: *Here's to Dear Old Haaren* ...The Graduating Class

14. Recessional: *The Corcoran Cadets March*—Sousa ..The Orchestra

Reprinted by permission of Haaren High School, New York City.

Concerts

(1)

THE CURTIS INSTITUTE OF MUSIC
CURTIS HALL, TWENTY-FOURTH SEASON

FACULTY RECITAL BY
MR. EFREM ZIMBALIST

Second Recital in Historical Series

MR. VLADIMIR SOKOLOFF at the Piano

TUESDAY AFTERNOON, DECEMBER 9, 19___
AT 5:15 O'CLOCK

PROGRAM

I

Sonata in A major, Opus 1, No. 1 ....GIUSEPPE TARTINI
Grave—Allegro—Presto

Adagio ....JOSEPH HAYDN

Sonata No. 10 in B flat major (K378) ..WOLFGANG AMADEUS MOZART
Allegro moderato
Andantino sostenuto e cantabile
Allegro

II

Concerto No. 22 in A minor ....GIOVANNI BATTISTI VIOTTI
Moderato
Adagio
Agitato assai

III

Sonata in C minor, Opus 30, No. 2 ....LUDWIG VAN BEETHOVEN
Allegro con brio
Adagio cantabile
Scherzo: Allegro
Finale: Allegro

Moses Fantasy ....NICOLÒ PAGANINI
(Variations for the G string)

Witches' Dance ....NICOLÒ PAGANINI

(2)

MUSICAL ORGANIZATION

CONCERT

MEMORIAL HALL, *Sunday,* March 9, 19___

_____

National Anthem

1.

Prelude "L'Arlésienne Suite"	*Bizet*
Intermezzo, *Cavalleria Rusticana*	*Mascagni*
Spirit of America	*Underwood*

The Orchestra
HANS NIX, *Conductor*

2.

St. Francis Walking on the Waves	*Liszt*
Etude in D Flat	*Liszt*
La Campanella	*Liszt*

JAMES T. FAULKNER, *Pianist*

3.

Psalm 150	*Franck*
The Erie Canal	*American Folk Song*
The Battle of Jericho	*Spiritual*

The Choristers
HENRY R. CASSELBERRY, *Conductor*

Ave Maria	*Schubert*

LYNN MARTIN, *Soprano*

4.

Normal	*Bennett*
Salute	*Seitzinger*
Our Director	*Bigelow*

The Band
HANS NIX, *Conductor*

(3)

OGDEN COMMUNITY—WEBER COLLEGE

GREATER CONCERT SERIES

Presents

GRANT JOHANNESEN, CONCERT PIANIST

OGDEN HIGH SCHOOL AUDITORIUM

January 21, 19__ 8:15 p.m.

———

—PROGRAM—

I. Fantasie and Fugue, A minor ....*Bach*

II. Sonata in F sharp, Op. 78 ....*Beethoven*
    Adagio cantabile—allegro ma non troppo
    Allegro vivace

III. Sonata in C minor, Op. 58 ....*Chopin*
    Allegro maestoso
    Scherzo—molto vivace
    Largo
    Finale—presto non tanto

—INTERMISSION—

IV. Humoresque in B flat ⎫
    Intermezzo No. 5   ⎬ ....*Schumann*
    Toccata, Op. 7   ⎭

V. Homage à Rameau ....*Debussy*
    Impromptu in F sharp minor ....*Fauré*
    Impromptu ....*Chabrier*
    Le Contentement de Soi ....*Poulenc*
    Scarbo ....*Ravel*

(4)

RUTGERS UNIVERSITY CONCERTS

KRAEUTER TRIO

KARL KRAEUTER, *Violin*

PHYLLIS KRAEUTER, *'Cello*

GRANT JOHANNESEN, *Piano*

Monday Evening, December 2, 8:30 o'clock

Presented in

THE VOORHEES CHAPEL

N.J.C. Campus

Trio in C major, K548 ....*Mozart*

Allegro

Andante cantabile

Allegro

Trio in A minor, Op. 50 ....*Tschaikowsky*

I. Pezze elegiaco

II. A. Temo con Variazioni

B. Variazione Finale e Coda

Intermission

Trio in A minor ....*Ravel*

Modéré

Pantoum. Assez vif

Passacaille. Très Large

Final. Animé

(5)

PROGRAM

I.

Sonata in G major, Op. 78 ....JOHANNES BRAHMS

> Vivace ma non troppo
> Adagio
> Allegro molto moderato

II.

Scotch Phantasy ....MAX BRUCH

> Grave—Adagio cantabile
> Allegro—Andante sostenuto
> Allegro guerriero

III.

Sonata (for violin alone) ....MAX REGER

> Allegro con grazia
> Andantino
> Prestissimo

IV.

Theme and Variations ....HENRY WIENIAWSKI

Havanaise ....CAMILLE SAINT-SAENS

Introduction and Caprice-Jota ....PABLO DE SARASATE

Reprinted by permission of Town Hall, New York City.

(6)

ROSA BOK, *Soprano*

ÁRPÁD SÁNDOR *at the Steinway*

Program

I.

Chère Rose "Zémire and Azor" ....*Grétry*

Arietta with variations
    Nel cor non piu mi sento ....*Paësiello*

Aria from "Il Pensieroso"
    Flute obbligato: John Wummer ....*Handel*

II.

An den Mond
Der Jüngling an der Quelle } ....*Schubert*
Geheimes

Auch kleine Dinge } ....*Wolf*
Elfenlied

III.

Concert Aria: "Mia Speranza Adorata" ....*Mozart*

Intermission

IV.

Il pleure dans mon cœur
    from Ariettes oubliées } ....*Debussy*
Chevaux de bois
    from Paysages belges

A Cupidon
    Chansons de Ronsard ....*Milhaud*

Pièce en forme de Habanera
    Vocalise ....*Ravel*

V.

La maja y el ruiseñor } ....*Granados*
Elegía Eterna

Cantares } ....*Turina*
Las locas por amor

Reprinted by permission of Town Hall, New York City.

(7)

1 Toccata and Fugue in D Minor ....Bach-Tausig
> Henry Strickrodt

2 Frühlingstraum ....Schubert
Ungeduld ....Schubert
Horch, Horch, die Lerch ....Schubert
> Greta Kirsten

3 Ballade in G minor ....Chopin
> Henry Strickrodt

4 Si, mi chiamano Mimi ....Puccini
from the opera "La Bohème"
> Greta Kirsten

—INTERMISSION—

5 Sonata quasi una Fantasia, Op. 27, No. 2 ....Beethoven
Adagio sostenuto
Allegretto
Presto agitato
> Henry Strickrodt

6 The Loreley ....Rogers
Agnus Dei ....Bizet
> Greta Kirsten

7 Valse in E major ....Moskowsky
> Henry Strickrodt

8 Ständchen ....R. Strauss
The Laughing Song ....J. Strauss
from the operetta "The Bat"

Reprinted by permission of Town Hall, New York City.

(8)

A PROGRAM OF ORGAN MUSIC

by

WILLIAM WATKINS

ORGAN PRELUDE—CANTILÈNE ....*Charles Marie Widor*

PROCESSIONAL HYMN ....No. 90
(The congregation is asked to stand as the choir enters and to join in singing the entire hymn.)

CALL TO WORSHIP *(Congregation seated)* ....DR. TIBBETTS

INVOCATION

SCRIPTURE

ORGAN
  PRELUDE, *from* SUITE, OPUS 5 ....*Maurice Duruflé*
  LARGO ....*G. F. Handel*
  FANTASY AND FUGUE IN C MINOR ....*J. S. Bach*

OFFERTORY
The services of worship and the work of this church are dependent upon the contributions of its members and visitors
  HEROIC SONG ....*Jean Langlais*
  SONG OF PEACE ....*Jean Langlais*
  GOD WITH US, *from* NINE MEDITATIONS FOR ORGAN
                                          Olivier Messiaen

PRAYER

RECESSIONAL HYMN ....No. 375
(The congregation is asked to be seated at the close of the last stanza to await the Benediction.)

BENEDICTION

Reprinted by permission of Riverside Church, New York City.

Appendix

LINEAR MEASURE

12 inches (in.)	= 1 foot (ft.)	320 rods	= 1 mile (mi.)
3 feet	= 1 yard (yd.)	1760 yards	= 1 mile
5½ yards—16½ feet	= 1 rod (rd.)	5280 feet	= 1 mile

SURFACE MEASURE

144 square inches (sq. in.)	= 1 square foot (sq. ft.)
9 square feet	= 1 square yard (sq. yd.)
30¼ square yards	= 1 square rod (sq. rd.)
160 square rods	= 1 acre (A.)
640 acres	= 1 square mile (sq. mi.)

CUBIC MEASURE

1728 cubic inches (cu. in.)	= 1 cubic foot (cu. ft.)
27 cubic feet	= 1 cubic yard (cu. yd.)
128 cubic feet	= 1 cord (cd.)

MEASURES OF CAPACITY

Liquid Measure		Dry Measure	
4 gills (gi.)	= 1 pint (pt.)	2 pints	= 1 quart (qt.)
2 pints	= 1 quart (qt.)	8 quarts	= 1 peck (pk.)
4 quarts	= 1 gallon (gal.)	4 pecks	= 1 bushel (bu.)
31½ gallons	= 1 barrel (bbl.)		
2 barrels	= 1 hogshead (hhd.)		

APOTHECARIES' WEIGHT

(Used in compounding medicines)

20 grains (gr.)	= 1 scruple (℈)
3 scruples	= 1 dram (℥)
8 drams	= 1 ounce (℥)
12 ounces	= 1 pound (℔)

The pound, ounce, and grain have the same weight as those of Troy Weight.

AVOIRDUPOIS WEIGHT

(For all articles except drugs, gold, silver, and gem-stones)

$27\frac{11}{32}$ grains	= 1 dram (dr.)
16 drams	= 1 ounce (oz.)
16 ounces	= 1 pound (lb.)
25 pounds	= 1 quarter (qr.)
4 quarters	= 1 hundredweight
100 pounds	(cwt.)
20 hundredweight or	= 1 ton (T.)
2,000 pounds	

1 lb. Avoirdupois = 7,000 grs.

The ton and hundredweight above given (often called the *short ton* and the *short hundredweight*) are those in common use in the United States.

The ton of 2,240 lbs., and the hundredweight of 112 lbs. (often called the *long ton* and the *long hundredweight*), are used at United States Custom Houses and in wholesale transactions in coal and iron, and are in general use in Great Britain.

TROY WEIGHT

(Used in weighing gold, silver, and precious stones)

24 grains (gr.)	= 1 pennyweight (pwt.)
20 pennyweights	= 1 ounce (oz.)
12 ounces	= 1 pound (lb.)

1 lb. Troy = 5,760 grains. In weighing diamonds, 1 carat = 3.168 Troy grains, and is divided into quarters, which are called carat grains.

THE METRIC SYSTEM

The metric system, which was determined by taking one ten millionth of the distance from the Equator to the Pole, is a decimal system. The basic units are the meter (39.37 inches), the unit of length; the liter (equal to a little more than one liquid quart and a little less than one dry quart), the unit of capacity; the gram (a little more than 1/30 ounce), the unit of weight; the hectare (10,000 square meters equal to 2.471 acres), the unit in surface measure.

The advantages of the system are:

1. The decimal relation between the units. The meter divided by 10, 100, and 1,000 gives the smaller units.

2. The uniform names of the units. The smaller units are distinguished by the Latin prefixes, *deci, centi,* and *milli;* the larger units by the Greek prefixes, *deka, hecto,* and *kilo.*

3. The simple relation of the units of area, length, weight, and volume to one another.

METRIC TABLES

Length

Myriameter	10,000 meters	6.2137 miles.
Kilometer	1,000 meters	0.62137 mile.
Hectometer	100 meters	328 feet 1 inch.
Dekameter	10 meters	393.7 inches.
Meter	1 meter	39.37 inches.
Decimeter	0.1 meter	3.937 inches.
Centimeter	0.01 meter	0.3937 inch.
Millimeter	0.001 meter	0.0394 inch.

Surface

Hectare	10,000 square meters	2.471 acres.
Are	100 square meters	119.6 square yards.
Centare	1 square meter	1,550 square inches.

Weight

Name	Number of grams	Weight of what quantity of water at maximum density	Avoirdupois weight
Metric ton, millier or tonneau	1,000,000	1 cubic meter	2,204.6 pounds.
Quintal	100,000	1 hectoliter	220.46 pounds.
Myriagram	10,000	1 dekaliter	22.046 pounds.
Kilogram, or kilo	1,000	1 liter	2.2046 pounds.
Hectogram	100	1 deciliter	3.5274 ounces.
Dekagram	10	10 cubic centimeters.	0.3527 ounce.
Gram	1	1 cubic centimeter ..	15.432 grains.
Decigram	.1	0.1 cubic centimeter.	1.5432 grains.
Centigram	.01	10 cubic millimeters.	0.1543 grain.
Milligram	.001	1 cubic millimeter ..	0.0154 grain.

Capacity

Name	Number of liters	Metric cubic measure	United States measure	British measure
Kiloliter, or stere..	1,000	1 cubic meter.	1.308 cubic yards.	1.308 cubic yards.
Hectoliter .	100	0.1 cubic meter.	2.838 bushels; 26.417 gallons.	2.75 bushels; 22.00 gallons.
Dekaliter .	10	10 cubic decimeters.	1.135 pecks; 2.6417 gallons.	8.80 quarts; 2.200 gallons.
Liter	1	1 cubic decimeter.	0.908 dry quart; 1.0567 liquid quarts.	0.880 quart.
Deciliter .	.1	0.1 cubic decimeter.	6.1023 cubic inches; 0.845 gill.	0.704 gill.
Centiliter .	.01	10 cubic centimeters.	0.6102 cubic inch; 0.338 fluid ounce.	0.352 fluid ounce.
Milliliter .	.001	1 cubic centimeter.	0.061 cubic inch; 0.271 fluid dram.	0.284 fluid dram.

Common Measures and Their Metric Equivalents

Common measure	Equivalent	Common measure	Equivalent
Inch	2.54 centimeters.	Dry quart, United States.	1.101 liters.
Foot	0.3048 meter.	Quart, imperial	1.136 liters.
Yard	0.9144 meter.	Gallon, United States.	3.785 liters.
Rod	5.029 meters.	Gallon, imperial	4.546 liters.
Mile	1.6093 kilometers.	Peck, United States ...	8.810 liters.
Square inch ..	6.452 square centimeters.	Peck, imperial	9.092 liters.
Square foot ...	0.0929 square meter.	Bushel, United States	35.24 liters.
Square yard ..	0.836 square meter.	Bushel, imperial	36.37 liters.
Square rod ...	25.29 square meters.	Ounce, avoirdupois ...	28.35 grams.
Acre	0.4047 hectare.	Pound, avoirdupois ..	0.4536 kilogram.
Square mile ..	259 hectares.	Ton, long	1.0160 metric tons.
Cubic inch ...	16.39 cubic centimeters.	Ton, short	0.9072 metric ton.
Cubic foot ...	0.0283 cubic meter.	Grain	0.0648 gram.
Cubic yard ...	0.7646 cubic meter.	Ounce, troy	31.103 grams.
Cord	3.625 steres.		
Liquid quart, United States.	0.9463 liter.	Pound, troy	0.3732 kilogram.

METRIC ABBREVIATIONS

Metric abbreviations are simply the initial letters of the respective units combined with the initial letters of the prefixes, set in lower-case, the same form being used for both singular and plural.

Prefixes and their meaning

m. milli = one-thousandth (0.001)
c. centi = one-hundredth (0.01)
d. deci   = one-tenth (0.1)
    [The unit equals 1]
dk. deka = ten (10)
h. hecto = one hundred (100)
k. kilo   = one thousand (1,000)

Metric units

m. meter (for length)
g. gram (for weight or mass)
l. liter (for capacity)

Length		Area		Volume	
km.	kilometer	km.^{2}	square kilometer	km.^{3}	cubic kilometer
hm.	hectometer	hm.^{2}	square hectometer	hm.^{3}	cubic hectometer
dkm.	dekameter	dkm.^{2}	square dekameter	dkm.^{3}	cubic dekameter
m.	meter	m.^{2}	square meter	m.^{3}	cubic meter
dm.	decimeter	dm.^{2}	square decimeter	dm.^{3}	cubic decimeter
cm.	centimeter	cm.^{2}	square centimeter	cm.^{3}	cubic centimeter
mm.	millimeter	mm.^{2}	square millimeter	mm.^{3}	cubic millimeter
μ	micron (0.001 mm.)	μ^2	square micron	μ^3	cubic micron
mμ	millimicron				

Weight		*Land area*		*Capacity of containers*	
kg.	kilogram	ha.	hectare	kl.	kiloliter
hg.	hectogram	a.	are	hl.	hectoliter
dkg.	dekagram	ca.	centare	dkl.	dekaliter
g.	gram			l.	liter
dg.	decigram			dl.	deciliter
cg.	centigram			cl.	centiliter
mg.	milligram			ml.	milliliter

A similar plan of abbreviation applies to any unit based on the metric system.

a.	ampere	h.	henry	kc.	kilocycle
A.	angstrom	j.	joule	kv.	kilovolt
c.	cycle (kc. only)	mc.	megacycle	mf.	millifarad
d.	dyne		ohm, not abbreviated	μf	microfarad (one-millionth of a farad)
e.	erg	v.	volt		
f.	farad	w.	watt	$\mu\mu$	one-millionth of a micron

GPO Style Manual

THE STATES OF THE UNITED STATES AND THEIR CAPITALS

State	*Capital*	*State*	*Capital*
Alabama	Montgomery	Montana	Helena
Alaska	Juneau	Nebraska	Lincoln
Arizona	Phoenix	Nevada	Carson City
Arkansas	Little Rock	New Hampshire	Concord
California	Sacramento	New Jersey	Trenton
Colorado	Denver	New Mexico	Santa Fe
Connecticut	Hartford	New York	Albany
Delaware	Dover	North Carolina	Raleigh
Florida	Tallahassee	North Dakota	Bismarck
Georgia	Atlanta	Ohio	Columbus
Hawaii	Honolulu	Oklahoma	Oklahoma City
Idaho	Boise	Oregon	Salem
Illinois	Springfield	Pennsylvania	Harrisburg
Indiana	Indianapolis	Rhode Island	Providence
Iowa	Des Moines	South Carolina	Columbia
Kansas	Topeka	South Dakota	Pierre
Kentucky	Frankfort	Tennessee	Nashville
Louisiana	Baton Rouge	Texas	Austin
Maine	Augusta	Utah	Salt Lake City
Maryland	Annapolis	Vermont	Montpelier
Massachusetts	Boston	Virginia	Richmond
Michigan	Lansing	Washington	Olympia
Minnesota	St. Paul	West Virginia	Charleston
Mississippi	Jackson	Wisconsin	Madison
Missouri	Jefferson City	Wyoming	Cheyenne

OTHER REGIONS ADMINISTERED BY THE UNITED STATES, AND THEIR CAPITALS

Territory	Capital
American Samoa Islands	Pago Pago
Canal Zone	
Guam	Agaña
Puerto Rico	San Juan
Virgin Islands	Charlotte Amalie
Wake and Midway Islands	

PROVINCES AND TERRITORIES OF THE DOMINION OF CANADA WITH THEIR CAPITALS

Provinces	Capitals
Alberta	Edmonton
British Columbia	Victoria
Manitoba	Winnipeg
New Brunswick	Fredericton
Newfoundland	St. John's
Nova Scotia	Halifax
Ontario	Toronto
Prince Edward Island	Charlottetown
Quebec	Quebec
Saskatchewan	Regina
Yukon Territory	Dawson
Northwest Territories	

COUNTRIES OF SOUTH AMERICA AND THEIR CAPITALS

Countries	Capitals
Argentina	Buenos Aires
Bolivia	La Paz
Brazil	Brasilia
British Guiana	Georgetown
Chile	Santiago
Colombia	Bogotá
Dutch Guiana	Paramaribo
Ecuador	Quito
French Guiana	Cayenne
Paraguay	Asunción
Peru	Lima
Uruguay	Montevideo
Venezuela	Caracas

COUNTRIES OF MIDDLE AMERICA AND THEIR CAPITALS

Countries	Capitals
British Honduras	Belize
Costa Rica	San José
Guatemala	Guatemala
Honduras	Tegucigalpa
Mexico	Mexico, D.F.
Nicaragua	Managua
Panama	Panama
El Salvador	San Salvador

PRINCIPAL ISLANDS OF THE WEST INDIES AND THEIR CAPITALS

Islands	Capitals
The Bahamas	Nassau
Barbados	Bridgetown
Bermuda	Hamilton
Cuba	Havana
Dominican Republic	Ciudad Trujillo
Haiti	Port-au-Prince
Jamaica	Kingston
Leeward Islands	
Puerto Rico	San Juan
Trinidad	Port of Spain
Virgin Islands	Charlotte Amalie
Windward Islands	St. George's

OTHER PRINCIPAL COUNTRIES AND THEIR CAPITALS

Country	Capital
Abyssinia (*see* Ethiopia)	
Afghanistan	Kabul
Albania	Tirana (Tirane)
Australia	Canberra
Austria	Vienna (Wien)
Belgium	Brussels (Bruxelles)
Bulgaria	Sofia (Sofiya)
Burma	Rangoon
Cambodia	Phnom Penh
Canada	Ottawa
Ceylon	Colombo
China (People's Republic of China)	Peiping (Peking)
China (Republic of China)	Taipei (Taiwan)
Czechoslovakia	Prague (Praha)

Country	Capital
Denmark	Copenhagen (Kobenhavn)
Egypt	Cairo
Eire (*see* Ireland)	
Estonia	Tallinn
Ethiopia (Abyssinia)	Addis Ababa
Finland	Helsinki
France	Paris
Germany (Federal Republic of Germany)	Bonn
Ghana	Accra
Great Britain and Northern Ireland	London
Greece	Athens (Athenai)
Hungary	Budapest
Iceland	Reykjavik
India	New Delhi
Indonesia	Djakarta
Iran (formerly Persia)	Teheran
Iraq (Mesopotamia)	Baghdad
Ireland (Eire)	Dublin (Baile Atha Cliath)
Israel	Tel Avív
Italy	Rome (Roma)
Japan	Tokyo
Jordan	Amman
Korea	Seoul
Laos	Vientiane
Latvia	Riga
Lebanon	Beirut
Liberia	Monrovia
Libya	Tripoli, present seat of government; Benghazi, king's residence
Liechtenstein	Vaduz
Luxembourg (Luxemburg)	Luxembourg
Morocco	Rabat
Nepal	Katmandu (Kathmandu)
Netherlands	Amsterdam, constitutional capital; The Hague (s' Gravenhage), seat of government
New Zealand	Wellington
Norway	Oslo
Oman	
Pakistan	Karachi
Persia (*see* Iran)	
Philippines	Quezon City

Country	Capital
Poland	Warsaw (Warszawa)
Portugal	Lisbon (Lisboa)
Rumania	Bucharest (Bucureşti)
Russia (*see* Union of Soviet Socialist Republics)	
Saudi Arabia	Riyadh, capital and king's residence; Jidda, temporary diplomatic center
Siam (*see* Thailand)	
Spain	Madrid
Sweden	Stockholm
Switzerland	Bern
Syria	Damascus
Thailand	Bangkok
Transjordan (*see* Jordan)	
Tunisia	Tunis
Turkey	Ankara
Union of South Africa	Cape Town, legislative capital; Pretoria, administrative capital
Union of Soviet Socialist Republics	Moscow
Viet-Nam (Vietnam)	Saïgon
Yemen	Sana'a
Yugoslavia	Belgrade (Beograd)

Index

A, an, use of, 201
A.M., capitalization of, 27, 87
Abbreviations
  academic degrees, 165–169
  airlines, 175–176
  American railroads, 174–175
  Army titles, 169
  book parts, 178
  books of the Bible, 177
  British money, 31
  British orders and honors, 170
  Canadian provinces and territories, 161
  capitalization of, 26–27
  Coast Guard titles, 169
  company, 161–162
  compass directions, 177
  corporation, 161–162
  dates, 53, 85–86
  days of the week, 176
  doctor, 162–163
  firm names, 161–162
  geographical names, 160–161
  government services, 173–174
  in bibliographies, 87–88
  in footnotes, 87–88
  junior, 164
  learned and professional societies, 171
  list of, 137–160
  metric system, 90, 537–538
  military titles, 169
  money, 179
  months, 176
  Navy titles, 169
  New Testament, books of, 177
  Old Testament, books of, 177
  orders of knighthood, 170
  personal titles following names, 163–164
  personal titles preceding names, 162–163
  plurals of, 136, 162
  possessive of, 137
  professional titles, 165–169
  punctuation of, 29, 53
  railroads, 174–175
  Saint, 161
  signs and symbols, 178–179

Abbreviations *(Cont.)*:
  sizes of books, 177
  social and religious organizations, 172
  societies, professional, 171
  states, 160
  titles, 162–164, 170–171
  United States, 161
  U.S. administrative boards, 173–174
  versions of the Bible, 178
Academic degrees
  abbreviations, 165–169
  capitalization, 4–5, 7
  order of writing, 163
Academic forms of address, 325–326
Academic functions, invitations to, 347–350
Acceptances
  to dinner invitation, 357, 363
  to luncheon invitation, 358
  to wedding invitation, 356–357
Acknowledgment, letters of, 240–242
Address on envelope, 237
Adjective clauses, punctuation of, 40
Adjectives
  after *appear, be, seem,* etc., 199
  agreement with nouns, 202
  capitalization of, 17, 27
  comma between modifiers, 33–34
  comparison of, 200–201
  ending in *ly,* 199
  hyphened, 65–66, 68
  proper, 27
Adjustment letters, 250–252
Administration, capitalization of, 10
Administrative boards of U.S., abbreviations for, 173–174
Admiral, form of address, 302
Adverbs
  comparison of, 200–201
  hyphen in, 65
  negatives, 201
  unnecessary, 202
  use of, 199–200
Ages, manner of writing, 89
Agreement
  of adjectives with nouns, 202
  of subject and predicate, 190–192

543

Air Force officers, form in letters to, 304

Air Force titles, 300, 304

Airlines, abbreviations for, 175–176

Alderman, form in letters to, 297

Alumna, plural of, 182

Alumnus, plural of, 182

Ambassador, American, form in letters to, 295

Ambassador, foreign, form in letters to, 294, 316

Amendment to constitution, 428

Ampersand, use of, 161

Anglican church officials, form in letters to, 319–320

Anniversaries, invitations to, 332–334, 341–342, 348, 350–351

Announcements
  business, 369–375
  wedding, 340–344

Apostrophe
  in abbreviations, 53
  in contractions, 53
  in plurals of figures and letters, 186
  in plurals of signs and symbols, 186
  in possessives, 50–53
  in titles, 51–52
  omission in possessive pronouns, 186

Apothecaries' weights, 534–536

Application, letters of, 254–260

Appointment, letters of, 274–275

Appreciation, letters of, 252, 275–278

Archbishop
  Anglican, form in letters to, 319
  Roman Catholic, form in letters to, 321

Army
  abbreviation of titles, 169–170
  capitalization of, 9
  form in letters to officers, 301–302, 303
  ranks and titles, 67, 299–301

Arrangement of degrees after a name, 163

Articles
  a or *an,* choice of, 201
  repetition of, 201
  the, capitalization, 5, 23–24

Assembly, member of, form in letters to, 293

Associate justice, form in letters to, 291

Association, capitalization of, 13–14

Associations, clubs, societies, form in letters to, 218–219

Asterisks, 62

At Home, invitations to an, 334–335, 343

Atlases, 492

Attention line, 224–225

Attorney, form in letters to, 217

Attorney General, plural of, 185

Avoirdupois weight, table of, 535

Bad, badly, 199

Ballots, writing of results, 89

Bank opening, invitation to, 354

Baron, form in letters to, 310

Baroness, form in letters to, 310–311

Baronet, form in letters to, 311, 313

Bible
  abbreviations of books of, 177
  abbreviations of versions of, 178
  capitalization of parts and versions, 18–19

Biblical, capitalization of, 19

Bibliography
  abbreviations in, 87–88
  compiling of, 465–467
  punctuation in, 35, 44, 47, 59

Biography, books on, 486–488

Bishop
  Anglican, 319–320
  Methodist, 323
  Protestant Episcopal in America, 319–320
  Roman Catholic, 322

Block style in letters, 42–43, 214, 227

Boards, form in letters to, 219

Book sizes, 177, 462

Book titles
  capitalization of, 25–26
  punctuation of, 56, 80

Books of the Bible, abbreviations of, 177

Botanical names
  capitalization of, 26
  italics, use of, 85

Brackets, 62

Brazilian letters, form in, 330

Brigadier General, form in letters to, 302

British decorations and honors, abbreviations for, 170

British money, abbreviations for, 31

British nobility, form in letters to, 307–313

British officials, abbreviations of titles, 170–171
British spelling, 93–95, 98
Brotherhood, members of, form in letters to, 325
Bureaus, form in letters to, 219
Business announcements
  admission of new members, 370–372
  change of address, 373–374
  change of firm name, 369
  death of member of firm, 374–375
  election to office, 370
  formation of company, 369
  opening of office, 372
  retirement of member, 374
Business titles
  capitalization of, 7
  in inside address, 214–217
Bylaws, 423–427, 429–432

Cabinet, capitalization of, 10
Cabinet members, form in letters to, 288–289, 290
Cablegrams, 385–386
Cadets, how addressed, 302
Canadian officials, form in letters to, 318–319
Canadian provinces and territories
  abbreviations, 161
  capitals, 539
Canon, form in letters to, 320
Capacity, measure, table of, 534, 536
Capitalization of
  A.M., 27, 87
  abbreviations, 26–27
  academic degrees, 4–5
  academic titles, 5–6
  adjectives, 17, 27
  administration, 10
  after a colon, 47–48
  army, 9
  association, 13–14
  attaché, 6
  avenue, 14–15
  Bible, parts and versions, 18–19
  Biblical, 19
  Biblical terms, 19
  bishop, 5, 20
  board, 9
  book parts, 24
  book titles, 23–26
  botanical names, 26
  buildings, 14–15
  bureau, 9
  business titles, 7

Capitalization of (*Cont.*):
  Cabinet, 10
  cantor, 6
  capital, 12
  capitol, 14
  Cardinal, 6
  cathedral, 18
  chapter, 25
  church, 18
  clergymen, 4–6
  club, 13–14
  code references, 24–25
  college, 8, 13–14
  commission, 11
  commissioner, 8
  committee, 9
  company, 13
  compass directions, 17
  complimentary close, 228
  compound words, 27
  congressman, 6
  constitution, 11
  consul, 6
  continent, 16
  courts, 9–10
  creeds, 21
  da, della, 4
  dean, 5
  degrees, 5–6
  Deity, 19–20
  department, 9
  Devil, 21
  directions: north, south, etc., 17
  documents, 11, 25
  "down" style of, 7, 11
  doctor, 6
  east, eastern, 17
  easterner, 17–18
  ecclesiastical titles, 5–6
  educational institutions, 13–14
  epithets, 3–4
  epochs, 26
  exclamations, 23
  ex-President, 8
  first word after a colon, 21–22, 47
  federal, 10
  first word of a line of poetry, 3
  first word of a sentence, 3
  foreign names, 4
  former President, 8
  general, 6
  geographical names, 15–18
  geological names, 26
  government, 10
  government departments, 9

Capitalization of (*Cont.*):
 government titles, 6–8
 governor, 8
 headings, 21
 historic events, 26
 holidays and holy days, 21
 interrogations, 23
 judge, 6
 junior, 164
 justice, 6
 legislature, 12
 madam, 8
 mayor, 6–7
 military titles, 9
 monsieur, 8
 monuments, 14
 musical compositions, 25
 nation, 12
 national, 12
 navy, 9
 newspaper usage, 7, 11, 13, 15
 north, northern, 17
 northerner, 17–18
 oriental, 17
 P.M., 27
 parenthetical statements, 23
 park, 14–15
 particles in American names, 4
 particles in foreign names, 4
 personifications, 24
 plays, 25
 political divisions, 18
 political parties, 13
 Pope, 20
 prefixes, 27
 President, 6–7
 President elect, 8
 priest, 6
 principal, 6
 professor, 5, 6
 proper adjectives, 27–28
 proper nouns, 3–4, 18
 questions, 23
 quotations, 22
 rabbi, 6
 rector, 6
 resolutions, 23, 405
 Roman numerals, 25
 sacred books, 18–19
 salutations, 217
 school, 18
 scientific terms, 26
 seasons, 24
 secretary, 6, 8
 senator, 6

Capitalization of (*Cont.*):
 sir, 8
 solar system, 26
 south, southern, 17
 southerner, 17–18
 species, botanical, etc., 26
 square, 14–15
 state, 12–13
 state legislatures, 12
 station, 9
 statues, 14
 street, 14–15
 synagogue, 18
 the
  in company names, 23–24
  in geographical names, 23
  in titles of books, plays, etc., 23–24
  with *Reverend,* 5
 titles
  business usage, 7
  in second person, 8
  in third person, 8
  newspaper usage, 7
  of government officials, 6–8
  of military officers, 9
  of rank, honor, or respect, 6–7
 trade names, 27
 university, 18
 van, von, 4
 west, western, 17
 westerner, 17–18
 zoological names, 26
Capitals of
 Canadian provinces and territories, 539
 Middle American countries, 540
 other principal countries, 538–542
 South American countries, 539
 United States, states and regions administered by, 538–539
 West Indies, 540
Captions, capitalization of, 25–26
Cardinal, form in letters to, 321
Cards
 of introduction, 270–271
 of invitation, 334–335
Case
 nominative of pronouns, 186
 objective of pronouns, 187
 possessive of nouns, 50–52
 possessive of pronouns, 187–188
 with gerunds, 53, 188
cede, ceed, words ending in, 110

Central American countries
  capitals of, 540
  names, 540
Cents, writing of, 88
Chairman
  form in letters to, 291
  use of word, 215
Chaplain
  form in letters to, 302–303
  form of address, 291
Charge accounts, letters relating to, 243–246
Chargé d'affaires, form in letters to, 296
Chemical symbols, writing of, 32
Chief Justice, form in letters to, 291
Citations, 494–507
City officials, form in letters to, 293, 297–298
City officials and wives, form in letters to, 298
Claim letters, 249–250
Clauses, punctuation of, 35–41
Clergy, form in letters to, 5–6, 163, 319–324
Closed punctuation, 42, 214
Clubs, form in letters to, 218–219
Co in compounds, 67–68
Coast Guard
  abbreviations of titles, 169
  form in letters to, 304
  titles of officers, 300–301
Code references, capitalization of, 24–25
Collection letters, 252–253
Collective nouns, agreement with predicate, 190–191
College
  form in letters to officials, 216–217, 325–326
Colon
  after formal salutations, 41, 47
  capitalization of word following a colon, 21–22, 47
  to introduce a list, 46
  to introduce formal quotations, 46–47
  to precede explanations, 47
  with figures denoting hours and minutes, 48
  with parentheses, 62
  with quotation marks, 56–57
Comma
  after British salutations, 306–312
  after salutations in social letters and notes, 41

Comma (*Cont.*):
  between adjectives, 33–34
  in bibliographies, 35
  in compound sentences, 39
  in dates, 37
  in direct address, 34
  in direct quotations, 40
  in letter parts, 41–43, 306–312
  in titles, 35
  omission of, with compound personal pronouns, 34
  to indicate an omission, 36
  with appositives, 34
  with *as, for example, namely,* 37
  with clauses, 37–41
  with *etc.,* 33
  with exclamations, 36, 50
  with figures, 37
  with *indeed, moreover, nevertheless,* 35
  with introductory expressions, 35, 37
  with inverted names, 35
  with nonrestrictive clauses, 40
  with parenthetical matter, 35–36, 61–62
  with phrases, 32–38, 41
  with quotation marks, 40, 56–57
  with transitional expressions, 35
  with words and phrases in a series, 32–34
Commandant, use of title in Coast Guard, 304
Committees
  form in letters to, 220
Commencement exercises
  invitations to, 347, 348, 349
  programs for, 521–525
Commissioner, form in letters to, 297
Company
  agreement of verb with, 190–191
  correct method of writing, 33, 161–162
  filing of names, 481–482
  form in letters to, 220–221
Comparison of adjectives, 200–201
Compass directions
  abbreviations of, 177
  capitalization of, 17
Complimentary close
  in British correspondence, 306–312
  in business correspondence, 228
  in military and naval correspondence, 301–302
  in official correspondence, 287–296
Compound adjectives, 64–65, 68

Compound nouns
  list of, 69–70
  plural of, 185
Compound personal pronouns
  omission of comma with, 34
  use of, 188
Compound sentences, punctuation of,
    39
Compound subjects, 192
Concerts
  invitations to, 346, 348
  programs for, 526–533
Conditions, subjunctive mood in, 195–
    196
Condolence, letters of, on death of a
      brother, 282
  business associate, 280–282
  father, 281
  friend, 282
  husband, 282
  mother, 281
  sister, 282
Condolence, telegrams of, 384–385
Confirmation, letters of, 273
Congratulation, letters of
  on a birthday, 279
  on a speech, 280
  on an airplane flight, 279
  on appointment to office, 279–280
  to committees, 278–279
Congratulations, telegrams of, 383–384
Congressman, form in letters to, 290
Congresswoman, form in letters to, 290,
    295
Conjunctions
  coordinate, 205–206
  distinction between, 205
  subordinate, 206
Constitutions
  examples of, 424–432
  form of, 424–425
Consul, form in letters to, 296
Continuation pages in letters, 227
Contractions, punctuation of, 53
Contrary-to-fact conditions, 195–196
Convocations, invitations to, 348
Coordinate conjunctions, 205–206
Corporate titles, rules for filing, 481–
    483
Cubic measure, table of, 534

Da, della
  capitalization of, 4
  filing of names with, 480
Dame, form in letters to, 312

Dances, invitations to, 337–338, 349–
    350
Dash, 57–59
Dates
  figures in, 85–87
  placement of, in letters, 212–213
  punctuation of, 37, 53
Days of the week, abbreviations of, 176
Dean, form in letters to, 216, 320, 323,
    326
Decimals, 31, 88
Dedications, invitations to, 351–353
Degrees
  academic degrees with abbreviations,
    165–169
  citations made in conferring of, 494–
    502
  order of, following name, 164
  punctuation of, 35
Deity, capitalization of, 19–20
Department, capitalization of, 9
Departments
  form of address in letters to, 219
Devil, capitalization of, 21
Dictator's initials, placement of, 231–
    232
Diction
  choice of words, 110–119
  French words and phrases, 131–134
  Latin words and phrases, 124–131
  pronunciation, 119–123
  words confused, 110–119
Dimensions, writing of, 90
Dinner, invitations to, 333–334, 361
Diplomats, form in letters to, 294–296,
    299
Direct address, punctuation, 34
Direct questions, punctuation of, 48
Direct quotations, punctuation of, 40–
    58
Directions: north, south, etc., capitali-
    zation of, 17
Directories and handbooks, 488–490
Distance, unit of, as subject, 192
Distances, writing of, 90
Division of words into syllables, 70–76
Divorced women, signature of, 230
Doctor
  abbreviation of, 6, 162, 166
  address in Armed Forces, 303
  British usage, 313
  plural of, 184
  with other degrees, 4–5, 163, 216–217
  with other titles, 5–6, 215, 216
Dots and asterisks, 62–63

Double possessive, 188
"Down" style of capitalization, 7, 11, 13, 14, 15
Dry measure, table of, 534
Duchess, form in letters to, 307
Duke, form in letters to, 305, 306–307

Each, 189
Earl, form in letters to, 305, 308
East, eastern, capitalization of, 17
Easterner, capitalization of, 17–18
Ecclesiastical titles
   capitalization of, 5–6
   usage in letters, 319–325
Educational institutions, capitalization of, 13–14
Either, 189–190
Emphasis by capitalization, 27
Enclosures, placement of, 231
Enumerations, punctuation of, 45–46
Envelope picture, 237
Epithets, capitalization of, 3–4
Epochs, capitalization of, 26
Esquire, 163, 297, 313
Etc., punctuation after, 33
Every, 189
Everybody, 189
Excellence, 314
Excellency, 296–297, 321–322
Exclamation point
   with exclamatory expressions, 49–50
   with parentheses, 61
   with quotation marks, 57–58
Exclamations, capitalization of, 23
Exhibitions, announcements and invitations, 343–345
Ex-officials, form in letters to, 297
Ex-President
   capitalization of, 8
   form of address, 297

Father, capitalization of, 4
Federal, capitalization of, 10
Figures
   ages, 89
   ballots, 89
   beginning a sentence, 85
   dates, 85–87
   decimals, 88
   dimensions, 90
   distances, 90
   fractions, 89
   in books, 83
   in editorials, 83
   in financial statements, 83

Figures (*Cont.*):
   in footnotes, 87–88
   in legal documents, 88
   in news items, 83–84
   measures, 90
   metric system, 90, 535–538
   plural form, 53, 186
   punctuation of, 37
   Roman numerals, 90–91
   round numbers in, 84
   street numbers with, 87
   temperature, 90
   time of day, 31, 48, 87
   weights, 90
   within a sentence, 85
Filing, rules for, 477–485
Financial statements, figures in, 88
Firm names
   abbreviation of, 161–162
   filing of, 481–483, 484
   singular or plural, 190–191
Firms
   salutations in letters to, 217–218, 220–221
   signatures of, 228–229
Footnotes, abbreviations in, 87
For example, punctuation with, 37, 45
Foreign names
   capitalization of, 4
   filing of, 480–481
Foreign plurals, 182–183
Foreign words and phrases
   italics of, 78, 79
   list of, 131–134
Forewords in reports, 438–440
Formal acceptances. *See* Acceptances
Formal invitations. *See* Invitations
Formal regrets. *See* Regrets
Former President, capitalization of, 8
Founders' Day, program for, 518–519
Fractions
   agreement of subject and predicate, 89, 191
   rules for writing, 89
French letters, form in letter parts, 314–315, 327
French words and phrases
   italics of, 78, 79
   list of, 131–134
Fund-raising letters, 246–248
Future tense, 193–194

General
   capitalization of, 6
   form in letters to, 301

Gentlemen, in letter salutation, 217–221
Geographical names
abbreviations of Canadian provinces
and territories, 161
abbreviations of states of the United
States, 160
capitalization of, 13–18
capitals of countries, 538–542
pronunciation of, 135–136
spelling of, 99–100
Geological names, capitalization of, 26
German correspondence, form in letter
parts, 328–329
Gerunds, possessive case with, 53, 188
Glossary of printing and publishing
terms, 261–264
Government, capitalization of, 10
Government boards, omission of periods in abbreviations of, 30
Government boards, commissions, etc.,
list of with abbreviations, 173–
174
Government officials, form in letters to,
287–297, 298
Government titles, capitalization of,
6–7
Governor
capitalization of, 8
form in letters to, 292
Governor General of Canada, form in
letters to, 318
Graduation exercises
invitations to, 347, 348, 349
programs for, 521–525
Grammar
adjectives and adverbs, 199–202
conjunctions, 205–206
nouns, 181–186
prepositions, 202–205
pronouns, 186–190
verbs, 190–199

Handbooks and directories, 488–492
Headings following a colon, capitaliza-
tion of, 21
Headings in letters, 212–214
Hence, punctuation with, 37, 45–46
High school
capitalization of, 16
commencement program, 525
Historic events and eras, capitalization
of, 26
Holidays and holy days, capitalization
of, 21
Honorable, use of, 297

Honorary degrees, citations for, 494–
503
Honourable with British titles, 312–313
House of Commons, addressing members of, 313
House of Lords, addressing members
of, 313
Hyphens
between prefix and proper names,
67
compounds with, 64–68
denoting division of syllables, 70–76
omission of
between prefix and stem, 67–68
in foreign phrases, 68
in titles, 66–67
with prefixes, 67–68
with adjectives, 65–66, 68
with adverbs, 65
with British titles, 67
with fractions, 66
with numerals, 65
with proper names used adjectively,
65
with *self,* 68
with titles, 66–67
with *well,* 68

In memoriam, 414–419
Indented style in letter parts, 41–42,
214, 227
Indexes and guides, 491, 492
Indexing
examples of, 475–476
rules for, 474–475
Indirect object, 187
Indirect questions, punctuation of, 48
Indirect quotations, punctuation of, 54
Infinitive, tenses of, 194–195
Informal acceptances, 363
Informal invitations, 361–362
Informal regrets, 364–368
Information, sources of, 486–493
Initials, punctuation of, 30
Initials of dictator and typist, 231–
232
Inscriptions, 508–517
Inside address in letters, 41–43, 214–
217, 218–223
Interrogation point
with parentheses, 49, 62
with questions, 48–49
with quotation marks, 48–49
Interrogations, capitalization of, 23
Interrogative pronouns, 188

Introduction
  card of, 270–271
  letters of, 267–270
Introductory expressions, punctuation of, 35, 37, 46
Inverted names, punctuation of, 35
Invitations, recalling of, 360
Invitations to
  academic functions, 347–350, 353
  anniversaries, 332–334, 341–342, 348, 350–351
  At Home, 334–335, 343
  city officials and wives, 298
  commencement, 347, 348, 349, 350
  concert, 348, 351
  dance, 337–338, 349–350
  dedication, 351–353
  dinner, 333–334, 361
  exhibition, 343–345
  government officials and their wives, 298
  lectures, 355–356
  luncheon, 339, 361
  opening of building, 354
  reception, 335–337
  recital, 346
  speaker, 362
  tea, 336–337
  unveiling of statue, 352
  wedding, 339–340
  wedding anniversary, 341–342
Irony, punctuation of, 49, 50
Italian letters, form in letter parts, 329
Italics
  abbreviations of foreign words, 77
  address lines of speeches, 82
  bibliographical usage, 79–80
  foreign words and phrases, 78
  legal usage, 80–81
  names of ships, 81
  omission of, 79–80, 82
  scientific names, 79
  titles of books, 56, 79–80
Its, 187
It's, 53

Judge
  capitalization of, 6
  form in letters to, 292
Junior
  abbreviation, 164
  capitalization, 164
  correct usage, 163, 165
  possessive, 50
Jury, as subject, 190

Justice. *See* Associate Justice, Chief Justice

Kind of, 202
Knight, form in letter to, 312
Knighthood, orders of, 170

Ladies, in salutation, 217–220
Lady, holder of title, 312
Latin words and phrases, 124–131
Lawyer, form in letters to, 217
Legal documents
  italics in, 80–81
  writing of figures in, 60
Learned and professional societies, abbreviations for, 171
Legislators, form in letters to, 290–294
Legislature, capitalization of, 12
Length, metric table of, 536
Letter pictures, 233–236
Letterheads, 212–214
Letters
  abbreviations of titles in, 162–164
  academic usage of titles in, 162–163, 216, 325–326
  attention line in, 224–227
  bibliography of, 284–286
  block style in, 42–43, 214, 227, 236
  Brazilian usage in, 330
  British usage in, 306–313
  business titles, placement of, 215–216
  closed punctuation in, 42, 214
  complimentary close in
    business correspondence, 41–43
    ecclesiastical correspondence, 319–325
    military and naval correspondence, 301–302, 304
    official correspondence, 287–296
  continuation pages, 227
  dates, placement of, 212–213
  enclosures in, 231
  form in letters to
    admiral, 302
    Air Force officers, 304
    alderman, 297
    ambassador, American, 295
    ambassador, foreign, 294, 316
    archbishop, 319, 321
    Army officers, 301–302, 303
    associate justice, 291
    associations, clubs, societies, 218–219
    attorney, 217, 297
    bishop, 319–320, 322, 323

Letters (*Cont.*):
 form in letters to (*Cont.*):
  boards, bureaus, 219
  brigadier general, 302
  British nobility, 307–313
  brotherhood, member of, 325
  Cabinet officers, 288–289, 290
  cadets, 302
  Canadian officials, 318–319
  canon, 320
  cardinal, 321
  chairman, 220, 291
  chaplain, 302–303
  chargé d'affaires, 296
  Chief Justice, 291
  city officials, 297
  city officials and wives, 298
  clergy, 5–6, 163, 319–324
  Coast Guard officers, 304
  college and university officials, 216–217, 325–326
  commissioner, 297
  committees, 220
  companies, 220
  congressman, 290
  congresswoman, 290, 295
  consul, 296
  dean, 320, 323, 326
  departments and offices, 219
  doctor, 215–217
  duchess, 307
  duke, 305, 306–307
  earl, 305, 308
  ecclesiastics, 319–325
  ex-officials, 297
  French officials, 314–315
  general, 301
  governor, 292
  Governor General of Canada, 318
  House of Commons, member of, 313
  House of Lords, member of, 313
  judge, 292
  knight, 312
  lawyer, 217
  lieutenant, 303
  lieutenant governor, 292
  major general, 301
  mayor, American, 297, 298
  mayor, French, 315
  mayor and wife, 298
  Medical Corps, 302–303
  men and women, 217–218, 219, 221
  minister from foreign country, 295

Letters (*Cont.*):
 form in letters to (*Cont.*):
  minister of the church, 5–6, 163, 319–324
  monsignor, 322
  Mother Superior, 324
  nobility, 305, 307–313
  nun, 324–325
  officials and wives, 298
  police commissioner, 297
  Pope, 321
  president of college or university, 216, 325, 326
  President of France, 314
  President of the United States, 287
  President of the United States and wife, 298
  priest, 322
  Prime Minister, British, 312
  Prime Minister, Canadian, 318–319
  prince, 306
  professor, 216, 326
  rabbi, 324
  representative, 293
  Roman Catholic officials, 321–322
  royalty, 306
  Secretary General of the United Nations, 315–316
  Secretary of Air, 290
  Secretary of Defense, 290
  Secretary of Labor, 289
  Secretary of State, 288
  Secretary of State and wife, 298
  Secretary of the Army, 290
  Secretary of the Navy, 290
  Secretary to the President, 289
  senator, 290, 293
  senator and wife, 298
  senator-elect, 290
  sisterhood, member of, 324–325
  Speaker of the House, 288
  superior of a brotherhood, 325
  United Nations, representatives to, 315–317
  vice admiral, 302
  Vice President, 288
  Vice President and wife, 298
  viscount, 309
  warrant officer, 303
  woman Cabinet member, 288–289
  woman member of the House of Commons, 312
  woman member of the House of Lords, 313
 French usage in, 314–315, 327

Letters (*Cont.*):
  German usage in, 328–329
  headings of, 41–42, 214, 227, 233–235
  indented style, 41–42, 214, 227, 233–235
  inside address of, 214–217
  Italian usage in, 329
  letterheads, 212–214
  of transmittal, 435–438
  open punctuation in, 41–43, 214, 218
  pictures of, 233–236
  punctuation of letter parts, 41–43, 214, 217–235
  quoted, punctuation of, 55
  reference line, 225–226
  reports in letter form, 445
  salutations in, 41–43, 217–224, 287–298, 301–312, 314–330
  signatures in, 41–43, 228–232
  Spanish usage in, 327–328
  stereotyped phrases in, 211–212
  subject line, 226–227
  titles in inside address, 215–217
  types of
    acceptances, 357–358
    acknowledgment, 240–242
    adjustment, 250–252
    application, 254–260
    appointment, 274–275
    appreciation, 252, 275–278
    charge account, 243–246
    claim, 249–250
    collection, 252–253
    condolence, 280–282
    confirmation, 273
    congratulation, 278–280
    fund-raising, 246–248
    introduction, 267–270
    invitation, 333–355
    order, 238–239
    recommendation, 262–266
    regret, 358–360, 364–368
    reminder, 272
    request for introduction, 267
    request for reference, 260–261
    reservation, 273–274
    resignation, 283
    resolutions in, 409, 412–413, 419
    sympathy, 280–282
    transmittal, 435–438
Letters of the alphabet, plurals of, 186
Lieutenant, form of address for, 303
Linear measure, 534, 536
Liquid measure, 534

Madam, in salutation, 217, 218, 219, 289, 290, 293
Madame, in salutation, 314, 327
Mademoiselle, in salutation, 327
Major general, form in letters to, 301
Manuscript
  preparation of, 460–461
  type sizes, 464
Marchioness, form in letters to, 308
Marine Corps titles, 300
Marquess, form in letters to, 308
Mayor, American, form in letters to, 297, 298
Mayor, French, form in letters to, 315
Mayor and wife, form in letters to, 298
Measures
  figures in, 90
  tables of, 534–538
Medical Corps of Armed Forces, form of address, 303–304
Memoranda, office, writing of, 283–284
Men and women, salutation in letters to, 217, 218, 219, 221
Mesdames, 184, 217–221, 223
Messrs., 184, 214–215, 220, 222
Methodist bishop, form in letters to, 323
Metric system, 90, 535–538
Middle America, countries and capitals, 540
Military service ranks, 299–301
Military titles
  abbreviations, 169–170
  capitalization of, 6, 9
  list of, 299–301
Minister of the church
  correct usage of *Reverend,* 5–6, 163
  form in letters to, 319–324
Ministers from foreign countries, form in letters to, 295
Minutes of meetings, 392–404
Miss, 216, 217, 221, 229
Misses, 184, 221, 222
Mr.
  British usage, 217, 313
  with other titles, 215–217
Mrs., 184, 216, 222, 229
Money
  abbreviations and symbols, 179
  British money, 31
  chargeable words in telegrams, 379–382
  writing of, 83, 84, 88
Monograms, writing of, 30
Monsieur, 8, 314–315

Monsignor, form in letters to, 322
Months, abbreviations of, 176
Mood, 195–196
Moreover, punctuation with, 35, 45
Mother Superior, form in letters to, 324

Namely, punctuation with, 37, 45
Nation, national, capitalization of, 12
Navy
  abbreviation of titles, 169
  capitalization of, 9
  form in letters to, 290, 302–304
  service ranks, 299
Negatives, double, 201
Neither . . . nor, 192
New Testament, abbreviation of books
  of, 177
Newspaper style of capitalization, 7, 11,
  13, 14, 15
Nobility of Great Britain, form in letters
  to, 305, 307–313
None, singular or plural, 189
Nonrestrictive adjective clauses, punctuation of, 40
North, northern, capitalization of, 17
Northerner, capitalization of, 17–18
Nouns
  collective, 190
  foreign plurals, 182–183
  formation of plurals, 181–186
  plurals of proper nouns, 184
  plurals of titles, 184
  quantity, distance, time, amount as
    units, 192
Number, with singular or plural verb,
  191
Numbers. *See* Figures
Nun
  form in letters to, 324–325

Office memoranda, writing of, 283–284
Officials and wives, letters to, 298
Old Testament, abbreviation of books
  of, 177
Omission of words indicated by punc-
  tuation, 36
Only, 201
Open punctuation in letter part, 41–43,
  214
Order letters, 238–239
Order of business in meetings, 425
Orders of knighthood, decorations, and
  honors, 170
Organizations, form in letters to, 217–
  221

Organizations, social and religious, abbreviations for, 172
Oriental, capitalization of, 17
Outlines
  for constitutions and bylaws, 424–427
  for minutes of a meeting, 390
  for reports, 434–435
  form for, 31

P.M., capitalization of, 27, 87
Pages, continuation, headings of, 227
Papal Household, members, form in
  letters to, 322
Parentheses
  around confirming figures, 60
  around explanatory matter, 60
  around parenthetical matter, 59
  with colon, 61–62
  with comma, 61–62
  with exclamation point, 61
  with interrogation point, 49, 62
  with period, 31–32, 61
  with semicolon, 46, 61–62
Parenthetical matter, punctuation of,
  35–36, 59–62
Parenthetical questions, punctuation of,
  49
Parenthetical statements, capitalization
  of, 23
Particles in American and foreign
  names
  capitalization of, 4
  filing of, 480–481
Parts of books, capitalization of, 24
Past perfect tense, 193
Past tense, 193
Perfect, 200
Period
  after abbreviations, 29–30
  after declarative sentence, 29
  after letters or figures in outlines, 31
  after requests, 29
  after Roman numerals, 30, 31
  before decimals, 31
  to indicate omission of words, 62–63
  with compass directions, 177
  with figures denoting hours and min-
    utes, 31
  with initials, 30
  with parentheses, 31–32, 61
  with quotation marks, 32, 56–57
  omission of
    after center, side, and running
     heads, 32
    after chemical symbols, 32

Period (*Cont.*):
  omission of (*Cont.*):
    after letters used as names, 30
    after signatures, 30
    with abbreviations for airlines, 175–176
    with abbreviations for broadcasting stations, 30
    with abbreviations for government boards, 30, 173–174
    with abbreviations for railroads, 174–175
    with military abbreviations, 169
Personal pronouns
  case, 186–188
  omission of comma with, 34
Personified words, capitalization, 24
Petitions, 387–389
Phrases
  French, 131–134
  Latin, 124–131
  idiomatic prepositional, 203–204
  punctuation of, 32–38
  stereotyped in letters, 211–212
Pictures, capitalization of titles, 25
Plays, writing of titles, 25, 56
Plurals of
  compound nouns, 185
  foreign nouns, 182–183
  letters of the alphabet, 186
  nouns, 181–186
  proper nouns, 184, 185
  signs and symbols, 186
  titles, 184
  words referred to as words, 186
Police Commissioner, form in letters to, 297
Political divisions, capitalization of, 18
Political parties, capitalization of, 13
Pope, form in letters to, 321
Possessive case
  double possessive, 52, 188
  of nouns, 50–53
  of pronouns, 187–188
  with gerund, 188
Postal guides, 492
Prefixes
  capitalization of, 27
  followed by hyphen, 67–68
Prepositions
  choice of, 202–203
  necessary, 204
  unnecessary, 205
Present perfect tense, 193
Present tense, 192–193

President and wife, form in letters to, 298
President of a college or university, form in letters to, 216, 325, 326
President of the French Republic, form in letters to, 314
President of the United States, form in letters to, 287
Priest, form in letters to, 322
Prime Minister, British, form in letters to, 312
Prime Minister, Canadian, form in letters to, 318
Prince, form in letters to, 306
Princess, form in letters to, 306
Principal parts of verbs, 196–198
Printing terms, glossary of, 461–464
Professor, form in letters to, 216, 326
Programs for
  commencement and graduation, 521–525
  concerts, 526–533
  Founders' Day, 518–519
  inauguration of college president, 520
Pronouns
  agreement with antecedent, 188–190
  case of, 186–188
  compound personal, 188
  interrogative, 188
  personal, 186–188
  relative, 189
Pronunciation, 72–76, 119–123
Pronunciation symbols for vowels, 123–124
Proofreaders' marks, 469–470
Proofreading, directions for, 470–472
Proper adjectives, capitalization of, 27–28
Proper nouns
  capitalization, 3–4
  hyphenation, 65, 66–67
  pronunciation, 135–136
  spelling, 99–100
Punctuation
  closed, 41, 233
  in letter parts, 41–43, 214, 217–235
  in telegrams, 330
  marks of
    apostrophe, 50–53, 186
    asterisks and dots, 62–63
    colon, 46–48
    comma, 32–46
    dash, 58–59
    exclamation point, 49–50

Punctuation (*Cont.*):
  marks of (*Cont.*):
    hyphen, 64–76
    interrogation point, 48–49
    parentheses, 59–62
    period, 29–32, 62–63
    quotation marks, 53–58
    semicolon, 42–46
  of requests, 29, 48
  open, 41, 234–236

Quantity, unit of as subject, 192
Queen, form in letters to, 306
Queen Mother, form in letters to, 306
Question mark. *See* Interrogation point
Questions
  capitalization of, 23
  punctuation of, 48–49
Quick, quickly, 199
Quotation marks
  double, 53–58
  single, 55–56
  with colon, 46–47, 56–57
  with comma, 32, 40, 56–57
  with dash, 57
  with exclamation point, 57–58
  with interrogation point, 48, 49, 57–58
  with period, 32, 56–57
  with quoted letters, 55
  with quoted paragraphs, 54–55
  with quoted questions, 48–49
  with semicolon, 46, 56–57
Quotations
  capitalization of, 22
  punctuation of, 53–58

Rabbi, form in letters to, 324
Radio stations, omission of periods with abbreviations for, 30
Railroads, American, abbreviations for, 174–175
Recalling invitations, forms for, 360
Receptions, invitations to, 335–337
Recitals, invitations to, 346
Recommendation, letters of, 262–266
Reference books
  atlases, 492
  biographical data, 486–488
  broadcasting, television, motion pictures, 493
  directories and handbooks, 488–490
  etiquette, 493
  indexes to books and periodicals, 491
  law, 489, 493

Reference books (*Cont.*):
  medicine, 489
  postal guides, 492
  quotations, 493
  styles of address, 488
  synonyms and antonyms, 491
  transportation guides, 492
Reference line in letters, 225–226
Regrets, formal and informal, 358–360, 364–368
Reminders, letters of, 272
Reports
  acknowledgments in, 441
  appendix in, 444
  conclusions in, 442–445
  examples of, 446–458
  foreword in, 438–440
  index in, 444
  introduction in, 435
  letter form of, 445
  letter of transmittal, 435–438
  outline for, 434–435, 445–446, 458
  recommendations in, 443–444
  summary of, 441
  table of contents in, 441
  text or discussion in, 441–442
  title page, 435
Representatives, form in letters to, 293
Request, letters of, 260–261, 267
Requests, punctuation of, 29, 48
Reservations, 273–274
Resolutions
  capitalization of parts, 23, 405
  examples of, 406–422
  expressing appreciation, 419–422
  in letters, 409–410
  on the death of an associate, 411–419
  purpose of, 405
Restrictive adjective clauses, punctuation of, 40
Reverend
  capitalization of *the* with, 5
  correct usage of, 5–6, 163
Roman Catholic officials, form in letters to, 321–322
Roman numerals
  in outlines, 30–31
  table of, 90–91
Round numbers, writing of, 84
Royalty of Great Britain, form in letters to, 306

Sacred books, capitalization of, 18–19
Salutations
  abbreviation of titles in, 162

Salutations (*Cont.*):
  Dear Madam, 217, 218, 219, 221, 289, 290
  Dear Sir, 217, 218, 219, 221, 288–290, 292–294, 296
  Gentlemen, 217, 218–225, 226
  in addressing academic officials, 325–326
  in addressing associations of men and women, 217, 218, 219
  in addressing Cabinet officials, 288–289
  in addressing city officials, 293
  in addressing committees, 217, 220
  in addressing companies, 217, 220–221
  in addressing ecclesiastics, 319–324
  in addressing government officials
    American, 287–296
    foreign, 294–295, 296, 312, 314, 315
  in addressing members of the Armed Forces, 290, 301–304
  in addressing men and women, 223–224
  in addressing representatives to the United Nations, 315–317
  in addressing women officials, 283, 293–294, 295
  in Brazilian letters, 330
  in business letters, 217–224
  in French letters, 314–315, 327
  in German letters, 328–329
  in Italian letters, 329
  Ladies, 217–220
  Madam, 217, 218, 219, 289, 290, 293, 294
  Madam Secretary, 289
  Mesdames, 184, 217–221, 223
  Sir, 288–296, 301–302, 305–306, 310–312, 316, 317, 318–319
Salutations, punctuation of, 41–43, 47, 217–224, 305–312
Scarcely, 201
School, capitalization of, 18
Scientific terms
  capitalization of, 26
  italics in, 82
Seasons, capitalization of, 24
Secretary
  capitalization of, 6, 8
  placement in letters, 231–232
  punctuation of, 82
Secretary, duties assigned in a constitution, 429

Secretary General of the United Nations, form in letters to, 315–316
Secretary of Air, form in letters to, 290
Secretary of Defense, form in letters to, 290
Secretary of Labor, form in letters to, 289
Secretary of State, form in letters to, 288
Secretary of the Army, form in letters to, 290
Secretary of the Navy, form in letters to, 290
Secretary to the President, form in letters to, 289
Self in compounds, 68
Semicolon
  in bibliographical references, 44
  with clauses, 43–45
  with enumerations, 45
  with *for example, hence, however, moreover, namely,* 45
  with names followed by titles or addresses, 44
  with parentheses, 46, 61–62
  with quotation marks, 46
Senator
  capitalization of, 6
  form in letters to, 290, 293
Senator and wife, form in letters to, 298
Senator-Elect, form in letters to, 290
Senior, use of, 165
Señor in address, 328
Señora in address, 327, 328
Señorita in address, 328
Series of words and phrases, punctuation of, 33–34
Shillings and pence, writing of, 31, 48, 87
Ships, punctuation of names of, 81
Signatures
  in business letters, 41–43, 228–232
  in telegrams, 379
  of a secretary, 231–232, 274, 365, 393–396, 398, 404
  of women, 229–231
Signs and symbols
  list of, 178–179
  plural of, 186
Sir
  capitalization of, 8
  in salutations, 288–296, 301–302, 305–306, 310–312, 316, 317, 318–319

Sisterhood, form in letters to members of, 324–325
Sizes of books, 177
Slow, slowly, 199
Societies
  learned and professional, abbreviations for, 171
  social and religious, abbreviations for, 172
Solar system, capitalization of, 26
Sort of, 202
Sources of information, 486–493
South, southern, capitalization of, 17
South America
  capitals, 539
  countries, 539
Southerner, capitalization of, 17–18
Spanish letters, form in letter parts, 327–328
Speaker of House of Representatives, form in letters to, 288
Spelling
  American, 93–95, 98–99
  British, 93–95, 98
  geographical names often misspelled, 100–101
  rules, 92–93, 95–99
  variant spellings, 93–95, 98–99, 108–109
  words ending in
    ance, 104
    ant, 102–103
    ence, 105
    ent, 103–104
    er, 105–107
    ible, 102
    ise or *ize,* 99
    or, 107–108
    y, 96–97
  words often misspelled, 99–102
Spring, capitalization of, 24
State legislatures, capitalization of, 12
States of the United States
  abbreviations, 160
  capitals, 538
  names, 538
Stereotyped phrases, 211–212
Street numbers in letters, 87, 214
Subject line in letters, 226–227
Subjects
  agreement with verbs, 190–192
  collective nouns as, 190–191
  compound, 192
Subjunctive mood, 195–196
Subordinate conjunctions, 205–206

Suffixes, hyphened, 67–68
Superior of a brotherhood, form in letters to, 325
Superior of a sisterhood, 324
Surface measure, table of, 534, 536
Syllabication, 70–76
Symbols
  list of, 178–179
  plurals of, 186
Sympathy, letters of, 280–282
Synonyms and antonyms, books on, 491

Table of contents in reports, 441
Tables of weights and measures, 534–538
Teas, invitations to, 336–337
Telegrams, 376–385
Temperature, writing of, 90
Tense
  future, 193–194
  of the infinitive, 194–195
  past, 193
  past perfect, 193
  present, 192–193
That, who, which, distinction in usage, 40
The, capitalization of
  in titles of books, 23
  with *Reverend,* 5
Theirs, 187
Time of day,
  unit of as subject, 192
  writing of, 31, 87
Titles. *See also* specific titles, as *mayor, senator*
  abbreviations, 162–164
  academic, 7
  Air Force, 300, 304
  Army, 169, 299, 301, 302
  capitalization of, 5–8
  corporate titles, filing of, 484
  diplomatic, 294–297, 299
  ecclesiastical, 5–6, 319–325
  Eminence, 321
  Esquire, 297, 313
  Excellency, 296–297, 321–322
  government, 6–8, 287–296
  Honorable, 297
  Honourable, 312–313
  hyphened and unhyphened, 66, 67
  in business letters, 7, 214–217
  in signatures
    of divorced women, 230
    of married women, 229, 230

Titles (*Cont.*):
  in signatures (*Cont.*):
    of secretaries, 231, 232, 274, 365, 393–396, 398, 404
    of unmarried women, 229
    of widows, 230
  Naval, 169, 299–301, 302–304
  of books, writing of, 25–26, 56, 79, 80
  of pictures, writing of, 25
  of plays, writing of, 25, 56
  plurals, 185
  punctuation of, 34, 35
  Reserve officers, 302
  United Nations representatives, 317
  Women in armed services, 301
  Women officials, 293–294
Trade names, capitalization of, 27
Transitional expressions, punctuation of, 35
Transportation guides, 492
Treasurer, duties assigned in a constitution, 430
Troy weight, 535
Type sizes, 464
Typist's initials, writing of, 231–232

Unique, 200
United Nations
  branches of, 315
  form in letters to, 315–318
  titles of representatives, 315
United States
  abbreviations of states, 160
  capitals of regions administered by, 539
  capitals of states, 538
  names of regions administered by, 539
  names of states, 538
Universal, 200

Van, von
  capitalization of, 4
  filing of names with, 480
Verbals, possessive case with, 53, 188
Verbs
  agreement of subject and predicate, 190–192
  infinitive, 194–195
  of the senses with adjectives, 199
  principal parts of, 196–198
  subjunctive mood, 195–196
  tenses, 192–198
Versions of the Bible, abbreviations of, 178

Vice President, form in letters to, 288
Vice President and wife, address in invitations to, 298
Viz., punctuation with, 37, 45

Weddings
  acceptances, 356–357
  announcements, 340–341
  invitations to, 339–340
  invitations to anniversaries of, 341–342
  recalling invitations to, 360
  regrets, 359
Weights
  tables of, 354–356, 358
  writing of, 90
West, western, capitalization of, 17
West Indies
  capitals, 540
  names of islands, 540
Whereas, writing of in resolutions, 23, 405
Which, who, that, distinction in usage, 40
Who, whom, case in questions, 188
Who's Who, 187
Widow's signature, 230
Winter, capitalization of, 24
Woman Cabinet member, form in letters to, 288–289
Woman mayor, form in letters to, 293
Woman member of House of Commons, form of address, 312
Woman member of House of Lords, form of address, 313
Women
  forms of salutations in letters to, 217–224
  ranks in Armed Services, 301
  signatures of, 229–231
Women Ambassadors, form in letters to, 295
Women officials, form of address, 293–294
Women representatives, form in letters to, 290
Women senators, form in letters to, 290
Words
  confused, 110–119
  foreign
    italicized, 78, 79
    list of, 124–134
    pronunciation, 72–76, 119–123